www.wadsworth.com

www.wadsworth.com is the World Wide Web site for Wadsworth and is your direct source to dozens of online resources.

At *www.wadsworth.com* you can find out about supplements, demonstration software, and student resources. You can also send email to many of our authors and preview new publications and exciting new technologies.

www.wadsworth.com
Changing the way the world learns®

THE WADSWORTH COLLEGE SUCCESS SERIES

Clason and Beck, *On the Edge of Success* (2003).
ISBN: 0-534-56973-0

Gardner and Jewler, *Your College Experience: Strategies for Success,* Media Edition, 6th Ed. (2005).
ISBN: 0-534-59392-5

Gardner and Jewler, *Your College Experience: Strategies for Success,* Concise Media Edition, 5th Ed. (2004).
ISBN: 0-534-60759-4

Gardner and Jewler, *Your College Experience: Strategies for Success,* Expanded Reader, 5th Ed. (2003).
ISBN: 0-534-59985-0

Gordon and Minnick, *Foundations: A Reader for New College Students,* 3rd Ed. (2005). ISBN: 0-534-62167-8

Hallberg, Hallberg, and Aschieris, *Making the Dean's List: A Workbook to Accompany the College Success Factors Index* (2004). ISBN: 0-534-24862-4

Hettich and Helkowski, *Connect College to Career: A Student's Guide to Work and Life Transitions* (2005).
ISBN: 0-534-62582-7

Holkeboer and Walker, *Right from the Start: Taking Charge of Your College Success,* 4th Ed. (2004).
ISBN: 0-534-59967-2

Petrie and Denson, *A Student Athlete's Guide to College Success: Peak Performance in Class and Life,* 2nd Ed. (2003). ISBN: 0-534-56999-4

Santrock and Halonen, *Your Guide to College Success: Strategies for Achieving Your Goals,* Media Edition, 3rd Ed. (2004). ISBN: 0-534-60804-3

Santrock and Halonen, *Your Guide to College Success: Strategies for Achieving Your Goals,* Concise Media Edition, 3rd Ed. (2005). ISBN: 0-534-59346-1

Steltenpohl, Shipton, and Villines, *Orientation to College: A Reader on Becoming an Educated Person,* 2nd Ed. (2004). ISBN: 0-534-59958-3

Van Blerkom, *Orientation to College Learning,* 4th Ed. (2004). ISBN: 0-534-60813-2

Wahlstrom and Williams, *Learning Success: Being Your Best at College and Life,* Media Edition, 3rd Ed. (2002). ISBN: 0-534-57314-2

STUDY SKILLS/CRITICAL THINKING

Jenkins, *Skills for Success: Developing Effective Study Strategies* (2005). ISBN: 0-534-63805-8

Longman and Atkinson, *CLASS: College Learning and Study Skills,* 7th Ed. (2005). ISBN: 0-534-62152-X

Sotiriou, *Integrating College Study Skills: Reasoning in Reading, Listening, and Writing,* 6th Ed. (2002).
ISBN: 0-534-57296-0

Van Blerkom, *College Study Skills: Becoming a Strategic Learner,* 4th Ed. (2003). ISBN: 0-534-57467-X

Van Blerkom and Mulcahy-Ernt, *College Reading and Study Strategies* (2005). ISBN: 0-534-58420-9

Walter, Knudsvig, and Smith, *Critical Thinking: Building the Basics,* 2nd Ed. (2003).
ISBN: 0-534-59976-1

STUDENT ASSESSMENT TOOL

Hallberg, *College Success Factors Index,*
http://success.wadsworth.com

SKILLS FOR SUCCESS

DEVELOPING EFFECTIVE STUDY STRATEGIES

CYNTHIA JENKINS

THE UNIVERSITY OF TEXAS AT DALLAS

THOMSON

WADSWORTH

Australia • Canada • Mexico • Singapore • Spain
United Kingdom • United States

THOMSON
★
™
WADSWORTH

Executive Manager: Carolyn Merrill
Assistant Editor: Stephen Marsi
Technology Project Manager: Joe Gallagher
Advertising Project Manager: Linda Yip
Project Manager, Editorial Production: Katy German
Art Director: Rob Hugel
Print Buyer: Lisa Claudeanos
Permissions Editor: Joohee Lee

Production: Mary Douglas, Rogue Valley Publications
Text Designer: Kathleen Cunningham Design
Copy Editor: Robin Kelly
Illustrator: Jan Troutt, Precision Graphics
Cover Designer: Ross Carron
Cover Image: Getty Images; *Photographer:* Ron Chapple
Text and Cover Printer: Quebecor World–Dubuque

Printed in the United States of America
1 2 3 4 5 6 7 08 07 06 05 04

For more information about our products, contact us at:
Thomson Learning Academic Resource Center
1-800-423-0563
For permission to use material from this text or product, submit a request online at
http://www.thomsonrights.com
Any additional questions about permissions can be submitted by email to
thomsonrights@thomson.com

Library of Congress Control Number: 2004102001

ISBN 0-534-63805-8

Wadsworth/Thomson Learning
10 Davis Drive
Belmont, CA 94002-3098
USA

Asia
Thomson Learning
5 Shenton Way #01-01
UIC Building
Singapore 068808

Australia/New Zealand
Thomson Learning
102 Dodds Street
Southbank, Victoria 3006
Australia

Canada
Nelson
1120 Birchmount Road
Toronto, Ontario M1K 5G4
Canada

Europe/Middle East/Africa
Thomson Learning
High Holborn House
50/51 Bedford Row
London WC1R 4LR
United Kingdom

Latin America
Thomson Learning
Seneca, 53
Colonia Polanco
11560 Mexico D.F.
Mexico

Spain/Portugal
Paraninfo
Calle Magallanes, 25
28015 Madrid, Spain

 FOR LAYNE, CAMILLE, AND BRENDAN

AND

ALL THE STUDENTS WHO HAVE HELPED ME BECOME A BETTER TEACHER

BRIEF CONTENTS

CONTENTS

③ EXCEL AT TIME MANAGEMENT 39

④ MAKE THE MOST OF YOUR CAMPUS EXPERIENCE 64

10 WRITE AND SPEAK ELOQUENTLY 224

PREFACE TO THE INSTRUCTOR

When I began teaching introductory psychology courses, I was fresh out of graduate school and was very naïve. I was completely unaware of what I would find when I took on the straightforward job of lecturing on the basics of human behavior. My eyes were quickly opened to a different reality. Students didn't understand their role in the classroom. They rarely asked questions, never took advantage of my office hours, didn't take assignments seriously, and performed poorly on exams. I've been on the other side of the podium for more than 12 years now, and the reality I encountered in those early semesters persists. Most students are unaware of the elements involved in college success.

I have found this to be the case with all types of students—those who come to college after earning their general educational development (GED), traditional college students right out of high school, older students who have been working and raising a family for the past decade, students who struggle to get accepted into college, and highly accomplished honor students. Clearly, understanding the skills as well as the attitudes necessary to achieve one's academic goals has nothing to do with how smart the student is. Even the most intelligent and competent students don't realize:

- The critical skill of good time management, deemed by many to be the key to surviving and succeeding in college
- What services and resources are available on campus or the benefits of using them
- The importance of taking the initiative to get to know their instructors, to feel confident enough to approach them when necessary, and to find instructors who can serve as advocates or even mentors
- That they can apply strategies and techniques to bring about a greater degree of success—from taking notes in class, to reading textbooks, to writing papers
- That applying test-taking strategies can reduce anxiety and improve their test performance

There has been a dramatic increase in the number of study skills courses offered at colleges and universities around the country. Some schools make such courses mandatory for graduation. At other schools, study skills courses are electives that are strongly recommended by administrators, advisors, and faculty. In either case, research has shown that students who take courses that introduce them to the issues and related strategies involved in college success are, in fact, more successful.

When I was a student, I did not have the opportunity to take a study skills course and I can see how beneficial it would have been. Although I was motivated and was a good student, I changed my major at a late date and did not earn the grades I would have liked until my senior year. I never made use of an academic advisor. Had I been aware of all that my campus had to offer and knew of some specific techniques to apply to my coursework, I would have met more of my goals and suffered less stress throughout my college career.

When I began my college teaching career, my psychology syllabus grew increasingly longer. I persisted in trying to help my students recognize what it took to do well in school, adding my own personal hints, tips, and suggestions to the information about the course. I even began to use valuable class time to teach specific techniques that would help students succeed. My ability to explore this critical aspect of college was frustrating because of the limited availability of helpful resources.

That is why I was so pleased to be able to write this book to share with more students the knowledge and skills that I believe will help them achieve academic success. My goals with this book are:

- To give students specific strategies that are proven to improve academic performance

- To impress upon students why strategies are valuable, and to demonstrate the benefits through example

- To connect college and career by showing students how applying the same strategies on the job after college can help them succeed throughout life

This book reflects my philosophy that strategies for achieving success involve two things: skill development and an accurate perspective. Chapter 1 introduces students to the role each of these plays in the college experience. Not only will students learn the techniques involved in taking good notes, writing well, and studying, but they also will discover the importance of adopting an optimal attitude for college and life success.

FEATURES OF THE TEXT

This book includes several special features to enhance students' learning experience and to give instructors some additional ways to engage their students. These features appear in every chapter and complement the strategies they highlight.

- **Student Scenario.** This feature provides students with a personal look at situations commonly experienced in college. Each scenario is a true story, either from my own days as a college student or from observations I have made as an instructor. The vignettes prompt students to think about the importance of the skills and perspectives highlighted, as well as their own behaviors and attitudes. Each one is followed by a series of open-ended questions that you could use as a homework assignment or for small group or full class discussion. Students may want to read through the scenarios before beginning the chapter to determine the issues they will be learning about.

- **Professor's Perspective.** This feature shares my own views, as well as those of my colleagues, on different aspects of the college experience, particularly as it pertains to students. With insight into the thoughts and perspectives of college instructors—and of how their instructors may perceive them—students can gain an advantage in how they relate to their own instructors. This feature offers an opportunity to explore the significance of the instructor's role in students' education. When students are aware of how their decisions and behaviors may be interpreted by the individuals who grade them, they have a greater understanding of why it is important to develop their skills and adopt an effective attitude.

- **Future Focus.** Success in college is only the beginning, as this feature demonstrates. Most students don't realize that the skills necessary for achieving their goals in school are the same as those that will bring them success in the future. Creating a link between what students are currently doing and what they hope to do in the future is a powerful boost to success. Instructors can expand on this feature with examples from their own career experiences and by encouraging students to talk with professionals about the skills fundamental to career success.

- **Skill Check.** This feature gives students the chance to assess their current strategies before they learn new techniques. It provides a set of questions for students to answer mentally or in writing to establish a starting point for developing their skills further. You can also use the questions for a class discussion.

- **Perspective Check.** The right attitude is critical for college success. For this reason, each chapter presents a structured opportunity for students to think about their point of view on specific aspects of the college experience. When they answer the questions honestly, they will learn about their attitudes and how those attitudes help or harm their success.

END-OF-CHAPTER LEARNING OPPORTUNITIES

- **Chapter Review Questions.** These questions cover the major points of the chapter. They are in short answer format to allow for writing skills practice, but you can also use them for class discussion instead. You can also introduce each chapter by posing the review questions and having students guess the answers—and then, of course, having them assess their answers as they read the chapter.

- **Skill Practice.** These exercises give students the chance to put into practice some of the specific techniques and ideas presented in the chapter. Practicing these skills will prepare students to apply the skills in their current courses. For the most part, the exercises are presented in isolation from content-specific material.

- **Current Course Application.** One of the benefits of a study skills class is the immediate payoff. Students can apply just about everything they learn right away. This section suggests ways in which students can put into motion the key strategies discussed in the book. Point out that doing homework for this class helps students get better grades in their other classes.

- **Take a Look Online.** The World Wide Web makes a tremendous amount of resources available to students. This feature lists a few websites and pages with information that relates to the chapter content. Most sites are from university learning resource centers and student help desks, and many of them are brimming with great tips and pointers, summed up in an easy-to-read format. Some sites reiterate points presented in the chapter, whereas others offer additional information and activities.

- **Student Scenario Discussion Responses.** As a follow-up to the chapter's Student Scenario, this section reviews the key points. You and your students may have different responses or different solutions to the issues, but these sample responses serve as guidelines based on the lessons presented in the chapter.

An Instructor's Manual/Test Bank to accompany the text is available from your local Wadsworth sales representative. In addition, a companion website with materials for both students and instructors is available at www.success.wadsworth.com/jenkins.

ACKNOWLEDGMENTS

Working on this project has been a tremendous experience, both personally and professionally. This book is the realization of a long-held vision, and I want to thank Annie Mitchell for opening the door of opportunity and helping me get up and running. Carolyn Merrill has been a wonderful editor and guide, providing answers to all of my (many, many) questions, along with much appreciated encouragement and support. This work would not be what it is without the insightful and thorough editing by Cathy Murphy. Her models have helped me grow as a writer. I also want to thank Ilana Sims, a colleague and friend who always "just listened" with a long-distance smile, and Amanda Santana, whose attention to detail kept the project moving forward. I owe the beautiful final form of this book to the amazing talent of the production staff. Thank you to Mary Douglas for all her words of encouragement and ability to coordinate the details, and much appreciation to Katy German, Robin Kelly, and Kathleen Cunningham for sharing their tremendous expertise on my project. I could not have persisted without the unwavering support of my husband Layne, daughter Camille, and son Brendan. Their understanding has meant everything to me. And thank you, John Santrock, for starting it all.

In addition, I would like to express my appreciation for the time, effort, and valuable insight given by everyone who reviewed this book as a work in progress. Thank you to

Kim Byrd
Casper College
Robert Flagler
University of Minnesota, Duluth
Christopher Fries
Northern Michigan University
Bill Horstman
Mesa State University
Barbara McLay
University of South Florida
Martha Olsen
Oklahoma State University
Janet Pickel
East Tennessee State University
Pamela Price
Mercer County Community College
Harold Russell
International College

Maria Salinas
Del Mar College
Linda Spaeth
University of Wisconsin, Eau Claire
Gretchen Starks-Martin
St. Cloud State University
Dave Strong
Dyersburg State Community College
Martha Van Cise
Berry College
Sue Wickham
Des Moines Area Community College
Robyn Wingo
University of Montana–Western
Janet Zupan
University of Montana

Every college student is different. Students enter the college environment with their own unique background, personal goals, motivations, and life circumstances. Therefore, there can be no single formula for guaranteeing success in college. As a study skills instructor, you can help students discover their strengths and identify the areas that need improvement, as well as the strategies that work best for them. Consider introducing this course and this text as learning tools to help them take control of their success.

Best wishes,
Cynthia Jenkins
The University of Texas at Dallas

Becoming a college instructor has opened my eyes to many things. Working with students as I do now makes me realize how little I knew about college success when I was a student. I worked hard and made decent grades, but they weren't always what I hoped they would be, and they came at a great price. I was constantly stressed. I often felt hopeless when faced with challenges, because I didn't know where to find help. I missed out on numerous learning and social opportunities simply because I didn't know they existed. In short, I was ill equipped to have an optimal college experience.

Working with students for the past 12 years has enabled me to see my own college days in a different, yet truer, light. I had been an honors student in high school and thought I knew all there was to know about being a great student. Many of the students I teach come into college with the same confidence I had as a freshman. Although believing in yourself is critical to success, believing there's no room for improvement is dangerous. Even with my rude awakening, I did not seek out the resources to help me become a better learner or to reach my full potential as a student.

One reason for this was that I didn't even know what I needed. No study skills courses were offered—at least none that anyone told me about. So I was on my own to figure everything out. I figured out some things, but many more things I did not figure out. For this reason, I have developed my passion for helping students learn about everything involved in college success. I have observed freshmen struggle with everything from taking good notes during lectures, to remembering what they have read in the book, to knowing where to go on campus for help. Recalling my own naïve experience, it is my primary goal as an instructor to teach students the strategies they can use to achieve their academic and life goals. I was pleased to be able to write this book to share the knowledge and skills that I believe will help you make the most of your college experience.

The goals of this book are:

- To provide you with proven strategies that you can use to improve your academic performance in college

- To give you specific examples that demonstrate how students just like you have learned and applied these strategies

- To show you how these strategies can benefit you—not just in college, but also in your future career

FEATURES OF THE TEXT

The following chapter features will help you learn, adapt, and benefit from the various strategies in this text.

- **Student Scenario.** We often learn best by watching others, and this is your chance to do just that. Each scenario is a true story based on students I have taught or on my own experience as a college student. Each situation is common and allows you to look into the thoughts, actions, and even mistakes of others. Doing so may help you avoid making similar problematic decisions.

- **Professor's Perspective.** This feature shares with you my own views, as well as those of other instructors, on the college experience, particularly as it pertains to students. I hope that by giving you insight into the typical thoughts and perspectives of college instructors you will be more comfortable, competent, and successful in class and during office hour meetings.

- **Future Focus.** Success in college is only the beginning. Then you can follow up your accomplishments in school with a satisfying, productive, and successful career. Often, instructors fail to connect college and career. The Future Focus feature shows you that the skills you are learning now to succeed in your classes will be necessary later for success on the job.

- **Skill Check.** This section precedes the strategies part of each chapter, giving you the chance to assess your current situation. What are you already good at? What could use some improvement? The Skills Check always presents a set of questions for you to answer mentally or in writing to help you assess your skills.

- **Perspective Check.** The right attitude is critical for college success. This feature prompts you to think about your point of view on specific aspects of the college experience. If you answer the questions honestly, you will learn a lot about your attitude and how it can help or harm your success.

END-OF-CHAPTER LEARNING OPPORTUNITIES

- **Chapter Review Questions.** These questions cover the major points of the chapter. If you can answer them correctly and completely, you are well on your way to understanding what it takes to succeed.

- **Skill Practice.** These exercises give you the chance to put into practice some of the specific techniques and ideas presented in the chapter. Practicing these skills will prepare you to apply them in all of your courses.

- **Current Course Application.** One of the benefits of a study skills class is the immediate payoff. You can apply just about everything you learn right away. This section suggests ways in which you can put into motion the key strategies discussed in this book. You can do this by working with the materials and experiences from the other courses you are currently taking. In other words, doing your homework for this course may help you get better grades in your other courses. This book can serve as a guide for future reference as you encounter new and different experiences in college. You may learn about some skills now but may not have the need to apply them until later. Brushing up on the strategies for success will help you tackle new academic challenges down the road.

- **Take a Look Online.** The World Wide Web makes a tremendous amount of resources available to you. I have collected a few resources for each chapter that I believe can further assist you in mastering the skills for success.

- **Student Scenario Discussion Responses.** As a follow-up to the chapter's Student Scenario, this section reviews the key points. The sample responses serve as guidelines for thinking about the situation. Your own responses or solutions to the issue may be different.

A companion website is available at www.success.wadsworth.com/jenkins. The website provides practice quizzes, additional exercises, and study aids.

Every college student is different. You enter college with your own unique background, personal goals, motivations, and life circumstances. There is no single formula for guaranteeing success in college. Therefore, it is up to you to discover your strengths and to identify the areas that need improvement, as well as the strategies that work best for you. As you work through the process, consider this text as a guide and a learning tool to help you take control of your success.

Best wishes,
Cynthia Jenkins, The University of Texas at Dallas

ESTABLISH YOUR VISION

In this chapter you will learn

- The variety of experiences you will have in college that make your education so valuable

- The differences between high school and college

- What skills are necessary for college success

- The role that your perspective plays in college success

- How this book will help you develop effective skills and perspectives for achieving college success

THE VALUE OF HIGHER EDUCATION

More people than ever are pursuing higher education. Nearly one-half of the students now graduating from high school are likely to spend at least some time in a college classroom.[1] This is due in part to the fact that institutions of higher learning are becoming more accessible to more people. Ultimately, though, it is because having a college degree is now recognized as necessary for pursuing better and more interesting jobs. If you want to work in any high-tech, computer-based field, you will need a college degree. Likewise, you will need a degree for a career in medicine, business, or education. Most students would agree that the career choices that require higher education are preferable to repetitive jobs that pay minimum wage.

What is it about earning a college degree that sets you apart from those who don't have one? Many believe it is all of the information you learn—the seemingly endless facts and figures you must commit to memory for at least a brief period of

[1]Boyer Commission (2001). Reinventing undergraduate education: A blueprint for America's research universities. Retrieved June 2002 from http://naples.cc.sunysb.edu/Pres/boyer.nsf/.

time. Years of going to class, reading textbooks, doing assignments and taking tests deserves some major recognition, right? That is definitely true, but there is much more to it than simply meeting your course requirements. The college experience goes well beyond the academic, both in terms of what it takes to succeed and what you will gain from it.

As you progress through your education, you develop as a person. Education inspires you to grow in new and different ways. When you persevere through the demands and challenges that come your way over the next several years, you emerge as a more knowledgeable, competent, and complete version of yourself. Therein lies the value of higher education.

AREAS IN WHICH YOU WILL GROW

College is rich with new and different opportunities. Doors of learning will open for you like never before. You will explore topics in amazing detail, and instructors will teach you in many different ways. You will learn about the world through both your courses and your classmates, who are likely to represent cultures from around the globe. You will discover the tremendous power you have to make your goals a reality and the higher standard of excellence expected from you.

EXPOSURE TO THE WORLD

Higher education offers you the chance to learn about things beyond your current life experiences. It also enables you to study familiar topics in greater depth under the tutelage of experts in their field. In a sense, you have the world at your fingertips. You can discover ancient peoples and their customs in anthropology. You can come to understand the origins and tenets of religions around the world. You can learn the rules of economics and apply them to develop your own business management scheme. You can gain a new perspective on the French Revolution, the Civil War, and the Vietnam War. You can take your own throat culture and look for strep bacteria under a microscope. You can learn to see the difference between a Manet and a Monet, and to hear the difference between Bach and Beethoven. This list reflects only a small portion of what you can gain from your time in college. The most difficult part for many students is deciding which things not to explore.

Regardless of your major, you will receive exposure to this wide variety of topics through a set of *core courses*—classes that all students are required to take early in their college experience. In most cases, you can choose which courses to take within each core category. Categories typically include humanities, social science, behavioral science, natural science, history, government, math, literature, and composition. If you have not yet decided on a major or are not completely sold on the one you have chosen, taking a variety of core courses can help you discover the field of study that interests you. Some students maintain their major while adding a minor area of focus because they find another field fascinating and want to study it in greater depth. Other students take as many courses as possible in different fields to gain a little knowledge about a lot of things.

Your ultimate goal is to study your major in depth and gain substantial command of the subject matter to earn a degree in that field. That will happen in time. However, if you only took classes in your major, you would have a very limited knowledge base. This could actually hinder your future possibilities. The world is becoming a much smaller place, and the overlap in once diverse fields is increasing. College does not provide training so you can do one specific job. Rather, it ensures that you will have a wide range of knowledge, which is important for you to be truly educated. Exposure to vastly different fields of study helps you relate better to a variety of people and understand more about who and what makes up our society and our international community.

NEW LEARNING EXPERIENCES

Your core courses and electives not only provide exposure to a variety of subjects, but they also present you with a diversity of class experiences. Obviously, learning about photosynthesis in biology—diagramming, labeling, and identifying the process by which plants convert sunlight into energy—is a very different experience from listening to Mozart's *Le Nozze de Figaro* in music appreciation or gaining a new perspective on the founding of the United Nations in your political science class. What goes into teaching each subject is different, so your modes and methods of learning must vary. Some courses rely on you to accomplish much of the learning on your own through reading and thinking about the material. Other courses involve hands-on activities so you can apply what you've read or heard from your instructor. In seminar or discussion-based courses, the instructor asks for input from you instead of providing information for you to memorize. Some classes require a great deal of written communication and others call on your public speaking abilities. You will enjoy some and will be challenged by others. Some course styles will be right up your alley, whereas others may clash with your preferred style of learning.

Through the collection of course experiences, you will develop many important qualities. Succeeding in a diverse sampling of classes necessitates processing information in a variety of ways. Therefore, your college degree demonstrates your flexibility in processing information as well as your ability to adapt to different learning environments. For example, if you are a computer science major, you are probably an analytical thinker. You most likely enjoy breaking things down into their component parts and working with concrete issues. Doing well in your psychology course involves abstract thinking on your part. You must consider theories about broad and intangible concepts, such as emotion and intelligence. Opinions and approaches to these topics are diverse, and your analysis must be of a more *holistic,* or broad and general, nature. It may be challenging to you, but it will undoubtedly enhance your thinking skills.

Life is not one dimensional. Your career will not be one dimensional, either. The medley of subjects offered to you during college provides the opportunity to learn about things beyond your chosen major as well as the chance to achieve in many different areas.

INTERACTIONS WITH DIVERSE PEOPLE

College brings you together with many different kinds of people. You will encounter people from different cities and countries, people of different religions and ethnicities, and people of various talents and intellectual capacities. You will experience these individuals in various roles—as teachers, campus staff, and classmates. You may have to work with a greater diversity of people than ever before.

Your college instructors may reflect a wide spectrum of personalities. Some you will like, but others you will clash with. Some may be difficult to understand due to a language barrier or a communication barrier. Some may express opinions that you fully agree with. Others may express opinions you find offensive. You will find it comfortable and easy to be around some instructors. You will find others to be brash and disagreeable. Regardless, you must find a way to succeed in each and every one of your courses. Instructors and teaching assistants play a major role in your class experience. Therefore, some classes will be more challenging simply because of who is in charge. You must follow the instructor's directions, try to understand information presented in lectures, and communicate on assignments and exams to the instructor's satisfaction. All of these situations can be demanding, and, when faced with an instructor who is different from you in some way, you may need a period of adjustment.

You may need to interact with other campus staff members over the course of your college career. For example, you may have an academic advisor who helps you complete your degree plan and suggests the appropriate classes for you to take each semester. You will use the library at some point, and you may need to ask the library staff for help. The health center, counseling center, tutoring lab, and financial aid office all offer services you may use. Taking advantage of these services involves interacting with the staff. You will need these services at various times throughout your stay in school, and successful outcomes will depend on your people skills. No single approach works with everyone. You must learn how to present yourself, convey your needs, and respond to a diverse group of people to get the help you need.

Your peers are another prominent group of people at college. Getting to know your classmates is important. In many cases you do not have a choice, because group projects and teamwork often are part of college class work. Also, participation in class discussions may be mandatory, and the professors may assess how well you interact intellectually with people from a variety of backgrounds. You may find yourself amid people with different cultural norms, different religious and ethical beliefs, and different societal roles. Your ability to cooperate successfully with others on course assignments, to communicate expectations and exchange important information, and to join efforts to create an effective end result demonstrates flexibility and adaptability with diverse people—a quality that is increasingly important today.

PERSONAL RESPONSIBILITY

Pursuing higher education requires a unique form of personal responsibility. Unlike working to pay the bills or caring for your children, going to school is an option. You do it because you want to do it. You take on the demands of college because you recognize that doing so will add value to your life. The greatest challenge to your personal responsibility stems from the fact that when the going gets tough, you can quit. When you are committed enough to persist—even in the face of frustration, confusion, and exhaustion—you demonstrate an impressive level of commitment. This is enhanced by the fact that college doesn't provide immediate and tangible positive reinforcement for your efforts. With a job, you earn a weekly or monthly paycheck, which you can then cash and spend on needs and wants. With your children, your care and attention (although tiring at times) is rewarded with hugs and kisses. The marks you receive on your assignments and exams are all you have to spur you on in school. Those scores are combined once every fifteen weeks or so to produce an official set of letter grades that represents your status as a student. This is hardly as satisfying as a paycheck or hugs and kisses.

Succeeding in college demands that you make sacrifices, delay gratification, and draw on your sense of internal motivation. The dedication you exhibit to earn your degree represents your high level of personal responsibility and an exemplary work ethic.

You get out of higher education what you put into it. The more you embrace the opportunity to learn new and different things—that is, the more willing and able you are to adapt to the variety of learning experiences you face, and the more positive your approach to interacting with diverse people—the more you will benefit educationally. College pushes you to push yourself. It can be the force of change if you let it. It can transform you into someone who uses education and experience to achieve a lifetime of personal growth.

THE ROLE OF SKILLS AND PERSPECTIVE IN ACHIEVING SUCCESS

Skills are specific techniques that can be learned and practiced to do something competently. We acquire skills for playing tennis, cooking, performing on a musical instrument, competing in chess, being a leader, and many other things. Specific skills are also necessary for academic success. These skills include concentrating during a lecture, taking effective notes, scanning a textbook chapter for meaningful information, studying for an exam, and communicating learned information according to someone else's standards. Mastering these academic skills is crucial to doing well in college, but higher education also draws on life skills and personal skills.

ACADEMIC SKILLS

You are already a successful student because you are in college. To get there, you proved yourself intelligent, competent in the classroom, and able to engage in effective learning. You may be wondering, "Why do I need a course in study skills?" Good question. Read on for your answer.

COLLEGE: A NEW DESTINATION

Imagine that you are a seasoned world traveler. You enjoy visiting new places, and you have seen many cities in many countries. Ready for a new adventure, you begin making plans to go somewhere you have never been before. The new destination is foreign to you. The inhabitants speak a language you do not know, and they follow social customs unknown to you. The city is vast and made up of various cultural districts. The weather for this time of year is unfamiliar, and the town has many interesting sights. To make the most of your visit, you invest in a travel guide that highlights your destination.

The travel guide helps you choose where to stay. You can know the location and the cost of your hotel ahead of time. The guide recommends a variety of restaurants, so you can sample different foods while on your trip. The guide suggests the best mode of transportation, informs you as to appropriate dress while sightseeing, and gives specific directions to points of interest. Reading through your guide and referring to it during your journey ensures that you experience everything you want while traveling. You can avoid wandering aimlessly through the city streets searching for places of interest, spending more money than necessary on lodging, and missing out on that once-in-a-lifetime cultural experience. Relying on a guide to help you navigate does not imply that you are an incompetent traveler.

College is a new destination. Although you have "traveled" through school for many years and have many academic experiences under your belt, you are still entering foreign territory. Most students need a period of adjustment to learn the social, cultural, and academic norms of college. This period affects students in different ways. Some students wander aimlessly through their first few semesters, not knowing where they're going or how to make the most of their journey. They may take courses that aren't right for them and then drop or fail those courses. Besides spending more money than necessary, they also miss out on important information that can help them determine their goals and learn how to achieve those goals. Those students may also struggle through classes, losing confidence in their abilities and not realizing there are resources to help them do better.

The goal of a course such as this one is to serve as a guide for you, the student. You have earned your way to this new destination, and now you have a chance to learn how to make the most of it. This course and this book will help you understand the college experience and will provide you with the strategies for success on your journey. Use the information as you would a travel guide—to familiarize yourself with where you are and what is expected of you. Learn to navigate through the circumstances and tasks you encounter. Find ways to interact with the people who help you along the way. Develop the skills that pave the way for advancement. Know how to approach challenges in the most effective way for the experience you want.

THAT WAS THEN, THIS IS NOW

Many students remain skeptical that any kind of guidance is necessary or even helpful upon entering college. They may claim that because they are highly intelligent, performed superbly in high school, and have been accepted to college, they have no need for a course in college success. After all, haven't they already proved that they know how to study? Doesn't their success in high school show that they are good students capable of achieving success on their own? The answer is both yes and no. Being a successful student in high school is good preparation for doing well in college. However, the skills necessary to succeed in college are in many ways different from the skills applied in the past.

In high school, teachers generally take more time to cover less material. Conversely, college courses cover a large amount of material in a brief period of time. You spend less time in class per week in college than you did in high school, and instructors have a great deal more to cover in a single term. This means that reading assignments may be longer than you are used to. What you might have taken four to six weeks to read in high school may now be one week's worth of reading, much of it containing information not covered in class.

In high school, your instructor probably wrote explicit notes on the board or distributed handouts that provided the important information you were responsible for. By contrast, college instructors provide information in a variety of ways. Some instructors write notes on the board and offer additional handouts or notes for purchase. The majority of instructors, however, give lectures on the material and expect students to determine what is important and to take adequate notes. Some instructors assign reading material as the main source of information. You must take more personal responsibility to acquire the critical information in college.

You probably had daily homework assignments in high school—for example, worksheets with questions to answer or problems to solve. Teachers assign homework to help students learn and remember the material. You see very little of this in college, though. In college, homework consists primarily of large amounts of reading, with research papers and other long-term projects making demands on students' time. Don't expect instructors to provide a means for working with the information on a daily basis. That is your responsibility.

In addition, most high school courses offer numerous tests and quizzes, providing frequent opportunities for students to demonstrate what they learned. The regular occurrence of tests and quizzes motivates students to pay attention in class and stay on top of assignments. This provides routine feedback as to how well students understand the material, and it gives teachers a lot of information on which to base course grades. Students have several chances to do well, and a bad day that results in a poor test performance most likely isn't critical.

Much to many students' dismay, college courses have far fewer examinations. This has two important implications. The first is that each test covers a greater amount of material. Remember, without regular homework assignments to keep you on top of things, you have a lot more information to be responsible for on each test. The other critical factor is that you have fewer assignment and test scores available to make up your semester grade. Thus, each exam has a much greater impact on your final grade.

In general, high school teachers have a lot of time to get to know their students. This helps them to be a little more flexible with assignment details and deadlines. You may have been able to explain why your paper was only five pages even though the teacher requested eight, if your teacher knew that your work was always top notch and your effort impeccable. If the paper was supposed to have been typed, your teacher might have accepted it if you had neat handwriting. In another instance, your teacher may have allowed a few days' extension on a report due if you were busy with a tournament for your debate team.

College professors, on the other hand, do not get to know their students as readily. In most cases, it is up to students to make themselves known to the instructor. Many classes are so large that it is not possible for the instructor to get to know the names of all students, let alone their reliability and standards as students. Therefore, don't expect leniency with assignments in college. When an instructor specifies requirements and a due date, stick to them. The same goes for exams. You must become familiar with an instructor's makeup test policy before an emergency causes you to miss an exam.

The greater demands of college require that you acquire some new skills and also improve some existing skills. It will not take you long to realize that high school and college are different. The sooner you adapt to your new circumstances, the more comfortable and successful you will be.

LIFE SKILLS

College also requires that you master several important life skills as well as developing new academic skills. *Life skills* are techniques that enable you to function competently in many aspects of life. Life skills include time management, goal setting, decision making and critical thinking, and interpersonal communication. All of these skills are necessary for success in college and in life.

TIME MANAGEMENT

Chances are you have already engaged in time management. If you had a part-time job while in high school or participated in any extracurricular activities, you would have planned out time for your tasks. You may be used to making schedules to accommodate school, work, sports, homework, and family. The challenge of time management increases in college, because you may actually have more time on your hands than you did in high school. You may spend a much smaller portion of your week in class—up to 15 or 16 hours at the most, compared to 35 or more in high school. You may feel you have all the time in the world, but be careful. You now have many more responsibilities to schedule on your own. You now decide when and for how long to study for each course. You determine when to go to the library to do research, and you decide how much research you want to do. You now have the freedom to choose your bedtime, mealtime, and social time. You must recognize the demands on the limited hours in your day and brush up on your time management skills. It is one of the most critical keys to college success.

GOAL SETTING

Part of successful time management is effective goal setting. You must identify what you want to achieve and by what time. Setting goals is the basis for developing priorities and planning a schedule. Most likely you have other obligations besides school, so you must assess the importance of your goals for the various aspects of your life. Losing sight of what you want to accomplish disrupts your ability to allot time for priorities. Understanding the importance of setting goals and knowing the steps to take to do so successfully play a large part in motivating you to do well in school.

DECISION MAKING AND CRITICAL THINKING

As you move into adulthood, you must make more significant decisions on your own. With freedom comes responsibility, and knowing the best course of action to take can be challenging. You must think critically in the classroom as in life. College is not a place of absolutes. You are expected to think for yourself—to analyze, assess, critique, and synthesize what you read and hear—and to express your opinion. Expanding your perception of the world benefits you tremendously in school, as well as in life.

INTERPERSONAL COMMUNICATION

Life is a parade of interpersonal interactions. Whether dealing with your peers and professors at school or hanging out with your family and friends, you must communicate your thoughts while trying to understand theirs. Working with other people is unavoidable, and the better you are at teamwork the more successful you will be. Your college experience paves the way for your future career, which likely will require that you interact successfully with a variety of individuals. Developing an ability to communicate well helps you experience positive outcomes from your interactions with others. Knowing how to approach people with problems or concerns, ask appropriate questions, and respond to inquiries and challenges provides you the best possible strategies for understanding others and being understood—both of which are key to success in all areas of life.

PERSONAL SKILLS

Personal skills are those abilities that enable you to assess and monitor yourself. It is important to recognize and understand how well you function in the areas that are critical to your success. Doing so helps you make necessary alterations to maximize your performance. You must honestly acknowledge your current level of success and pinpoint the specific behaviors that led you there. If you are doing well, you certainly want to know what it is that you are doing right so that you can keep doing it. Also important is the ability to acknowledge your weaknesses. You must identify the areas in which you are struggling to achieve and then determine why. Knowing yourself well enough to determine your limitations and the areas that need improvement gives you an advantage as you pursue your goals.

Once you have assessed your abilities and level of skill development, you must determine how to adapt to your circumstances and learn which tactics will help you succeed. Ask yourself, "Am I accomplishing what I want?" "Do my efforts yield the desired results?" "What skills do I need for improvement?" "What techniques have I not tried?" Your honest answers to these questions will lead you to meet your challenges effectively. You can't improve, however, without first knowing where you stand.

Self-assessment is a continuous process. You should always be aware of the extent to which you are in control of your success. If this concept is unfamiliar to you, begin now to develop your personal skills and open the door to understanding yourself. You can't be successful otherwise.

PERSPECTIVE

Your *perspective* is your point of view—the meaning you make of the world around you. Your perspective influences your behaviors. The way you interpret the situations you encounter guides your personal decisions and actions. In college, your perspective determines the extent to which you learn, develop, and apply skills. You will judge the degree of importance of various demands placed on you. You will consider the role you must play in each course and your learning experience. You will determine that some requirements are fair or unfair, that some information is valuable or not valuable, and that some skills are necessary or unnecessary.

Many students get "tripped up" in college—not because they lack intelligence, have poor skills, or are unable to meet the challenges, but because they have negative, problematic, or even harmful perspectives that hinder their ability to make the decisions necessary for them to reach their goals. Errors in judgment can cloud a person's vision. The result is faulty decisions and problematic actions that derail your progress. The Student Scenario "I Know What I'm Doing," presented later in this chapter, shows the importance of having an appropriate perspective.

College requires adjusting and adapting to many new experiences. Besides recognizing which skills are important and developing those skills, you must understand the significant role your personal perspective plays. Your perspective can motivate you to accomplish your goals, or it can prevent you from taking steps toward success. But you aren't expected to know how to approach the college experience. Along with presenting the skills necessary for increased academic performance, this book will help you understand many of the subtleties involved in college success so you can adopt an optimal perspective that will help you reach your goals.

HOW THIS BOOK WILL HELP YOU ACHIEVE SUCCESS

Learning takes place in numerous ways. This book's organization and content, special features, and diverse exercises and activities give you significant information on the various skills involved in college, career, and life success. This book will introduce you to specific college demands and will give you insight on the importance of developing academic and life skills more fully. It provides specific techniques and ways to apply them to improve your learning and performance in school. Each chapter gives you the opportunity to think about the topics as they relate to your own personal style and point of view, as well as the chance to practice and put those skills to use immediately in the classes you are now taking.

ORGANIZATION OF THE BOOK

This book progressively introduces you to the critical elements for achieving college success. Each of the four sections—You As a Student, In the Classroom, Assignments, and Exams—contains a few chapters that explain the importance of the college experience and that teach you the skills for mastering that realm. The sections build on each other, with the earlier sections laying the foundation of knowledge and skills for those sections that follow. This first section introduces the basics of functioning and perceiving yourself as a college student. You will learn how to incorporate being a college student into your personal identity so you can approach school with a maximum level of commitment.

Connecting with your values and the process of goal setting helps you think about how to make your dreams a reality and helps you recognize that your daily tasks are significant steps toward getting where you want to go. Chapter 3 guides you in the techniques of time management so you can get organized to make the most of your life. Chapter 4 describes the variety of resources and support systems available through your campus. Much of your success will come from understanding how to take advantage of the services at your school.

Success in school comes more readily when you understand your strengths and challenges as a student. Chapter 5 gives you the opportunity to discover how you learn best and how you prefer to be taught. You will learn the optimal ways to approach your courses, based on your learning style. Chapter 6 introduces the elements of good critical thinking. It prepares you to process information in the new and different ways expected of you in the classrooms of higher education.

Section 2, "In the Classroom," will help you become a better listener through improved motivation and concentration. Taking effective lecture notes is critical for getting the information you need to perform well on exams. A variety of techniques capitalize on different learning styles. Choose the best techniques for you, and your classroom experiences will be much more rewarding.

Section 3, "Assignments," focuses on specific coursework requirements. You will learn strategies for getting the most out of all reading assignments: textbook chapters, professional journal articles, imaginative literature, and poetry. The chapters discuss common mistakes that students make when reading, how to avoid such mistakes, and how to read more effectively. College courses strongly emphasize communication through both written and oral projects. You will learn how to research your topic and manage your time so you can actually get ahead on long-term assignments.

The final section of the book, "Exams," will help you learn to prepare for and take different kinds of college exams. This book frequently addresses the concept of mentally processing information. You will learn just how your brain processes information for learning. Some study methods build on this process and are the most effective. You will learn how to use those study methods while studying and while taking exams.

SPECIAL FEATURES

This book has several different box features to help illustrate important points about the college experience. The information in these features is as beneficial as that presented in the text, so read them carefully.

STUDENT SCENARIO

Each chapter includes a story about one or more students. All of these true stories highlight the perspectives and actions of students in various college situations. Following each scenario is a series of questions that prompt you to think about what you just read. By answering these questions, you gain insight to your understanding of the circumstances and demands of the particular situations. You can see how some responses might be problematic and can identify ways to avoid these experiences yourself. To guide your thinking, suggested discussion responses appear at the end of the chapter. The Student Scenario demonstrates the importance of taking the right perspective so as not to endanger your learning.

STUDENT SCENARIO: I KNOW WHAT I'M DOING

Corey was planning his first semester of college courses with his academic advisor when the subject of math came up. "I took calculus in high school," he told her, "so I need to take Calculus II now." Corey was pleased that his hard work from last year would pay off with one less math requirement in college.

"Actually, you still need to take Calculus I," his advisor replied. "Although you had calculus before, we require that you take all of your calculus here."

"What!?" Corey gasped. "No way! I've already had it. I'm not taking it again."

"You really haven't had *all* of it," the advisor explained. "What you covered in your semester in high school makes up only a portion of our entire Calculus I course. You need to cover a lot more material before you take Calculus II."

Corey had no choice but to sign up for Calculus I to fulfill his math requirement, but he couldn't understand why his high school even offered calculus if the course wasn't really going to count in college.

When school began, Corey felt vindicated from his meeting with his advisor. He sat through his first three calculus lectures knowing everything. "I know what I'm doing," he thought to himself, just as he had told his advisor. He was angry to be wasting his tuition money on this class when he really felt he should be in the higher-level course. Because his first few weeks in calculus proved to be a review, he decided that he did not need to go to class. He noted the exam date on the syllabus and planned to show up for the exam. "At least I won't be wasting my valuable time anymore," he thought.

Corey was horrified when he began to take the exam. He recognized only two of the fifteen problems on the test, and the rest of the material was completely unfamiliar. He stumbled through, fully aware that he would most likely fail the exam. When he asked a classmate about the test afterward, he learned that the pace of the course had increased by the third week and that most of the problems on the exam covered the most recent material. Corey now understood what his advisor had been telling him and the reasons for beginning again with Calculus I. Unfortunately, it was too late.

Consider the following:

- What was Corey's first mistake?

- How did Corey's problematic perspective result in a bad decision?

- If Corey were concerned about wasting his valuable time in class, what might he have done instead of stop attending class?

- What challenges and consequences might Corey now face since failing his exam?

- Corey's absence from class caused him to miss critical material covered on the test. What other problems might result from repeatedly missing class?

- What beneficial perspective could you take if you find yourself in a course that reviews the material learned in a previous course? What actions would follow this perspective?

PROFESSOR'S PERSPECTIVE

Throughout your college career, you must demonstrate to your professors that you deserve the grades you desire. It is important to perform well on your course assignments and exams, earning the points necessary for a desirable term grade. However, academic performance is not the only means of communicating your savvy as a student. Your behavior and choices in many situations communicate your ability and desire to learn and do well. Also, the course requirements may be diverse enough that they require a variety of important decisions and actions on your part.

To present yourself as a conscientious student, it takes some insight into how professors see their role, your role, and different academic situations. The Professor's Perspective feature presents the viewpoints of college instructors, along with a discussion of how instructors are likely to interpret specific student behaviors and responses. Pay attention to their thinking style and approach to the college learning experience. The more you understand the perspective of professors, the greater your chances for impressing the individuals who determine your course grades.

PROFESSOR'S PERSPECTIVE: NO NEED TO APOLOGIZE

Professors understand their role in your education quite clearly: to provide you with the materials and means of learning the relevant information and to expose you to experiences that help you discover how to learn. They know that the education you seek is for you—a fact you may not even fully realize yet. It is not uncommon for students to perform poorly on their coursework or exams and subsequently apologize to their instructor for not doing well. An instructor might get an essay exam back with questions left blank except for a personal note that says, "I'm sorry, I just don't remember this," or "Please forgive me, I just didn't have time to study this material." Or the instructor might receive an apology when a student sleeps in and misses class.

Students who express such regret to their professors may be looking for a break or may simply want to ease their guilt. Whatever the reason, it demonstrates an important thing to the instructor. Apologizing for a poor performance shows that students don't understand they are doing the work for themselves rather than for the instructor. This is a critical mistake.

You should recognize that when you miss a lecture or don't do well on assignments or exams, only you will suffer the consequences. You are not hurting your instructor's feelings or making him or her feel bad when you don't know the material. When you let yourself down by doing less than your best in class, instead of apologizing for what you didn't do, approach your professor about what you can do to make sure it doesn't happen again.

FUTURE FOCUS

Notice that the title of this book is not *Skills for College Success,* or *Skills for Academic Success*. Rather, it is *Skills for Success,* because the skills and perspectives presented will be important well beyond the few years you spend in college. Almost every skill necessary for succeeding in college will continue to be necessary once you establish your career. You may be surprised by this and may wonder how learning to take good notes will be important once you are working. Your professional job will require that you gain new information on a regular basis—from weekly or monthly staff meetings, to annual training courses. In addition, all jobs, regardless of the field, involve reading texts, manuals, reports, and other significant information. You will be expected to read and understand this information in a short period of time. Communicating orally and through the written word is one of the most valued skills in any field. To effectively communicate, you must be able to research important information and present it well. Even exams may make an appearance beyond your time in college, because many jobs require periodic licensing exams, retraining and testing sessions, and aptitude assessments for promotions and job changes.

The Future Focus feature of this book illustrates how the skills and perspectives for achieving success in college will benefit you long after graduation. You can see the benefits of enhancing your skills now, and the tremendous value those skills will have throughout your life.

FUTURE FOCUS: THERE'S ALWAYS ROOM FOR IMPROVEMENT

No matter how intelligent, skilled, or adept you are at the things you do in life, there is always room for improvement. Even the top professionals in their field recognize that there is always more to learn and there are new ways to look at things. Employers also take this perspective with employees. You may be outstanding in what you do; however, if you adopt the attitude that you know everything about your field and believe you've reached the peak of your potential, you will quickly lose respect as well as opportunities.

As you begin your college career, use this course as an opportunity to develop in ways that help you realize improvement. Make it a goal to improve your abilities by strengthening your skills and fine-tuning your perspectives. Your efforts will be rewarded. Demonstrate your awareness of one of the most fundamental keys to success: There's always room for improvement.

EXERCISES AND ACTIVITIES

To help you actively develop your skills and perspectives, this book offers a variety of exercises and activities. Some are presented within the body of the chapter and are designed to encourage you to think about particular issues as they are discussed. Those at the end of each chapter offer different formats for working with the material.

SKILL CHECK

The Skill Check feature within each chapter asks questions about your current level or mode of functioning with regard to the highlighted topic. The purpose of this feature is to prompt you to think about how you have approached a particular skill until now—that is, to consider your starting place for developing that skill. When you are aware of your current method or approach to doing something, you can see where you need to go from there. You can consider how you have done things previously as you read the discussion in the book, which gives you a clearer picture of your strengths as well as areas to target for growth.

PERSPECTIVE CHECK

Similar to the Skill Check feature, Perspective Check prompts you to think about your current perspective on a specific issue related to the college experience. Addressing this set of questions helps you more objectively assess your thoughts and attitudes regarding an important issue. You can then determine how effective your point of view might be, based on how you are likely to act, given your perspective. In many cases, it is not a student's skills that hinder him or her, but rather an inability to understand how to view the situation.

CHAPTER REVIEW QUESTIONS

A set of short-answer essay questions addresses the main points covered in the chapter and helps you review the facts and methods discussed. Read through them *before* you begin reading the chapter, because they can introduce you to the important lessons of the chapter. This strategy is an excellent way to get more out of what you read.

SKILL PRACTICE

At the end of each chapter, you have an opportunity to practice the skills that the text presents. Exercises require you to work with the material in a specific way. As you experience these skills firsthand, you get used to doing things in potentially new ways, and can see their effectiveness.

CURRENT COURSE APPLICATION

The purpose of this book is to help you develop skills for success during your college career, so everything presented has a practical use in your current courses. The Current Course Application exercises prompt you to employ the chapter skills in other courses you take. They show you how to use the skills now, whereas the Skill Practice exercises allow you to get a feel for the skills independent of a particular application.

TAKE A LOOK ONLINE

The Internet has such a wealth of information, it should be no surprise that it offers a great deal of material related to skills for success. At the end of each chapter is a list of websites for further exploration of the topics presented in the text. Some will be informative articles, but most are interactive sites that will provide self-assessments, quizzes, activities, and tips for improving the skills that will take you far.

You are at the beginning of an exciting journey. Make the most of it and keep in mind that your education is something you do for yourself. What you can gain from the college experience is invaluable, because learning facts and figures is only a means of teaching you so much more. If you establish your vision and are committed to your goals, you will grow tremendously in ways you never imagined.

CHAPTER 1 REVIEW QUESTIONS

1. In what ways does the value of higher education go beyond academic learning?

2. How is going to college a unique and particularly challenging personal responsibility?

3. What are the three kinds of skills necessary for college success? Provide specific examples of each.

4. Explain the ways in which the experience of college differs from that of high school.

5. Why is your perspective so important in college?

TAKE A LOOK ONLINE

For three articles highlighting the many benefits of higher education, check out the following links:

www.dfes.gov.uk/highereducation/benefits.shtml

www.ulusofona.pt/inst/eventos/esrea/abstracts/john_bynner.pdf

http://education.umn.edu/pepsc/products/RowleyHurtado.pdf

STUDENT SCENARIO DISCUSSION RESPONSES

- **What was Corey's first mistake?** Corey's first mistake was to adopt the perspective that he knew the prerequisites for college math courses and that his academic advisor was incorrect in her guidance.

- **How did Corey's problematic perspective result in a bad decision?** When it appeared that the class was a review, he viewed it as confirmation that he had known what was best for him. This prompted him to decide to skip class and just show up to take the exam.

- **If Corey were concerned about wasting his valuable time in class, what might he have done instead of stop attending class?** If a college course seems to be a review, look carefully at the syllabus and discuss the content with your instructor. If the information comes easily to you, take advantage of it. Use class time to confirm your thorough understanding and build your confidence about how you will perform on the test. Enjoy relaxing while listening to the lecture, and really listen to what the instructor says without having to take notes frantically. Corey could have solved additional math problems in the text and even looked ahead to future topics. He could then have considered the familiar lecture material in the context of how it would prepare him for the upcoming material.

- **What challenges and consequences might Corey now face since failing his exam?** The impact of Corey's poor test grade depends on the total number of exams given during the semester. The fewer the exams, the more difficult it will be for Corey to raise his grade. If Corey has only a few more opportunities to earn points for the course, he may not be able to earn an adequate grade in the course. Also, Corey now must return to class in the middle of new and unfamiliar material. He must learn all of the missed material on his own. This comes at a time in the semester when the demands of all of his other courses increase as well. If he can't catch up and performs poorly on the next exam, he may face not passing the class or choosing to drop the course. In either case, he has to take the course again, putting him behind in his college plans.

- **Corey's absence from class caused him to miss critical material covered on the test. What other problems might result from repeatedly missing class?** Corey was fortunate that the exam was actually held on the day he showed up to take it. The assignments, due dates, and test times on a syllabus are always subject to change. Instructors often announce changes in course requirements and scheduling during class time. Students who are not in attendance won't know about the changes. Instructors also might provide critical information regarding testing policies and procedures, as well as helpful hints for preparing effectively for exams. Skipping class can cause you to miss significant information that will directly affect your grade.

- **What beneficial perspective could you take if you find yourself in a course that reviews material learned in a previous course? What actions would follow this perspective?** As mentioned before, if you find yourself in a course in which the material comes easily to you, relax and make the most of it. Enjoy listening, questioning, and participating more in class, rather than having to take copious notes. Recognize the benefit of getting credit for a course that is not stressful or demanding of your time and effort. Capitalize on getting a higher grade with less work than another course might involve. If the material interests you, see if you can learn more through a special project or additional research. You may even use your established knowledge to get to know your instructor better, and he or she might even become your mentor.

MAKE COLLEGE PART OF YOUR LIFE

In this chapter you will learn

- The importance of defining yourself as a college student

- How your values help you achieve your goals

- The characteristics of attainable goals

- Steps for achieving your goals

ARE YOU REALLY A COLLEGE STUDENT?

WHAT DOES A COLLEGE STUDENT LOOK LIKE?

The image of a college student used to be clear-cut. Students were young, recent high school graduates who were taking time out from "real life" while pursuing a college degree. They wore sweatshirts emblazoned with their school's mascot, and, when not in class or the library, they could be found cheering their team on during Saturday's game or sharing a pizza in the local hang-out. Most students lived on campus and graduated after four years. Not so anymore.

Colleges around the country are seeing increasing numbers of *non-traditional students*—students who have been out of high school for several years, are already established in the workplace, and possibly have a home and are raising a family. These students commute to college and typically plan their school schedule around their work schedule. They are not enrolled in college to socialize or "find themselves." They have a more practical purpose for being there. They may be young or old, single or married, workers, parents, and even grandparents. There is no uniform description of a non-traditional college student.

The image of traditional students is changing as well. Many young adults who enter college immediately after high school have much more going on in their lives than just school. More young college students than ever are holding down jobs while working toward a degree. Some must work to pay tuition and other college expenses. However, in many cases students are working so they can afford their own apartment, a car, a computer, a cell phone, and other luxuries. The college years are no longer considered a transitional time between childhood and adulthood, but rather as part of a full-blown grown-up life.

THE NEED TO ESTABLISH YOUR STUDENT IDENTITY

Although the image of the college student may now be blurred, one thing is clear: Life today is more complex and more demanding than ever for those who choose to further their education. Few students are privileged with a carefree college existence in which the only requirement is to enjoy campus life while steadily progressing toward a degree. For most students, going to class is a task to be checked off the daily to-do list. College course attendance takes its place among the numerous other demands of life and, if everything goes well, the students will make it to class most of the time.

What this scenario describes is not truly a college experience. Higher education involves much more than simply going to class. Unfortunately, many students don't realize that by taking this approach to school they are cheating themselves out of some tremendous learning opportunities. They don't get their money's worth, and they may limit their future possibilities. The Student Scenario presents an all-too-common view of the college experience.

STUDENT SCENARIO: I SHOULD NOT HAVE TO DO THIS!

Alex received the syllabus for his Introduction to the Arts course and was curious about an assignment titled "Experience University Art." He asked the instructor what was involved and Dr. Ross explained. "You are required to attend an art-related event that takes place on campus, then write a brief summary of your experience. Although you should make the effort to write a sufficient summary, the purpose of the assignment is to attend an event—anything from a musical performance to a theater performance, or check out the student union art gallery."

Alex asked for confirmation that this assignment was really a requirement. "Dr. Ross, I commute to class every day and I have a busy schedule. I work about 30 hours a week and, with my homework, I don't have time to come back to campus for something that's not class." Dr. Ross explained that numerous events were taking place on campus, that certainly something would fit his schedule. "In fact," he added, "the art exhibit currently in the union is open for viewing all day every day for the next six weeks. You can view it at any time."

"I only come to campus for classes. Because of my work schedule, I need to leave right after class is over. I should not have to do this! It's fine for those who live on campus, but I do not think it is fair that you base a course requirement on something that takes place outside of class time." Dr. Ross responded by informing Alex that this may be the first time but it certainly won't be the last time he will be expected to do just that.

Consider the following:

- What was the value of the "Experience University Art" assignment?

- Why was Alex opposed to returning to campus for the assignment?

- Why is it acceptable for instructors to require an assignment such as this, even for students who commute?

- What could Dr. Ross be trying to tell Alex when he says it won't be the last time Alex will be required to do something that takes place outside of class time?

- What should Alex do to respond to college demands such as this assignment?

As you read in Chapter 1, what makes college so valuable is the collection of experiences you acquire as you progress toward your degree. Most of the critical experiences—things that help you develop and grow intellectually and personally—do not take place in the classroom. The time you spend in class is extremely valuable, and it is necessary for you to obtain information and input critical to your success. However, class time does not encompass the essence of your learning or provide the ultimate benefit of going to college. If you view your role as a college student simply in terms of going to class, you are doing yourself a great disservice.

To give yourself the greatest opportunity for success, you must incorporate the role of college student into your self-image. When you consider the question "Who am I?" you may answer with your name, then some descriptors such as *waiter, skateboarder, music fan, girlfriend, husband,* or *parent.* Along with each of these roles comes a set of thoughts and behaviors from which you draw your identity. Perceiving yourself in a specific role helps you function optimally in that role. Roles are a part of who you are; they define you. Explore your roles as you read the Perspective Check.

PERSPECTIVE CHECK: COLLEGE AND MY LIFE

Think about yourself as a college student. What do you envision? Have you integrated your new role into your perception of who you are, or is going to college something external to your self-image? Do you want to immerse yourself fully in the college experience, or do you view college as a set of class times that you plan around your current work schedule? Are you determined to make continuous progress toward your degree, or are you unsure of your goals at this time? Does having a college degree enhance the image of the person you hope to be, or is it necessary to qualify for the job you'd like to have? As you consider your responses to these questions, recognize the perspective that shapes the responsibilities of a college student.

If you want to do well in college, you must define yourself as a college student. This role can coexist with the other roles in your life, but you must fully incorporate the image of yourself as someone committed to pursuing higher education if you expect to succeed, and you must meet the demands that go with the role. As

Chapter 1 mentioned, college offers a unique challenge of personal responsibility: When the going gets tough, you can quit. It is much easier to quit if you don't internalize your fundamental role as a college student. To keep from quitting, make going to college a part of who you are, not just something else you do.

THE KEYS TO MAKING COLLEGE ESSENTIAL

To incorporate college into your life requires identifying your values and setting goals. Acknowledging your values, or what you find meaningful, lays the foundation for the direction you take in life. Knowing what's important to you is the key to setting goals. Identifying education as one of your values will help you take on the role of college student. Mapping out the specific steps to take follows naturally. The remainder of this chapter guides you through the process, helping you to connect with what you believe is important and to establish your true goals. You will discover the way to make college a part of your life so you can stay committed to your education and prepare a definite plan for achieving success.

IDENTIFY YOUR VALUES

How frequently do you think about what is important to you? For many people, life is fast-paced and packed with responsibilities and obligations. They are always on the move, going from one activity to another. Even their leisure time tends to have a frantic quality. They might run the track during lunch hour or settle on attending their children's various sporting events as a way of experiencing the great outdoors. You are probably used to your routine, but does it really reflect what you want out of life? Can you identify what you value in your daily life? Are you even aware of what holds the most meaning for you? Read the following list and choose those things that are most important to you. Don't be tempted to focus on those things that others believe are necessary or satisfying. Think only of yourself, and see if you can rank the activities according to their significance for you.

_____ Having a family

_____ Spending time outdoors experiencing nature

_____ Being financially secure

_____ Working at a job you love

_____ Being cultured or having sophisticated taste

_____ Keeping a nice house

_____ Traveling

_____ Maintaining deep, close friendships

_____ Being your own boss

_____ Raising healthy and happy children

_____ Having a college degree

_____ Being a skilled athlete

_____ Making a lot of money

_____ Having time to pursue a hobby

_____ Engaging in creative activities

_____ Being able to communicate effectively with a variety of people

_____ Having a choice of where you live and work

_____ Helping those in need

_____ Being physically fit

_____ Holding a position of power and influence

_____ Working with others

_____ Being challenged intellectually

_____ Being knowledgeable on a wide range of subjects

_____ Understanding world cultures

_____ Having a great deal of leisure time

_____ Being highly respected by those who know you

_____ Being on the cutting edge of technology

This is not an exhaustive list of things that may be meaningful to you. However, you can use it to get started thinking about what you value. Identifying your values is important to getting where you want to go.

Values fuel motivation. Your drive and desire to accomplish something derive from your sense that the activity is worth doing. You want to commit the time and effort to those things that are important to you. For example, if you value being in good physical shape, you are motivated to make time in your schedule to exercise, and you are likely to monitor the foods you eat.

The fact that you are currently taking college courses implies that you value some things in life related to the experience of furthering your education. You may find meaning in the education itself, or you may just want to get a job that pays more money. Perhaps you want to accomplish something no one in your family has ever done, or you may dream of traveling the world. Viewing college as the key to having the things you want is a valuable step in the process. Going to college is important to you because it is part of living your life more meaningfully.

With all of the challenges that college presents, you must draw upon your sources of motivation frequently. Begin by reconnecting with your values. Concentrate on those things that you believe make life worth living. When you think about what's important, tap into the power that their meaning holds. See how pursuing your education is moving you toward your personal vision of a valuable existence, and make the most of the motivation it provides.

 ## SET GOALS FOR YOURSELF

When you are motivated to achieve something, you generally are ready to take the necessary steps to achieve it. These desired achievements are goals. Each of us has numerous goals at any one time.

GOALS OF OUR LIVES

Your life is not one dimensional, so your goals most likely are varied. You may not have identified all of your goals. Most likely, though, you want to accomplish some things in the following areas:

- *Education.* You are in college, so you probably hope to accomplish several things while you are there. A degree may be the ultimate goal, but you may also have other goals in mind, such as maintaining a particular grade point average, exploring specific subjects through your elective courses, and developing effective communication skills.

- *Career.* Whether you are currently working or just preparing for a career, you probably have some idea about what you want in your future career. Your goals may apply to a certain field of study, and you may not have identified a specialty yet. Or you may have mapped out a time line for your progress on a career ladder, perhaps even with specific companies. Maybe you want to be your own boss, work in the technology industry, or conduct research at a university.

- *Financial.* Most people have goals that involve money—particularly how to make it and spend it. You may be looking for ways to make it easier to pay for school, or you may be considering how much money to save. You may have goals for investing money and ensuring the kind of retirement you want. Financial goals are present in every stage of adult life.

- *Social.* What kinds of friends do you want? What aspect of your current relationships do you want to improve? Do you want to see friends more often or to meet a wider variety of people or to develop an intimate relationship? Your social goals include whatever you want to achieve from your circle of acquaintances.

- *Spiritual.* Wanting to grow in your understanding of and connection to a higher power comprise spiritual goals. These are highly personal and evolve over the course of life.

- *Lifestyle.* What you want for your day-to-day existence makes up your lifestyle goals. How you hope to spend your time, where you want to live and work, whether you have a family, and what you do in your free time reflect the goals for how you live life.

The complexity of life is unavoidable. However, it is advisable to limit the number of goals you pursue at any one time.

CHALLENGES TO SUCCESSFUL GOAL SETTING

Modern American society is goal oriented. For example, think about New Year's resolutions. Perhaps you can recall some of yours. Most people have good intentions with their New Year's resolutions, but their resolve often falls by the wayside before February. This is because most people don't understand what makes a good goal, and they don't understand the process by which goals can actually be reached. Stating or thinking about goals is not enough. Really wanting to achieve them is not enough. You must also know the critical steps involved in reaching your goals.

KNOWING WHAT YOU WANT

Sometimes people set goals simply because they think they should. They have heard it's a good idea, so they quickly put together a list of things to accomplish. But choosing goals out of a sense of obligation decreases the chance that you will actually reach them.

Many students declare a major without having the slightest idea what they really want to do later in life. Parents or administrators may encourage them to just list something for the record, or the students themselves feel some pressure to determine a specific path immediately. They don't feel any particular drive to pursue the goals associated with what they've selected, and, after a period of frustration and disillusionment, they change direction.

Your goals should state what is important to you. It won't work to set goals randomly or under pressure. You may pursue the goals for some time, but eventually you will discover you aren't motivated to reach them and you will discard them. Make sure that you spend time thinking about your values first and considering what's important for you to pursue.

OWNING THE RESPONSIBILITY

Goals are typically challenging, so you must work to achieve them. When you veer from your goals, it is important to recognize that you have the power to find your course again. Too often, people don't reach their goals because they blame others or look to someone else to ease the burden when the going gets tough. For example, students may believe they are doing poorly in class because the instructor's teaching style is ineffective or the exams are unfair. Such excuses thwart achieving success. It may be true that a professor is not a skilled teacher or the exams are unduly challenging. However, if you want to do well in the class, you must determine what it takes, regardless of other factors. The Professor's Perspective gives further insight on the expectation of personal responsibility in college.

When you set goals, the responsibility to reach them lies with you alone. Of course, some goals require the use of resources and various support systems. Nevertheless, the only person who can actively engage the process for making progress is you.

PROFESSOR'S PERSPECTIVE: DO WHAT IT TAKES

The college experience involves the pursuit of numerous goals, both large and small. You may have the desire to make the dean's list or graduate with a grade point average of 3.5. To accomplish these things requires the successful completion of smaller goals, such as performing well on all of your exams and earning high marks on your assignments. Sometimes even the brightest and most driven students find themselves having a hard time reaching these smaller goals. An instructor may be hard to follow or may provide poor examples and explanations of the concepts. The instructor may have an obscure grading system that no one seems to be able to figure out. Meeting up with such frustrations can lead some students to place the burden of their challenge on the instructor. In response, a student may think, "He's impossible to understand" or "No one can ever get an A out of her." These thoughts reflect that the student feels helpless and believes that trying to achieve success in the class is a pointless endeavor.

Every professor and every course has the potential to pose challenges. Instructors recognize that their style and approach to the course will not appeal to all students. However, if your goal is to do well, then you must do what it takes to reach that goal. Instructors will not personally contact you to find out if you need their help. They will not distribute names of good tutors or suggest additional reading that can help you with the material—unless you ask. Your goals require your effort at determining what needs to be done and taking the time to do it.

UNDERSTANDING THE POWER OF SETTING GOALS

You probably realize by now that setting goals is a process that involves a fair amount of thought. This is exactly what makes goal setting such a powerful activity. Too often people think they don't need to state specific goals. They may drift through life, carrying out their tasks and responsibilities, giving little thought to whether their actions have meaning. They may feel frustrated and dissatisfied because they don't know what they're doing, why they're doing it, or where they're going. They need goals.

When you think about what you want in life—both now and in the future—and you make a plan for how to get there, your choices and efforts take on special significance. By setting specific goals, you find a focus and a direction. Your actions, then, are purposeful because they enable you to connect with what is important, and the path ahead of you is clear and rewarding.

FOLLOWING A PLAN

One reason many people do not reach their goals is that doing so requires following a plan. If you are spontaneous and free-wheeling, you may believe that taking steps to reach a designated goal is too constrictive. But you can't expect to reach your goal haphazardly. Identifying goals means mapping out the things you must accomplish along the way. You need to establish a time line for specific milestones in your quest. When the commitment to a plan dissolves, the goal falls by the wayside.

LEARNING HOW TO SET GOALS

Learning how to set goals makes a difference in whether you achieve them. Neglecting the critical first step of connecting with your values, or failing to understand what is a good goal will hinder your ability to set realistic goals. Goal setting requires much more than just imagining something you would like to do or pursue.

When you learn the specific steps to take in setting goals, and when you become aware of the challenges to accomplishing them, you can engage in a worthwhile process that ensures success.

LIMITING YOUR FOCUS

Everyone pursues multiple goals at any one time. For example, you may have relationship goals as you become closer to someone special. You may have lifestyle goals as you adapt to the independence of adulthood. You may have education and career goals as you begin to pursue your education in a particular field. And you may have spiritual goals to help you find a direction during this time of great transition. Although it's good to know what you want from each element of your life, it is important to narrow your focus with regard to goal setting. Establishing too many goals can be overwhelming. Trying to accomplish too many things, regardless of how far in the future some goals are, can result in your giving up on everything—something you definitely don't want to do.

One of life's greatest challenges is to develop priorities. Note, however, that the different stages in your life bring about different opportunities for personal growth. You have chosen this time to further your education, so school should be a priority and your goals should center around academic accomplishments. This doesn't mean that other interests can't receive your attention and dedication. It simply means that *some* interests have a lower priority than your education at this time. Interests that are not a priority now may command your time and effort later, but you must be selective in what you take on or you will find you aren't getting anywhere with any of your goals. For more insight into the importance of being selective in your goal setting, read the Future Focus.

FUTURE FOCUS: PURSUE A PARTICULAR PATH

When you are established in your career and are familiar with the intricacies of your field, you may consider more specific career goals. It is difficult to do this before working in your field, so expect to first spend some time getting to understand the possibilities available to you. The same process you are learning about now applies to setting goals in the future. You must first decide which areas within your field represent your values. Does one path enable you to work more closely with other people? Can you become specialized in a more analytical aspect of your field? Are there opportunities for leadership, travel, or working from home?

Once you learn what opportunities exist, you can begin pursuing a particular career path. You must identify the specific steps that will help get you where you want to go and then apply your efforts accordingly. Take responsibility for reaching your goals by sharing them with your coworkers and particularly your boss. They will respect and admire your commitment to finding and following your personal direction in the field.

FACING YOUR FEARS

Reaching for some goals may challenge us in new ways and may require things we aren't certain we can do. In essense, goals can be scary. Sometimes going for a goal means facing your fears—standing up to concerns of weakness, inability, embarrassment, and failure. This is no small task, but it is the way we grow. This is how we make something of ourselves—how we become self-confident individuals that we can be proud of.

Your goals have meaning to you because you realize they represent the best part of you. If you let fear derail your dreams, you know you have let yourself down. Use your resources and seek support if necessary, but prepare to push through your perceived limitations to discover your true, strong self.

CHARACTERISTICS OF ATTAINABLE GOALS

Before facing the challenges to successfully reaching your goals, you must first have effectively stated those goals. All attainable goals have specific traits. If they don't exhibit these characteristics, it will be much more difficult for you to make them a reality.

GOOD GOALS ARE PERSONAL

The goals you pursue need to be yours. They should not be your parents' goals, your friends' goals, or society's goals. Why? Because you aren't nearly as likely to achieve them, and, if you persist, it will be quite a struggle. It isn't that your parents and friends don't have admirable, worthwhile hopes for you. If they are suggesting you work toward something, they probably believe it will benefit you and bring you satisfaction. They may be right, in which case it is still necessary for you to accept the goal as your own and not something you are doing to meet others' expectations. If they are wrong, then you must discover for yourself what you need and want. Remember, your goals must reflect your values. That isn't the case if the goals represent what is important to someone else.

GOOD GOALS ARE SPECIFIC

Have you set any goals for college yet? A popular goal expressed at the beginning of the school year is to do well in school. It's an admirable goal, but what does it mean? You may think it refers to earning good grades. What are good grades, then? Do you have to make straight A's to qualify as having earned good grades? Are A's and B's acceptable? If you earned all A's but get a C in your most difficult class, did you fall short of your goal? Suppose you have a difficult semester being on your own or having to support yourself for the first time and you simply manage to pass all of your classes. Did you "do well" in school?

The simple goal of doing well in school is, in fact, ambiguous. It is a *nebulous* goal—that is, it is too vague. What constitutes "doing well" for one person may be different from how another person sees it. Their concept has no objective definition. Good goals, then, have specific definitions.

When you state a goal, try to define specifically what it means to you. That way, you'll know if you've reached it. If your goal is vague, it's difficult to know how to go about reaching it. The more specific the goal, the greater your chance of attaining it. The following list illustrates the difference between nebulous and specific goals.

Nebulous Goals	Specific Goals
I want to do well in school.	I plan to earn at least a 3.2 this semester.
I want to get a bachelor's degree.	I plan to get a B.A. in accounting.
I want to start studying for my exam soon.	I plan to start studying on Friday.
I want to get a summer job.	I plan to find an internship in my field.
I want to do my math homework today.	I plan to do my math homework from 3:00 to 4:30 today.

Nebulous Goals	Specific Goals
I want to make more money.	I plan to earn $200 more each month.
I want to spend more time with my kids.	I plan to devote each Sunday to spending time with my kids.

GOOD GOALS ARE REALISTIC

It's important to set your sights high and hold yourself to elevated standards. Your goals should be challenging, or they aren't good goals. You should be excited about growing and pushing yourself, but you should also stay grounded. If you become too *grandiose* in your visions (that is, if you exaggerate what you believe you can accomplish), you may set yourself up for disappointment, discouragement, or failure. When you determine your goals, be realistic about yourself and your situation. As you know, there is no single type of college student. What you bring to your college experience is personal and is based on your unique set of talents, abilities, desires, and life circumstances. Your goals should reflect those qualities. Realize that your goals most likely will differ from those of your peers.

The next section discusses how to determine your goals. Before you formulate your goals, you must first consider what you are capable of. Of course, it is important to challenge ourselves throughout life, and, as you've learned, goals can serve the purpose of helping us push ourselves to grow. Don't go overboard, though. For example, if you have a family or must work full-time to pay for school, registering for 16 semester hours and setting a goal of earning a 4.0 may be too ambitious. Taking a smaller course load or setting a target of 3.0 or better may help you tackle the challenge more successfully. If you are taking a required chemistry course and chemistry has always given you trouble, consider a goal such as making an increased effort to do well through meeting regularly with your instructor, joining a study group, or seeking tutoring from a graduate student. Following through to achieve this goal will bring success in class. Regardless of the particular grade you receive, you will leave the course knowing that you made the greatest effort possible to do well and learn. Consider the difference between the following two sets of goals:

Goals That May Not Be Realistic	Goals That Are Realistic
Earn a 4.0 my first semester.	Make all A's and B's my first semester.
Take 15 course credits and work full-time.	Take 9 hours, work, and earn good grades.
Become best friends with my roommate.	Get along comfortably with students in the dorm.
Join several clubs and become popular.	Find an organization that suits me, and make some new friends.
Play sports on my college team.	Get involved with intramural sports.
Volunteer for a charitable organization in addition to attending school and working.	Excel at time management to see if I can do some volunteering later.
Find someone to fall in love with.	Make the effort to meet lots of new people and begin dating.
Be completely independent of my parents.	Make as many decisions as I can on my own and ask for help as little as I can.

We all have limits. Recognize yours and keep your goals within reach. Setting attainable goals enables you to achieve what you set out to accomplish. The momentum that our triumphs bring has incredible power for our future endeavors. Keep it real and make it happen.

GOOD GOALS HAVE A DEFINITE TIME FRAME

By definition, every goal has an end point. You identify what you want, and you work toward achieving it by some given time. Imagine running a race but not knowing where the finish line is. How could you feel you were getting anywhere if you didn't know how far you had left to go? How would you pace yourself? After a period of time, you might get discouraged. This is why a good goal has a definite time frame. Part of specifying exactly what you want to accomplish is indicating the time by which you want to accomplish it. If you neglect to state the time frame, you may flounder in your efforts.

SETTING DIFFERENT TIME FRAMES

As part of developing priorities for your goals, you can categorize your goals into three basic time frames—short-term, intermediary, and long-term. Short-term goals are those that you need or want to accomplish relatively soon. You may expect to achieve intermediary goals between a month and a year from now. Long-term goals are much farther down the road, possibly several years away. Regardless of how far away your goals are—weeks, months, or years—you still need to be as specific as possible with the desired deadline. You can always change the time frame if you need to, but you should set the deadline when you set the goal. The following goals are organized by time frames.

Long-Term Goals

Early retirement (age 55?)

Have a cabin in the mountains by retirement (about 36 years or so)

Send my children to the college of their choice (20–25 years after getting married)

Get married on a beach in Hawaii (after dating at least 2 years!)

Earn a graduate degree (6–8 years)

Write a book (during retirement or before?)

Intermediary Goals

Earn a bachelor's degree in finance management (4 years)

Establish myself with a company through an internship program (eligible in 2 years)

Compete in a triathlon (the summer after next)

Be selected as a resident assistant (at the end of this school year)

Participate in Alternative Spring Break (next spring)

Short-Term Goals

Complete and submit my grant application by Tuesday

Ace my finance exam next week (begin reviewing on Saturday)

Go to the library to research my paper (today or tomorrow)

Meet with my history study group on Friday

Work out at least four days this week

Complete the remaining calculus problems in the chapter before Monday's class

SPECIFYING YOUR LONG-TERM GOALS

Long-term goals are the most difficult to define, both in terms of the target date of completion and exactly what you want to accomplish. For example, you may have set the goal of earning a college degree, but you may not have a major. It may take you longer than four years to graduate, and this circumstance limits your ability to state the time frame with certainty. This scenario is common. Nevertheless, although you have many decisions to make in the future, you can still proceed toward your goal. The steps you take toward your long-term goals often enable you to determine exactly where you are going.

Let's expand on the example just given. Working with an academic advisor ensures that you start taking the core courses required for any degree. You can also round out your schedule with some elective courses in areas that you find interesting. Other beneficial steps related to your goal include visiting your campus career center and talking with staff who can help you discover your talents and interests, attending workshops and seminars on career choices, and exploring resource guides on career opportunities. Through these experiences, choices will emerge for your major. Most students identify their field of study by the end of their sophomore year.

Perhaps you have enjoyed your business courses as well as several art electives you've taken. You decide to pursue business as a major while continuing to take art classes for fun. Your goal is somewhat clearer (earning a degree in business) but still is not fully defined. As you proceed through your required business courses, you discover that you can combine a career in business with your enjoyment of art by majoring in advertising. You officially declare your major accordingly. Having taken this step, you consult the college catalog and your academic advisor to plan your program. You now have a specific long-term goal with a known date of completion. This process may have taken you a year or two, but you didn't lose any time in pursuing your goal. Without completing the earlier steps, you wouldn't have been able to define your goal more specifically. This is the case with many long-term goals. They begin as rather nebulous dreams—ideas of something you would like in your life. By taking preliminary steps in the general direction of where you want to go, your destination will emerge.

HOW TO ACHIEVE YOUR GOALS

Reaching your goals takes more than just thinking about what you want to achieve in life and going for it. A specific process is necessary to ensure that you proceed toward your goals and ultimately reach them. Like those discarded New Year's resolutions, goals that are approached haphazardly with no specific plan will easily lose momentum and stagnate until you give them up. Take a moment to consider how you plan to reach your goals by thinking through the Skill Check.

> ### SKILL CHECK: GETTING WHERE YOU WANT TO GO
> You know at least some of what you want out of life—now and in your future. So what are you doing about it? Do you have a plan for getting there? Do you actually set goals, or do you just know in general where you're going? If you have goals, do you systematically map them out so you know exactly where to begin and how to proceed? Do you try to identify a time frame for completing specific steps in your quest to reach your goal? How does your approach to getting where you want to go help or hinder your progress?

START WITH A DREAM

The American author Napolean Hill said, "A goal is a dream with a deadline." This statement captures the nature of our most important goals—the things we truly dream of achieving. You, too, can translate your dreams into goals by simply putting that all-important time frame on them. Begin your goal setting by writing your dreams. Don't hold back. Include everything you hope to have, accomplish, and experience. Next, give them some form—at least in your imagination. Determine what they look like in reality. If you have lots of dreams, consider how they are related. Will reaching one goal help you attain another? Is one dream a stepping stone to the next? Nothing reveals your values more clearly than your dreams. Spending time daydreaming will start you on your way to identifying and setting truly meaningful goals.

WRITE DOWN YOUR GOALS

Even if you are aware of your goals and are convinced that you won't forget them, it's critical that you put pen to paper when setting your goals. Use a notebook to keep track of your goals, to map out your plan for reaching them, to monitor your progress, and to note any changes that you may need or want to make. Keeping all of your thoughts about the future in one place makes it easier to keep your vision clear. The following text describes what you might write in your goal notebook, and Figure 2.1 illustrates how to go from dreaming it to doing it.

State your goals in a positive way. Goals are things that you want to accomplish and experience, not things you want to avoid. It may be the case that you don't want to get into debt, but you shouldn't make it a goal to stay out of debt. Rather, focus on the positive aspect of what you want to achieve. Plan to "Create and maintain a workable budget for my lifestyle" or "Keep spending within my means" and "Save any extra money each month to put toward paying off student loans after graduation." These goals give you a positive direction to take, not a path to avoid, traveled in fear.

HIGHLIGHT REWARDS AND ACKNOWLEDGE CONSEQUENCES

When you spend time writing about your dreams and goals, it's important to specify the rewards they will bring when you achieve them and the consequences you will face if you don't. Remember, your goals should be beneficial in some way. Be certain to highlight this as you journey toward them. Indulge yourself as much as you'd like in visualizing what you set out to achieve. The more you can keep this image in the forefront of your thoughts, the more motivated you will be to persist.

On the other hand, you may be motivated more by the notion that you might not achieve success. Even if this is not the case, it is still important to recognize the alternative to attaining your goals—acknowledging the reality of not succeeding. What will life hold for you? What will you have given up? What opportunities may be lost? What will you do instead? It is important to identify the consequences of not succeeding, possibly by listing the circumstances that may result. This can help you understand more clearly just how important it is to take the necessary steps to reach your goals. Here's an example:

Goal: Earn a bachelor's degree in computer science

> ### Rewards:
>
> Lots of career opportunities
> > Different kinds of companies
> > Different areas of specialization
> > The independence of starting my own business and working from home
>
> Choice of living locations that interest me
> > East Coast
> > California
> > Europe or Asia
>
> Substantial salary
> > Pay off student loans quickly
> > Own a condo

Figure 2.1
Goal Notebook

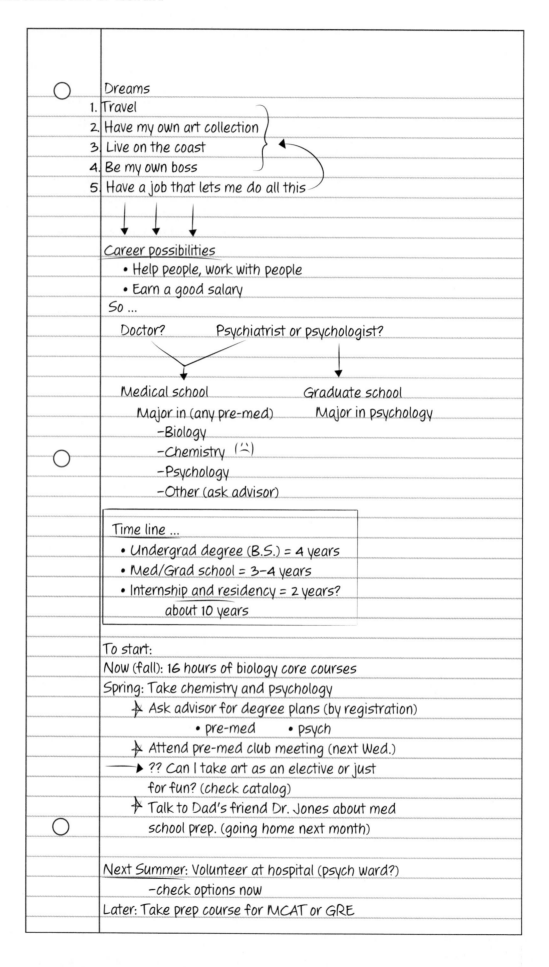

Finally have a nice car

Travel

Consequences of not finishing school:

Jobs are limited

Retail

Food or restaurant business

Labor

Punch a time clock (little freedom)

Low pay

Will have little to pay off student loans I already have

Limited living options (cheaper locations—live at home or rent)

Struggle to make ends meet, have few luxuries or leisure opportunities

No financial security (can't start a family with my girlfriend)

Friends will move on or will move away

Lose momentum for returning to school

Study skills will fade (more challenging to go back if necessary)

This student's goal is to earn a bachelor's degree in computer science. He identifies several benefits of realizing this goal. He also lists several possible consequences of not achieving this goal, along with the resulting circumstances. As you can see, the consequences are a significant deterrent to quitting.

CREATE SUB-GOALS

You can break most goals down into *sub-goals,* or smaller tasks that will help you reach your larger goal. Very few goals are accomplished in one fell swoop. Attaining significant goals requires an extended effort and achieving many sub-goals. Once you've established your main goal, start identifying the individual steps necessary to get there. The smaller the sub-goals, the more readily you can achieve them and see progress toward your destination. Create sub-goals that you can easily carry out in a short period of time. As you proceed through these, you will gain momentum to take on the larger tasks involved in reaching your main goal. Be sure to specify and assign deadlines to your sub-goals. Identifying the steps and knowing when you will complete them are necessary to achieving your long-term goal. Here's another example:

Goal: Graduate with honors

Sub-goals: Make the dean's list each semester

Specific goals for this semester:

Earn A's in Algebra, Psychology, and Economics

Earn at least a B in English Composition and Greek Literature (the most challenging courses)

Tasks to accomplish:

Attend class each day

Keep up with required reading (at least one hour each class day)

Turn in all assignments on time or early (see calendar)

Attend writing workshop sponsored by Learning Resource Center (Friday, October 23)

Ask for professor's feedback on rough drafts for composition and literature papers one week prior to due dates (check syllabus)

Set up a study group for Economics by next Wednesday (call Paul, Monica, Hashim, and Veda)

Attend exam review sessions for Psychology (9/16, 10/14, 11/18)

Solve all algebra problems in the text, even if they're not assigned

Talk with instructors during office hours when necessary

Complete the extra-credit story analyses for literature (due on finals day)

As you can see, this student has the long-term goal of graduating with honors. She has identified the sub-goal of making the dean's list each semester, which will ensure that her grades are high enough for her to achieve honors status at graduation. She then narrows her focus to the current semester, recognizing the courses that she is likely to make A's in and the more challenging classes in which she will accept a B. With her course performance goals clearly in mind, she lists the specific tasks required to reach her desired grades, along with the time frames for carrying them out. There is no question as to where she is going and how she will get there. She has a solid plan for success.

BE HONEST ABOUT OBSTACLES

Another reason many people do not reach their goals is that they believe that by simply setting the goal they will achieve it. Many people, for example, make the same resolution year after year. What is it about this new year that they think will be different from last year? They didn't reach their goal then, so what will enable them to reach it now? Most people would respond, "Well, this year I *really* want to accomplish it!" The truth is, they didn't want to achieve their goal any less a year ago. In fact, most people fail to honestly acknowledge the obstacles that are likely to keep them from reaching their goals.

Few worthwhile goals are easy to reach. They take time and effort to accomplish. We wouldn't typically set a goal of having fun at Disneyland. It's pretty much an effortless thing to do. True goals challenge us. They represent a place we want to go that doesn't come easily. When you identify the things that challenge you the most when striving for your goal, you must prepare to face them and find ways to overcome them.

Consider the example of the student who identified her goals and sub-goals. She recognized the courses that were the most challenging to her and adjusted her goals accordingly. To earn the necessary grade point average to make the dean's list, she set her sights on making A's in those classes she felt most confident about and allowed for the possibility of B's in two difficult courses. The tasks she planned to accomplish include several things to boost her chances for success—particularly in the difficult courses. She planned to attend a writing workshop, turn in papers early for feedback, take advantage of extra credit opportunities, and visit her instructors if necessary. This demonstrates the next important step in achieving your goals: making use of your resources and support systems.

Clearly identifying obstacles that could prevent you from reaching your goals is an important step in achieving those goals. The following example shows a list of what the student would like to accomplish, followed by a list of the challenges associated with each goal.

Goal: Attend class regularly

Obstacles:

I have trouble getting up early, and I have three early morning classes.

The instructor's monotone voice puts me to sleep.

Class is at the same time as my favorite TV show.

Goal: Earn high grades on assignments

> *Obstacles:*
>
> I am a serious procrastinator and put off writing large papers until the last minute.
>
> I don't always understand the concepts presented in lecture so I'm not sure how to approach the assignments.
>
> The instructor has a reputation for never giving A's.

Goal: Make a variety of new friends

> *Obstacles:*
>
> I'm always either in class or at work.
>
> I am very shy and take a long time to warm up to people.
>
> I don't enjoy going out to bars or partying.
>
> I don't live on campus.

Creating lists of obstacles allows you to plan a course of action for avoiding them, and ultimately reaching your goals. When you want to make it to every class but are concerned about the early morning hour, you can design your schedule to get more sleep the night before. Also, you can attend a time-management workshop to help you overcome a tendency to procrastinate, and you can arrange for a tutor to help you with difficult classes. Identifying and using your resources and support systems give you the power to overcome the obstacles to your goals.

IDENTIFY YOUR RESOURCES AND SUPPORT SYSTEMS

Don't feel that you have to accomplish your goals all by yourself, even though they are *your* goals. Colleges have numerous resources to help you get where you want to go. Chapter 4 presents an extensive list of resources available on your campus. In addition to the services and opportunities for assistance through your school, you can establish a personal support system that includes anyone close to you who may be able to help you reach your goals. Family and friends are an obvious place to start, but also consider your roommate, fraternity brothers or sorority sisters, resident assistant, campus personnel such as librarians or career counselors, or even an instructor with whom you've developed a good relationship.

Once you have identified the obstacles you might encounter while pursuing your goals (or if you encounter an obstacle suddenly), seek help from an appropriate resource. Whether you use some of the services on campus or call upon a variety of individuals to lend a helping hand, know that turning to others is an important part of the process. Few great goals, if any, have been accomplished single-handedly by individuals keeping to themselves. The more extensive your list of resources and supporters, the more readily you'll be able to deal with the obstacles you face.

MONITOR AND REVISE YOUR GOALS REGULARLY

As you take steps toward your goals, check your progress. Keeping a notebook of your goals enables you to review your tasks and assess how many you have completed and whether you are making your deadlines, and to note if anything needs to be updated. Don't forget to cross off those tasks you have accomplished. It is satisfying to do so, and it motivates you to do more.

Regularly monitoring your progress—noting what you have accomplished and where you need to exert more effort—helps you maintain focus, ensures that your goals are realistic and meaningful, and enables you to make any necessary changes to your plan. Have you discovered the need to add some new sub-goals? Can you eliminate any redundant tasks? Should you alter the time frames for reaching speci-fied points? Expect to make minor revisions periodically. Sometimes, however, the changes you make may be much larger in scope.

Once you state a goal, it is not set in stone. Many things can change as you progress toward your accomplishments. What you want to accomplish can change as well. You may find that your values change. It is not unusual to discover new and different meanings in life as a result of your college experience. You are exposed to different people and different ways of thinking. You take classes in subjects you have never studied before. You make decisions independently, often without input from anyone else. All of these things can cause you to rethink what is important to you and can lead you to replace old values with new ones. Such changes can alter your goals.

Your life circumstances may change as well. You may find yourself in a better or worse financial situation. You may become involved in a new relationship or may end an old one. You may face illness or family discord. Any of these changes can affect your current goals. You may have to change your priorities and shift your focus for the time being.

You may discover that what you are getting is not at all what you had expected, and you may need to revise your plans accordingly. These are some of the reasons that it is important to monitor both your progress and your continued desire to achieve your stated goals. If your life and your values change significantly, your goals must follow. Just because you have been working toward a particular goal doesn't mean you must carry it through to completion if it no longer represents something you want to achieve. Of course, be careful not to jump the gun and desert a goal because it poses a challenge. Consider critically and carefully what led to your change of heart, and give yourself time to revise your plans.

CHAPTER 2 REVIEW QUESTIONS

1. Why is it critical that you incorporate the notion of being a college student into your personal identity?

2. What two things are fundamental to making college an essential part of your life, and how do they relate to one another?

3. In what areas of life do most people have goals?

4. What are the challenges to successful goal setting? How can you overcome them?

5. Discuss the roles of dreams and reality in successful goal setting.

6. What are the characteristics of attainable goals? Provide examples of each characteristic.

7. What steps can you take to help reach your goals?

SKILL PRACTICE

1. Here are some typical, vaguely worded goals from students. Rewrite each one so it is well defined and specific.

I want to do well in school.

I want to get involved on campus.

I want to improve my writing.

I want to work harder in math.

I want to have a healthier lifestyle.

I want to spend more time with my children.

I want to make things better with my roommate.

2. Choose three of the goals above and list some possible sub-goals to help accomplish each one.

3. Begin a goal notebook.
   a. Start by writing down all of your dreams—everything you would like to accomplish, to have, and to experience. Don't hold back—this is completely personal.
   b. Try to put an estimated time frame on achieving these dreams. When would you like to reach them, ideally?
   c. Translate your dreams into specific, realistic goal statements. Make sure you have defined exactly what you want and need to do.
   d. List the steps or sub-goals required to achieve each goal.
   e. Create a time line for completing the sub-goals.
   f. Identify all of the steps you can begin working on now to reach your goals, and provide specific dates for completion.
   g. Consider the obstacles that you may face—now or later on—that will require some extra effort or the use of additional resources to accomplish your tasks. Describe these obstacles.
   h. Brainstorm possible resources (people, campus services, and so on) that can help you overcome those challenges. List them.
   i. Continue to modify and update your goals, sub-goals, time lines, and resources. Keeping track of your progress and additions in one place helps you make those goals a reality.

CURRENT COURSE APPLICATION

1. Think about how you perceive yourself in each of your classes. How do you think your perspective influences the experiences you have in each class? Reflect on your current classes and answer the following questions.

Does the course satisfy a requirement in your chosen major, does it satisfy a general requirement, or is it an elective that interests you?

How do you feel about your role in each course? Do you see yourself differently in each class?

Do you feel confident in some classes but uncertain and intimidated in others?

How might you be able to alter the way you view your place in each course to develop a sense of belonging or to feel that you are growing personally in this academic environment?

What could this do to change your chances of success in college, in your future career, or generally in life?

2. What experiences have you had in college so far that have affected your personal values? Consider the following questions as you formulate your answer. Explain as thoroughly as possible.

Have you discovered a new interest or developed a passion for something new?

Has anything you have done or seen caused you to reassess your values?

Have any of your classes introduced you to a subject and/or a way of thinking that has influenced what you believe is important?

3. Identify at least one way in which each of your classes is contributing to the achievement of one of your personal goals. Consider how the experiences of each course are leading to your growth in many ways. Perhaps you are taking even more steps than you initially realized toward achieving what you want in life.

4. View the upcoming requirements for each of your courses as goals in and of themselves. Identify what you want to accomplish with each, including the specific grade that you hope to earn. Make a list of the steps you can take to achieve each one. Then identify any obstacles that you might face on your way. How will you overcome these? Make specific plans now for exactly what you will do, how you will do it, and when you will do it. Describe your plan.

TAKE A LOOK ONLINE

To explore your values in greater depth, visit the following website, where you will find a vast list of potential values to contemplate along with the various roles that values can play in your life.

www.gurusoftware.com/GuruNet/Personal/Topics/values.htm

For very specific goal-setting activities and tips, see

www.topachievement.com/goalsetting.html

www.mindtools.com/page6.html

STUDENT SCENARIO DISCUSSION RESPONSES

- **What was the value of the "Experience University Art" assignment?** The assignment gave students the chance to apply what they were learning in class by experiencing different kinds of artistic presentations firsthand. It also introduced them to the opportunities to do so on campus. Many performances and exhibits are available to students on college campuses, and they often provide interesting and enjoyable experiences for a reduced student rate, or even for free.

- **Why was Alex opposed to returning to campus for the assignment?** Alex was most likely opposed to returning to campus because it didn't easily fit into his schedule. The problem is that Alex wants to attend college only on the condition that it fits into his schedule. A complete college experience is a dynamic and often-changing set of demands, requiring that the student accommodate a variety of different learning experiences. Alex doesn't really view himself as a college student, but rather someone who takes some college classes.

- **Why is it acceptable for instructors to require an assignment such as this, even for students who commute?** Students find numerous reasons to be on campus when they are not in class. Sometimes review sessions are offered, which all students should take advantage of. Study group opportunities with classmates often are scheduled to take place on campus. All students are required to make use of the library over the course of their study in college, and professors won't use class time to enable them to do so. Nearly all schools have campus organizations that can help students in their particular majors; services that provide assistance in math, writing, careers, and personal development; and guest speakers who will enrich students' understanding of important course material. As a college student, you are expected to immerse yourself in the resources of your institution—during class time or otherwise.

- **What could Dr. Ross be trying to tell Alex when he says it won't be the last time Alex will be required to do something that takes place outside of class time?** Throughout your college experience, you will be expected to attend and take advantage of the experiences and resources available to you outside of class time. Professors frequently assign research papers—assignments that inherently require that students spend time in the library outside of class time. Group projects require time that students spend time working with others outside of class time. Some instructors expect students to attend additional review sessions (particularly if grades are low), and others require attendance at presentations from invited speakers. Even if some of these activities are for extra credit only, it is a good habit to attend all recommended events.

- **What should Alex do to be able to respond to college demands such as this assignment?** Alex should establish priorities for his goals and should determine where his education fits in. If it is important for him to work toward a degree, he should incorporate the notion of being a college student into his self-concept. He can't approach school in terms of fitting in his courses, attending, then checking them off his to-do list. He must recognize the broader scope of engaging in higher education and be prepared to work his schedule around school as much as possible. Defining himself as a college student will help him understand that the expectations and requirements are there to provide worthwhile learning experiences.

SKILL PRACTICE ANSWER SUGGESTIONS

1. Here are some typical, vaguely worded goals from students. Rewrite each one so it is well defined and specific.
- I want to do well in school.
  I want to earn a grade point average of at least 3.5.
  I want to make the dean's list.
  I want to make A's in all courses related to my major.
- I want to get involved on campus.
  I want to join a fraternity.
  I want to run for student government.
  I want to join the campus pre-law organization.

- I want to improve my writing.
  I want to learn how to better organize my papers.
  I want to learn how to present research information more effectively in a paper.
  I want to improve my use of grammar.
- I want to work harder in math.
  I want to work with a math tutor on a weekly basis.
  I want to complete my math homework as soon as possible after class.
  I want to organize a study group to work through problems together.
  I want to read the text more carefully before I attempt the problems.
- I want to have a healthier lifestyle.
  I want to do aerobic exercise at least three times a week.
  I want to stop drinking cola drinks that contain sugar.
  I want to eat a serving of fruits or vegetables at every meal.
  I want to walk instead of drive wherever I can.
- I want to spend more time with my children.
  I want to devote at least 30 minutes before bedtime to read to my children.
  I want to volunteer at my child's school at least once a month.
  I want to devote at least one full morning or afternoon on weekends to an activity with my children.
- I want to make things better with my roommate.
  I want to make sure my roommate is not studying before I bring my friends to the dorm to socialize.
  I want to clean my messes up immediately after I make them.
  I want to make sure I have the food and supplies I need so I don't borrow from my roommate.

2. Choose three of the goals above and list some possible sub-goals to help accomplish each one.
   Here are three sample suggestions:
   - I want to make the dean's list.
     Find out the minimum grade point average required to make the dean's list.
     Determine what grades I must earn in each of my courses to earn the necessary GPA.
     Monitor my grades weekly in all classes to be constantly aware of what I must earn on each assignment and exam to achieve the grade I desire.
     Attend all review sessions, complete extra credit assignments, and form a study group to master the material.
   - I want to walk instead of drive wherever I can.
     Determine how far I am able to comfortably walk.
     Identify the stores and services that are within that radius.
     List the ways in which I can make use of those stores and services.
     Be prepared to dress according to the weather and buy good walking shoes so that I will be comfortable.
   - I want to make sure my roommate is not studying before I bring my friends to the dorm to socialize.
     Sit down and discuss my roommate's preferred study schedule. Plan social time at home accordingly.
     If I am not at home, call my roommate to see if she is open to my bringing friends to the dorm.
     Tell her if I have special plans with friends in our dorm room and ask if she will make plans to study or socialize elsewhere during that time.
     Find other common areas where my friends and I can spend time, rather than hanging out in my room.

EXCEL AT TIME MANAGEMENT

In this chapter you will learn

- How time management relates to your goals

- The importance of being realistic when managing your time

- How to avoid procrastinating

- Strategies for using time effectively

- Three primary schedules for time management success

BE REALISTIC ABOUT TIME MANAGEMENT

Time management is the most critical factor in college success and can determine whether you reach your goals. Consider the following two profiles of college students:

Student A

This individual gets a lot out of life. She does well in school, always keeps on top of her homework, but seems to have plenty of time for fun, too. She has lots of friends and makes an appearance at most parties. She's also healthy and in great shape from working out on a regular basis. She sees the progress she makes toward her goals and feels confident about reaching them. When challenges arise, she adapts her schedule, calls upon her resources, and moves on. She is a success.

Student B

This individual can't remember when she wasn't stressed to the max. She is always behind in her responsibilities and feels the constant pressure of not being prepared. Her whole life is characterized by flying by the seat of her pants, and, although she makes sure she has a social life, she doesn't enjoy it very much. There is always some unfinished task hanging over her head, and she wishes she could take a month off of life just to catch up.

The fundamental difference between these two students' lifestyles is time management. When you manage time effectively, you have a better chance of living the life you want and achieving your goals. When you are disorganized and approach life haphazardly, you may feel as if you're engaged in a constant battle for time and control. Life passes you by and you have little to show for your effort.

Connecting with your values and setting goals are the first steps in good time management. Remember, these are the motivating forces. When you are determined to accomplish certain things, you will devise a plan to do so. Creating a schedule for your daily life and sticking to it can be challenging. When you recognize that the schedule is a path to reaching your dreams, then following it will be easier and of greater importance.

REALITY REVISITED

Good goals are realistic. The same is true for managing your time. You must have realistic expectations and must work around your circumstances.

Media messages perpetuate the notion that we can do it all and have it all—an idea particularly aimed at women. Numerous magazine articles promote the image of a "superwoman," combining family, career, physical fitness, personal growth, and spiritual growth. The fact is, there are only 24 hours in a day, seven days in a week, and there is a limit to what you can do. Life requires making choices—even sacrifices—to attain certain things.

Succeeding in college takes a great deal of time. You cannot breeze through it or pursue it as an afterthought. If one of your goals is to earn a degree, then you must commit the necessary hours to course work and studying. (See the Professor's Perspective for some insight on the expectations of your time in college.) Commitment to college requires that you lessen the time you give to other endeavors. You may find it frustrating at first, but you will recognize the value once you see the progress you are making. Work within your time constraints.

PROFESSOR'S PERSPECTIVE: A REASONABLE REQUEST

Each degree plan requires the completion of a specific number of *credit hours* for graduation. This number reflects the cumulative time spent in the courses related to your major. Each course you take is assigned a number of credit hours. Typically, courses range from one credit hour (a physical education course, for example), to five or six credit hours (for courses with lab requirements). Most courses count three credit hours. The number of credit hours reflects the number of hours you spend in the classroom each week, but it also has implications beyond class time.

Typically, for every one hour spent in class each week, you should expect to spend three hours working outside of class. For a history course of three credit hours, for example, you would spend three hours each week in lecture and nine additional hours each week reading and studying the textbook or additional material. Of course, you will do this for each of your classes. If you are taking

12 credit hours this semester, then you go to class 12 hours each week and should plan to focus on school for 36 more hours throughout the week. That's a total of 48 hours dedicated to school each week. That's why you are considered a full-time student.

Not all of your classes will be so demanding as to require a full nine hours per week on reading and assignments—at least not every week of the semester. However, most professors recognize this "three hour rule" as a fair basis for their expectations of your time. You may feel overwhelmed by your weekly reading assignments and research projects. When you allot nine hours a week for every course of three credit hours, you should be able to stay on top of the course work.

PRIORITIZE TO ORGANIZE

You will certainly work toward numerous goals simultaneously, including long- and short-term college and career goals, relationship goals, goals related to your current job, social goals, and spiritual goals. Some goals will be directly linked to your dreams, whereas others will be more immediate—those related to family or work responsibilities. Pursuing multiple goals requires organization. In other words, you need to arrange your goals according to their priority, or order of importance. Here are the steps to take when you determine priorities.

1. *Begin with obligations.* You absolutely must do some things even if you don't want to. These mandatory tasks are your responsibility, or *obligation.* Ignoring obligations such as paying bills, providing childcare (if you are a parent), going to work (if you have a job to support yourself), and maintaining your car (if the car is your only means of transportation) gets you into trouble. Neglecting such tasks can disrupt your ability to attend class or pursue your studies. Obligations must take priority because everything else that you want to do rests on their routine accomplishment.

2. *Specify your dreams.* Don't be content to keep your ambitions in your head. Write down as explicitly as possible what you want out of life. Include the details and the time frame by which you would like to accomplish these things. Continue writing the specific steps you can take to reach those goals. Identify the tasks that you can work on *now,* in your day-to-day life.

3. *Assess where you are in life.* Each stage of life brings with it a new focus and a different set of circumstances in which we can pursue our dreams. Rarely do things stay the same, including our goals and the ability to work toward them. It is important that you recognize what you can realistically do now to achieve success in the areas you want. For example, if you are struggling financially, this is the time to commit yourself to working and saving so you can establish some security and move forward with other goals. On the other hand, if you have earned a scholarship or your parents are willing to pay for college, you are in the best position to further your education with relatively few distractions.

   To help you decide which goals to focus on, consider which ones are optimal for this stage of your life. Can you realistically function as a full-time student? Is it more feasible for you to go to school on a part-time basis? With school as your focus, perhaps you don't have any immediate relationship goals. Maybe your newfound independence enables you to pursue some new spiritual goals. Keep in mind that it is not possible to work effectively toward too many goals at one time. Think about which goals you are most able to work toward, given your current life circumstances.

4. *Choose what's most important.* Once you have narrowed down your goals to those that are right for you to pursue now, list them in order of importance. Simply decide which are most meaningful to you and, ultimately, what you want to give the most time and effort to accomplishing. For example, you might decide that earning a degree is your top priority, followed by having a part-time job to earn enough money to pay for your car, spending time with your girlfriend, and training so you can run a marathon some day. With school as your primary goal, your schedule is dominated by going to class, reading, writing, and studying. You restrict your work hours to less than 20 hours a week, and you have an agreement with your girlfriend to see her a couple of evenings a week. You work out or go running as a study break or when you have less homework.

Choose activities that are most important to you on a small scale, too. Determine the priorities, for example, for the academic tasks that lead up to your goal of earning a degree. Which classes pose the greatest challenge and therefore require more study time? Will earning A's and B's in courses related to your major open the door to getting the paid internship you want for the summer? Can you take some easier courses that require relatively little work? Determining the priorities for the specific tasks leading to your goals helps you plan how to spend your time.

BUILD ON THE BASICS

This chapter addresses the specifics of designing a schedule later. Before you determine the specifics, though, you must consider the basics. Several things are fundamental necessities to living our lives, and this is where your time management plan must start.

PHYSICAL NECESSITIES

First and foremost, every day we must eat and sleep. New college students tend to neglect both of these fundamental needs. Eventually they pay the price—typically under the worst conditions.

Most people need seven and a half to eight hours of sleep a night to function effectively. A good night's sleep helps you think and concentrate on important tasks. Despite this truth, many students try to get by on a mere four to five hours of sleep a night and some students actually pride themselves on pulling all-nighters. It is, in fact, possible to function in a seemingly normal state for some time on such a schedule. Lack of sleep catches up with you, though—right about finals time. Just when you have the most to learn, remember, and communicate—often, the point at which your course grade is decided—your body may succumb to utter exhaustion. You are highly susceptible to illness and fatigue when you deprive yourself of sleep, even for a short period of time. Imagine the resources your body must use if you deprive it of significant rest over a couple months' time. There literally won't be anything left to give to the demanding mental tasks required for successfully preparing for and performing on exams. When you get a good night's sleep each night, you maximize the potential for productivity.

Proper nutrition is another necessity for clear thinking and productive work. Fast food and snacks fit our busy lives but leave our bodies demanding more and better nourishment. When we don't make time in our days for decent meals, the options are poor—vending machines or drive-thrus, candy bars, diet soda, greasy chicken, burgers, and fries—none of which sustains us for long and may cause sugar lows or upset stomachs. Taking the time to eat a healthful breakfast and a well-balanced lunch won't set you back. Rather, it will give your body what it needs so you don't have to seek snacks later in the day.

Personal hygiene is important, too. It is not necessary to spend inordinate amounts of time meticulously grooming yourself, styling your hair, and applying makeup. However, it's important to bathe regularly, wear fresh clothes, and brush your teeth daily. When you are clean and presentable, you feel better and are approachable to those around you. Plan time to take care of yourself physically.

SUPPORTIVE RELATIONSHIPS

We all need other people to make our lives complete. Our endeavors are made more meaningful—and sometimes simply possible—by the support of those who are closest to us, whether it is our parents or siblings, spouse, romantic partner, or close friends. Neglecting the people who are closest to us can be harmful in many ways: We may lose the assistance of people we rely on to enable us to pursue our goals; we may feel isolated and helpless, which could result in the loss of motivation; and we may find that there is nothing comforting to balance our efforts, nothing soothing to offset our challenges.

Spend time with the people who support you and who make you feel loved, cared for, and motivated. Be sensitive to the time and attention they need from you, but be honest about the time demands of working toward your goals. Work together with your friends and loved ones to reach an understanding, and create a plan for the time you spend together. If you have moved away from home to attend college, talk to your parents about when you can visit throughout the school term and how often you will call or contact them by e-mail. If you are in a dating relationship, discuss the frequency with which you will go out, meet for lunch, or talk on the phone. If you are married, agree on how often you will focus only on each other, tuning out all other responsibilities, for the sake of maintaining a healthy relationship.

Life is demanding even without college. With the added demands of college, it is critical to create a time management plan that accommodates the people important to your happiness and, ultimately, your success. As you plan your schedule, be truthful about the time you need for your studies. At the beginning of each school term, when you have collected your syllabi and have an idea of your scholastic demands, you can determine the days and times to give to the people in your life.

CHILDCARE

If you have children, you must work school around your responsibilities as a parent. Depending on the ages of your children, you will have various childcare issues to consider when developing your time management plan. Because the well-being of your children must be a top priority, their needs are the place to start.

Before planning your course schedule, identify the times that you must be home with your children. Determine if you can read or study when your children are napping, or arrange for friends or relatives to spend time with the children. Note all of your children's school events or activities on your calendar first. You won't be able to concentrate in a review session if you know you are missing a ballet recital or a holiday pageant. College requires many sacrifices, but try to minimize those sacrifices that involve your children. Taking care of your children and spending time with them is not an option. Let childcare dictate your time management approach.

KNOW YOURSELF

When you set out to manage your time, take a moment to reflect on yourself. Identify the ways and times you function best so you can create the most effective schedule. For example, if you are a morning person, plan to accomplish significant tasks early in the day and save evening for your down time. If, on the other hand, you are a night owl, do not sign up for an 8:00 a.m. class. Many students make the mistake of signing up for early morning classes, ignoring the fact that they are likely to struggle with getting up and arriving to class on time. Once there, they have difficulty listening and concentrating in their groggy state.

How are you at keeping up momentum? Do you prefer to get on a roll and maintain the pace, or do you work better with periodic breaks? If you know that you have a hard time resuming an activity when your momentum is broken, plan your schedule accordingly. Take consecutive classes each day so you can remain in the mode of listening and taking notes. Avoid blocks of free time between classes so you're not tempted to leave campus for the rest of the day while killing time before your next class. Allocate longer periods of time to read, write, and work math problems, and follow them up with extended breaks that allow you to relax and unwind. Consider going to class and then working on necessary tasks for the rest of the day so you can have the entire evening free. Try devoting all of Saturday or Sunday to schoolwork so you can take the other day off entirely. This strategy may keep you productive and motivated.

If you lose your focus after a relatively short period of time, create a schedule that alternates work and play. Sign up for classes that are spaced throughout the day so you can refresh yourself. Eat, take a walk, or do some light reading in the interim so you can concentrate again. Use the same strategy when you do homework. Focus as long as possible. Then stop and do something enjoyable. Be aware that when you take breaks more often, they should be shorter in length so you spend most of the time on your required tasks and responsibilities.

When planning your daily schedule, consider all aspects of how you work best. Do you read more effectively before or after you've eaten? Can you focus better after you've worked out for the day, or will you be too tired then? Do you prefer to use the library when no one else is there? Are weekends the best time for you to "dig in" to your schoolwork? Arrange your schedule for whatever works best for you. Do not plan your schedule according to anyone else's time frame, except for group projects or meetings. However, take an honest look at the ways in which you work most effectively and the times of day when you focus best, and develop your plans around those natural preferences. It will make a difference.

DON'T PROCRASTINATE

Everyone occasionally *procrastinates,* or delays doing things they must do. Procrastination can be very dangerous in college, though. Your weekly workload is likely to be great enough that getting significantly behind is costly. Some people claim to work better under pressure. Even so, at some point they simply won't have enough time to get all of the work done.

EVERYBODY DOES IT

We procrastinate for several reasons. Understanding the causes of procrastination can help you overcome the temptation to delay. Here are some typical reasons for procrastinating:

- *It's boring.* We put off things that we don't want to do. One reason we may not want to do something is that it is not interesting. Reading numerous pages from your economics textbook, for example, may simply be the most boring thing you can imagine. If the task is uninspiring, you may avoid it as long as possible.

- *It's time-consuming.* When you are assigned a research paper that you know will require many hours in the library, reading a variety of materials, and writing and revising extensively, you may take comfort that the due date is a month away. Putting off tackling a large project keeps the misery at bay.

- *It's challenging.* If your latest math lecture was confusing and hard to follow, you probably aren't looking forward to doing the homework on your own. You envision struggling through complex formulas and difficult equations, and you are not in a hurry to do this.

- *A fear of failure.* If you aren't confident that you can be successful on an assignment, project, or exam, you may avoid working on it. This not only keeps you from confirming your fear (trying and failing), but it also provides a comfortable excuse when you fail as a result of having procrastinated. Your work may be poor (as you worried it would be), but you feel better about it because you can attribute the quality to not having had enough time.

- *A fear of the unknown.* When we don't know what to expect from a situation, we often are hesitant to find out. Suppose your instructor requests a meeting after returning your exam to you. You may be intimidated by the one-on-one meeting, and you may not know what to expect. Putting off the meeting as long as possible postpones the uncertainty.

- *No goals in sight.* If you don't connect a task to one of your goals, you will not be motivated to work at it. Tasks you perceive as busywork, rather than valuable steps toward accomplishing something you want, are good candidates for procrastination.

- *Poor time management.* When you have many tasks to accomplish at once—especially if you don't know exactly what you are doing or when you are doing it—it is easy to let things slide. You may be aware of all you need to do, but unless you specifically identify a time for doing each task, something will get left behind. If you approach your goals and responsibilities haphazardly, you will spend a lot of time on some tasks and rush others. You will waste time but also neglect some things unintentionally.

Unfortunately, it is easy to procrastinate and to justify it. Excuses flow readily. We may have good intentions, but we convince ourselves that something else requires our attention.

BREAK THE HABIT

You can kick the habit of procrastinating by incorporating some techniques into your time management schedule. Here are a few techniques to consider.

SHORT AND SIMPLE STARTS SUCCESS

Large, time-consuming tasks are primary targets of procrastination. It is often difficult to begin something that looms large ahead. You see no end in sight and you haven't even taken the first step. Therein lies the problem. You are viewing the task like a trek up Mount Everest, when you should simply be concerned with taking your hiking boots out of the closet. Many tasks can be broken down into smaller, more manageable tasks. Chipping away at a large task bit by bit helps you avoid putting it off and develops your momentum for completing it. Let's look at an example.

Suppose your communications professor assigns a group project requiring that you and several of your classmates film a public service announcement for a local nonprofit organization. The project isn't due for another month. Currently, you can't imagine the work that's involved. You have no idea which organizations are available, what issues you'll need to address, how to write the script, or how to film it. Everyone in your group is waiting for someone to call all the shots, but no one does.

It's time to change your perspective. Instead of seeing it as one huge project, view it as a series of small tasks spread over a longer period of time. Here are some strategies for tackling this project.

- First, meet as a group and get to know each other better. Let every person share what they believe their strengths will be relative to the project. Exchange phone numbers and e-mail addresses, and designate your next meeting time. The first task for everyone is to identify a couple of organizations to consider.

- At your next meeting, everyone presents their list of organizations and, after discussion, the group decides which ones are most interesting. Either select one at this time or narrow the list to three to investigate further. Schedule your next meeting.

- After you have chosen an organization to showcase in your announcement, list the main tasks for the project and divide the tasks among your group. Some group members will research the organization, one or more group members will write the script based on the information obtained, someone will read the script on camera, and others will do behind-the-scenes filming or other tasks such as preparing props. Establish time lines and due dates for each aspect of the project.

- If your designated tasks must be accomplished at the beginning (researching or interviewing), most of your work will be done early on. If you have a job that can only be done after other work has been completed, use the downtime to get ahead on your other course assignments and readings.

- Be ready for your part of the project. Make sure you have the time available to do what is necessary without the stress of other school demands. Plan to be available for putting the service announcement together.

- If one or two group members are not doing their part of the project, divide their tasks among the responsible group members (and talk with your professor).

Working together, the group can break down the project into a series of manageable tasks that everyone can handle on their own. Group projects can make large assignments easier, but individual projects can be simplified in the same way. Chapter 10, which discusses how to research and write a term paper, shows how to break down an individual project into manageable parts.

When you create sub-goals for large tasks, you will be motivated to begin and complete each step. Planning to visit the library for a mere 20 to 30 minutes to gather some sources helps you avoid the temptation to put it off. Once you've achieved something—even something as small as checking the library catalog to locate possible sources—you feel a change. You experience accomplishment, and it will both relax you and motivate you to do more. You relax because you see progress and realize that you are one step closer to finishing the project. This, in turn, gives you the desire to keep going and do more because you see the end in sight.

The opposite occurs when you procrastinate. The longer you neglect a task that you put off, the more anxious you become. The task hangs over your head like a dark cloud, and the only way to get rid of the anxiety is to get started. With time running out, getting started becomes an even less appealing prospect. Then you are forced to accomplish a great deal in a short amount of time. It is no longer possible to break down the project and spread the work out over time. In addition, it is diffi-cult to concentrate because of the pressure of the looming deadline. Clearly the process of progress feeds on itself in either direction. Make sure you're going the right way.

INCLUDE REWARDS

Completing your tasks and reaching short-term goals are rewards in and of them-selves, but it doesn't hurt to consider some external ones as well. We often procrasti-nate by doing other things we prefer instead. Try reversing the sequence. Choose something special to do once you've finished your work. Schedule small, individual tasks to be followed by your reward. It will be more appealing to read and take notes on your history chapter, for example, if you know that afterward you'll go to the student union for some ice cream or watch a favorite television show. Small rewards propel you through arduous little tasks. Use larger rewards after completing larger projects. After turning in a big paper or taking an exam, plan a day relaxing by the pool, take your family to the zoo, or go on a road trip with your friends.

INVOLVE OTHERS

When you know you are likely to procrastinate on a task, try to involve other people. If you have a test coming up, schedule a study group or some one-on-one time with a classmate to review the material. When you know that someone else will be counting on you to be there, you are less likely to put it off. You and your roommate can help each other too, by agreeing to set aside specific times to study or read when you are both at home. Set the timer for 45 minutes and commit to individually working on a necessary task during that time. Don't answer the phone or the door, and hang in there for the entire study period to respect the other person's quiet time. Afterward, go run together, get a slice of pizza, or play a two-person video game. If you live at home, ask someone to keep track of time for you. Work alone and don't watch the clock. When you've finished, enjoy the company of others. You will be much more fun to be around when you have accomplished something and feel good about making progress. If you are stressed about having a lot of work to do, you will not be good company. Enlist the help of others to assist you in avoiding procrastination.

WISE WAYS TO USE YOUR TIME

Good time management is a learned skill, and there are many things to consider. Creating a composite plan for your day-to-day life that enables you to accomplish your goals requires the use of several specific strategies—blocking out your time, fitting tasks in where you can, making sure you include time for yourself, and so on. First, think about your current method for controlling your time. Read the Perspective Check and answer the questions.

PERSPECTIVE CHECK: HOW DO YOU APPROACH TIME?

How do you view the time you have each day? Do you wake up each morning and decide to just see what happens in the next 24 hours? Or do you know exactly what you will accomplish and in what sequence? You may combine these approaches—planning a few things but remaining uncertain about the rest. If you just entered college right out of high school, you'll recall that a great deal of your day was accounted for by other people's plans. You had no choice but to attend school most of the day. If you worked or participated in extracurricular activities, even more of your day was arranged for you. Now, most likely, you face more time to do with as you please. Do you have a plan? Do you think you need one? Do you feel confident that you can meet all of your obligations and make progress toward your goals? What are the strengths and weaknesses of your time management approach? Do you think you lack certain things in your life because you don't have enough time? Does this include any of your goals? What might you do to change the situation?

ELIMINATE DISTRACTIONS

Managing your time begins with making the most of what you are doing at the moment. Therefore, when you sit down to work on school tasks, make it a habit to reduce the potential for distractions. If you can't focus because your environment is too noisy or too hot or too cold, or because the view outside your window encourages daydreaming, or because you are uncomfortable or too comfortable, you will waste valuable time. The solution is to adjust your environment. If you are likely to be tempted by computer activities—surfing the Web, visiting a chat room, or playing games—schedule specific times during the day to check e-mail, and turn the machine off otherwise. Reading, writing, and studying productively require the right environment.

When you are working at home or in the dorm, don't leave the television, stereo, or computer on. Close the shades so the sights outside don't draw your attention away from what you are doing. Turn the ringer off on the phone and lower the volume on the answering machine. Sit upright at a desk or table. Sprawling out on your bed will make you too comfortable and may result in a nap rather than the study time you had intended. If you study elsewhere on campus, choose a quiet spot rather than a popular social hang-out. Libraries have study carrels for this purpose, located well away from the noisier student areas. Some dorms have study lounges, and student unions offer quiet study areas. Find the places at your school where you can successfully get your work done.

Don't allow others to pull you off track and hinder your ability to accomplish things. Make it clear to your friends and family the times you have set aside to work, and stick to your plan. Learn your roommate's schedule so you can be home to study when he or she isn't (unless you have arranged study time together). If you have a family, plan your time with them and then focus on your schoolwork when you can. Provide special toys and books for children to use during your study time, or do your course reading when your spouse goes out.

STICK TO STRUCTURE

One sure way to get something done is to plan a specific time frame for doing it and then stick to your plan. When you block out your schedule for top-priority tasks, you can see how much time you have to accomplish everything. Begin with events that have set times—classes, work, club meetings, and so on. Plan around set events and then add the time frames for accomplishing the other tasks on your list. You can determine when and for how long to focus on these tasks. Make use of your optimal mode of functioning. When are you most receptive to reading? At what point are you likely to concentrate best on math problems? What is your attention span for reviewing your notes? If you can only focus for 30 minutes or so, don't block out an hour for a mentally demanding task. Remember, it makes a difference in your productivity if you carefully set up your schedule according to how you work best. Use your preferences to guide you in blocking out times to work on particular tasks.

Things often take more time than we expect. When you plan your schedule, get in the habit of trying to overestimate the amount of time each task will take. For example, some history chapters may take only an hour of concentrated effort to read through and understand, whereas others may require an hour and a half or more. Math problems that primarily review what you did last semester can be completed quickly. However, be prepared to take more time as the semester progresses and the material becomes more difficult. If you end up blocking out more time than you need for a task, you can fill the time with something else. That's easier than dealing with the consequences of not having planned enough time for a task. In that case you'll find yourself getting behind.

For this to work, you must commit to your schedule. When you assign particular times to accomplish things, you must stick to your schedule. The key to effective planning is that during the times you have designated for reading, studying, and writing you must concentrate and carry out the task to completion. This allows you to relax and enjoy the time designated to having fun. If you slack off during your scheduled work periods, you won't accomplish much and you'll know it. Your schedule may tell you to move on to the next task, but you'll still be stressing over what you didn't get accomplished earlier.

Imagine blocking out an hour to read your political science text, followed by 30 minutes of hanging out with a buddy. Suppose you end up spending most of your reading time glancing up at the clock, watching coeds out your window, and generally daydreaming. When the hour is up, you go to see your friend but spend the entire time complaining about how nervous and unprepared you feel about the upcoming exam in your political science class. Not only did you lose an hour of productive reading time, but you also lost a healthy period of relaxed socializing. Instead, make every effort to focus during designated times so you can play when it's time to do so.

STUDENT SCENARIO: I CAN SQUEEZE IT IN

Kendra felt good about the semester so far. She had purchased a day planner in the campus bookstore and had thoroughly scheduled her weeks and days. Not only did she highlight the most important dates for exams and assignment deadlines, but she also divided each day into blocks of time to accomplish specific tasks, including reading for class, working on her research project in the library, doing algebra problems, and studying for the next test.

When she arrived for work one evening, Kendra's boss mentioned that he had scheduled her for extra hours that month. "I know you are always struggling a little with money," he said, "and you are one of my best employees, so I wanted to give you the chance to work more." Kendra was pleased that her boss appreciated her hard work and knew the extra money would relieve some of the pressure. As much as she wanted the work hours, she was hesitant. "I've got everything mapped out for this month," Kendra thought. "I don't know what I'll give up to make time for more work." Giving in to her employer's encouragement, Kendra convinced herself that she could somehow squeeze in the extra hours. Besides, she enjoyed where she worked. Her coworkers were mostly college students and were a lot of fun to be with. After work, Kendra joined them for a late movie, coffee, or just a night of swapping stories.

The financial boost that month was nice, but Kendra had never been so stressed. Her calendar became meaningless with the revised work hours and unplanned social time. Because her plan was completely disrupted, she felt out of control and gave up trying to do any specific time management. Kendra refused another month of extra work hours, especially because she had a lot of catching up to do in school. Her assignment and exam grades dropped once she made no attempt to systematically approach working on them. Playing catch-up was not going to be fun.

Consider the following questions:

- What benefits did Kendra enjoy as a result of her careful scheduling?

- Why was her employer's offer so challenging?

- What should Kendra have done in this situation?

- Was it possible for Kendra to accept the extra hours and maintain her schoolwork? Explain.

- Discuss the importance of setting priorities in Kendra's situation.

- What would you do if you were in Kendra's situation and your boss offered you more hours every month? What factors would contribute to your decision?

DON'T FORGET THE FUN

You may think that you need to block off time only for your obligations and responsibilities, but it's not true. It is equally important to designate specific times for doing the things you enjoy. Your social events, family time, leisure activities, and study breaks should fit prominently into your schedule. You must have downtime to be productive in the other areas of your life. When you map out specific times to enjoy, you guarantee that you can have that time without sacrificing valuable hours necessary for studying.

BE FLEXIBLE

Make it a habit to follow your schedule as much as possible. Plan well and commit to carrying out your plan. Things change, however, so you must be ready to accommodate new situations and unexpected demands. Not only do demands and priorities shift, your schedule must also accomodate moods, motivation, and well-being. You may have scheduled an activity for a given day but, for whatever reason, your heart just isn't in it. You may be distracted by a personal issue, you may not feel your best, or you may realize you just aren't motivated to carry out your original plan. Allow yourself to rearrange your schedule so you can function. There is no point in using a block of time trying to study when your mind is elsewhere.

If you have a bad headache during the time allotted for going to the library, reschedule the visit and take a nap instead. You might consider missing an hour at the gym the next day to accomplish your library task. Suppose you just can't concentrate on school, even though you had planned several hours of reading. What other necessary tasks can you accomplish instead? Consider grocery shopping, working out, cleaning your desk, or doing laundry. The time originally scheduled for these tasks will then be free so you can study when you are more focused. Whatever your situation, keep in mind the ultimate goal of using your time as efficiently as possible.

MAKE EVERY MINUTE COUNT

One of the best ways to be efficient with your time is to make use of the bits and pieces that add up each day. The time you drive to school, wait for class to start, eat lunch alone, and use a treadmill are all likely to be wasted. Instead, make use of these periods. You may be surprised by how valuable they are.

Commuting can take a little or a lot of your time. In either case, you can put it to good use. If you have a tape deck in your car (or a portable tape player), consider listening to recorded class lectures or a prepared recording of your class notes. If you are working on a paper, use driving time to brainstorm topic ideas or to review your research and organize the paper in your mind. Use a tape recorder to record ideas as they come to you. If you are too busy to read books for pleasure, consider listening to books on tape during your commute. Many books on tape are available at public libraries. You can relax and enjoy this time instead of worrying about traffic or class. If you carpool with the students in any of your courses, consider the drive time for an informal study group. You can review material by sharing thoughts, opinions, and concerns—all of which help you learn the material.

Apply these ideas to other circumstances in which you have just a little time to spare. Brainstorm in the shower, jot down new vocabulary words while eating breakfast, review course notes in the few minutes before class starts, or skim chapter headings and subheadings while on the treadmill to prepare for later reading. Consider each of these opportunities a chance to accomplish small but important tasks. Remember, breaking down larger tasks into smaller ones is a great way to make progress and motivate you to do more later. Even if you spend five to ten minutes while waiting in line at the bank prepping to read your next biology chapter, you will feel ready to immerse yourself in it more fully when the time comes. You may even free yourself for additional leisure time later on.

IF YOU MUST WORK

A recent national study found that 74 percent of full-time college students worked while attending college, and 84 percent of those students worked simply to meet college expenses. The same national survey indicated that working more than 25 hours a week interfered with students' academic achievement.[1] However, 63 percent of students who work more than 25 hours a week reported that they had to work that much to pay for college.

---

[1] T. King and E. Bannon. "At what cost? The price that working students pay for a college education." Washington, D.C.: U.S. Department of Education, State Public Interest Research Groups' Higher Education Project (April, 2002).

WORK WITH CAUTION

It takes a lot of money to get a college education, but it also takes a lot of study and hard work. The effort spent earning tuition and fees may hinder a student's progress toward earning the degree itself. Students who work many hours each week are at greater risk for failing or dropping courses, resulting in the loss of money. In addition to having lost those fees, they will most likely have to register—and pay for—those courses again so they can graduate. Thus, although you earn more money by working more hours, you actually end up losing both money and time when work interferes with your success in school. It makes more sense to work fewer hours and pass your courses the first time. However, many options are available, so take the time to investigate what works best with your needs and goals.

INVESTIGATE WORK STUDY AND INTERNSHIPS

Work-study programs offer students the chance to work a limited number of hours either on campus or in the community. Such programs recognize that students need substantial time for schoolwork to be successful. Finding an on-campus job is beneficial for many reasons, but one reason in particular is that there is no commute time. You may want to investigate paid internships related to your major. Many local companies hire students on a part-time basis as a way of finding potential future employees. An internship provides a valuable experience working in your chosen field and helps you learn about your future career. In addition, employers that offer internships usually are sensitive to the needs of students. Because they want you to do well in school, they are likely to work around exam and paper due dates and to recognize the need for time off during midterms and finals.

LOOK FOR JOBS WITH LIGHT WORKLOADS

Some jobs require your physical presence but don't necessarily involve constant effort and may allow time for some schoolwork. If you enjoy children, you might consider offering your services as a babysitter or part-time nanny. Although childcare involves a high degree of responsibility and attentiveness to the children, you may have the chance to read, review, or outline ideas for a paper while the children nap or play in their rooms by themselves.

Working a switchboard or an airport tollbooth may also provide study opportunities. Whereas your focus on the responsibilities of your work must be first and foremost, some jobs offer limited breaks from the flow of demands, freeing you to spend time on school tasks.

BE YOUR OWN BOSS

If you have a talent to share with others, use it to your advantage to create a job that works best around your school schedule. If you play a musical instrument, competitive tennis, or have an artistic flair, consider giving private lessons. You may be an excellent typist or have a great deal of computer know-how. These skills can be applied to freelance work. Being your own boss, you can choose when and how much to work.

BE ASSERTIVE IN SEEKING YOUR IDEAL JOB

Jobs will not just come to you. You must seek them out, especially if you are looking for something different from traditional food service or retail store employment. Those jobs are popular but may not allow you the freedom and time to succeed in school. Many jobs, particularly internships, are not advertised. You may be able to secure an internship by speaking with professors in your major and declaring your need and interest. Job availability around campus may simply travel by word of mouth. If you are interested, talk to people in different positions in various departments. If you think you know where you would like to work, call the company or visit in person. Communicate your sincerity in finding a job that fits your schedule as a student. Some employers respect and appreciate students and believe they are responsible and reliable workers. Find a balance between earning the money you need and doing well in school to discover and land the right job for you.[2]

GET A HEAD START

Nothing relieves stress like getting ahead in your work. When you have lighter loads during specific times in the semester, take advantage of the opportunity to accomplish tasks that reduce your workload in the future. The beginning of each semester is often the easiest time because tests are not scheduled for many weeks, large projects are not due for a while, and instructors allow time for you to get into the groove of school once again. It is an ideal time to do some extra things to prepare for the heavy load ahead.

Read ahead so when the material is covered in class it will be familiar to you. You will most likely need to read it again. Having read it once, though, you will find it easier to understand and will learn the information more thoroughly. Begin exploring topics for papers by doing a preliminary search of sources in the library. Later, when you need to determine a direction and begin your research, you will already have some ideas. If a class involves weekly assignments, try to complete some earlier than required so you can lighten your load during midterms. Getting a head start doesn't mean taking time from other demanding tasks or sacrificing your valuable leisure time. It is something to consider when the opportunity presents itself.

CREATING YOUR SCHEDULE

Are you aware of all that is involved in effective time management? Read the Skill Check to assess your understanding of how to approach your days. When you are ready to make your schedule, you must think about several things—the tools for planning and referring to your schedule, the time frames for your schedule, where to start, and how to adjust the schedule. Once you decide on your approach, you can begin managing your time effectively.

SKILL CHECK: LIFE PLANNING

If you want to get a handle on your time and make the most of your days, how do you do it? Are you savvy enough to keep it all in your head? Should you? How important is it to write it down, and where is the best place to write it? How do you decide which tasks to do when? Should you always schedule everything, or can you be spontaneous and still manage your time well? How can you make sure you don't forget important dates and events? Do you have a sense of how much time you spend on goal-related tasks and how much goes to unplanned, unexpected activities? Do you waste a significant amount of time? How do you know? Being able to answer these questions with certainty helps you identify how far along you are in your time management abilities.

---

[2] John W. Santrock and Jane S. Halonen, *Your Guide to College Success,* 3rd ed. (Belmont, California: Wadsworth, 2004), pp. 140–143.

TOOLS OF THE TRADE

The first step in getting organized for managing your time is to select the tools for keeping track of your schedule. Do you prefer high-tech gadgetry and digitalized spreadsheets? Or are you a pencil-and-paper person? There is no ideal system for time management. Find the one that works best for you. If you aren't certain what will prompt you to continue scheduling consistently, take some time to explore your options.

PAPER-AND-PENCIL PLANNERS

Most stationery and office supply stores offer a variety of management tools, from the most basic calendars—monthly, weekly, and daily—to extensive notebooks with multiple calendars, pages for notes, personal contact information, and more. If you prefer maintaining a written schedule, consider having two different calendars—one displayed prominently at home, and another one that is portable. Display your main calendar by your desk, next to your computer, or on the refrigerator. Consider it your master calendar—an all-encompassing calendar of your commitments and activities over the course of the school term. When you view your master calendar, you see what lies ahead over the next couple of months or several upcoming weeks.

Keep a smaller calendar to carry around with you to school, work, and club meetings. This enables you to see what you have scheduled on which days and times so you can make further plans or changes accordingly. If instructors change course exam dates, assignment times, or meeting locations, you can note it immediately. Relying on your memory to mark it down when you get home could get you into trouble. Choose a small day planner or minicalendar that fits easily into your purse or backpack.

COMPUTER TIME MANAGEMENT SOFTWARE

If you spend a great deal of time working at your computer and prefer to have all of your important information consolidated there, consider using time management software. Some e-mail packages include a calendar function. You can type in activities and appointments at 30-minute or one-hour intervals throughout the day and view a day, a week, or even an entire month at a glance. If the application is running, it will even sound an alarm or use a pop-up window to remind you about scheduled events. Of course, this function is useful only if you are using your computer at the moment. However, you can print out the schedules that you create and post them on your bulletin board or refrigerator, and carry them in your notebooks. You can revise and reprint them quickly and easily as needed.

ELECTRONIC PLANNERS

Electronic planners (handheld computers) are small, portable time management tools. They work very well for long-term, multilevel tasks, and can store names, phone numbers, e-mail addresses, and other personal information that you can keep with you at all times. Should you ever need to contact anyone on the spur of the moment to rearrange your plans, you have everything you need at your fingertips. You can program monthly, weekly, and daily schedules and change them instantly. Electronic planners let you cross-check items on your calendar with personal notes about meeting locations, materials, and assignment specifics. Most planners can be linked to a desktop computer for printing documents such as a to-do list. Some advanced cell phones also offer many of the features of these electronic time management tools.

FUTURE FOCUS: ALL IN A DAY'S WORK

If you think you have a lot to keep track of, get used to it. The need for time management will likely increase once you begin your career. Right now you have to keep on top of reading assignments, homework, and exams. In a professional job, you will most likely juggle multiple projects, handle several accounts, or work with a variety of clients, all of which have different objectives and make various demands on your time. You'll have to make time for meetings and reports and will have to schedule everything from business lunches to travel plans. If you don't have a plan, you could be in trouble.

Organization is the key to doing your best work. For school or your job, it is imperative that you master the skills of using your time efficiently and creating a schedule to refer to on a regular basis. Your success depends on it.

SURVEY YOUR SEMESTER

Your time in college is most likely marked by the semester or quarter, with each class you take lasting approximately 15 weeks. Therefore, it is a good idea to begin your time management plan by mapping out the next several months. Gather the syllabi for all of your classes and mark very clearly on your semester calendar each critical date, including quiz and exam dates, term paper due dates, assignment dates, and any unusual course events such as an announced change of venue or the presence of a guest speaker.

Once you plot all of your critical course information, you have a picture of what school will bring for you during the semester. You can see immediately if you have multiple exams on the same day or if a major research paper is due on the same day that an exam is scheduled. Plotting the semester helps you prepare for the challenges you will face regarding course work.

Next, mark every date that is significant in some other way—for example, project deadlines at work, family and social plans, children's activities, vacation plans, scheduled visits from friends or family. Does your daughter have a ballet recital? Note every event that will significantly affect your time throughout the semester. Figure 3.1 shows a sample calendar. Place your semester calendar in a prominent location where you will see it regularly—on your desk, next to your computer, on the fridge, or by the phone. Consider making a small copy to place in the front of each of your course notebooks. Professors will show no sympathy for the declaration, "I forgot we had a test today!"

WHAT'S UP FOR THE WEEK?

Critical time management takes place primarily on a weekly and daily basis. You should always be familiar with what your week holds so you can plan your days accordingly. Begin by transferring all of your critical dates and events from your semester calendar to your weekly calendar and highlighting them. Then fill in your known obligations and responsibilities for each day, including the times you must be in class, the hours you work, the meeting times for any organization you belong to, the study group session you planned, your usual time at the gym, and the lunch date with your mom. Once you have listed all of your time

Figure 3.1
Semester Calendar

SEPTEMBER

	Monday	Tuesday	Wednesday	Thursday	Friday
Week 1		Algebra Quiz		Homecoming Float Meeting 2:00–3:00	English Comp.– Library Tour
Week 2		ALG. Quiz			
Week 3		ALG. Quiz / History Exam I			
Week 4	Work: Client Report Due	ALG. Quiz		Jenna: Parent-teacher conference 2:00	Work: Employee Training 4:00

OCTOBER

	Monday	Tuesday	Wednesday	Thursday	Friday
Week 5		ALG. Quiz		Homecoming Float MTG. 3:30–5:00	
Week 6		ALG. Quiz	Biology class meets at Pond		English Comp. Paper Outline due
Week 7		ALG. Quiz			Dentist 11:00
Week 8	Biology Lab Practical	ALG. Quiz / History Exam II	Biology Midterm		

Figure 3.1
(Continued)

NOVEMBER

	Monday	Tuesday	Wednesday	Thursday	Friday
Week 9	Meeting with Advisor 1:00	ALG. Quiz		*History: Guest speaker –WWII	
Week 10		ALG. Quiz			Homecoming Float Construction Parade!
Week 11		ALG. Quiz			English Comp. Paper DUE
		⊢——— Preregistration Week ———⊣			
Week 12		ALG. Quiz / History Exam III	Leave for home after class	Thanksgiving	

DECEMBER

	Monday	Tuesday	Wednesday	Thursday	Friday
Week 13		ALG. Quiz			Jenna's dance recital dress rehearsal 6:30
Week 14		ALG. Quiz	Dead Week (No Class) ——→		Dance Recital 7:00
Week 15	Lab Practical	ALG. Quiz / History Final	BIO Final / COMP. Review Paper DUE		
Week 16					

commitments, you can then establish priorities for the remaining tasks and plan your days.

Because the demands on your time vary from one week to the next, you should approach each week as it comes. If you have an exam on Thursday, block out some time to prepare for it. If you are handing in sources for an upcoming research report, decide when to visit the library to gather them. You may have a heavier reading load one week, so you will need to allot times throughout the week to complete it, working around the set times of your other obligations. Weekly scheduling requires that you keep your course syllabi handy for reference. Check what is on the agenda for each class each week, and make sure your weekly schedule accurately reflects your responsibilities. Figure 3.2 illustrates what this might look like. Anticipate brief periods of unscheduled time and find quick tasks to fit them. Carry texts, notebooks, and other materials with you so you can use them on short notice.

DESIGN YOUR DAYS

The reason for effective time management is so you can balance the completion of necessary tasks and the pursuit of pleasurable ones. Once you have planned your week, you have a picture of what each day is likely to bring, but changes can arise. When you arrive at class on Thursday, the professor may announce a change for class on Tuesday (perhaps no quiz). Your mom may call and cancel dinner plans, or the homecoming float committee may decide to meet Wednesday afternoon instead of Thursday. As you learn about each change, mark it on your weekly calendar and adjust your schedule accordingly. What will you do with the time you would have spent at dinner with your mom or reviewing for the quiz? What if you had planned to do research at the library Wednesday afternoon, but now need to attend your committee meeting? You must be flexible and rearrange your daily plans as necessary.

Every night, review your schedule for the next day. Get up each morning with a daily to-do list to guide you (see Figure 3.3). When you know what is coming, you can prepare mentally for the structure of the following day. You can be more efficient and can carry out the expected tasks more smoothly.

REVIEW AND REWORK

Time management is a dynamic process that involves continuous monitoring of obligations, events, and changing priorities. Don't just glance at your calendar on occasion to note the date and to determine how many class periods there are before the next test. Calendars are tools to be used on a daily basis and representations of our ever-changing lives. Refer to your schedules regularly and modify them frequently. Reviewing and reworking your schedule is fundamental to effective time management.

There is no point in developing a plan for using your time if you don't consult that plan often. People who believe they can manage their time—and their lives—strictly by memory are at risk of forgetting responsibilities, neglecting commitments, and wasting valuable time. Documenting your plans for managing your semester, your weeks, and each day gives you power. It denotes firm decisions about what you will accomplish and when. You are less likely to abandon a plan that you have documented purposefully.

A good manager is adept at rearranging schedules that must be changed. Reworking doesn't just mean crossing off tasks that cannot be completed as planned or switching the order of activities and events. It requires critically thinking about the best overall plan. Effective time management is an occupation—a position that is responsible for optimizing daily functioning and taking control of your life so you can reach your goals.

Oct. 18   Oct. 24

Figure 3.2
Week at a Glance

	Sunday	Monday	Tuesday	Wednesday	Thursday	Friday	Saturday
6:00							
7:00							
8:00		Biology	Algebra Quiz	Biology	Algebra	Biology	Walk
9:00	9:30 Church	English COMP.	— 9:20 —	English COMP.	— 9:20 —	English COMP. Outline Due!	Study History Notes
10:00		Walk	Work	Walk	Work	Walk	Pick up J's Friend
11:00		Lunch 11:30 BIO Lab		Lunch Comp. Paper Ideas...		Lunch / Read BIO Lab Info.	Read BIO CH 13
12:00				Work		Work	Lunch
1:00	Read HIST CH 9 Break	— 1:30 —					Read BIO CH 14
2:00	Review BIO Notes	Work	Grocery Store		Computer Lab to print outline		Review History
3:00	Mom's for Dinner				Float Meeting		Algebra Problems
4:00			Jenna: Dance Class Review BIO				Relax &
5:00			Dinner		Dinner		Laundry
6:00	6:30	Dinner	History	Dinner	History	Baby Sitter Dinner & Movie	Dinner
7:00	Jenna: Bath & Bed	Jenna Bedtime	— 7:20 — Jenna Bedtime	Jenna Bedtime	— 7:20 —		Prep. dish for church potluck
8:00	Read History CH 10, 11	Review BIO Flashcards	Read BIO CH 12 Read History	Finalize Comp Paper Outline	Study Group (Library)		Call Mom
9:00		Finish Algebra Problems •Review			— 9:30 —		
10:00							
11:00							

Figure 3.3
Daily To-Do List

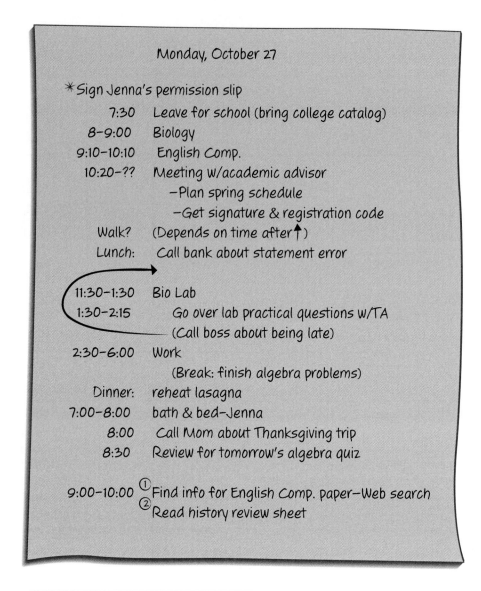

CHAPTER 3 REVIEW QUESTIONS

1. What does it mean to "build on the basics" in time management?

2. What things should you consider about yourself when approaching time management?

3. Discuss how to overcome the desire to procrastinate.

4. What job possibilities help make the most of your time?

5. What three basic kinds of schedules keep track of your time best?

6. How is time management a dynamic job?

SKILL PRACTICE

1. Make a list of your priorities.

> Begin with all of your obligations and responsibilities.
>
> Create a list of the goals you are currently working on, in the order of their importance.
>
> List specific tasks associated with each goal and identify the time frame in which you want to accomplish them.

2. Get to know yourself. Make a list of requirements for you to be your best at what you want and need to do.

> What does your body need in terms of sleeping, eating, and exercising?
>
> When should you eat the biggest meal of the day?
>
> When are you most alert and able to concentrate on schoolwork?
>
> What is your attention span for concentrating on different tasks?
>
> Under what circumstances are you most able to relax?
>
> How much time do you need to be with friends and family?
>
> What other conditions help you perform your best and accomplish tasks?

3. Use the chart at the end of this chapter to keep track of how you use your time for a week. After you have filled out the chart, answer the following questions:

> How much of your time was spent on personal obligations?
>
> How much time did you spend in activities related to achieving your goals?
>
> How much time did you spend in self-scheduled study or reading time?
>
> At which times were you most productive? On average, how much time were you truly productive?
>
> At which times of the day did you tend to waste time? On average, how much time did you waste each day?
>
> What is your overall assessment of your current time management ability?
>
> What specific techniques could you use to improve your time management?

4. Develop a list of people who can help you with time management.

> Can family members help you with childcare, meals, laundry, or other household chores?
>
> Is your roommate willing to commit to some quiet hours to guarantee a good study environment?
>
> Could you carpool with any of your classmates so you can discuss topics from class while commuting?
>
> Are any classmates available for a regular study or discussion session that could deepen your knowledge of the material?

CURRENT COURSE APPLICATION

1. Identify a short-term goal to accomplish within the week. Break it down into a set of sub-goals. Block out specific times on your calendar to work on these tasks. What can you accomplish today?

2. Consider your current school schedule and your list of priorities from the Skill Practice.

How well does your schedule match your optimal levels of functioning?

What have you learned about scheduling classes and fitting school into your life, based on what you are currently experiencing?

What challenges do you face as a result of not having considered your ideal functioning needs prior to creating your schedule?

What will you change next semester to have a more efficient and satisfying schedule, and what things will remain the same?

3. Identify any brief unscheduled periods of time that exist throughout your schedule. Make a list of specific course-related tasks that you could work on during these times.

4. If you have to work while in school, consider some job possibilities that might allow you to make more of your time.

Are there any jobs on campus to eliminate a commute to work?

Are any internships available that might better accommodate your academic schedule?

What jobs in your area might allow you to study during specific periods?

What skills or talents do you have that might enable you to have your own business?

TAKE A LOOK ONLINE

For a comprehensive look at time management and to discover how you use your time, go to

www.uni.edu/walsh/linda7.html

You can find additional information on time management at

http://web.mit.edu/arc/learning/modules/time/assessment.pdf

www.mindtools.com

STUDENT SCENARIO DISCUSSION RESPONSES

- **What benefits did Kendra enjoy as a result of her careful scheduling?** She was in control of her life. She knew what she was doing and when she was going to do it. She was assured that she had enough time to accomplish what she needed and wanted to do. This most likely would lead to confidence and low stress levels (along with academic success).

- **Why was her employer's offer so challenging?** First of all, having to worry a little less about her financial situation and have some extra money was very attractive to Kendra. Also, her employer's appreciation of her work made it hard for her to turn him down. Socializing with her friends was an added bonus to working more. However, the extra work hours conflicted with her carefully planned schedule.

- **What should Kendra have done in this situation?** Kendra should either have refused the offer (after thanking her boss and explaining her reason, of course) or have asked if she could think about it and let him know the next day. She also might have given up some of the after-work socializing to replace study time lost due to the extra work hours.

- **Was it possible for Kendra to accept the extra hours and maintain her schoolwork? Explain.** Kendra may have been able to work the extra hours and still accomplish her school tasks if she had reviewed and adjusted her carefully planned schedule. She may or may not have been able to fit it in, depending on how she allotted her time. Sometimes there are just not enough hours in the day to do everything. Revising her schedule may have helped Kendra resist the temptation to socialize after work.

- **Discuss the importance of priorities in Kendra's situation.** Kendra had to decide what was most important to her. In this case, she chose making more money but discovered that she had to pay the price in other important ways. If she had been living on what she earned before the offer, she could have continued to do so and keep up her grades.

- **What would you do if you were in Kendra's situation and your boss offered you more hours every month? What factors would contribute to your decision?** You might begin by reviewing and reworking your schedule to see if it would be possible to add the extra hours and still have sufficient time for schoolwork. You would consider how much stress you would be under, what leisure activities you might have to reduce, and how much the extra money would mean to you in relation to your performance in school.

DAILY TIME CHART

In each area of the chart, note what you did with your time. Be honest. You can improve your time management only if you are aware of how you spend your time. Indicate whether something is obligatory (O), goal related (G), or self-scheduled schoolwork (SW). Indicate if you were productive (P) or wasted time (W).

	Sunday	Monday	Tuesday	Wednesday	Thursday	Friday	Saturday
12–6 a.m.							
6–7							
7–8							
8–9							
9–10							
10–11							
11–noon							
12–1 p.m.							
1–2							
2–3							
3–4							
4–5							
5–6							
6–7							
7–8							
8–9							
9–10							
10–12							

MAKE THE MOST OF YOUR CAMPUS EXPERIENCE

In this chapter you will learn

- The sources for valuable information to function effectively on your campus

- How you can benefit from the services and resources provided on your campus

- How to use your campus library effectively

- Why you should develop relationships with your instructors

- How to get to know your instructors

 ## SCOPE OUT YOUR SCHOOL

As you know, pursuing your goals is not a solitary venture, so it is important to seek a variety of resources and personal support. Your school is a great place to start. College campuses are not just buildings with classrooms and laboratories but, rather, communities of people and services that can help you reach your goals. This chapter helps you identify the resources available to you—to learn what you can expect from staff and faculty, and how to make use of what your institution offers. Begin by doing the Skill Check to find out how familiar you are with your campus.

USE YOUR COLLEGE CATALOG

A critical aspect to college success is understanding how your institution works. Let's start with your college catalog, which contains a great deal of necessary information. Not only does the catalog provide detailed descriptions of degree requirements, courses, and faculty credentials, but it also contains important school policies. When you become familiar with these basics, you can navigate smoothly through the logistics of school and avoid costly oversights and unforeseen errors.

SKILL CHECK: KNOW YOUR WAY AROUND

How well do you know your school? Are you confident that you can use it to the maximum capacity? Do you know all of the critical procedures for students? For example, do you know the best time to register for classes? Is it necessary to obtain signatures to register, withdraw from a course, or change your major? If so, do you know whose signature is required? If you don't know, how can you find out? Where can you go for assistance?

Do you know what services are available on campus? If you are struggling in math, for example, should you hire a private tutor or could someone in the math department help you for free? Are you aware of all of the options for financial aid? Are you certain you don't qualify for a monetary grant?

What are the hours for the library? How can you access the online catalog or use the databases for research? What is the fine for overdue books? Can you reserve meeting rooms at your library for study groups?

What personal services does your campus offer? Is there a place to buy stamps? An ATM? Help for stress management?

Knowing the answers to these questions helps you make the most of your time at school. Start exploring your campus. Learn about the resources right there at your fingertips.

- *Important dates and deadlines.* The catalog you receive when you enter school is valid through your graduation date (assuming you finish in a timely manner). It provides critical dates for registration, fee payment, dropping and adding classes, graduation applications, holidays, and so on.
- *Student status information.* The catalog informs you of admission requirements for new students, transfer students, and international students. It provides course credit transfer information, college entrance exam requirements, and advanced placement (AP) exam credit procedures. It also explains what determines your rank as a freshman, sophomore, junior, or senior.
- *Degree plans, registration, and attendance procedures.* The catalog outlines procedures for declaring and changing majors, academic advising, registering for classes, and different registration options (such as auditing courses or taking courses for no credit). It lists core courses, elective options based on your major, and specific course tracks to choose from within each major.
- *Expectations for scholastic performance.* The catalog outlines your institution's grading format and grade point average (GPA) expectations for transfer and established students. It shows how to calculate your GPA and indicates the GPA value that will result in your being placed on academic probation or suspended from the university. It also indicates the necessary GPA for participating in the honors program or for graduating *cum laude, magna cum laude,* and *summa cum laude.*
- *The foundation for degree requirements.* The catalog provides an overview of your institution's curriculum requirements, including the elements of the core curriculum and the requirements for choosing a double degree, a double major, or a minor. It also explains graduation requirements and application procedures.

- *Tuition and fees.* The catalog discusses tuition and additional fees for lab courses, student union, computer accounts, parking, and other services. It describes payment options and deadlines, refund policies, and campus policies for student responsibility.
- *Financial aid.* The catalog provides a brief overview of financial aid services and opportunities provided through your institution. It also discusses study abroad and on-campus work-study programs.
- *Student resources, services, and organizations.* The catalog presents a brief overview of the special student services and organizations on your campus.
- *Specific degree plans for every major.* The catalog explicitly states the requirements for each major and summarizes every course within each major. It includes credit hours for each course and lab, along with the total credit hours required for graduation.
- *Faculty and administration credentials.* The catalog identifies the institutions at which all professors earned their degrees, as well as their area of specialization. It also lists the degrees of all high-level administrative personnel.

EXPLORE YOUR CAMPUS WEBSITE

Many schools have their entire catalog online. Some campus websites provide a more detailed description of services and organizations available to you. Often, the home page links to the academic programs, faculty and staff, student government, campus services, news and upcoming events, and clubs and organizations. When you follow up with these links, you find a great deal of information about how these elements of your campus work, how to make use of them, contact them, and become involved. Your campus website is one of the most valuable tools that your school has to offer.

TUNE IN TO CAMPUS PUBLICATIONS

Most colleges publish a variety of print material and distribute it throughout the campus. You can learn a lot about your campus environment from a campus newspaper. Articles alert students to important issues that affect them and offer reviews of past events and previews for upcoming speakers, shows, and seminars. You will also find classified ads for roommates, local job opportunities, and typing and tutoring services.

Some campuses also publish weekly or daily flyers to highlight important events such as time management workshops, on-campus job fairs, or intramural team sign-ups. Bulletin boards in various buildings around campus—particularly the student union and student housing areas—display a vast array of notices of upcoming events of interest to students. They announce club meetings, cheerleader tryouts, AIDS awareness week activities, and many other campus events in hopes of generating student participation. Check out what's happening on campus. You may discover some helpful and even enjoyable things.

KNOW YOUR CAMPUS SERVICES AND RESOURCES

Most colleges provide services to further students' success in school. This chapter profiles the most common services and resources found on college campuses. Remember, they are there for you to use.

The particular services available to students vary from school to school. Many services—including resources for personal, academic, and social enrichment—are standard. The Professor's Perspective illustrates how readily students are expected to take advantage of campus services.

> ## PROFESSOR'S PERSPECTIVE: NO EXCUSES
>
>
> Many students rush to school, attend class, and leave campus as quickly as possible. They are not interested in discovering what help is available or the services that might facilitate attending school. Professors are aware of these services, though, and they expect students to use them. If your home computer is down or your printer runs out of ink the night before an assignment is due, your professor expects you to use the computer center on campus. If you are struggling in math and can't understand the concepts presented during class, free tutoring may be available in the math lab, and your professor may expect you to use such services without suggestion. If you don't know where to find the required resources for your sociology paper, you are expected to ask the reference librarians. Their job is to help students locate information.
>
> Your campus is there to support you. Make use of what it offers so you can fulfill your responsibilities and maximize your chances for success. Instructors know what services are available to help students, and they are not likely to accept any excuses.

BE AWARE OF THE BASICS

When you start familiarizing yourself with campus services, make sure you note the most basic information. Get a schedule of operating hours along with contact information. Does the service have a link from the campus website? Find out if there is a fee for using the service. It is rare for campus services to charge students, because the student fees paid along with tuition cover the cost of most services. However, some medical tests or procedures at the health center may incur a fee, or the number of pages you can print free at the computer lab may be limited. Find out ahead of time if a service will cost you anything.

Learn about the procedures for using the service, too. Find out if you need to present your student ID card or if you need to make an appointment. Are you charged if you cancel your appointment or don't show up? Is there a time limit for using the service? Once you understand how a service works, you will be more comfortable trying it for the first time and will be more likely to use it regularly without penalty.

Many universities are like little cities—designed to centralize services and opportunities so students can function almost entirely on campus. Even if you commute, you may find that you can accomplish a great deal—besides going to class—without leaving campus. Taking advantage of school services can be a great time management tool. You can eliminate driving time and the hassle of running around town by making use of your school's facilities.

- *Studying.* Your campus probably has numerous locations for studying. The library may have quiet study areas for both individual use and group study sessions. Some student unions have a separate study lounge or areas that are not heavily populated during the day. If you can focus easily, a shady bench or a tranquil spot under a tree may be the perfect location for you to read and write.

- *Eating.* Your campus is likely to have several places for refreshments—from a cup of coffee to a complete meal. You can read or study while you eat, and you can suggest that your study group meet in the cafeteria or at picnic tables.

- *Exercising.* If your campus has a gym, you most likely paid fees to use the facilities. Take advantage of them by running the track or playing racquetball between classes. Use the weight room or swim laps to get energized for more studying.

- *Supplies and postage needs.* Student bookstores sell self-help books, career guides, best-sellers, paper, envelopes, pens, highlighters, notebooks, dividers, calculators, and other supplies. Many campus bookstores sell postage stamps and have a U.S. mailbox as well as FedEx and UPS stations.

- *Leisure activities.* If you need some time to relax or you are looking for something fun and interesting to do, your school may be just the place. You can probably find a quiet place on campus to just sit and relax on nice days, and the student union may have a lounge with comfortable chairs and sofas and even a television. College campuses often host numerous entertainment events, including festivals and rallies, musical concerts, theater productions, and art exhibits. Students often get reduced-price tickets or even free admission.

CONSIDER FINANCIAL AID

The campus financial aid office can assist students by arranging for grants, loans, scholarships, and work-study programs. The staff should be able to identify the most appropriate financial aid and help students fill out the necessary paperwork. A wide variety of financial opportunities exist, and it is beneficial for all students to explore their options. Ask financial aid counselors about the following options:

- *Scholarships.* These are a form of gift aid—monetary awards that the student does not need to pay back. Many organizations and schools provide money for scholarships, which usually are rewarded on the basis of academic merit or a particular talent or skill, such as athletics or music. Some take into account financial need, but others do not. Many are awarded to the most qualified students who meet the eligibility requirements, such as membership in a specific organization (Future Business Leaders of America, Debate Club, Girl Scouts, Boy Scouts, and so on) or participation in a group (church, band, thespians). Children of parents who work for a specific business or who are members of a civic group (Kiwanis or Shriners, for example) may be eligible for scholarships awarded by that group.

- *Grants.* Typically, grants are awarded on the basis of financial need. The most common grant is the Federal Pell Grant, and the amount available to students each year is based on the funding allotted by Congress. For example, the awards for 2002–2003 ranged from $400 to $4,000. A combination of factors—including whether the individual is a full-time or part-time student (both are eligible for aid), the cost of attending school, and how much money the student's family can contribute—determine the grant amount. The government uses a specific formula to calculate this figure, based on information the student provides in the "Free Application for Federal Student Aid" (FAFSA). No academic requirements or GPA minimum is necessary to receive a Pell Grant; however, some schools are not eligible. The financial aid office can provide applications and information regarding grants.

- *Loans.* Students can also apply for loans to help pay for college education. The largest source of loan money comes from the federal government. Government loans are appealing because the interest rates are low, the credit requirements are fairly relaxed, and repayment can be deferred or spread over a longer period of time.[1] A financial aid counselor can help you determine which type of loan is best for you.

TAKE ADVANTAGE OF ACADEMIC ADVISING

Most institutions require that students meet with an academic advisor prior to registering for classes each semester. An academic advisor can help you develop your degree plan once you have chosen a major and can keep you on track as you progress through your required courses, making sure you take the courses you need when you need them. If you have not yet chosen a major, an advisor can assist you in exploring possible interests and can help you choose core courses that will benefit you and fulfill school requirements in a timely manner.

Academic advising is not limited to informing students about required classes. Ideally, you can develop a long-term relationship with your advisor. Meet with your advisor regularly so he or she can get to know you. Advisors are trained to listen and recognize your needs and goals to help you succeed in school and beyond. They can help students with goal setting, time management, study skills, and test preparation. They also can refer students to other resources on campus that support their efforts. The more you work with your academic advisor, the more complete your college experience will be.

Many academic advisors are knowledgeable about the formats of classes and the characteristics of individual instructors. Once your advisor gets to know your learning style and course preferences, he or she can make suggestions for specific class sections and for professors that you may enjoy and learn from the best. If you hear other students speak of "good" classes and "bad" classes, "good" instructors and "bad" instructors, your academic advisor will tell you that there's no such thing. Classes and instructors are simply *different:* Classes have various formats, with different assignments and requirements; instructors have different personalities and teaching styles. It is important to recognize that one student may love a certain course and thrive with a certain teaching style, while another may find the same course and same instructor almost unbearable. Make use of your advisor's knowledge so you can enroll in the classes best suited to your academic needs and wants.

CONSULT THE CAREER CENTER

Many freshmen and sophomores perceive the campus career center as a useful service only for students nearing graduation. In fact, most college career centers have valuable services to offer all students—particularly those who have yet to determine a major area of study. They provide assessment services, matching student profiles with career options.

Career centers have literature on almost every occupation, as well as information about which schools offer the best undergraduate and graduate degree programs in each field, future job projections, and salary ranges. Many campus career centers help students find on-campus or local job opportunities, including career-related internships. They provide seminars on résumé writing and interviewing techniques and host on-campus job fairs. Check out your career center to collect information related to your major or to explore possibilities for your future.

---

[1] John Santrock and Jane Halonen. *Your Guide to College Success,* 3rd ed. (Belmont, California: Wadsworth, 2004), pp. 143–145.

CURTAIL COMPUTER PROBLEMS BY USING COMPUTER LABS

Your campus probably has one or more computer labs for student use. When you pay tuition, you can also pay a fee for a computer account that gives you access to the Internet, databases, and a personal e-mail address. Some schools charge additional fees for printing—or at least printing beyond the established page count included in the account. By having computer access on campus, you may not need a home computer or Internet service where you live. Chances are good that there will be a computer and printer available when you have a typed assignment due.

On-campus computer access offers another great way to make the most of your time. You can catch up on e-mail and personal correspondence in addition to using such services as online banking and shopping. You can surf the Internet between classes, research a project topic, or edit a term paper. With a computer lab at your disposal at school, you don't have to worry about your computer crashing.

INVESTIGATE TUTORING SERVICES

Many colleges have learning resource centers to help students who have difficulties with math and writing assignments. The centers are free of charge but may require appointments. Essentially, they are free tutoring services—paid for, most likely, by student fees. Many students use on-campus tutoring, and it can make a difference in your academic performance. You can make a one-time visit for a specific issue or go routinely to help you through a particularly challenging class.

SEEK SUPPORT THROUGH THE COUNSELING CENTER

Campus counseling centers offer both personal and academic support. They are staffed with certified counselors who can provide individual, couple, and group counseling for various issues. They guarantee confidentiality and often deal with everything from mild homesickness to serious depression. Services provided on campus are free of charge, and counselors can provide referrals for more serious problems. Counseling centers also provide other services such as seminars on time management, stress management, roommate relationships, and dealing with academic challenges.

USE THE HEALTH CENTER

Taking care of yourself is critical to performing well in school and making progress toward your goals. The student health center on your campus can provide convenient and inexpensive (if not free) basic health care. Special tests such as throat cultures or blood tests are likely to incur a minor fee, but you can have quick access to medical staff who can assess your condition and prescribe any necessary medication. Health centers also typically offer seminars on health-related topics such as nutrition, weight loss, and stress relief. They may provide free condoms, offer information on birth control options, and provide counseling for students diagnosed with a sexually transmitted disease. Some colleges also offer low-cost student health insurance.

 LEARN ABOUT THE LIBRARY

The library is an invaluable campus resource, and you will use it many times throughout your college career. Finding the information you need in libraries has become both easier and more difficult over the years, so it is important to become familiar as soon as possible with how your library functions.

FIND YOUR WAY AROUND

College libraries are vast resources. They offer a huge number of books and periodicals and access to even more sources. Until you become familiar with your school library, it may seem complex and intimidating. When you visit the library for the first time, don't expect to know exactly how to find what you are looking for.

Most libraries offer tours that help students find their way around, both physically (where resources and services are located in the building) and informationally (which materials and tools help users locate resources they need). Suppose you had to find documentation on the Food and Drug Administration's ruling on the use of a particular drug. Would you know how to find it, or would you wander through the library without knowing what to look for, where to search, or how to access the information? Asking a reference librarian for assistance saves you a great deal of time. Sometimes even the librarians have to do some research to locate a source, so imagine if you tried it on your own. Observe the librarian as he or she works. Notice the systematic approach to locating information, and learn from your observation. Become familiar with how to use your library efficiently and effectively, and get to know the reference librarians.

WHAT'S IN IT FOR YOU?

The exact content and accessibility of information differs from one library to the next. All libraries have some basic elements in common, though. Nearly all libraries have shelved books, shelved and archived periodicals, reference books, and systems of organization.

BOOKS

To locate books on a chosen topic, you use the library's *catalog,* which lists all of the books available. Most libraries have an *online catalog,* but they also may use a card catalog, which notes holdings on small cards filed in a cabinet. To find information on a specific topic, you must physically go to the cabinet and flip through cards filed under the first letter of the topic you are looking up.

Online catalogs are faster and easier and provide numerous search opportunities by which to locate potential research materials. You can search for books by the exact title, author's name, the general subject matter, a keyword in the description, or a combination of topic prompts. This helps you quickly narrow your search.

For example, if you are interested in researching prisoners in the Bastille during the French Revolution, you could type in each of the primary requirements: *prisoners + Bastille + French Revolution.* The online catalog immediately provides you with a list of books that meet all of those criteria. Where would you start if you were using a card catalog? Looking up *French Revolution* would probably yield a huge number of books on every aspect of the topic—the people involved, the political issues, the guillotine, and battles. Weeding through the results would be time-consuming. Looking up *Bastille* may narrow your search, but it would still include other information you are not interested in, such as the construction of the prison, its destruction, or its use at other times than during the revolution. Searching for materials with the online catalog streamlines your research and saves you time.

Once you have identified potential sources of interest, the catalog indicates if the library has the book, whether the book is currently available, and, if your school library is linked to the city or county public library system, where you can find the book if your school library does not own it. Books that are in stock at your library have a *call number,* or identification that tells you where to find it in the *stacks,* or shelves. Libraries use one of two systems to organize their collections—the Dewey decimal system or the Library of Congress system. Each system categorizes books by subject matter, so when you look up a specific book you can find it among others on the same topic. If the source turns out to be not as useful as you had expected, then you can look at the other books on the shelf nearby. Once you begin using the library frequently—particularly for research related to your major—you begin to know where books on the same subjects are located within the building.

PERIODICALS

Your library also has a variety of *periodicals,* or materials that are published periodically—weekly, monthly, bimonthly, or quarterly. These include newspapers, magazines, and professional and technical journals. As you do more research at the college level, you tend to use periodicals more than books because they offer the latest findings in the field of study they represent. Books may offer a good foundation for fundamental theories and concepts, but detailed information can become outdated quickly when new developments occur.

You can use several different tools to locate articles of interest to you. The *Reader's Guide to Periodical Literature* is a monthly index that lists articles published that month in various magazines and professional journals. Each entry includes the necessary bibliographic information so readers can locate the article. Some entries include *abstracts,* or brief summaries of the articles. The *Reader's Guide* is organized alphabetically by topic. Most libraries have the *Reader's Guide* index dating back several years. Figure 4.1 shows a sample entry in the *Reader's Guide.* The title is followed by the authors' names, the name of the periodical, the volume number, the initial page number, and the date of publication. This entry also has an abstract, which enables you to quickly determine if the article really deals with your interests.

Note that articles from magazines for the general public are listed along with those from professional research journals. In college, you are expected to use primarily the latter. Make sure you know your professor's expectations as to the kinds of periodicals to use for your paper. You wouldn't want to cite sources from the popular magazine *Psychology Today* if you are supposed to research findings in *Journal of Educational Psychology.* If you are uncertain whether a particular publication is a professional journal, also called a *peer-reviewed* journal, ask the reference librarian, who can consult a list of all peer-reviewed publications.

Some periodicals have their own indexes. Some newspapers, like the *New York Times,* publish a monthly index of articles. Libraries also keep specialized indexes for different disciplines, including humanities, social science, psychology, and art. Because so much information is available dating back decades, libraries can't keep hard copies of everything. Therefore, you may find the articles you're looking for on *microfilm* or *microfiche*—formats that preserve articles greatly reduced in size—and that enable the library to store millions of articles. Because they are so small and there are hundreds of articles contained on one sheet, viewing them requires the use of a special magnifying machine. Libraries do not allow users to check out microfilm, but users can make a printed copy of any articles they need.

Figure 4.1
Entry in *Reader's Guide to Periodical Literature*

Peer interactions and friendships in an ethnically diverse school setting. Howes, C & Wu, F.—authors.

Child Development. 61 : 537 Apr '90

Abstract: Peer interaction, social status, and reciprocated friendships were examined in two ethnically diverse groups of children: 104 kindergartners and 106 third-graders. There was no correlation between social status and ethnicity. Third-grade children formed more cross-ethnic friendships and engaged in more cross-ethnic positive peer interaction than kindergartners. Children with more cross-ethnic friendships and more cross-ethnic peer interaction were no different in social status than children with fewer cross-ethnic experiences.

REFERENCES

All libraries have numerous reference sources, such as

- *Dictionaries.* There are many different kinds of dictionaries, including the *Oxford English Dictionary,* which includes an extensive history of word origins along with pronunciations, definitions, and examples of usage, and specialized discipline dictionaries that focus on terms as they are defined and used in particular fields such as medicine or law.

- *Encyclopedias.* The entries in an encyclopedia are arranged by topic, in alphabetical order. An encyclopedia—either a general edition or a specialized set—contains an index and is a good starting place to gain a broad perspective on a topic.

- *Almanacs.* Almanacs present a variety of information based on calendar days. They discuss topics such as cycles of the moon and tides, times for sunrise and sunset, and other astronomical phenomena. They also provide historical weather data, weather predictions for the future, crop planting guides, and additional statistics.

- *Atlases.* Atlases are collections of maps, charts, and tables for geological, geographical, agricultural, and political information from around the world.

THE WORLD (WIDE WEB) AT YOUR FINGERTIPS

Research is no longer limited to books, magazines, and newspapers contained within the library building itself. With Internet technology, we can access materials from just about any library in the world and many other sources. Many indexes for periodicals, including the *Reader's Guide,* are available online. Some are available on CD, which you can use at a computer in your library.

In addition, you can access dozens of databases—on health, performing arts, business, genealogy, and many other topics—at your library or via the Internet. Figure 4.2 shows just a sample of the databases that are available via the Internet. Numerous search options help you focus on specific information. Conducting an

---

Here is a sample list of databases available online. Some may be accessible only to subscribers such as your school library. Which ones interest you?

Academic Search Premier	Los Angeles Times
Biography and Genealogy Index	MathSci
Book Review Digest	Medline
Clinical Pharmacology	Military Library
Congressional Universe	National Geographic Map
Consumer Index	New York Times
Contemporary Women's Issues	Oxford English Dictionary
Criminal Justice Abstracts	Public Affairs
DOE (energy) reports	Patent Database
Historical Abstracts	Philosopher's Index
Inter-Plays (play index)	Population Index
International Index Performing Arts	Sage Urban Studies
Iter (Medieval/Renaissance)	Statistical Universe
Lexis-Nexis	Wall Street Journal
Linguistics	Web of Science

Figure 4.2
Online Databases

Figure 4.3
Critically Thinking About
the Web

Consider the following when visiting a website for the purpose of obtaining valid, reliable information.

- What names, credentials, and affiliations are presented for the website sponsor?
  Is it a school or university website?
  Is it a government website?
  Is it a commercial or business website?
  Is it a media source website?
  Is it an individual's website?

- What appears to be the purpose of the website?
  To provide valid, objective information on a specific topic or set of topics?
  To solicit business?
  For personal entertainment?
  As a forum for people to share opinions, ideas, and experiences?

- Does information at the linked sites correlate with that presented on the main site?

- Do other independent sites provide the same information?

- Can this information be verified?

- How recently was the site updated? Does it contain outdated information?

- Do you need to pay to access most of the information?

- Does the website ask you for personal data?
  For what purpose?
  Can you obtain the same information from another site for free?

---

effective database search takes skill, so work with a reference librarian to learn how to make the most of your search time.

Information from these databases can take a variety of forms. Some *hits,* or matches for your topic, simply list the bibliographic information so you can search your library for the hard copy. Other listings include an abstract, and some even let you *download,* or save to your computer, the entire text of the article. If you are working at the library you can print out the information you retrieve from the database or, in some cases, e-mail it to yourself.

Many students are turning to the World Wide Web for research. Although a tremendous amount of material is available, you should be careful about using information from websites that you find without the guidance of a reference librarian. There are no requirements for posting information on a website. There is no process to ensure that individuals who make statements and present facts on the Internet are qualified to do so, or that the facts are indeed true. Consequently, you should be wary of the sources. With all of the reliable databases available, most librarians—and professors—prefer that you use material from those sources. That way, you can be sure that the information you gather is current, scholarly, and authoritative. Many instructors won't accept resources from a general World Wide Web search. When this is the case, be sure to restrict your search to acceptable sources. If you are allowed to surf the Web to find information, consider each site carefully to determine its integrity. Figure 4.3 offers some guidelines for assessing websites. When in doubt regarding any aspect of a particular website, err on the side of caution.

 GET INVOLVED

Your college campus can offer you growth opportunities through social involvement. Being part of a campus organization helps you feel more connected to your school and strengthens your perception of yourself as a student. The deeper your connection to college life, the more committed you will become and the more likely it is that you will continue with school.

Most campuses support a variety of organizations dedicated to bringing students together to meet and interact with new people and to share some common ground outside of class. Some are primarily social, but most offer service to the university or community in some way.

Fraternities and sororities have a rich history. Each chapter, or local fraternity and sorority, is a branch of a national group of the same Greek name. Some campuses have entire houses for the members of each chapter to live in while attending school. Fraternities and sororities have officers and committees to oversee the activities and projects they are involved in. Members must meet specified academic standards and weekly study time requirements, and they must participate in service projects. However, fraternities and sororities are mainly social organizations.

The goals of other Greek organizations—honor societies, music brotherhoods, and discipline-based groups—are to bring students together who share academic interests and pursuits. These organizations broaden students' peer and faculty contacts and offer special opportunities such as meeting experts in a discipline, traveling to study special topics, and participating in internships and research projects.

Many campus clubs offer a place to share hobbies and special interests with other students. You can play intramural sports with students from your dorm or biology class. You can watch the latest high-tech cartoons and meet others who like Japanese anime. You can plan a trip to Paris with the French Club, campaign for your favorite candidate with the Campus Democrats, explore career possibilities and strengthen your oratory skills with the Pre-Law Society, or share the latest video game strategies with the Gamer's Group. Check out the social clubs at your school, or start your own.

Joining a service organization gives you the opportunity to offer some of your time to helping others while connecting you to the community. Many nonprofit organizations recruit enthusiastic students to volunteer for them. Big Brothers and Big Sisters and Habitat for Humanity are national organizations that offer opportunities for you to get involved. These groups and many others promote the "Alternative Spring Break" program, in which students work on a major community service project—either locally or at a site that requires travel—while on break from school in the spring. Some professors incorporate service learning into their courses, whereas others award extra credit for participation. Working alongside your peers to help others can be personally rewarding and satisfying.

ON-CAMPUS COURSE BOOSTERS

Doing well in your classes sometimes involves more than just taking careful notes and performing well on tests. You can get a boost in your learning and performance through getting to know your classmates and taking the time to do a little extra.

PEERS

As you know, college is not an experience that you want to spend alone. The time requirements and intellectual demands are tough and, if nothing else, you must seek a support network of family and friends. Don't overlook your peers. Classmates and other students can be a tremendous support to each other as they tackle similar obstacles and work toward shared goals.

Your peers understand what you are going through better than anyone else. They may not share the same life circumstances, but as far as school is concerned they know what challenges and pressures you face. It is powerful and comforting to talk with others who understand what you are experiencing and feeling. Simply sharing stories about difficult assignments, frustrating professors, and test anxiety can help you overcome the sense that you are a tiny fish in the huge ocean of college. Many other people are thinking and worrying about the same topics, and they have the same questions you have. They are performing at the same level and, like you perhaps, are wondering if they will ever make it to graduation. There is strength in numbers—even mental strength. Develop confidence by talking to your peers. Ask for their advice and give some of your own. Explore your campus resources together and encourage each other as needed.

Getting to know your peers can be a matter of practicality. Studying with a partner or a study group is a highly effective way to learn and ensures that you will in fact study. Make an effort to meet students who attend class regularly, ask questions, participate, and seem interested in learning. They can inspire you and play an important role in your success. Compare schedules and plan a regular time to meet. That way, even if you don't feel like studying, you will continue with your plans because someone is counting on you.

Study sessions with peers don't always have to be serious meetings. Get together for coffee just to compare notes, debate topics from class, and quiz each other on the challenging material. Compare lecture notes. You may be surprised at what others noted but that you missed. Working together, talk through the course subject matter. Fill in the blanks in your notes and see if your idea of "the big picture" matches your classmates' interpretation. If you get together on a weekly basis to review material with your peers, you will be amazed at how much you already know when it's time to study for the exam.

Some courses require group projects in which classmates create an end product or presentation. Group projects give you the chance to get to know more of your classmates and discover how they think and work. We all learn a great deal through observing other people's thought processes and creative approach to problem solving. Interacting with people who think differently can expand your own thinking and open your eyes to new ways of working. Capitalize on this idea when you are part of a group project. Don't dominate the meetings, even if you are capable of doing the required work. Contribute freely but learn from the input of others.

Most professors value group work, especially when students are working in diverse groups. Many campuses have a significant international student population, so you may find yourself learning about cultural differences and group dynamics in addition to the course topic your group is exploring. Working with others is an important part of most careers. The more effectively you can interact, cooperate, and communicate with different people, the greater your chance for future success. Start developing these skills with your peers.

FROM EXTRA ACTIVITIES TO EXTRA CREDIT

Despite meeting three or more hours a week, a college course is limited, given the scope of what there is to learn. Some professors get frustrated at not having enough time to cover the subject matter as they would like, or because they are restricted in what they can teach in class. Professors may offer extra learning opportunities outside of class, and it is highly beneficial to take advantage of them.

THE BROWN BAG

A *brown bag* meeting is an informal gathering of students and faculty to discuss a specific topic more in depth. Brown bags often occur around lunch time—hence the term—so you can bring food or the host may provide it. A brown bag may include a guest speaker who presents new research findings or a unique perspective on a subject, or it may simply offer students the opportunity to explore any issue they choose. The presence of one or more faculty members makes a brown bag a particularly worthwhile experience—not just because of the professional input from experts but because students can get to know the faculty personally. These casual get-togethers with an academic twist can add to your knowledge and motivate you to dive deeper into your education.

GUEST SPEAKERS

Colleges and universities often invite guest speakers who are revered in their discipline to lecture on campus. Instructors for courses related to the topic usually alert students and recommend attending. They themselves will likely attend, and your presence demonstrates your interest in learning more about the topic. A question-and-answer period may follow the presentation, as well as a reception, which may give you the opportunity to meet the guest of honor. Students who share an interest in the field have a rare opportunity to make a connection by talking with the guest. They may even be invited to work on a special research project or participate in a prestigious internship.

REVIEW SESSIONS

If an instructor or a teaching assistant offers a review session outside of class time prior to an upcoming exam, make every effort to go. It is valuable to study with someone who knows the material and the test questions well. Besides, it is unlikely that the person will waste time in an optional review session covering topics that are not important.

Attending a review session may give you a slight advantage. First of all, the instructor or teaching assistant may give you clues or direct information about what is on the test. Educators want you to learn the critical information, so when they are preparing you for the exam they will tell you what you need to know. Secondly, instructors notice which students make the effort to attend optional review sessions. Your attendance makes a significant impression and may work to your advantage during grading. If there is any doubt as to whether you understand a concept, the instructor may recall that you sat in on the review session and may give you the benefit of the doubt.

EXTRA CREDIT

Some instructors offer students the chance to earn extra credit. You should always take it if possible. Even if you are already doing well in the class, you should not view extra credit as optional. Barring any major time management issues, do any and all extra credit assignments that come your way. Don't forego or skimp on the required elements of class. Doing so would cancel the benefits of the extra work. However, extra credit assignments are worthwhile because you learn from them, you earn points for them, and they show that you want to succeed to the highest degree possible. In addition, they may help you unexpectedly. An emergency may prevent you from taking an exam or preparing sufficiently for one, you may have unforeseen difficulties with an assignment, or you may have overlooked a requirement on the syllabus and may have no opportunity to make it up. Extra credit assignments are rare in college. When they come along, incorporate them into your time management plan.

BUILD RELATIONSHIPS WITH YOUR INSTRUCTORS

You see your instructors often. They grade you and are the catalysts to your learning. How important is it to get to know them? Consider your feelings about this issue as you read the Perspective Check.

PERSPECTIVE CHECK: JUST A NUMBER

College differs from high school in several ways, not the least of which involves your experience in the classroom. You probably have noticed that your classes are bigger (maybe much bigger) than those in high school. Most classes meet two or three times weekly instead of every day, so professors are not likely to know your name. You may feel like "just a number" to your professors—just one of the many students they assign point values to and submit a final grade for.

Does it frustrate you that your teachers don't know you as a unique individual? Do you believe that it's just the way college is? What can you do about it? Should you make the effort to get to know your instructors or do you think they would consider it immature? On the other hand, is it acceptable to simply fade into the background in a class—to do the assigned work, perform well on exams, and collect your grade? What do you think? Are you content to be just a number? Should you hope for anything more?

WHO ARE YOUR INSTRUCTORS?

Most of your professors probably earned Doctor of Philosophy (Ph.D.) degrees in a specific field of study. They may have contributed new and unique information to their area of specialization and may be considered experts in their field. Most professors, particularly at research universities, continue to conduct studies and bring in grant money for their institution to further understanding on their topic. Some universities distinguish between professors based on their length of time at the school, their accomplishments, and whether they have been awarded tenure—a permanent position at the school based on the individual's contributions and performance. The instructor's position—associate professor, assistant professor, or full professor—reflects these distinctions.

Visiting professors or lecturers—called *adjuncts*—do not have full-time positions on the faculty but teach for a limited period. Some instructors or lecturers may have a master's degree and some may be graduate students in the process of earning a master's degree or Ph.D. Graduate student instructors, called teaching assistants (TAs), typically are guided by a full-time faculty member. In some cases, the teaching assistant is the only instructor for a class. Many lab sections are led by teaching assistants, for example. In other cases, the TA simply assists the professor in the teaching of his or her courses.

Regardless of the status of your instructor, he or she is there to provide you with the necessary information and materials to learn the subject matter and complete the course requirements. Like all of us, college instructors represent a range of personalities and characteristics. Some enjoy teaching and interacting with students in the classroom, and their enthusiasm and talent are obvious. Others are more preoccupied with their research endeavors and many teach only because they are required to do so. As a student, you must try to succeed in your courses regardless of the instructor's interests, personality, or talents. Try to gather information ahead of time about the teaching style and format of each course so you can find the best match possible. However, when you recognize a challenge in your circumstances, seek the resources to help you succeed.

WHY IT'S IMPORTANT TO GET TO KNOW THEM

Instructors are some of the most valuable resources you have—for many reasons. They determine the requirements for completing a course successfully. They create the assignments and exams, set the standards, and assess your work. They judge how well you understand the content and have mastered the material. You should go directly to your instructors if you have questions or concerns about a topic or want to know how to prepare effectively for exams or find out the characteristics of a paper that meets expectations.

The first source of information about your instructor's requirements and expectations is the course *syllabus*. The syllabus is an overview of the course material and important information pertaining to taking the class. Figure 4.4 shows a sample syllabus, and includes the following features:

- *Course title and number.* The syllabus lists the name of the course and any prerequisite or corequisite courses. Check that you are in the right class and have completed all prerequisites, in addition to being enrolled in corequisite courses (usually lab courses).

- *Instructor name and contact information.* Instructors typically note their faculty status (adjunct, full professor, teaching assistant), along with their office location, office hours, phone number, and e-mail address.

- *Required materials.* The syllabus lists textbooks or other materials required for the class, along with any optional materials. Be sure you have the correct edition of the textbook and most current version of the materials. Problems can arise if you purchase used books that are outdated for this instructor's course.

- *Course objectives.* The syllabus describes the goals of the course—what you are expected to learn and accomplish—so you can understand the scope of the course content and what the course involves.

- *Assignments and exams.* The syllabus specifies the course requirements, including research projects, oral presentations, papers, and exams. The instructor may provide detailed assignment descriptions later.

- *Course schedule.* The syllabus provides an outline of the course, with the sequence and pace of topic coverage, along with assignment due dates and exam dates.

- *Grading scheme.* The syllabus explains how the instructor determines students' course grades. Grading may be on a point or percentage basis, and the instructor may grade on a curve (that is, awarding individual grades as they relate to the entire class).

- *Course policies.* Some instructors list on the syllabus any policies they have regarding student behavior and work-related issues.

You might view the course syllabus as a contract between the instructor and the student. The instructor makes clear his or her expectations of you, and you are responsible for knowing those expectations and following through with course policy. It is important to keep your syllabus handy so you can easily see it and refer to it. Don't just read through it once or discard it. You may need to check your syllabus continuously for reading assignments, upcoming quizzes and exams, and information about how to contact your instructor.

Part of every instructor's job is to set aside time outside of class to be available to students. If you have questions that you don't have the opportunity (or courage) to ask in class, make an appointment to talk with the instructor during office hours. If you have concerns about a grade on an assignment or exam, discuss the problem with the instructor. However, you must contact the instructor. He or she will not seek you out to ask if you need help. Take responsibility for your success. Go to your instructors before your grades become a problem.

Figure 4.4
Sample Course Syllabus

Course: Psy 3302—Life Span Development (3 credit hours)

Prerequisite: Psy 1302—Introduction to Psychology (1 credit hour)

Concurrent Lab: Psy 3302L—Life Span Observation Lab

Instructor: Dr. Beth Stark, Professor of Psychology

Office Hours: MWF 12:30–2:30 p.m. North Bldg. A406

Contact Information: 555-1234, bstark@college.edu

Required Texts: *Life Span Development* 4th edition
Observing the Young Child—2nd edition, lab workbook

Required Materials: Stop watch, clipboard

Course Objectives: Students will compare and contrast the physical, emotional, cognitive, and social changes that take place at each stage of life, from birth to death. The course emphasizes the varying contributions of growth and development and explores genetic and environmental influences. Students will leave the course with a firm understanding of what triggers the onset of different developmental periods as well as the variety of factors contributing to developmental delays and disruptions.

Assignments: Students will take four exams over the course of the semester, write a research-based paper, and present findings orally from lab observations.

Grading:

Exams	400 points (100 points each)
Paper	100 points
Oral presentation	100 points
Total	600 points

Semester grades will be determined according to a strict scale in which
90–100% = A   80–89% = B   70–79% = C   60–69% = D   Below 60% = F

Class Policies:

- No food is allowed in the classroom. Drinks are allowed.
- If students routinely arrive late, the door will be locked at the start of class time.
- Disruptive, noisy, and disrespectful students will be asked to leave class.
- If your cell phone rings, you will be asked to leave class.
- Late work is *not* accepted.
- Makeup exams are available only to students who speak to me *before* exam time and have a reason that I find valid for missing the original exam.
- Makeup exams are entirely essay in format.

Course Schedule:

Week 1	Class Introduction and Overview Read Chapters 1 and 2
Week 2	Physical and Cognitive Development in Infancy Read Chapters 3 and 4
Week 3	Social and Emotional Development in Infancy
Week 4	Exam (Intro and Infancy, Chapters 1–6) Read Chapters 5 and 6
Week 5	Physical and Cognitive Development in Early Childhood Read Chapters 7 and 8
Week 6	Social and Emotional Development in Early Childhood Read Chapters 9 and 10
Week 7	Physical and Cognitive Development in Middle Childhood Read Chapters 11 and 12
Week 8	Social and Emotional Development in Middle Childhood
Week 9	Exam (Childhood, Chapters 5–12) Read Chapter 16

Figure 4.4
(*Continued*)

Week 10	Adolescence (research paper topic due) Read Chapter 17
Week 11	Young Adulthood Read Chapters 18 and 19
Week 12	Marriage & Parenthood (research paper outline due) Read Chapter 19 and 20
Week 13	The Middle and Retirement Years Read Chapter 21
Week 14	Old Age, Death, and Dying Review session, Monday 2:00 (optional)
Week 15	Exam, research paper due

FUTURE OPPORTUNITIES AND RECOMMENDATIONS

Instructors who teach classes in your major can be particularly valuable to know. They are likely to know what's involved in earning undergraduate and graduate degrees in that field as well as career possibilities. They know which courses you have to take, and they can inform you of specific demands, assignment requirements, and additional readings. They can guide you in selecting the electives best suited to your style or interests. Some professors have contacts with professionals in the community and may help you get an internship. They may even employ you to work on their own research projects, which looks good on a résumé.

To get this special assistance from your professors, you must get to know them first. Your academic performance in their class does not ensure that you will stand out. Read the Student Scenario to explore the importance of developing a true relationship with your instructors.

STUDENT SCENARIO: GOOD GRADES AREN'T ENOUGH

Rashid is a junior and a microbiology major, excited to finally be taking upper division courses. He enjoyed last semester's course, "Microbial Physiology," and his current favorite class is "Techniques in Medical Microbiology." Rashid found an opening for an intern at a local hospital, working in the blood lab. He realizes how important it is to get experience in his field of study, and his professors repeatedly urge students to pursue internships.

After filling out the application for the lab position, he discovered that he must include a letter of recommendation from a professor in the biology department. He was certain that his Microbial Physiology instructor would oblige, because Rashid earned a solid A in the course. All of Rashid's grades have been excellent since he began college, so he was confident that he would be selected for the intern position.

When he approached Dr. Minett to ask for the letter, he had to introduce himself and remind her which course he had taken last semester. He explained about the internship and told Dr. Minett that he had earned a 98 percent average in her class. Dr. Minett reviewed her records from the previous semester and confirmed Rashid's claim, but she also informed him that she could not in good conscience write him a letter of recommendation.

Rashid was completely shocked. He asked Dr. Minett what the problem was, and she responded, "You are clearly a very competent learner, Rashid, and you should be proud of your grade. It will serve you well in the future when prospective employers look at your transcript. However, that grade is all I know of you as a student. You never asked questions in class, you never participated in class discussions, and you never came to see me during my office hours." All this was true, Rashid thought, but that was just the kind of student he was. He didn't like asking questions in front of everyone. If he didn't understand something, he'd look it up later. Class discussions were interesting to listen to, but he never felt the desire or need to participate. He also didn't see the need to visit Dr. Minett in person, because he was doing fine in the class.

Dr. Minett continued, "A letter of recommendation informs those who are considering hiring you as to who you are as much as it informs them of your knowledge of course information. They are asking me to describe your strengths—your ability to critically analyze information, to effectively communicate your thoughts, and to realize your goals. I know none of those things about you, Rashid, because you never demonstrated them to me. All I have is a record of your test scores. I'm truly sorry. You'll have to ask someone who knows you better." The problem was that no one in the biology department knew Rashid any better.

Consider the following questions:

- Was Rashid qualified for the internship? Why or why not?

- Dr. Minett stated that a 98 percent semester grade does not indicate that Rashid could function successfully in the internship. What reasons could she have given?

- If students choose not to speak up in class or visit the instructor to develop a personal relationship, does it indicate they are less competent? Explain.

- Was Dr. Minett too harsh for not writing the letter? Could she have been responding to a personal issue?

- What should Rashid do at this point? Should he change the kind of student he is? Why or why not?

MENTORING

A *mentor* is someone who inspires and listens to another person and who offers assistance and moral support as the person works toward his or her goals. Many individuals can serve as a mentor, including professors in your field of study. They can offer encouragement and advice to pave the way for you to reach your academic and career goals. They can help you gain valuable hands-on experience, either through working directly with them, or connecting you with others who can advance your opportunities. They can offer suggestions for taking on challenges in the classroom, managing your time, and planning for the future.

An instructor becomes a mentor primarily through a student's efforts. When you take steps to show the instructor who you are, you lay the foundation for a significant and beneficial relationship. Many professors enjoy getting to know their students, particularly those majoring in their field, and they want to help them succeed.

HOW TO GET ACQUAINTED

You can make a good impression on your instructors in many ways, and the classroom is the place to start. Sitting in the front enables them to see you every day in class, make eye contact with you during the lecture, and chat with you before or after class. During class, ask questions, confirm your understanding of a concept, discuss a topic-related article you read in the newspaper—anything that briefly engages the instructor and shows that you are involved with the course material.

Ask questions that are well thought out, intelligent, and related to the topic. Don't disrupt the flow of the lecture or dominate the class at the expense of others' ability to participate. It is important to be an active participant who contributes valuable ideas to class discussions rather than spouting unsolicited personal opinions, ignoring or belittling the input of classmates, or preventing others getting a word in edgewise.

Make a point of visiting your instructors during their designated office hours. Here are some things to keep in mind when you do so:

- *Respect office hours and appointment policy.* Professors are busy, often teaching several classes with 100 or more students to keep track of. They also have other responsibilities on campus, such as sitting on advisory boards or faculty senate meetings, and chairing graduate student thesis committees. Visit only during the posted office hours or appointment times. Demonstrate that you respect their time.

- *Stay for a reasonable amount of time.* Limit your office visit to cover only the issues at hand. Other students may have scheduled to visit, or your professor may have a particularly busy day. Just showing up for a lengthy casual visit may annoy rather than impress the instructor.

- *Have a specific agenda.* Make a list of questions, problems, or concerns to address during your visit. Try to be explicit, and bring your notes, assignments, and exams to make the most of your time. This demonstrates your maturity in communicating your needs and may help the instructor view your future visits positively.

- *Treat them with respect.* Some teachers are professional with students, whereas others are casual and personable. In either case, treat them with the respect their position deserves. Like employers, they have authority over you. Although a close relationship can develop between a professor and a student, at no time should you speak to your instructors or treat them as a peer.

As your relationship develops, these rules may relax. However, you should follow your instructor's lead. He or she may eventually encourage you to stop by the office any time or may engage you in conversation about things other than class or school. Let the instructor broaden the parameters of your interactions; don't try to push the boundaries yourself.

Don't expect to develop close relationships with all of your instructors. However, it is important that you feel comfortable approaching each one when you have questions or issues in the class. Let your instructors know who you are as a student. When you participate in class and make yourself known, you give the instructor more information on which to determine your success in the course. When you don't do as well as you had hoped on an exam, following up with your instructor demonstrates that you are determined to improve and do well in class. When you ask questions, it shows that you are tuned in to the material and want to understand it fully. When you participate in class discussions, it helps you think critically and communicate about the topics. You don't have to be outgoing or feel like you have mastered the course content to show that you are a conscientious student who cares about his or her grade. This lays the foundation for a future of connecting with people you meet and work with in your career. Read the Future Focus for a look at the ongoing importance of getting to know those around you.

FUTURE FOCUS: IT'S WHO YOU KNOW

You have probably heard the expression, "It's not *what* you know; it's *who* you know." Being competent in your field of study and other endeavors opens the doors of opportunity, but the people you encounter along the way can often be the doors themselves. *Networking* is important in today's job market. People often get where they are going through the connections they make with others. If you are an employer looking to hire someone, you feel more confident choosing a person that you know. One of the best ways to learn about a person's strengths, work ethic, leadership ability, and other characteristics is through a mutual friend or respected colleague. If everything else is equal, a personal recommendation is a powerful bonus.

The more people you know—and who get to know you—the more opportunities will come your way. When you make a positive impression on those you meet, your horizons broaden. Remember, they know people who know people who know other people who know more people.

CHAPTER 4 REVIEW QUESTIONS

1. What valuable sources can you use to help you navigate successfully around your college campus?

2. How can your campus help you make the most of your time?

3. How has technology changed library research?

4. Why might it be important to get involved in an on-campus organization?

5. Describe the different kinds of instructors you are likely to find on your college campus.

6. Why is it important to interact with your instructors and to develop positive relationships with them?

7. What guidelines should you abide when approaching instructors?

SKILL PRACTICE

1. Examine your college catalog, website, or schedule of classes to find the following information.

Critical dates for dropping courses and receiving tuition refunds, withdrawing from a course without penalty, registering for next semester, and paying tuition

Grade point averages required for graduating with honors, avoiding academic probation, getting off of academic probation, and avoiding academic suspension

How to audit a course and how to take a course for no credit

The consequences for having outstanding parking or library fees

2. Using the schedule of classes, find out the meaning of course prefixes and numbers. What indicates that a course is offered only in the spring? How can you determine if there are prerequisites? Identify all special case indicators associated with course listings.

3. Study the degree plan for your major (or for a few majors, if you haven't declared one yet).

What school or department is the major in?

How many credit hours are required for graduation?

What courses look most interesting to you?

Are there related minors you can pursue with your degree?

4. Conduct a Web search of your institution's website to find the following information:

Upcoming campus events

Student government issues and opportunities

Tips from the counseling and career centers

Library hours and services

Other services and resources available to students

A faculty member's Web page

The Web page of two campus clubs

A map of your campus to identify the location of various services

Online job opportunities for students

Financial aid information

5. If you aren't already familiar with your library, arrange to take a tour or spend some time on your own locating the following resources:

The online catalog

The reference desk

Computers available for using Internet databases

The area in the stacks with books on world leaders

The area that has professional journals

The microfilm and microfiche viewing area

Sets of encyclopedias

The quiet study carrels

The copy machines

CURRENT COURSE APPLICATION

1. Consider the challenges you face now or anticipate in each class you are currently taking. What on-campus services or resources can you use to help you overcome those challenges? Cite the location, hours of operation, and any other necessary information for each service or resource named.

2. If you have not done so already, meet with an academic advisor. Discuss your degree plan or the core courses you plan to take next semester. Ask for specific information about class formats and instructor styles to help you determine which ones might best suit your own personality and learning style. Plan another meeting prior to registration to confirm your course selections.

3. Spend some time at your campus computer center. Work on an assignment, check e-mail, or surf the Internet.

4. Brainstorm some topics for a library research paper due later in the semester. If you don't have a paper due this semester, consider some topics of personal interest to explore.
   a. Identify some books using the online catalog.
   b. Use the *Reader's Guide to Periodical Literature* to find some articles in a peer-reviewed journal.
   c. Explore the index for a major newspaper.
   d. Ask a reference librarian to recommend some Internet databases to search.
   e. Do a Web search to compare general information available to that provided by the databases. Assess the sites for quality and usefulness.

5. Consider your instructors.

Who is the most approachable?

Who intimidates you the most?

Who might be most helpful for your future endeavors?

Who would you like to get to know better?

What steps could you take to get to know your instructor better?

How could you get to know the least approachable instructors?

6. Make an appointment with one of your instructors. Prepare a list of questions— either regarding specific course content, general study tactics, or general academic success—and other particular issues that you'd like to address. Meet with your instructor and write a summary of your experience.

Was it easier or more difficult than you had anticipated?

Did the instructor effectively answer your questions?

Did you get more information than you sought?

Did the visit give you confidence to approach other instructors?

Might you continue to try to develop a relationship with this instructor? Why or why not?

TAKE A LOOK ONLINE

For a list of do's and don'ts for interacting with faculty, go to

www.reshall.berkeley.edu/academics/resources/faculty

For some tips on getting along with your professors, check out

www.ctl.ua.edu/CTLStudyAids/StudySkillsFlyers/GeneralTips/
gettingalongwithprofs.htm

If you need some guidance on how to approach your professor for help, visit

www.counsel.ufl.edu/selfHelp/approachProf.asp

STUDENT SCENARIO DISCUSSION RESPONSES

- **Was Rashid qualified for the internship? Why or why not?** We don't know if he was qualified. Rashid was a capable student who earned an outstanding grade in Dr. Minett's class as well as his other courses, but we don't know if he was able to work with others or communicate effectively.

- **Dr. Minett stated that a 98 percent semester grade does not indicate that Rashid could function successfully in the internship. What reasons could she have given?** The ability to perform well on tests does not necessarily indicate being able to perform well in the workplace. Because Dr. Minett didn't remember Rashid, she didn't know if he came to class regularly or on time. She didn't know if he was willing to seek and accept guidance from others, if he could perform as part of a team, communicate with others effectively, or deal with real-world challenges.

- **If students choose not to speak up in class or visit the instructor to develop a personal relationship, does it indicate they are less competent? Explain.** Rashid was highly competent with regard to his course work. Dr. Minett was considering the fact that Rashid was seeking an opportunity beyond the classroom. For this, she needed more information than his course grade provided. She needed personal information about how he functioned on a variety of levels.

- **Was Dr. Minett too harsh for not writing the letter? Could she have been responding to a personal issue?** Instructors like to see their students succeed. It is satisfying to observe progress with those they have taught. Therefore, it is unlikely that Dr. Minett had any personal reason for not writing the letter, particularly because she didn't even remember Rashid. Employers or institutions that request letters of recommendation often have a specific list of characteristics they expect the letter writer to address. Such letters are not simply a statement of a student's academic performance. Therefore, Dr. Minett was being honest about not being qualified to write a letter for Rashid. She truly was not able to provide the information the letter needed to contain.

- **What should Rashid do at this point? Should he change the kind of student he is? Why or why not?** As Rashid continues with courses specific to his major, he should become more involved. He should consider his goals and what he hopes to accomplish prior to graduation (laying the groundwork for career options) as well as after graduation (putting together his résumé, applying for jobs, and interviewing). To accomplish his goals, he should make sure the faculty in the microbiology department get to know him and his assets as a student, a hard worker, a team player, an effective communicator, and a critical thinker. He can only convey this by interacting with those around him, including his classmates, teaching assistants, and instructors. If he continues to "fly solo," he will have a more difficult time progressing in his career.

BROADEN YOUR LEARNING  5

In this chapter you will learn

- What learning styles are and how they affect your college experience

- Five major theories of learning styles and characteristics of distinct types of learners

- Strategies and techniques that optimize learning based on your learning style

- How your learning style can help you declare a major and lead you to a career that's right for you

- Specific career ideas that match particular learning styles

RECOGNIZE YOUR LEARNING STYLE

Your personal style reflects who you are in the things that you enjoy (such as the music you listen to), the way you express yourself (such as your manner of dress), and how you respond to the world around you (such as whether you're an optimist or a pessimist). Your *learning style* reflects how you learn. Learning is the way we process information—encoding it, making sense of it, connecting it to what we already know, remembering it, and communicating about it.

We all have our own set of preferences for how we process information. For example, some people like to experiment with new things—to dig in and get a feel for a process. Others prefer to sit back, watch, and listen before trying something new. Some people are analytical. They like to identify all of the elements that make up a problem and consider them one by one. Others approach problems as a whole, looking at the big picture and thinking about it as a single but complex unit. Some people learn best when they share the process with others, seeking the input of peers. Others are more introspective, searching for ideas and solutions on their own.

How we prefer to learn is a function of both our general personality traits and the specific ways in which our brains function. This chapter helps you discover your own learning style and presents ways in which you can apply or adapt your style to become a more productive learner.

Your information processing preferences determine your strategies for learning—participating in the classroom, organizing your notes and other course materials, reading and study methods, taking an exam, and so on. Capitalizing on your strengths as a learner and approaching your academic tasks in the manner that suits you best enables you to learn more effectively and even enjoy it more.

UNDERSTAND THE MULTIDIMENSIONAL DEMANDS OF COLLEGE LEARNING

As a first-year college student, you are probably required to take math, lab science, literature, history, and composition courses. Each of these courses calls for a particular approach to learning. Applying algebraic formulas and solving problems require different strategies than planning and writing a creative story or understanding the issues related to the Vietnam War.

Lab science courses involve hands-on interaction with problem solving and tools of the trade. Behavioral science courses often involve data collection, research, and communicating your findings through essays and papers. Social science and philosophy courses require a great deal of critical abstract thinking. For these classes, you may need to come to class prepared to discuss your ideas and opinions with others. Many lecture-based courses allow you to demonstrate your learning through exams, which can themselves take on a variety of different forms.

TRY A VARIETY OF PRESENTATION STYLES

The subject matter may dictate a specific mode of presentation. Teaching learners how to solve math problems requires a different approach than teaching them how to write an effective argumentative essay. Presentation styles differ even within a subject, because individual teaching styles develop from the learning preferences of your instructors. The ways in which your instructors process information are reflected in the way they teach you. (See the Professor's Perspective.) Some prefer to tell you the information they want you to learn. Others expect you to learn by discussing the information in class. They may pose questions for you to answer aloud, or they may prompt group discussion or debates. Some teachers provide graphical organizers—charts, outlines, and notes on the board—and prepared study guides. They may also require a lot of writing, through essays, homework questions, and journaling. Some instructors demonstrate concepts, involve students in role-playing scenarios, or use stories or examples to deliver important points. The format of your classes most likely will follow your professor's preferred learning style.

PROFESSOR'S PERSPECTIVE: I'LL DO IT MY WAY

As a student, you must deal with information as it is presented to you by your instructor. If you become an instructor, you are no longer bound by anyone else's styles or methods of thinking about and organizing information. If you have the task of teaching others, you will do so in a way that makes the most sense to you. Of course, professors want their students to understand and learn the material, and they most likely believe that when they present it to you from their perspective you will comprehend. Unfortunately, this doesn't always happen.

Instructors are aware that students' learning styles differ, and they understand that some students have a difficult time with their delivery style. If you discover that your learning style and the instructor's mode of teaching clash, speak with your instructor about it. Identify the issue (for example, you need to see new concepts in writing rather than just hearing them). The instructor may be willing to work with you. Don't expect your professor to change the presentation style just for you, but he or she may make some changes—or allow you to—so you can get what you need from the course.

ADAPT AND BE FLEXIBLE

You will have many course experiences in college. Some of them will fit right in with your optimal learning style and others will clash. In the former case, you are likely to enjoy those courses more, feel more at ease and more confident about succeeding in them, and learn more readily. Courses in which the presentation style conflicts with your learning style are the ones that pose the greatest challenges. (To see how prepared you are to deal with these mismatches, do the Skills Check.) This doesn't mean you're doomed to struggle or that you must accept less than ideal course outcomes. Your learning style is flexible and it can grow.

SKILL CHECK: HOW WILL I MAKE IT THROUGH?

Have you ever sat in class on the first day as the teacher was introducing the topic and course requirements and felt an impending sense of dread for what the semester would hold? Have you ever wondered how in the world you would tolerate hours of lectures that seemed to ramble and had no accompanying visuals, or how to participate in discussion-based class meetings for which you never felt prepared? Have you ever been given assignments that felt awkward or that you just couldn't imagine completing to the instructor's satisfaction? What did you do? What would you do if it happened now?

If you are faced with a course that's a mismatch for your learning style and you can't transfer to another section or withdraw without losing your money—or if you must take it as a degree requirement—how will you make it through? What strategies could you use to make sure you take in all of the necessary information from the lecture? How can you make sure you keep up with the required reading and other course assignments? If you must contribute to a group project and are shy and prefer to work independently, how can you adapt? What about preparing sufficiently for exams?

Brainstorm some answers to these questions. List some ideas. What strategies have worked for you in the past, and which ones failed?

Once you understand how you learn best and discover the specific strategies that you can employ to accomplish your learning, you can apply this knowledge to all of your classes. (The Student Scenario illustrates how important this is.) For example, if you prefer to have information presented to you visually and have diffi-culty isolating important points from a lecture, ask your instructor if you can tape-record the lectures. That way, you can invest more effort in listening and processing what the instructor says, because you can listen to the lecture on tape. This enables you to reshape the content in a visual form. Another technique is to read the text-book chapter before the lecture so you already have a good idea about the lecture content.

Our learning preferences are not set in stone. How we learn is flexible, and with practice we can incorporate numerous additional ways of processing information. A combination of styles facilitates learning.

STUDENT SCENARIO: ONE OF THE WORST PROFESSORS EVER!

Julie's government class was a challenge. She was no stranger to the college classroom; she already had taken a variety of courses at several colleges over the years. Now she was in college full-time and was excited about the opportunity. What she was not excited about was the way her government professor taught the class. Every day he lectured according to an outline of the material presented with an overhead projector. He changed the transparencies as the lecture progressed, so there was a constant stream of talking and visu-als. Julie felt overwhelmed by the information and had a difficult time dealing with it. She couldn't believe that he expected them to both listen and look at the written notes to copy. Her exam grades—C's and D's—reflected her problems obtaining all of the necessary information. Despite her poor performance, Julie never spoke with her instructor. However, she shared her frustration with a classmate at the end of the semester when they compared grades.

"How did you do in that class?" Julie asked LaShondra.

"I did really well—a solid A. It was actually a pretty easy class, given Dr. Tyrell's lectures. He made the material so clear and understandable," LaShondra replied.

Julie was shocked. "You're kidding, right? I barely passed. It was ridiculous how he ran the class. I couldn't keep all of that information straight. I've had many instructors throughout all my years in college. Let me tell you, he has got to be one of the worst professors ever!"

Consider the following questions:

- Why was this course so difficult for Julie, given her previous college experience?

- How could Julie and LaShondra view the same class so differently?

- Why did Julie feel overwhelmed by the information? Were the content and concepts too difficult for her?

- What could Julie have done as soon as she recognized the challenge she faced during class and began receiving low test scores?

- How would you respond if someone told you about a terrible instructor?

DISCOVER HOW YOU LEARN BEST

Are you aware of your learning preferences? Use the Perspective Check to identify your approach to processing information. You may then recognize elements of your unique learning style.

You can learn more about specific learning styles through a preference assessment, which includes a list of questions that enable you to indicate specifically how you like to learn. Your academic advisor, campus career center, or counseling center probably offers preference assessments. Professionals are trained to administer, score, and accurately interpret responses.

There are many theories that classify learning styles, including the hemispheric dominance theory, the sensory preferences theory, the multiple intelligences theory, the personality type theory, and the experiential learning theory. They are not mutually exclusive, nor does identifying how you learn according to one theory override what you discover from another theory. Together, the theories address numerous aspects and modes of thinking that are important to learning.

This chapter presents a description of each theory and a brief inventory for you to complete. These inventories give you a basic idea of the nature of each approach and help you recognize what type of learner you are. Follow these up with a visit to a professional on your campus for a more substantial and reliable evaluation.

Each assessment includes a list of characteristics of the types of learners identified by that theory, as well as specific strategies for learning based on what comes naturally and most comfortably to the learner. Once you discover the methods that are optimal for you, try to apply them whenever possible.

PERSPECTIVE CHECK: YOUR LEARNING WAYS

Are you aware of how you learn best? Which subjects are the easiest and most enjoyable to you? Can you immediately tell when a class is going to be stimulating or a struggle to get through? Consider your favorite teachers from the past. What made them appealing to you, and how do you think the appeal reflects your learning style? What about those you didn't like? Was there a personality conflict, or was it something about the way they taught?

What aspects of your learning preferences led to your major? If you haven't declared a major, think about the classes you've always enjoyed taking. What elective courses appeal to you, and what does it say about how you like to learn? Reflect on the positive and negative academic experiences that you have had so far, and identify your learning style.

LEARN HOW YOUR BRAIN WORKS: THE HEMISPHERIC DOMINANCE INVENTORY

Answer the following questions as they apply to you.[1] Go with your first response rather than analyzing the question.

   1. How do you prefer making decisions?
   _____ **a.** intuitively   _____ **b.** logically

   2. Which do you remember more easily?
   _____ **a.** names   _____ **b.** faces

---

[1] From *Class, College Learning and Study Skills,* Sixth Edition by Longman and Atkinson, © 2002. Reprinted with permission of Wadsworth, a division of Thomson Learning: www.thomsonrights.com.

3. Do you prefer

____ **a.** planning your activities in advance?   ____ **b.** doing things spontaneously?

4. In social situations, do you prefer being the

____ **a.** listener?   ____ **b.** speaker?

5. When listening to a speaker, do you pay more attention to

____ **a.** what the speaker is saying?   ____ **b.** the speaker's body language?

6. Do you consider yourself to be a goal-oriented person?

____ **a.** yes   ____ **b.** no

7. Is your main study area

____ **a.** messy?   ____ **b.** neat and well organized?

8. Are you usually aware of what time it is and how much time has passed?

____ **a.** yes   ____ **b.** no

9. When you write papers, do you

____ **a.** let ideas flow freely?   ____ **b.** plan the sequence of ideas in advance?

10. After you have heard music, are you more likely to remember the

____ **a.** words?   ____ **b.** tunes?

11. Which do you prefer doing?

____ **a.** watching a movie   ____ **b.** working a crossword puzzle

12. Do you frequently move your furniture around in your home?

____ **a.** yes   ____ **b.** no

13. Are you a good memorizer?

____ **a.** yes   ____ **b.** no

14. When you doodle, do you create

____ **a.** shapes?   ____ **b.** words?

15. Clasp your hands together. Which thumb is on top?

____ **a.** left   ____ **b.** right

16. Which subject do you prefer?

____ **a.** algebra   ____ **b.** trigonometry

17. In planning your day, do you

____ **a.** make a list of what you need to accomplish?   ____ **b.** just let things happen?

18. Are you good at expressing your feelings?

____ **a.** yes   ____ **b.** no

19. If you are in an argument with someone else, do you

____ **a.** listen and consider the point of view of the other person?   ____ **b.** insist that you are right?

20. When you use a tube of toothpaste, do you

____ **a.** carefully roll it up from the bottom?   ____ **b.** squeeze it in the middle?

Shade the boxes that indicate your responses. The grid that has more shaded boxes indicates your brain hemisphere preference.

Left-Brain (Linear) Learner									
4b	7b	9b	10a	18b	20a	14b	1b	13a	11b
19b	5a	17a	6a	3a	16a	12b	2a	8a	15a

Right-Brain (Global) Learner									
9a	6b	17b	2b	18a	4a	13b	8b	1a	15b
5b	11a	16b	3b	10b	19a	12a	7a	14a	20b

WHAT THIS INVENTORY MEASURES

For decades psychologists have been studying the roles of the two different halves, or *hemispheres,* of the brain. Each hemisphere controls some elements of thinking and the physical functioning of the opposite side of the body. If you are right-handed, you are considered to be left-brain dominant. However, brain hemisphere dominance involves much more than hand use preference. Your learning reflects the functioning of the dominant hemisphere and the brain activity it controls. People tend to prefer learning in the style associated with the information processing modes of the dominant hemisphere of their brain. The chart that follows compares and contrasts the characteristics of left-brain and right-brain learners.

Left-Brain (Linear) Learners	Right-Brain (Global) Learners
Thinking and processing information	
Process information in a sequential, or *linear,* fashion: Begin with details in a problem and progress toward the whole to draw conclusions	Process information in a holistic, or *global,* fashion: Begin with outcome and work backward to identify details
Function in reality: Accept rules and adhere to them	Think intuitively and challenge reality: Consider rules optional
Think logically: Base problem solving on formal principles of reasoning, drawing inferences from evidence	Think visually or spatially: Pay attention to images, forms, and placement of objects
Think abstractly: Consider and explore theoretical and hypothetical ideas without concrete representation	Think concretely: Solve problems using visual, auditory, and tactile elements; prefer hands-on approach
Optimal subjects	
Language subjects that focus on grammar and syntax (rules of forming sentences from words and phrases)	Language subjects that have subjective or emotional focus: creative writing, literature, poetry
Algebra-based math	Geometry-based math
	Art: Visual forms, patterns, colors, faces
Music: Time and rhythm (linear learners make good percussionists)	Music: Melodies (patterns of pitch and chord structure)
Preferred form of receiving information	
Lectures: Explicit presentation of facts in an orderly way	An overview of the topic that makes connections and shows relationships between all elements involved (the "big picture")

Left-Brain (Linear) Learners	Right-Brain (Global) Learners
Preferred form of receiving information	
Outline: An orderly format that identifies main points and gives supporting points in sequence	Illustrations: Visuals, including charts, graphs, maps
Details: Present all information as it relates to main points	Generalizations: Broad understanding of the material, filling in details later
Textbooks: Information presented in much the same way as lecture, with outlines, and main points followed by supporting details	Stories and examples: Verbal illustrations to clarify key points
Logic-based arguments: Examples that demonstrate step-by-step process of drawing conclusion based on inferential reasoning	Practical application: Beyond the facts, the purpose of the material and how it can be used

STRATEGIES FOR OPTIMAL LEARNING

If you are a left-brain (linear) learner, become an active listener in class. Lectures tend to provide information in the way that most linear learners prefer. The more you focus on the lecture, the more you learn when the material is first presented. Here are some other strategies.

- Organize your notes and course materials, because you work best with order and structure. When you keep your notes and other related information in an obvious sequential fashion and everything has a designated place, you more easily make sense of it and feel in control. Analyze the information you need to learn. Find the connections between related elements.

- Make use of textbook features designed for linear learners, including chapter summaries, outlines, and bulleted lists. Make lists of important facts to study. Spend time committing facts to memory along with formulas and new vocabulary words. Identify categories of information to make details more meaningful.

If you are a right-brain (global) learner, read any assigned material before attending a lecture or ask your instructors for a summary of what they will discuss in the next class. When you go to class already having an overview in your mind, you can fit the details into what you already know. All of the specifics that your instructor presents have a framework within which you can place the information.

- Take complete notes of lectures. Visualize the lecture as you review your notes. This helps global learners assimilate detailed information. Create tables, charts, graphs, maps, or other graphical organizers to help you make sense of the subject matter. You can do this during or after class time.

- Ask your instructor for examples or illustrations of phenomena, if he or she hasn't already provided them. For example, if your psychology professor presents a lecture on compliance, ask for an example of how a person can gain someone's compliance. The example may trigger a meaningful memory for you. Your personal experience with the topic helps you understand it more completely as you make the connections between the interrelated elements.

- Create a mental picture of the material. As you are listening to the information being presented, or at a later time, produce a movie of it in your head. That is, combine the details of the information into a coherent whole through a dramatic visualization of it. This way, you can see what you need to recall and understand. When you learn about the crash of the stock market in 1929, think about people's reaction to their losses. Imagine the chaos on Wall Street and the sudden appearance of breadlines in your town. Intertwine the details with a mental movie of the precursors, the consequences of the event, and the reactions of the cast of characters.

- Make use of the textbook features designed for global learners, including figures, tables, overviews, charts, illustrations, graphs, and maps.

- Interact with others. Discussing the material, debating it, providing examples, and listening to the views of others can help global learners grasp the information more fully. Make the information more concrete by telling stories, discussing practical applications, and exchanging ideas about how each of you understand and interpret the subject matter.

LEARN YOUR SENSORY PREFERENCES: LEARNING STYLES INVENTORY

Carefully read the following statements in this inventory.[2] If the statement relates to you *all* or *most* of the time, check YES. If the statement is *seldom* or *never* true for you, check NO.

	YES	NO
1. I like to listen and discuss work with a partner.	____	____
2. I could likely learn or review information effectively by hearing my own voice on tape.	____	____
3. I prefer to learn something new by reading about it.	____	____
4. I often write down directions someone gives so I do not forget them.	____	____
5. I enjoy physical sports and exercise.	____	____
6. I learn best when I can see new information in picture or diagram form.	____	____
7. I am easily able to visualize or picture things in my mind.	____	____
8. I learn best when someone talks or explains something to me.	____	____
9. I usually write things down so that I can look back at them later.	____	____
10. I am aware of the rhythm or the individual syllables of multisyllabic words when I hear them in conversations or music.	____	____
11. I have a good memory for the words and melodies of old songs.	____	____
12. I like to participate in small group discussions.	____	____
13. I often remember the sizes, shapes, and colors of objects when they are no longer in sight.	____	____
14. I often repeat out loud verbal directions that someone gives me.	____	____

[2] Linda Wong, *Essential Study Skills,* 4th ed. Copyright © 2003 by Houghton Mifflin Company. Reprinted with permission.

	YES	NO

15. I enjoy working with my hands.

16. I can remember the faces of actors, settings, and other visual details of movies I have seen.

17. I often use my hands and body movements when explaining something to someone else.

18. I prefer standing up and working on a chalkboard or flip chart to sitting down and working on paper.

19. I often seem to learn better if I can get up and move around while I study.

20. I would need pictures or diagrams to help me with each step of the process to assemble something, such as a bike.

21. I remember objects better when I have touched them or worked with them.

22. I learn best by watching someone else first.

23. I tap my fingers or my hands a lot while I am seated.

24. I speak a foreign language.

25. I enjoy building things.

26. I can follow the plot of a story on the radio.

27. I enjoy repairing things at home.

28. I can understand information when I hear it on tape.

29. I am good at using machines or tools.

30. I find sitting still for very long difficult.

31. I enjoy acting or doing pantomimes.

32. I can easily see patterns in designs.

33. I need frequent breaks to move around.

34. I like to recite or write poetry.

35. I can usually understand people with different accents.

36. I can hear many different pitches or melodies in music.

37. I like to dance and create new movements or steps.

38. I enjoy activities that require physical coordination.

39. I follow written directions better than oral ones.

40. I can easily recognize differences between similar sounds.

41. I like to create or use jingles or rhymes to learn things.

42. I wish more classes had hands-on experiences.

43. I can quickly tell if two geometric shapes are identical.

44. The things I remember best are the things I have seen in print or pictures.

45. I follow oral directions better than written ones.

	YES	NO

46. I could learn the names of fifteen medical instruments more easily if I could touch and examine them. ____ ____

47. I often need to say things aloud to myself to remember them later. ____ ____

48. I can look at a shape and copy it correctly on paper. ____ ____

49. I can usually read a map without difficulty. ____ ____

50. I can "hear" a person's exact words and tone of voice days after he or she has spoken to me. ____ ____

51. I remember directions best when someone gives me landmarks, such as specific buildings and trees. ____ ____

52. I have a good eye for colors and color combinations. ____ ____

53. I like to paint, draw, or make sculptures. ____ ____

54. I can vividly picture the details of a meaningful past experience. ____ ____

To calculate your score, look at the item number of every YES response. Circle those item numbers in the boxes below. Count the number of circled items for each category (visual, auditory, and kinesthetic) and write the total in the space provided.

Visual					Auditory					Kinesthetic				
3	4	6	7	9	1	2	8	10	11	5	15	17	18	19
13	16	20	22	32	12	14	24	26	28	21	23	25	27	29
39	43	44	48	49	34	35	36	40	41	30	31	33	37	38
51	52	54			45	47	50			42	46	53		
Total _____					Total _____					Total _____				

WHAT THE INVENTORY MEASURES

One of the most widely recognized theories of learning styles is based on the notion of *sensory learning modalities,* which refers to a person's preference for taking in and processing information through the senses—namely, sight (visual mode), hearing (auditory mode), or touch (kinesthetic mode). Your highest total from the assessment you just completed indicates your primary sensory learning modality—the way in which you prefer to process information. If you have two high totals that are close to each other, you are likely to rely on both senses to learn, which is not unusual. Most people use all three senses to some extent. The more sensory information you gather and make use of, the more complete your learning experience will be. A low score in one area indicates that you use that mode very little. With opportunity and practice, you can expand your learning styles to maximize the mental tools at your disposal. Here are the primary characteristics of learners whose strength lies in a particular sensory modality.

Visual Learners

• Learn by seeing information (presented on the chalkboard, overhead projector, or computer monitor)

• Make good use of class notes and handouts

• Learn readily by reading the textbook

• Enjoy visuals such as charts, graphs, diagrams, maps, and illustrations

- Learn from visual displays of information in films, videos, and in-class demonstrations
- Can visualize information and related scenarios in their mind
- Can gain additional meaning from speakers' body language and facial expressions

Auditory Learners

- Learn by hearing information (usually from instructors who simply talk without presenting any visuals)
- Easily remember things told to them, both in lecture and in conversation
- Have strong language skills such as extensive vocabularies and the ability to articulate thoughts and communicate effectively
- Enjoy and benefit from in-class discussions and talking with others about the material
- Learn foreign languages easily
- Tend to be musically inclined, quickly learning different rhythms, identifying pitches, and following melodies

Kinesthetic Learners

- Learn by doing. They enjoy "hands on" experiences—touching, manipulating, and moving materials.
- Enjoy physical activities such as sports, dance, and drama
- Tend to be physically coordinated, with strong motor skills
- Prefer courses that involve physical components, such as lab experiments, fieldwork, and role-play

You can probably figure out a set of learning strategies based on the characteristics of each type of learner. To make it easier for you to understand and process incoming information, you simply need to make use of the sensory mode that is optimal for you. There are no rules. You can be as creative as you want, as long as your idea capitalizes on the characteristics described in each learner profile. For example, if you are a visual learner, you prefer written information and charts, diagrams, tables, or illustrations related to the material. If none are provided for you, create your own. Read the textbook and study the visual aids within the chapters. Record your thoughts, questions, and conclusions about what you read in your textbook. Develop mental movies of events, processes, and examples of important concepts in your mind.

Everyone should try to incorporate all of the sensory modalities in their learning process. As you consider strategies relevant to each learning preference, you find that many of the techniques apply to more than one sense. Some even apply to all three, thus enabling you to approach learning from your most comfortable standpoint and also employ your other senses. Here are just a few learning strategies and the sensory modalities they appeal to. Consider this a start for developing your own strategies.

If you are a visual learner, note taking probably appeals to your need to see the information. Taking notes gives the kinesthetic learner an in-class activity. Are you an auditory learner? Try reading your notes aloud later, or tape-recording and listening to them while studying for an exam. This technique may help you learn the material more completely.

Auditory learners tend to enjoy lecture courses. They like having the instructor tell them the information, and they also enjoy hearing their classmates' questions and answers during discussions. Discussions engage kinesthetic learners, too, because they can participate actively in the class and talk animatedly with others about the material. Visual learners may listen carefully and take notes on the discussion for later viewing.

Lab courses can appeal to all kinds of learners. Hands-on opportunities are the defining pleasure of kinesthetic learners. Auditory learners can verbalize each step of an experiment as they progress, stating the materials and processes involved and announcing the results. Visual learners benefit from labs because they can see a process or phenomenon take place. They learn through the visual images encoded into memory and enhance their notes with illustrations or diagrams of the physical components of lab work.

Reading usually appeals to visual learners. Auditory and kinesthetic learners may benefit from verbally summarizing sections of the text or even acting them out. This activity may help make reading more worthwhile. Highlighting with a marker is an easy way to get involved with the reading. Using different colors to code the information (blue for people, green for places, pink for events) enhances the kinesthetic activity. Of course, this activity is only beneficial if it is not overdone. Making notes in the text margin also helps you read more actively and provides you with additional material when you summarize the chapter.

Auditory and kinesthetic learners can deepen their understanding of the material by teaching it to someone else (even if it's just the cat) using the textbook or class notes. Students who put themselves in the role of instructor and take on the task of verbally explaining the material—in their own words—learn a tremendous amount, and it doesn't matter if anyone else is present. You can feel free to stand up, pace the room, gesture wildly, and pound your lectern. Visual learners might consider writing the material for someone else to learn and understand.

Good class notes and a textbook are the foundations of learning course material, but you're not limited to those things. To engage your visual, auditory, and kinesthetic senses, make additional learning tools—flash cards (which are great for reading, verbalizing, and handling), charts, maps, graphs, diagrams (which give kinesthetic learners the chance to use rulers, colored pens, and highlighters, as well as an opportunity to explain the information verbally), lists, time lines (tools for memorization and storytelling), and three-dimensional models.

Study groups allow visual learners to swap notes with others and to collect additional sources of written information. They give auditory and kinesthetic learners a chance to share ideas, interpretations, opinions, and theories with other students. Students can take turns teaching the material, perhaps using flip charts and other tools for visual learners. Role-play is another effective way to learn material.

IDENTIFY YOUR INTELLIGENCE: MULTIPLE INTELLIGENCES INVENTORY

Indicate your strengths by identifying all of the characteristics that apply to you in this inventory. Write 0, 1, or 2 according to the following values:

> 2 = very much like me
>
> 1 = somewhat like me
>
> 0 = not like me

Multiple Intelligence Inventory

Verbal-Linguistic

_____ I love a good crossword puzzle.

_____ It is important to me to improve my vocabulary.

_____ I like puns and plays on words.

_____ I would rather get the news from talk radio than watch it on television.

_____ I have a good memory for things I've read and heard.

Logical-Mathematical

_____ It interests me to manipulate symbols when problem solving.

_____ I like to do calculations in my head.

_____ I enjoy the challenge of solving problems and analyzing situations.

_____ I have a habit of picking apart the logic of people's arguments.

_____ I appreciate hearing people debate interesting issues.

Musical

_____ I often sing to myself or drum on things.

_____ I can tell when someone is singing off-key or an instrument is out of tune.

_____ I like to compose little melodies.

_____ I like the thought of learning to play different instruments.

_____ I can be inspired by instrumental and orchestral music.

Bodily-Kinesthetic

_____ I like hands-on experiences.

_____ I like to be active most of the time.

_____ I am a pretty good athlete.

_____ It feels good to move my body in a strong, coordinated athletic way.

_____ I like my body.

Spatial

_____ I have good imagery skills.

_____ I have an appreciation for beauty of all kinds.

_____ I have a good sense of direction and can follow a map easily.

_____ I love to draw, color, and do crafts in my spare time.

_____ People often tell me that I have a great sense of style.

Interpersonal

_____ I am very social and seek interpersonal relationships.

_____ I am good at recognizing and naming people I have seen before.

_____ I enjoy the fact that people consider me a leader.

_____ I can sense the intricate differences that make people unique.

_____ I am highly tuned in to other people.

Intrapersonal

_____ I like to work alone.

_____ It is pleasurable to sit in peace and quiet.

_____ I am an emotional person.

_____ I engage in a great deal of self-exploration.

_____ I like to have a small, intimate circle of friends rather than a lot of acquaintances.

Naturalist

_____ I am interested in learning about the intricacies of nature.

_____ I always try to identify patterns in the world around me.

_____ I prefer to spend my time outdoors.

_____ I enjoy the detailed nature of science courses.

_____ I keep my things organized and arranged in the way I see fit.

Add up your scores in each category. The categories in which you have higher scores indicate the intelligence areas in which you are stronger. Those with low scores are your weak areas.

WHAT THE INVENTORY MEASURES

For decades, intelligence has been conceptualized as a single entity and represented by a score consisting of one number, your IQ. This intelligence quotient presumably indicated an individual's potential for thinking, learning, and academic accomplishment. In the early 1980s, Harvard psychologist Howard Gardner proposed a different idea about human intelligence. Instead of the notion of a singular intellectual capacity based on the combined performance scores in the areas of verbal ability, mathematical reasoning, and visual-spatial functioning, Gardner theorized that individuals have a set of multiple intelligences—the potential to think, reason, and excel in different areas. Certainly people enjoy and are good at different things. Gardner's theory views this obvious notion from the perspective that _intelligence_—the skilled use of reason—takes many forms and can be measured relative to different areas of human interest and functioning. In fact, the different forms of intelligence help us understand personal learning styles.

Gardner named eight different intelligences but believes that more will be identified in the future. As you probably discovered from your responses to the inventory you just completed, people are not limited to strengths, skills, and interests in just one or two areas. Most people have reached or are developing potential in a few different intelligence domains. Several skill areas are associated with each domain. You may not be strong in every skill. However, if you have many abilities in a particular intelligence domain, it will likely be easy and desirable for you to progress with the other skills.

The concept of multiple intelligences has relevance to your college learning experience in the same way as the other learning style theories. Based on your individual strengths and areas of potential, you are more likely to take in, respond to, and process information in a specific way. Your intelligence profile may help you gain a clearer picture of the subjects that you are likely to learn easily and comfortably, and you may better understand the areas that challenge you. As you read the following descriptions of the different intelligence domains, think about how having strengths in some areas can be used to expand your potential in other areas.

Verbal-Linguistic Intelligence

- Has an appreciation and affinity for language—both verbal and written
- Focuses on the sounds of words and how they are used to communicate meaning and elicit emotions, as through literature and poetry
- Engages in and develops word puzzles, games, rhymes, and puns and has a strong memory for the specifics of language use
- Is effective in many kinds of communication—oral presentations, debates, storytelling, creative writing, poetry, and journals

Logical-Mathematical Intelligence

- Employs systematic logic and reasoning to engage in problem solving, looking for patterns, and using the scientific method

- Enjoys hypothesizing, researching, testing, analyzing, and drawing conclusions based on test results
- Thinks both concretely and abstractly to engage in solving complex mathematical operations

Musical Intelligence

- Possesses finely tuned auditory capabilities, including a strong memory for sounds, rhythm, and melodies
- Is highly sensitive to all aspects of sounds and music, including pitch, timbre, and harmony
- Expresses personal emotions and creativity through performance and composition of vocal and instrumental music
- Understands music theory and symbolism
- Appreciates many different kinds of music and can often be observed singing, humming, or drumming rhythms

Bodily-Kinesthetic Intelligence

- Possesses a strong sense of the physical self, with an awareness of bodily strengths and capabilities
- Exhibits good bodily control and coordination with regard to balance, strength, flexibility, dexterity, and speed
- Enjoys gross motor activities such as sports, exercise, dance, and drama
- Enjoys fine motor activities such as arts and crafts, building, and repairing objects

Spatial Intelligence

- Is attuned to the visual world—shapes, colors, patterns, designs, and textures
- Prefers graphic representation of ideas and is highly capable of visualizing images
- Is highly imaginative
- Enjoys the arts—drawing, painting, sculpting, and photography

Interpersonal Intelligence

- Tunes in to others' emotional states, behavior patterns, and intentions, and accurately perceives and interprets nonverbal information, such as facial expressions and body language
- Possesses effective social and interpersonal communication skills
- Wants to connect, socialize, and develop relationships with others
- Demonstrates leadership qualities in addition to being able to cooperate in a team
- Wants to help others and serve the community

Intrapersonal Intelligence

- Has a strongly developed sense of self and is aware of his or her own feelings, beliefs, capabilities, motivations, and intentions
- Expresses pride and self-confidence and uses it to face life's challenges, which are viewed as learning experiences from which to grow
- Has a sense of personal responsibility for decisions and actions and is likely to set goals and strive to progress in his or her accomplishments
- Enjoys times of introspection about the self, values, and the meaning of life
- Is highly adaptable

Naturalist Intelligence

- Focuses strongly on the natural world and the things in it
- Is interested in gaining a deep understanding of nature—the environment, plants, animals, cycles, and seasons
- Tends to classify elements of the world, adhering to existing categories or creating new ones for mentally sorting things

LEARNING STRATEGIES FOR THE INTELLIGENCES

As you read through the descriptions of each intelligence domain, you can probably guess which classes appeal to students with strengths in each domain. You can't limit yourself to courses that match your intelligence profile, though. To succeed in classes that require skills in areas other than those in your profile, consider how to put your strengths to work. Here are some learning strategies for each intelligence domain.

- *Verbal-Linguistic.* All courses require listening, reading, and communicating effectively. Even in math-based courses, draw upon your language skills to help you understand your instructor's verbal explanation of problem solving and the text's written description of steps required. Interact with classmates to share your understanding of the concepts, and discuss what you must learn and do to succeed.

- *Logical-Mathematical.* Strong logical reasoning skills are applicable to many courses. If logical-mathematical intelligence is your strength, you can use your skills in classes that emphasize language skills. In those instances, rely on your abilities to think sequentially, hypothesize, and research to create coherent, well-organized papers or speeches. Focus on topics that require a more analytical stance or that would benefit from the inclusion of factual information. Social science and behavioral science courses make use of the scientific method and often require the ability to think abstractly—both areas in which you are likely to excel if this is your strong domain.

- *Musical.* If domain is your strength, you probably have keen auditory processing skills. You probably do well in lecture-based courses. To increase opportunities to hear the information you need to learn, consider becoming involved in a study group or seek a study partner. To memorize details, create jingles, rhymes, or rhythmic chants.

- *Bodily-Kinesthetic.* If this is your strong domain, you may find it easy to take detailed notes, illustrate them, and make them more dynamic. By writing constantly and embellishing what you learn from lecture, you can create useful study material. Bring notes to review or texts to read while using a treadmill. While running, listen to a tape-recorded lecture or a recording of yourself reading your notes. Or get a jogging buddy who's in your class so you can talk about the material while on the move. When you study for exams, try role-playing, model building, or detailed diagramming of information. Consider different ways to make course material part of your active routine.

- *Spatial.* In classes that have minimal visual elements, create your own. Translate the information into visual images in your notes. Develop diagrams, make charts, and label illustrations. Retype your notes into a graphical presentation program such as PowerPoint, and include graphics to help you understand and remember. Try to create a mental movie of the material in your mind, putting yourself in the middle of the action. Or try viewing an event, process, or concept as an objective observer. This technique can transform mundane principles into colorful, dynamic images. Use your visual sense to create scenes of the concepts presented in class and the topics you must learn.

- *Interpersonal.* Learning always involves other people. If you have strong interpersonal intelligence, pay close attention to the nonverbal cues your instructor communicates about the significance of various facts. Participate in class by asking questions, addressing the instructor's questions, and involving yourself in class discussions. Start a study group that meets regularly to share ideas and to discuss issues from the class. Visit your instructor during office hours to address any concerns or questions prior to the exam or about an assignment. To get through challenging courses, make use of your human resources.

- *Intrapersonal.* If your intrapersonal skills are strong, it will be obvious to you when a course offers a particular challenge. You are likely to know what is at the root of the difficulty and how to deal with it. Strengths in this domain enable you to adapt to a variety of courses, instructors, and demands. Use your self-confidence and introspective abilities to seek the resources to tackle the most difficult learning experiences.

- *Naturalist.* If you have a strong naturalist intelligence, you can adapt your perception of the natural world to help you focus on details required for other areas of study. Capitalize on your skills in categorizing and organizing information in a logical manner. Apply your approach with nature to other course material to help you make sense of it and remember it. Look for the systems, cycles, and processes that exist in other fields of study and create analogies to those in nature.

EXPLORE PERSONALITY TYPES: STUDENT PERSONALITY TYPE INVENTORY

Answer the following questions as carefully, honestly, and quickly as possible.[3] The only right answers are the best answers for you. Select either a or b for each item.

1. When you come to a new situation, you usually
   ____ **a.** try it right away and learn from doing.
   ____ **b.** watch first and try it later.

2. Do you think people should be more
   ____ **a.** sensible and practical?
   ____ **b.** imaginative and inspired?

3. When you come to an uncertain situation
   ____ **a.** you usually trust your feelings more.
   ____ **b.** you usually trust your thinking more.

4. Would you say you are
   ____ **a.** a little more serious?
   ____ **b.** a little more easygoing?

5. Do you spend most of your time
   ____ **a.** in bigger groups, seldom alone?
   ____ **b.** in smaller groups or alone?

6. It is better to
   ____ **a.** be able to accept things.
   ____ **b.** want to change things.

7. Is it worse to
   ____ **a.** do mean things?
   ____ **b.** do unfair things?

[3] The Paragon Learning Style Inventory, version 48a. Copyright © 2000, 2001, 2002, 2003. (Available online at www.oswego.edu/CandI/plsi/plsi48a.htm.). Reprinted with permission.

8. Do you prefer when things are
____ **a.** planned and structured?   ____ **b.** spontaneous and
                                                         unplanned?

9. After a day spent with a lot of people, do you
____ **a.** feel energized and   ____ **b.** feel drained and want to
         stimulated?   be alone?

10. When you need to get something important done, you prefer to
____ **a.** do it the way that   ____ **b.** do it a new way that you
         worked before.   just thought of.

11. Which is a bigger compliment?
____ **a.** "He or she is really   ____ **b.** "He or she is really
         nice."   smart."

12. When it comes to time, are you more likely to
____ **a.** be on time?   ____ **b.** be pretty flexible?

13. When you are in a group, do you usually
____ **a.** do a lot of the talking?   ____ **b.** mostly listen and talk
                                                       a little?

14. Are you more interested in
____ **a.** what really is?   ____ **b.** what can be?

15. When you look at two things, you mostly notice
____ **a.** how similar they are.   ____ **b.** how different they are.

16. Do you tend to get along better with
____ **a.** people who are a lot   ____ **b.** lots of different kinds of
         like you?   people?

17. Most other people seem to see you as
____ **a.** rather outgoing.   ____ **b.** rather shy and reserved.

18. When it comes to exact and detailed work,
____ **a.** it is pretty easy for you.   ____ **b.** you tend to lose interest
                                                       in it quickly.

19. When your friends disagree, it is more important to you
____ **a.** to help them agree or   ____ **b.** to help them come to the
         come together.   right answer.

20. When you get up in the morning,
____ **a.** you know pretty much   ____ **b.** every day seems pretty
         how your day will go.   different.

21. When it comes to using the phone,
____ **a.** you use it a lot and make   ____ **b.** you use it most when
         most of the calls.   others call you.

22. When you work on group projects, do you prefer
____ **a.** to help make sure the project   ____ **b.** to help devise the ideas
         gets done and works?   and plans?

23. Others often describe you as
____ **a.** a warmhearted person.   ____ **b.** a coolheaded person.

24. Which expression is more like you?
____ **a.** to "do the right thing"   ____ **b.** to "just do it"

25. When you talk to strangers you've just met, you
____ **a.** talk pretty easily at length.   ____ **b.** run out of things to say
                                                       pretty quickly.

26. When it comes to work, you
_____ **a.** prefer steady effort and a regular routine.
_____ **b.** tend to work in spurts— on and then off.

27. Is it worse to be
_____ **a.** too critical?
_____ **b.** too emotional?

28. Would you rather have things
_____ **a.** finished and decided?
_____ **b.** open to change?

29. When it comes to news at school, you seem
_____ **a.** to find it out quickly.
_____ **b.** to be one of the last to know.

30. Are you more likely to trust
_____ **a.** your experience?
_____ **b.** your hunches?

31. Do you prefer teachers who are more
_____ **a.** caring and supportive?
_____ **b.** knowledgeable and expect a lot?

32. Is it more your way to
_____ **a.** finish one project before you start a new one?
_____ **b.** have lots of projects going at once?

33. Which is more true for you?
_____ **a.** You often act and talk without thinking much first.
_____ **b.** You spend too much time thinking and not enough time doing.

34. Children's games would be more fair if the kids
_____ **a.** would just follow the rules.
_____ **b.** would just use good sportsmanship.

35. It's usually easier for you to tell
_____ **a.** how someone else is feeling.
_____ **b.** what someone else is thinking.

36. Which is the more useful ability?
_____ **a.** to be able to organize and plan.
_____ **b.** to be able to adapt and make do.

37. At a party or gathering
_____ **a.** you usually introduce others.
_____ **b.** others introduce you more.

38. Which do you think about more?
_____ **a.** what is going on right now
_____ **b.** what will happen in the future

39. Do you usually
_____ **a.** show what you are feeling?
_____ **b.** refrain from showing your feelings?

40. You are the kind of person who
_____ **a.** must have things a certain way.
_____ **b.** does things any old way.

41. When you get done with an assignment,
_____ **a.** you feel like showing it to someone.
_____ **b.** you like to keep it to yourself.

42. Things would be better if people were
_____ **a.** more realistic.
_____ **b.** more imaginative.

43. Would you say you are more concerned with

_____ **a.** being appreciated by others?

_____ **b.** achieving something important?

44. It is better that people

_____ **a.** know what they want.

_____ **b.** keep an open mind.

45. Friday night after a long week you usually

_____ **a.** feel like going to a party or going out.

_____ **b.** feel like renting a movie or relaxing.

46. When you do a job, it's usually your approach to

_____ **a.** start from the beginning and go step-by-step.

_____ **b.** start anywhere and figure it out as you go.

47. When you tell a story, you mostly talk about

_____ **a.** how the people involved were affected.

_____ **b.** what happened in general.

48. You feel most comfortable when things are more

_____ **a.** planned and you know what to expect.

_____ **b.** unplanned and flexible.

Record your answers on this grid.

1.	2.	3.	4.
5.	6.	7.	8.
9.	10.	11.	12.
13.	14.	15.	16.
17.	18.	19.	20.
21.	22.	23.	24.
25.	26.	27.	28.
29.	30.	31.	32.
33.	34.	35.	36.
37.	38.	39.	40.
41.	42.	43.	44.
45.	46.	47.	48.
a's_____	a's_____	a's_____	a's_____
Extrovert, or E, score	Sensing, or S, score	Feeler, or F, score	Judger, or J, score
b's_____	b's_____	b's_____	b's_____
Introvert, or I, score	Intuitive, or N, score	Thinker, or T, score	Perceiver, or P, score

Total each column. Count the a's and b's separately and record the totals for that column. Then record the higher total for each column here:

_____ EXTROVERT or INTROVERT—E or I (first column)

_____ SENSING or INTUITIVE—S or N (second column)

_____ FEELER or THINKER—F or T (third column)

_____ JUDGER or PERCEIVER—J or P (fourth column)

Your score gives you a four-letter learning style type—for example, ESTJ, INFP, ISFJ, or ENFP.

WHAT THE INVENTORY MEASURES

This inventory is based on the study of *personality*—the complex set of characteristics that make up an individual—and particularly on the theories of psychologist Carl Jung and, more recently, studies conducted by Isabel Briggs Myers. A popular tool for assessing personality is the Myers-Briggs Type Inventory (MBTI), which creates a personality profile based on four basic dimensions of how individuals act and react to the world around them. The results indicate an individual's preferences along the lines of (1) being an extrovert or an introvert, (2) sensing or intuiting information, (3) focusing on thoughts or feelings, and (4) tending to judge or perceive. Your particular functioning in each of these areas can affect your learning experiences, so the inventory you just took adapted the format of MBTI to take a more specific look at your personality as related to school issues.

To understand your four-letter profile, begin by reading the characteristics associated with each dimension. Your personality is the combination of traits you exhibit along each of the dimensions. Thus, there are 16 different personality types.

Extrovert or Introvert: How do you relate to others? Do you enjoy socializing or prefer to spend time alone? Your affinity for interacting and working with others is the focus.

- *Extroverts:* You look to others to inspire and energize you. You have an outward focus when working and approach assignments in an energetic, yet quick and possibly scattered manner.

- *Introverts:* You prefer to think things through on your own. Your approach to working and problem solving is measured and well thought-out. You can concentrate and persevere better than most people.

Sensing or Intuitive: How do you take in and process information? Do you like facts and figures, or do you prefer to "go with your gut"? The kind of information you prefer to work with is the focus.

- *Sensers:* You are firmly grounded in reality as you focus on information gathered through your five senses. You work with information you can see, hear, and touch, and you view the practicality of what you are dealing with.

- *Intuitive persons:* You have that extra sense of just knowing how things are. You prefer to consider abstract notions and creative ideas when problem solving. You tune in to the big picture and are not as concerned with specific details.

Feeling or Thinking: What forms the basis for your decisions? Do you systematically consider the facts or the emotional elements of a situation? The information you use to evaluate and draw conclusions is the focus.

- *Feelers:* You are highly tuned in to human emotion, which helps you interpret and respond to the situations you encounter in life. Everything is relevant to you based on the personal elements involved. Your focus is personal, which makes you flexible.
- *Thinkers:* You are logical and motivated to use objective criteria to solve problems. Your approach to the world is straightforward, fair, and unemotional.

Judging or Perceiving: How do you approach the world around you? Do you like to make sense of your circumstances immediately and then move on, or do you need time to consider various factors? The goals you have for understanding what you encounter are the focus.

- *Judgers:* You need to draw conclusions quickly. You are single-minded in your focus, but you strive to deal with it and move on. You like structure and checking off accomplishments. You like to get things done—the sooner, the better.
- *Perceivers:* You are in no hurry. It is important and desirable for you to take in all the information you can and consider all aspects of a situation. You enjoy the process of making a decision and reaching a conclusion—so much so that the conclusion isn't especially important. You are flexible and go with the flow.

The combination of your individual dimensions yields the profile that illustrates your approach as a student. Try to identify those characteristics that serve you well across your learning experiences. Use those aspects of your personality that provide your learning strengths, and think about how you can employ them to succeed in any academic situation. Here are a few ideas to stimulate thought.

Extrovert or Introvert: Extroverts should include others in their learning. They should take inspiration from instructors and classmates, interact with them, learn from them, share with them. Introverts should make the most of their solitary endeavors. They should learn from reading, embellish notes to study later, explore ideas for paper topics, tune in to what they need for success.

Sensers and Intuitive Persons: Sensers should seek the facts and map details to the big picture, seeing the collection of tangible information. Intuitive persons can assimilate concrete data into a conceptualized whole. They can get creative with the concrete, letting it lead them to the preferred holistic image.

Thinkers and Feelers: Thinkers should identify objective elements related to a subject. Then they can allow themselves to venture beyond the logical but use it as an anchor when exploring emotions. Feelers should recognize that concrete facts and situations are often the basis for emotions. They can apply a personal touch to the objective and still consider and respond to concrete information from their own personal perspective.

Judgers and Perceivers: Judgers can approach large issues and tasks by drawing a series of conclusions. Working with material broken down into smaller units of meaning enables them to process information quickly without overlooking significant material. Perceivers should learn to recognize a definite conclusion and end point to some issues. However, being able to perceive many contributing variables enables them to learn material thoroughly.

INVESTIGATE THE LEARNING EXPERIENCE: EXPERIENTIAL LEARNING INVENTORY

Check each item that is applicable to you.[4]

When I have to learn how to operate a new piece of equipment, I

_____ **1.** Watch someone who knows how to operate the equipment.

_____ **2.** Carefully study the owner's manual.

_____ **3.** Fiddle with the dials until I produce a desired effect.

_____ **4.** Ignore the instructions and make the equipment suit my purposes.

What I like best about lectures is (are)

_____ **1.** The chance to record the ideas of an expert.

_____ **2.** A well-constructed argument about a controversial issue.

_____ **3.** Illustrations using real-life examples.

_____ **4.** Inspiration to come up with my own vision.

My class notes usually look like

_____ **1.** Faithful recordings of what the instructor said.

_____ **2.** Notes embellished with my own questions and evaluations.

_____ **3.** Outlines that capture key ideas.

_____ **4.** Notes with drawings, doodles, and other loosely related ideas or images.

I prefer assignments that involve

_____ **1.** Emotional expression.

_____ **2.** Analysis and evaluation.

_____ **3.** Solving practical problems.

_____ **4.** Creative expression.

In class discussion,

_____ **1.** I'm a watcher rather than a direct participant.

_____ **2.** I'm an active, sometimes argumentative, participant.

_____ **3.** I get involved, especially when we discuss real-life issues.

_____ **4.** I like to contribute ideas that no one else thinks about.

I would rather work with

_____ **1.** Stories about individual lives.

_____ **2.** Abstract ideas.

_____ **3.** Practical problems.

_____ **4.** Creative ideas.

My learning motto is

_____ **1.** "Tell me."

_____ **2.** "Let me think this out for myself."

_____ **3.** "Let me experiment."

_____ **4.** "How can I do this uniquely?"

[4] From *Your Guide to College Success: Strategies for Achieving Your Goals,* Media Edition, 2nd edition, by Santrock/Halonen © 2002. Reprinted with permission of Wadsworth, a division of Thomson Learning. www.thomsonrights.com.

Tally the total for each time you checked 1, 2, 3, and 4. The number that you checked the most indicates your preferred experience for learning.

If you checked mostly **1**s, then you prefer learning by reflecting.

If you checked mostly **2**s, then you prefer learning by critical thinking.

If you checked mostly **3**s, then you prefer learning by doing.

If you checked mostly **4**s, then you prefer learning by creative thinking.

WHAT THE INVENTORY MEASURES

Psychologist David Kolb's theory of experiential learning states that optimal learning takes place through an orderly cycle of complementary phases, each of which reflects a particular area of cognitive development and builds on the previous phase.[5] Kolb identified the phases as (1) concrete experiences, (2) reflective observations, (3) generalizations about experiences, and (4) active experimentations. He acknowledged that, although we benefit from progressing through all four stages, each of us has our own particular learning style. In this case, learning preferences differ based on how we like to experience information best. When presented with new material, do you like to analyze it, mentally manipulate it to consider hypothetical situations, hypothesize about it, and make judgments about it? Do you prefer to spend time reflecting on its elements, its meaning, and the ways in which you can relate to it personally? Would you rather think "outside the box" and develop your own approach to working with the material, focusing on the abstract elements rather than the concrete? Are you eager to begin working with the material yourself, solving problems, experimenting, and getting involved with it?

Learning styles based on Kolb's model can be summarized as follows:[6]

Learn by Reflecting: Learners express the desire to contemplate information rather than work with it. Reflecters enjoy discovering personal meaning in material and making an emotional connection to it.

Learn by Critical Thinking: Learners express the desire to learn through the use of mental operations, based on both concrete and abstract ideas and information. Critical thinkers enjoy theoretical subject matter and interactive courses that emphasize logical reasoning.

Learn by Doing: Learners express the desire to become actively involved with the information. They enjoy hands-on experiences and being immersed in the material.

Learn by Creative Thinking: Learners express the desire to approach information in a unique way and not limit experience to standard methods or requirements. Creative thinkers seek the big picture and develop ways of researching, problem solving, and theorizing about it.

By now, you probably recognize how to make the most of your learning strengths and how using your preferences can help you adapt to classes that don't directly cater to your strengths. The way in which you like to experience information is the key to getting the most out of your courses. The category names (for example, learning by doing) suggest the optimal strategies for approaching all material if possible. Even when your teacher doesn't structure the course in a way that maximizes the use of your experiential preference, you can still manipulate the material to maximize your learning.

---

[5] J. S. Atherton, *Learning and Teaching: Learning from Experience* (2002). Available online at www.dmu.ac.uk/~jamesa/learning/experien.htm.

[6] John W. Santrock and Jane S. Halonen, *Your Guide to College Success,* 2nd ed. (Belmont, California: Wadsworth, 2002).

LET YOUR PREFERENCES LEAD THE WAY: LEARNING STYLES AND CAREERS

You now know about the importance of recognizing your personal learning style to increase your odds of success in college. In addition, your preferences for thinking about, learning, and working with information should be your guide to what you pursue for the future. As you progress in your college career, pay attention to your preferences. Your interest in some topics, the courses that you find easy, and the assignments that appeal to your way of thinking and working all help answer the question of what you should do in the future. Capitalize on your learning style by pursuing a career that lets you work in an area that interests you and requires your approach to thinking and solving problems. When you match your learning preferences and intellectual functioning with a line of work that requires the characteristics that you possess, you increase your chance for success and joy in work. The Future Focus highlights how important it is to know your style when it comes to making career decisions.

FUTURE FOCUS: YOUR CAREER CALLING

Have you ever known people who just love what they do? You've probably read profiles of individuals who have a passion for their jobs, enjoying their career to the fullest—not workaholics, but rather people who are truly happy with their choices in life. Those individuals didn't end up with satisfying careers because of good luck. They made the right choices by knowing what they wanted.

The media often attribute such success to a miraculous vision. They describe happy, successful people as "following their heart" and "realizing a dream." These things may be true, but the foundation for their dream really comes from understanding their learning style and intellectual preferences. People who are highly successful in their careers know how they think best. They recognize their method of approaching and solving problems and how they like to exercise their mental abilities. They pursued fields that required their individual strengths, enabling them to shine in areas that come naturally to them. These actions fed the joy and even passion they felt for what they do. Their thinking is successful, which results in a great deal of personal satisfaction and motivates them to continue their efforts. The cycle of positive experiences in an area of interest produces an ongoing love of the mental stimulation involved. When you tune in to who you are and how you work intellectually, you can make the choices and follow the path to your ultimate career calling.

CAREERS TO CONSIDER

Working through the assessments in this chapter and reading about the characteristics of individuals with different learning preferences, you probably have noticed that the categories are not mutually exclusive. We can easily see the similarities and overlap in the types of learners distinguished by these theories. For example, if you are primarily a kinesthetic learner, you also probably score high in the area of bodily-kinesthetic intelligence and prefer to learn by doing. All of the approaches to learning styles tap into the fundamental aspects of information processing. They simply conceptualize the origins and variables differently. Regardless of the specifics of the theories or the style names, the preferences themselves relate to intellectual strengths. When you visit your campus career center and complete the official learning styles inventories available, a career counselor can then present you with a list of potential careers that match your style. Here are some brief lists that show the connections between learning strengths and job possibilities.

Careers Based on Multiple Intelligences			
Verbal-Linguistic	**Logical-Mathematical**	**Bodily-Kinesthetic**	**Musical**
Author	Engineer	Artist	Composer
Attorney	Mathematician	Actor	Performer
Teacher	Astronomer	Athlete	Music educator
Advertising professional	Computer analyst	Coach	Conductor
Politician	Physicist	Dancer or choreographer	Singer
Spatial	**Interpersonal**	**Intrapersonal**	**Naturalist**
Architect	Social worker	Writer	Conservationist
Surgeon	Psychologist	Psychologist	Museum curator
Painter	Politician	Philosopher	Botanist
Web designer	Sales manager	Advice columnist	Agriculturist
Fashion designer	Health care provider	Journalist	Librarian

SOURCE: From Holland, *Making Vocational Choices*. Published by Allyn and Bacon, Boston, MA. Copyright © 1973 by Pearson Education. Reprinted by permission of the publisher.

Careers Based on MBTI Categories			
ISTJ	**ISFJ**	**INFJ**	**INTJ**
Accountant	Counselor	Psychologist	Economist
Engineer	Librarian	Special teacher	Computer programmer
Dentist	Nurse	Novelist or poet	Administrator
Pharmacist	Real estate agent	Human resources specialist	Mathematician
School principal	Artist	Environmental attorney	Civil engineer
Stockbroker	Musician	Job analyst	Judge
ISTP	**ISFP**	**INFP**	**INTP**
Private investigator	Physical therapist	College professor	Writer
Pilot	Chef	Occupational therapist	Architect
Chiropractor	Geologist	Minister or rabbi	Photographer
Coach or trainer	Elementary teacher	Journalist	Neurologist
Marine biologist	Botanist	Editor or art director	Chemist
Software developer	Social worker	Legal mediator	Biologist

Careers Based on MBTI Categories			
ESTP	**ESFP**	**ENFP**	**ENTP**
Land developer	Veterinarian	Speech pathologist	Venture capitalist
Entrepreneur	Fundraiser	Newscaster	Politician
Insurance agent	Exercise physiologist	Actor	Literary agent
Technical trainer	Public relations specialist	Nutritionist	Art director
Aircraft mechanic	Athletic coach	Marketing consultant	Talk show host
EEG technologist	ER nurse	Housing director	Restaurant owner
ESTJ	**ESFJ**	**ENFJ**	**ENTJ**
Pharmaceutical salesperson	Social worker	Entertainer	Attorney
Computer analyst	Teacher	Recreation director	Chemical engineer
Factory supervisor	Retail owner	Travel agent	Personnel manager
General contractor	Credit counselor	Translator	Mortgage broker
Electrical engineer	Bilingual educator	Sales trainer	Media planner or buyer
Dentist	Sales representative	Drug or alcohol therapist	Business consultant

SOURCE: U.S. Department of Interior, Career Manager. (From www.learningchoices.com.)

Careers Based on Experiential Learning Preferences			
Reflecting	**Critical Thinking**	**Creative Thinking**	**Doing**
Dietician	Actuary	Advertising manager	Architectural drafter
Counselor	Anesthesiologist	Drama coach	Chef
Historian	Cartographer	Landscape architect	Corrections officer
Detective	Ecologist	Medical illustrator	Dental technician
Personnel recruiter	Economist	Graphic designer	Exercise physiologist
School administrator	Market analyst	Copywriter	Forester
Librarian	Software engineer	Photographer	Optician
Community planner	Technical writer	Architect	Quality control manager

SOURCE: From Holland, *Making Vocational Choices.* Published by Allyn and Bacon, Boston, MA. Copyright © 1973 by Pearson Education. Reprinted by permission of the publisher.

These lists are only intended to stimulate ideas for your major and career direction. They should in no way limit your possibilities. Use them as a starting point to help you visualize where your potential can take you. Remember, if you discover a passion for something, follow that lead and connect with your style. It will show you the way to success.

CHAPTER 5 REVIEW QUESTIONS

1. What are learning styles and why should you be able to recognize yours?

2. In general, what are some things you can do if the subject or format of a class does not match your learning style?

3. What are some of the major theories of learning styles?

4. What is a linear learner? What is a global learner?

5. What is meant by *multiple intelligences*?

6. What are the four dimensions of personality assessed by the Myers-Briggs Type Inventory, or MBTI?

7. David Kolb's experiential learning theory describes four preferences. Identify some specific activities that learners of each preference would enjoy.

SKILL PRACTICE

1. After taking the assessments in this chapter, you have five different perspectives on your learning preferences. Describe your overall learning style, referring to where you scored on each of the inventories. Present your answer in a form that best suits your learning style.

2. Choose ten careers listed in the final charts of the chapter and indicate which sensory learning style(s) they would most appeal to. Briefly explain why.

3. List at least five jobs or careers that were not identified in the charts. Categorize them by type of learners, referring to the different theories.

4. Choose one college core course (a course most students are required to take). Create a course design (in-class teaching format, assignments, projects, and so on) that would appeal to different types of learners. You can do this by
   a. Designing a course that would appeal to the greatest number of learners possible. Consider what it would take to make the course easy and enjoyable for most students.
   b. Designing a course in several different ways to optimize the learning of each different group of learners. Consider what elements must be fundamentally different to do this.

5. Create your own course evaluation form based on what you have learned about learning styles. Students would fill out this evaluation after completing a course, and the information it provides would tell prospective students if the course is right for them. Consider keeping the course evaluation forms on file at your fraternity or sorority or campus organization so students can look through them prior to registration each semester.

CURRENT COURSE APPLICATION

1. Assess your current courses in terms of how they match your learning style and preferences.
   a. Which subjects do you most enjoy?
   b. Which subjects are easiest for you?
   c. How do these subjects relate to your major or future career possibilities?
   d. Which instructors appeal to you the most because of how they teach?
   e. What aspects of their teaching help you learn the most?
   f. Which course textbook do you most enjoy reading?
   g. What elements of the text make it appealing to you?
   h. What course assignments do you enjoy or look forward to doing the most? Why?
   i. What other courses listed in your college catalog are likely to contain the same elements as the classes that appeal to you?
   j. How might you find out about other courses and instructors prior to taking them, to find the best ones for you?

2. Assess your current courses in terms of how they challenge you. Be as specific as possible in identifying the important issues to work on.
   a. What courses do not hold your interest? Why? Is the subject matter uninteresting, or is the problem related to other factors such as a challenging instructor, unfavorable time of day, or difficult lab requirements?
   b. What subjects (interesting or not) are the most difficult for you academically? What specifically is the problem?
   c. Which instructors are the most difficult for you to understand and learn from? Can you identify the problem? (Is it the instructor's method of presentation, tone of voice, visual aids, organization of concepts?)
   d. Which textbook do you have the most difficulty reading? Why? Is it written at a higher level than you're used to? Does it lack visual aids? Is the subject matter the source of difficulty?
   e. What assignments are the toughest for you? Do they require working in ways that don't appeal to you (such as hands-on activities, group activities, or lots of reading)? Do they require a style of thinking that is uncomfortable or challenging to you? Provide specific examples.

3. For each of your responses to question 2, list at least three strategies that you can use to adapt to the particular challenge. Focus on how you learn best and what you like to do when you are in a learning situation.

4. Read the descriptions in your college catalog of each course for your degree plan, including electives. If you have not yet chosen a major, select a degree plan that interests you currently.
   a. Overall, do the courses seem to involve topics that match well with your learning preferences?
   b. Which courses seem most interesting and exciting?

    c. Which ones could be challenging, because of your interest or the course format?

    d. How certain are you that your major is right for you? Write a list of pros and cons.

5. Identify some upcoming class tasks—assignments, projects, or exams. For each one, list some strategies based on your learning style that will help you complete the assignment better and enjoy it more. Make a plan for carrying out these exercises or activities and begin incorporating this into your regular approach to learning.

TAKE A LOOK ONLINE

For a good site with several online inventories and links to other sites on learning styles, go to

    http://snow.utoronto.ca/Learn2/mod3/

For a more detailed look at David Kolb's theory, check out

    www.infed.org/biblio/b-explrn.htm

The following site has several articles on learning styles and their role in different elements of college life, along with some inventories and other general information:

    www.indstate.edu/ctl/styles/articles.html

For more information on Howard Gardner's theory, check out

    www.pz.harvard.edu/PIs/HG.htm

STUDENT SCENARIO DISCUSSION RESPONSES

- **Why was this course so difficult for Julie, given her previous college experience?** No college course can really prepare you for the teaching style of a future instructor. The format of the lecture was apparently different than anything Julie had encountered before, and she was not prepared to follow the presentation in class.

- **How could Julie and LaShondra view the same class so differently?** The two students have different learning styles. LaShondra easily tuned in to both the visual and auditory aspects of the lecture. In fact, having both seemed to help her learn the material. Julie, on the other hand, had difficulty processing any information with both presentations going on at once. She couldn't tune in to either presentation because she was distracted by the other. The teaching style simply clashed with her learning preferences.

- **Why did Julie feel overwhelmed by the information? Were the content and concepts too difficult for her?** We don't have enough information to know if the material was too difficult for Julie. She certainly felt overstimulated by the material. Experiencing sensory overload is an obvious hindrance to effectively identifying, gathering, and encoding the necessary facts to learn.

- **What could Julie have done as soon as she recognized the challenge she faced during class and began receiving low test scores?** After recognizing that the class format posed a challenge for her, Julie could have tried to identify which of the two presentation modes (auditory or visual) she preferred and then concentrate on that mode alone (for example, not copying the notes from the transparency and just listening or taking her own notes). It might have taken some effort for the first few class periods, but she could have discovered some ways to become more comfortable in class—possibly sitting in a different location in the room to alter her view. She could have asked if the transparencies were available online or at the library so she didn't have to copy them in class. She also could have asked to tape-record the lecture so she could focus on the notes without worrying about missing what the instructor said. Julie should have immediately talked with Dr. Tyrell after getting the results of her first exam. Dr. Tyrell could have provided some pointers for preparing more effectively or getting more out of class or the readings. If nothing else, she would have demonstrated that she was concerned and wanted to improve.

- **How would you respond if someone told you about a terrible instructor?**
Remember that teaching styles are subjective. When inquiring about teachers and their courses, ask about the style of teaching, the format of the class, and the requirements for the course. These are the things that will help you decide whether a specific class or instructor is right for you. Once you are fully aware of your learning style, you can use this information to help you choose the most appropriate classes.

DEVELOP YOUR CRITICAL AND CREATIVE THINKING

6

In this chapter you will learn

⚙ The importance and benefits of critical and creative thinking

⚙ What to consider when assessing information

⚙ The specifics of inductive and deductive reasoning

⚙ Your personal thinking limitations and ways to overcome them

⚙ Techniques for enhancing creativity

⚙ EXPAND YOUR THINKING

UNDERSTAND THE REALM OF COLLEGE THOUGHT

College learning is all about active thinking, also known as *critical thinking*.[1] Critical thinking involves mental manipulations that ensure a more effective, accurate, and useful understanding of the world around you. It helps you process information to consider all relevant points and reduces errors in judgment. It requires moving beyond your comfort zone of personal opinion and leads you to challenge strongly held beliefs and assumptions. Critical thinking is the key to learning and is necessary to move beyond an egocentric perspective.

The mental manipulations of critical thinking include identifying, assessing, analyzing, comparing, contrasting, synthesizing, evaluating, and applying information. For example, imagine that your government professor schedules an exam for next Wednesday but then gives the class the opportunity to postpone it until the

[1] Linda Wong, *Essential Study Skills,* 4th ed. (Boston: Houghton Mifflin, 2003).

PERSPECTIVE CHECK: WHAT WILL CHANGE?

This is the beginning of your journey through the world of higher education. In a few years you will graduate with a degree that makes you a more valuable candidate for a career-track, higher paying job. So, what will change during your time in college? Certainly you will learn a great deal of facts, figures, concepts, corollaries, theories, and theorists—too abundant to count. Must you have all of that material readily accessible in your brain the moment you receive your diploma? Hardly. The details of your time in class and hours of studying will have faded, but something else will have emerged. How would you describe the expected change? What is it about higher education that creates the person you have become by graduation? What is college learning really about?

following Wednesday. He calls for a vote. Some students vote to postpone the exam, believing it's better to put off the unpleasant task as long as possible. Other students begin to ask the professor some questions: "Why are you considering changing the exam date? Why is it up to us? Will we cover more material than originally planned, thus increasing the scope of the test? Will it alter the date of remaining exams?" These students want to consider the pros and cons of the entire situation after receiving answers to their questions. They may decide that keeping the test as scheduled may be preferable to postponing it. Waiting an additional week could make the test too comprehensive. It could be more demanding on their schedules and disrupt the rest of the semester. Only after carefully considering the options and discussing them thoroughly will these students make their decision. These students are thinking critically.

This kind of mental functioning doesn't happen automatically. Critical thinking requires a purposeful effort—although, when practiced enough, many operations become habit. This chapter addresses strategies for improving the ability to think critically in school and in life. Figure 6.1 presents a brief overview of the differences between those who think critically and those who do not.

IN THE CLASSROOM

Professors don't provide information so that it simply spills out in their students' notes. It is the students' responsibility to be involved participants in their learning, both internally and externally. Internally, it's important to assess, analyze, compare, contrast, and synthesize what you hear. Listen to what your classmates ask and pay attention to the comments they make. Be an active listener. Speak up and ask questions to clarify points of confusion and explore beyond the basics of the information presented. Use class discussions to challenge your initial beliefs and conclusions about a topic. Move from your usual position on occasion to defend an opposing point of view. Present both pros and cons of an issue without being asked to do so. If you don't get to interact during class time, enhance your notes with ideas, reactions, concerns, and conclusions. If a topic interests you, gather a few classmates for lunch and have an informal debate. All of these techniques enhance learning.

READING ASSIGNMENTS

Most college courses require a great deal of reading. The same rules apply to reading as to active listening. It's normal to feel overwhelmed by college reading assignments. They may seem long, dry, boring, or complex compared to what you read in high school. Reading passively—that is, taking in the information without

Good Thinkers	Poor Thinkers
. . . look at an issue, react to it, and then examine their reaction before accepting it.	. . . look, react, and accept their reaction uncritically.
. . . carefully determine the kind and amount of evidence needed to solve a problem and conduct their inquiry patiently.	. . . either ignore the need for evidence or rush through their inquiry carelessly.
. . . draw the conclusions to fit the facts, keeping their judgment tentative wherever the facts will not support a firm answer.	. . . let their feelings shape their conclusions, and prefer "pat" overpositive views to balanced, moderate ones.
. . . when faced with a new problem that is similar to one they have met previously, resist the temptation to use the previous, ready-made solution.	. . . spare themselves the effort of thinking whenever they can.

Figure 6.1
Which One Are You?

SOURCE: From V. R. Ruggiero, *Beyond Feelings: A Guide to Critical Thinking,* 2nd ed. (Mountain View, California: Mayfield, 1984). Reprinted with permission from McGraw-Hill Companies.

actively thinking about it—may compound this response. However, you can maximize the reading you do by applying active, effective reading techniques.

As you read the descriptions, concepts, theories, and ideas in texts, think about them. Ask yourself questions about the material and about your own reactions to it. Argue with statements you are reading. Challenge your own beliefs. What meaning does the material hold for you or for others, and why? Can you create new meaning or generate new ideas from it? What do the pictures say to you? Can you learn more from the graphs, tables, or diagrams? How would you present the information more effectively or describe it differently? For example, imagine that your political science textbook presented the table shown in Figure 6.2.

As you can see from the table, different United Nations (UN) forces were created at various times over the past 50 years or so, they are located in all areas of the world, and they greatly differ in size. Suppose you obtain a copy of a world map and color the areas where the forces exist, to help you visualize the UN presence worldwide. You could also indicate the size of the force and how long it has been in the region. To further analyze the peacekeeping efforts in the year 2000, you could transfer the information from the table and map onto a chart that compares and contrasts the regional support from the United Nations. Use all of your data to assess which areas of the world have a greater UN presence. Look at the number of countries in the region, as well as the number of troops in the area. Why do these areas command such intervention? Can you relate this to the history of the area, noting when the force was created? What factors contributed to the development of more recent UN forces? Link the information to world events, country and regional politics, and leadership changes. You can interact with this material in numerous ways. The more critical your approach, the greater the impact of the text.

COMMUNICATING

Written assignments, research papers, oral reports, and exams are all opportunities to demonstrate what you have learned. You are expected to digest the information, thinking critically about the topic or assignment, and then do something meaningful with the material in the context of the assignment. Your interpretation, analysis, application, and conclusions demonstrate the thought processes you employed while working with the topic.

Figure 6.2
United Nations
Peacekeeping Forces,
2000

Member states of the United Nations provide troops and officers for UN peacekeeping forces that are periodically sent to crisis areas around the world. In the year 2000, there were more than 47,000 UN military personnel in the field.		
UN Force (year created)	**Location**	**Troops**
UN Truce Supervision Organization (1948)	Israel	143
UN Military Observer Group in India and Pakistan (1949)	India and Pakistan	46
UN Peacekeeping Force in Cyprus (1964)	Cyprus	1,253
UN Disengagement Observer Force (1974)	Golan Heights (Syria-Israel border)	1,040
UN Interim Force in Lebanon (1978)	Southern Lebanon	5,643
UN Iraq-Kuwait Observation Mission (1991)	Iraq-Kuwait	1,104
UN Mission for the Referendum in Western Sahara (1991)	Western Sahara	1,309
UN Protection Force in Bosnia and Herzegovina (1992)	Bosnia-Herzegovina	8,566
UN Observer Mission in Georgia (1993)	Georgia	102
UN Confidence Restoration Operation in Croatia (1996)	Prevlaka peninsula	27
UN Interim Administration Mission in Kosovo (1999)	Kosovo	1,870
UN Mission in Sierra Leone (1999)	Freetown, Sierra Leone	13,000
UN Transitional Administration in East Timor (1999)	Dili, East Timor	9,229
UN Organization Mission in the Democratic Republic of the Congo (1999)	Democratic Republic of the Congo and the subregion, including Namibia, Rwanda, Uganda, Zambia, and Zimbabwe	262
UN Mission in Ethiopia and Eritrea (2000)	Ethiopia and Eritrea	4,200
		Total 47,794

SOURCE: Data provided by the United Nations, "Current Peacekeeping Operations," online at www.un.org/Depts/dpko/dpko/cu_mission/body.htm.

This is true on exams as well. Any time you find subjective or essay questions on a test, your instructor is giving you the opportunity to show how you have thought about the content of the lectures and reading assignments. The instructor checks for some objective pieces of information but also looks for evidence of your mental manipulation of what he or she has taught. See the Professor's Perspective for a look at an important element of class success.

PROFESSOR'S PERSPECTIVE: WELL THOUGHT-OUT!

When you demonstrate your ability to think critically about course topics, you make a significant impression on your instructors because this is what they hope to see. Even when you find yourself struggling with details or concepts, try to show clear, logical reasoning supported by sound evidence. You might earn a higher grade because of it. On occasion, two students may present contrasting arguments supported by seemingly conflicting evidence and may be awarded the same grade. Instructors don't always look for right and wrong answers. Rather, they look for well thought-out arguments. Proving you have the ability to think critically in a variety of situations with different demands sets you apart and indicates your potential as an apt learner.

Compare the two responses to the following exam question. Can you see why student 2 received an A (and the comment, "Well thought-out") when student 1 received a B, even though the response more clearly answered the question?

Exam Question: What theory of personality best explains human behavior?

Student 1 (grade = B): *The trait theory of personality provides the best explanation of human behavior because it is concrete and includes traits that are measurable. Aspects of human behavior, such as "aggressive," "friendly," and "motivated" can be broken down into specific observable behaviors that can then be assessed in individuals. For example, kicking, hitting, shoving, and name calling are observable behaviors for "aggressive." Behavior scores can be used to further explore patterns of related behavior and other similar traits.*

Student 2 (grade = A): *Each theory of personality explains human behavior from a different perspective. The key to understanding a theory's contribution to our knowledge of human behavior is to consider whether it is useful. Although there are strong advocates of each theory, as well as those who adamantly oppose concepts proposed by some theories, one thing is true: Each theory has its strengths and weaknesses, and together they cover the variety of issues that make up human behavior. The trait theory enables psychologists to measure individual characteristics. The psychoanalytical approach explains the power of the unconscious mind to influence behavior. The humanistic approach highlights the importance of our own motivation and desires for ideal behavior. And the behaviorist approach demonstrates the impact that the environment and circumstances have on what we do and don't do.*

APPROPRIATE CREATIVITY

Creative expression has a place in the college classroom but must be used judiciously. Before making any major changes to an assignment, you should get to know your instructor so you can tell how he or she might react to students taking creative license in the course. If you can't tell based on the time you spend with the instructor in class, visit him or her during office hours, introduce yourself, and have a frank discussion about your different ideas. Always treat your instructor with respect, and politely accept a refusal to allow your changes if that happens. Some instructors simply don't want to deal with unique elements presented to them, or they may feel other students would take a negative view of your special contributions.

Many instructors welcome evidence of creative thinking, which reflects deeper processing of the material and, if manifested appropriately, demonstrates a greater understanding of the topic and an ability to apply what has been learned. Some assignments require critical thinking.

Consider a history assignment that requires analyzing critical events of the Revolutionary War, writing a report, and presenting it to the class. In this case, critical thinking is a necessity, because the professor expects students to take into account different perspectives of individuals fighting on each side. You gather the relevant information, assess its value to the project, and consider the most effective context in which to present it. Then you put your imagination to work. You recall that news traveled fairly slowly during the eighteenth century. Only the most important individuals received firsthand news of critical events. You wonder what the atmosphere of the war would have been and what events might have taken place if CNN had been around at the time. To put a creative twist on the report, you collect your information, analyze the appropriate events and perspectives, but present your report in the context of modern-day news reporting. You decide to incorporate a program that includes reports from embedded reporters—those marching with George Washington's troops—as well as interviews with key figures, such as Paul Revere and Thomas Jefferson. You also include on-location feedback from correspondents at the British camps. Your creativity may help you stand out. Most instructors appreciate unique efforts that maintain the integrity of the course material and assignments. Such efforts are likely to gain you some strong faculty supporters.

LIVING IN THE INFORMATION AGE

As wonderful as modern technology is, it can be overwhelming at times. The amount of materials that people throughout much of the world can now access is an incredible privilege. Sorting and evaluating the abundant information is a daily challenge.

THE INTERNET

What would have taken many hours of searching through library stacks to obtain years ago can now appear almost instantly with the click of a button. Disseminating information on the World Wide Web is not limited only to professionals, though. Computer technology enables anyone to put together a highly professional looking website. Anyone can develop a home page that includes written, audio, or visual information. No credentials are required. Although this provides for an even greater number of cyber experiences, it also opens the door to the proliferation of false or misleading information, scams, and fraud. Therefore, we must think critically about what we find on the Internet.

The Internet also requires little accountability. It is an anonymous place, and some sites even encourage anonymity. Chat rooms and Web bulletin boards often require users to create a different name, called a handle, so they don't have to reveal their true identity. Even sites that present the names, titles, degrees, professional associations, and qualifications of their sponsors do not necessarily tell the truth. When using the Internet for both personal information gathering and academic research, you must increase your critical assessment of the sites you visit.

THE EVER-PRESENT MEDIA

We have become a society of voyeurs. Americans apparently want to see and know everything—especially as it is happening. Television bombards us with information about the world around us.

There are both positive and negative aspects to the information explosion. On the positive side, direct reporting, up-to-the-minute coverage, and unedited viewing enable us to have access to more information that we can assess, analyze, and synthesize. More media outlets mean more experts offering their perspectives. However, "more" doesn't guarantee fairness, balance, or a greater variety of viewpoints. On the negative side, the abundance of information makes it difficult to evaluate. Individuals are responsible for evaluating what they see and hear rather than accepting it at face value, regardless of how realistically the information is presented.

Any information you receive first goes through a human filter. Even a journalist reporting from the inside of a tank on the front lines of battle has only the information that he or she is told (which could be a small or distorted part of the story) and undoubtedly is in a highly emotional situation. The media are not supposed to influence what they tell the viewer, but they are motivated to make the news worth watching. Furthermore, they cannot cover every story, so someone must choose the news that viewers receive. In "reality TV" programming (so-named because it claims to present life as it really is, rather than using a fictional script performed by actors) we learn that the editing of the shows greatly distorts reality. An entertainment genre that gained momentum based on showing real people in real situations is now coming under fire for being as contrived as a made-for-TV movie of the week. Now, more than ever, we must actively think about what is real, true, and worthy of our trust.

When you gather information from a media source, ask yourself the following questions:

- How reliable is the source? What is its reputation for delivering accurate, unbiased reporting?

- What is the purpose of presenting the information? Is the purpose to inform, warn, promote, provide an opinion, or entertain?

- Does the information include facts and statements supported by evidence?

- How evenly does the source present both sides of an issue (the pros and cons)?

- Where else might you find this information to check the accuracy?

When you critically think through these questions, you can make a more informed decision about the information you receive.

MAKING PERSONAL AND CAREER DECISIONS

As an adult, you are faced with many independent decisions, some of which affect the rest of your life. You must be prepared to make wise, well-informed decisions based on valid and reliable information. Valid information is based on logical reasoning and is thus justifiable. For example, if your roommate tells you his biology professor is a terrible instructor, is it valid information? In other words, can your roommate justify his statement with logical reasoning? If he also explains that the professor is always late, rushes through the material, forgets what he has already covered, can't provide satisfactory answers to students' questions, and gives exams that don't reflect the assigned material, you might be more confident that his assessment is valid.

To gain more information about the biology professor's teaching ability, you need input from reliable sources. If other students identify the same characteristics in this professor, the description "poor instructor" becomes more sound. Repeated instances of a phenomenon demonstrate that it is not a fluke, and that the information is trustworthy. (If, on the other hand, students describe the biology teacher as a bit unusual but basically a good teacher, you would question your roommate's judgment.)

When you get in the habit of critically thinking through the issues at hand and carefully considering the nature of the information, you are more likely to make choices that will have the expected and desired result. Snap decisions may be flawed if the information that led up to them was inaccurate or misinterpreted. Consider some of the major decisions you will make in your life—decisions with your major and career direction, relationships, children, lifestyle and health, and personal money management. In each case, you will want to have as much accurate information as possible leading to your decision. It is your responsibility to effectively assess the validity and reliability of the information you receive.

EMPLOY CRITICAL THINKING

Before reading about the techniques you can use when assessing information, perform the Skill Check to find out about your current critical thinking skills.

SKILL CHECK: HAVE YOU HEARD THE LATEST?

What is your first reaction to new information? Do you respond immediately with a judgment? Do you begin sharing compelling information with friends and family to see their reaction or to share your interest and amazement? Do you react differently to information you get from different sources? Are you more likely to believe something you hear on the radio or read in the newspaper than what you see on television? Do you make further distinctions within these categories of media? What about things that other people tell you? Do you immediately question what they say and ask where they heard it, or do you trust that they share only reliable information? Do you consider your professors to be absolute experts—that your textbooks are the ultimate source of factual material?

Take an honest look at your approach to information in your world—all kinds, from all sources. Decide what you think about it and why. Then consider how you will do with upcoming critical thinking strategies.

IDENTIFY INFORMATION BY TYPE

When you encounter a *claim* (a statement put forth to convey information), the first thing you should do is determine whether it is a *fact*—something that can be proved true through objective observation and experimentation, or an *opinion*—an individual's personal belief about something, which may or may not be based on facts. This task is not as easy at it may seem, because many things presented as fact are not and many opinions are stated so they sound like facts.

One way to determine if a claim is valid is to analyze the vocabulary that it uses. Remember, a fact is something that can be proved. Look for terms and phrases that indicate the claim's validity, such as *research shows, studies have demonstrated, in tests performed, observations have revealed,* and *findings indicate.* Look for more information about who performed the tests, studies, or observations, and when and where they were conducted. The more information you can collect about the specifics behind the so-called fact, the more you know about whether to accept or reject the claim. When you hear or read terms such as *believe, feel, consider,* and *assume,* you should be cautious of what follows. These terms, even when used by professionals, indicate opinions and personal conclusions rather than facts.

Moderating terms such as *may, might, sometimes, occasionally, in some cases,* and *somewhat* can intentionally mislead individuals about the validity of information. People who seek a convincing factual statement could easily overlook those words or phrases in a statement. Few phenomena are true in all cases. Moderating terms can disguise the likelihood of the phenomenon.

Sometimes a claim uses vague or undefined terms—terms that are *relative* to the person using them rather than having an absolute value. In other words, you could define the term by your standards and someone else could define it by theirs. For example, what if your friend tells you there is an exhibit of some great art at the local gallery? What is meant by *great?* You and your friend may define it very differently, and you could be disappointed by the art display. Any time you see a word like *great* in a statement of supposed fact, you probably are reading an opinion. Read these two examples and the analysis that follows each one. The subject is the same, but the information is presented in a different way. Focus on specifics and on the language used.

Dr. R. Johnson of the University of Texas Southwestern Medical School reports that studies he conducted on individuals over the age of 60 demonstrated that exercising three or more times a week lowers blood pressure as much as 30 percent and reduces fatigue, resulting in the need for only seven to eight hours of sleep per night.

The statement in this example is likely to be a fact. Here are some reasons:

- The statement identifies a specific professional, Dr. R. Johnson.
- It identifies a respected affiliation of Dr. Johnson's, the University of Texas Southwestern Medical School.
- The term *reports* indicates an objective presentation of information.
- The phrase *studies he conducted* is an accepted means of validating information, carried out by a named individual.
- The term *demonstrated* indicates an objective observation.
- The phrases *three or more times a week, 30 percent,* and *seven to eight hours of sleep per night* are specific details that define the amount of exercise, blood pressure reduction, and new sleep requirements, respectively.

Researchers believe that exercising on a regular basis might help some individuals reduce their cholesterol levels if they maintain a healthy diet.

The statement in this example is questionable as a fact. Here are some reasons:

- The statement mentions only "researchers," unnamed individuals with no professional affiliation.
- The term *believe* indicates an opinion, with no mention of objective studies conducted.
- The phrase *exercising on a regular basis* doesn't define how much exercise is required.
- The statement *might help some individuals* is vague and includes two moderating terms (*might* and *some*), which indicates a randomness.
- The phrase *reduce their cholesterol levels* fails to specify the amount; the reduction could be too insignificant to count.
- The phrase *healthy diet* doesn't indicate what it entails.

Just because something isn't a proven fact doesn't mean it isn't important information. There is an appropriate time and place for opinions, especially by people who are qualified to give them. *Expert opinions* are beliefs and feelings expressed by professionals in the relevant field. Their opinions are more significant because of their education, experience, and knowledge of the subject matter. Experts often acknowledge when they are presenting an opinion instead of an established fact. Experts who make it clear they are only making an educated guess probably do not intend to mislead listeners.

CONSIDER THE SOURCE OF THE INFORMATION

The source of information can help you determine its validity. Consider the reputation of the source. Who or what is the source? How well respected is it? Has the source demonstrated that it presents valid and reliable information to the best of its ability? Do professionals rely on the source for accurate information they can use to make informed decisions? How does it compare with other sources of its kind? Consider the reputation of the following sources of information:

Time magazine	*People* magazine	*National Enquirer*
Wall Street Journal	*USA TODAY*	Your campus newspaper
National Public Radio	Your local pop music	CNN
Your textbooks	disc jockey	Your friends
	Your parents	

Consider the individuals behind the source of information. What are their credentials? What are their professional affiliations? What role do they play in making sure the source provides truthful information? What is their reputation? Are they respected by others in their field? Are they individuals of sound character and good judgment?

Consider the purpose for the information. Does it exist simply to inform the public, or is the purpose to make money? Does it promote a person or an idea? Is it trying to sell you something? Does it have an agenda?

If the purpose is promotion, sales, or support for a hidden agenda, it is considered *propaganda*—information that is distributed to influence people's thoughts or support a cause. A propaganda message may be true in part, but it doesn't represent the truth as a whole and thus is misleading.[2] Propaganda can be implemented as innocently as advertising, making an idea or a product appear desirable and worth having. (Think of cola commercials that show attractive, athletic, or energized people drinking the product.) Propaganda also can take the form of brainwashing, altering an individual's thought processes to achieve power. People are easily persuaded by the claims made through propaganda, so your best defense against it is to be a critical thinker. Words are often used to manipulate. Only through thinking critically will you be able to gain a clear understanding of the true message.

The source, the individuals involved, and the method and purpose for presenting information can all interact with each other, thus compounding your task of understanding. Consider the following scenarios:

- A tobacco company presents findings on the impact of smoking on health, stating, "Smoking cigarettes poses no more of a risk of lung cancer than living in a densely populated urban area with the resulting pollution levels." Research was conducted by an in-house lab staffed with company researchers.

- The chief executive officer (CEO) of a large corporation announces predictions for first-quarter earnings.

- A women's magazine features a popular celebrity on the cover who shares her personal struggle with breast cancer.

- Your parents tell you about a television news program they watched that investigated student credit card scams on college campuses, filling you in on all the critical details and suggesting you no longer use your credit card.

- A popular tabloid presents an in-depth exposé on police corruption in major U.S. cities.

- A political ad touts the "tough on crime" stance of one candidate while listing statistics purporting increased criminal activity during the leadership of the other candidate.

Think critically about each of these scenarios. Note the unresolved questions and issues with each one. How valid is research carried out by scientists who are employed by a company that seeks results related to its product? Might a CEO have

---

[2] From website www.santarosa.edu/~dpeterso/permanenthtml/PropagandaListFRAME.html

an agenda for making a positive or negative prediction regarding company earnings? Will the drama of a beautiful celebrity's struggle generate more magazine sales than a story of kitchen makeovers? Would a popular tabloid bank on a story about police corruption to sell more copies?

Sometimes you can't tell for sure if information is reliable. (See the Student Scenario.) Even when the information is verifiable, it may be too difficult or too time-consuming for most people to do so. Critical thinking helps you determine your own position on controversial issues. It helps you become a more informed consumer and a better citizen when you vote. You also make better personal decisions for yourself and your family. Your brain is the most powerful tool you have. Learn to use it well.

STUDENT SCENARIO: GUESS I JUST WASN'T THINKING . . .

"How did registration go?" Amy asked her roommate, Amanda.

"Great!" replied Amanda. "I got all the classes I wanted and I even lucked out with my bio professor."

"You got into Dr. Goodwin's class?" Amy asked.

"No! I was saved from taking Goodwin. I got the other prof—Welgelhausen, I believe, is his name," Amanda said. "It was so lucky that I just happened to run into Mark's roommate on my way to sign up. He warned me that Goodwin was horrible, that she is completely unfair, and that the tests were ridiculous. They had questions that came out of the blue, and no one could do well enough for her to earn a decent grade. Goodwin's so bad that he's actually campaigning for her to get fired! I am so relieved!"

"You're a fool! Goodwin is *the* biology prof to have! She was teacher of the year a couple years ago, and everyone who has had her always tries to take her upper division classes."

Amanda was shocked. "But, from everything Mark's roommate said, she sounded terrible! I was sure that it had to be Welgelhausen that everyone loved."

Amy replied, "Why would you listen to Mark's roommate? You don't even know his name! Do you know why he's always over at Mark's when we're there? Because half the time he doesn't go to class. Of course he's failing and can't pass the tests. He doesn't do the reading and he doesn't study."

"I know all that. He's a terrible student, but why would he be so adamant about turning students against her?" Amanda asked.

"He wants to blame her because he's such a lousy student," said Amy. "He thinks he'll look better by making her look bad." There was silence. "I'm sorry, Amanda, I think you would have really enjoyed Goodwin."

"I can't believe I did that! Guess I just wasn't thinking."

Consider the following questions:

- What made Mark's roommate's comments so noteworthy that Amanda acted on his advice?

- What factors would Amanda have considered if she had thought critically about the message she received?

- Does this scenario represent a common occurrence? Explain.

UNDERSTANDING ARGUMENT

Determining the validity of a claim is particularly important when you are faced with the task of assessing *arguments,* or sets of claims. The first claim presented in an argument is referred to as the *premise,* and the final claim is considered the *conclusion*. A solid argument enables you to take logical steps from the premise to the conclusion, although you may encounter twists and turns along the way. Some arguments fail to hold up to critical analysis.

INDUCTIVE REASONING

There are two fundamental approaches to thinking through arguments—inductive reasoning and deductive reasoning. *Inductive reasoning* is the process of using specific pieces of information gathered from observations, personal experience, or outside sources and generating conclusions of a broad nature. In the following examples, the word *therefore* signals the conclusion.

- *My mother and my friend's mother always nag us about everything—from money to doing well in school. Therefore, all mothers are probably nags.*
- *My philosophy class was unbelievably boring. Therefore, philosophy is likely to be a boring subject.*
- *Our football team has won four out of the past five games. Therefore, the team should get a post-season bowl bid.*

The weakness of inductive reasoning is that the conclusion can only offer support for the original observation while also suggesting bias and stereotypes.[3] When you apply inductive reasoning, you often work from assumptions and previously held beliefs. The information may represent your own personal perspective and interpretation rather than objective consideration. Conclusions use moderating terms such as *probably, likely, could, should, might,* and *may,* which reveal that the conclusion is still in question. For example, you may have experienced a lot of nagging mothers, but you cannot say for certain that all or even most mothers are nags. Your experience in philosophy may have been an unfortunate one, but with different circumstances the course could be one of the most interesting you ever have. And the football team? Is it possible that they played the easiest five games of the schedule? Have most of the games been at home? What if the star quarterback gets injured? The team has done well *so far,* but you cannot know for sure what the rest of the season will hold. Critically evaluate your conclusions to check for a reasonable and valid assessment, but keep in mind that inductive reasoning produces a limited degree of understanding.

DEDUCTIVE REASONING

Deductive reasoning works in the opposite way to inductive reasoning. You begin with a generalization, mentally develop a hypothesis, test your assumptions, then reach a specific conclusion. Here are some examples.

Premise: All colleges require students to take three credit hours of lab science.

Conclusion: You will take at least one lab science course.

Premise: The career center offers every learning styles inventory published.

Conclusion: You can take the Myers-Briggs Type Inventory at the career center.

Premise: Your history professor never offers makeup exams.

Conclusion: If you miss a history test, you will not be able to make it up.

If the premise is true, then with sound reasoning the conclusion will be 100 percent true. This is the power of deductive reasoning. However, not all statements

---

[3] From website www.santarosa.edu/~dpeterso/permanenthtml/PropagandaListFRAME.html.

associated with an argument are true, and you must carefully consider each one. Here are some examples.

> *Premise: All chickens have two legs.*
>
> *Premise: My brother has two legs.*
>
> *Conclusion: My brother is a chicken.*

In this argument, both premises are true but the conclusion is obviously in error. The first premise states that all chickens have two legs but does not state that chickens are the only things that have two legs. This leaves the possibility that other two-legged things exist, one of which includes my brother.

> *Premise: Honor students participate in student government.*
>
> *Premise: Hector participates in student government.*
>
> *Conclusion: Hector is an honor student.*

Again, both premises are true and the conclusion is reasonable but not necessarily true. Just because Hector is involved in an activity that attracts honor students does not mean that he is an honor student. We don't know if participation in student government is restricted to honor students. Without that information, we cannot conclude that Hector is an honor student.

> *Premise: The valedictorian is the smartest student in the senior class.*
>
> *Premise: Vinjay is valedictorian.*
>
> *Conclusion: Vinjay is the smartest student in the senior class.*

The logic that leads to the conclusion is sound but the first premise is flawed. The valedictorian is typically the student in the senior class with the highest grade point average, which does not correlate directly with intelligence. Furthermore, one student may have higher grades overall than another student but may not have taken classes considered as difficult.

OVERCOME BIAS, STEREOTYPES, AND DOUBLE STANDARDS

BE AWARE OF BIAS

Bias is a conclusion drawn rapidly from a set of *assumptions*—beliefs about reality that are taken as fact. To put it simply, bias enables you to see what you want to see. Let's say your mom stayed home to raise you when you were growing up. You firmly believe it was the best thing for you, and that all children should have the same experience. You are aware there is a lot of research on the subject that claims children do just fine when both parents work, but you simply won't consider it. You view working mothers with a critical eye. Without considering both sides of the issue, you have biased judgment.

Be careful not to fall victim to simply confirming your personal perspective—a process called *confirmation bias*. You may have the intention of thinking through an issue but then inadvertently limit your search of significant information to that which supports your beliefs. Consequently, you find evidence to support your claim but ignore all other information that might otherwise prove you wrong. For example, paying attention only to findings that cite the negative aspects of daycare while refusing to acknowledge any opposing results would confirm your views at the expense of your seeing the whole picture.

SIDESTEP STEREOTYPES

A *stereotype* is a judgment that is based on some aspects of reality but that ignores contradictory evidence. When you allow stereotypes to sway your thinking, you are in a sense engaging in confirmation bias. You only see the instances that support the limited notion of the stereotype and ignore or discount any information to the contrary. Stereotypes are useful because they allow us to make quick, easy judgments of people and situations. (*Dumb jocks, air-headed blondes,* and *elderly people who are poor drivers* are all stereotypes.) People tend to categorize the things they experience, and it is much easier to do when they can make generalizations about incoming information.

For example, you may feel more secure in your decision to stay home to raise your children yourself (or have your spouse stay home) when you come in contact with children who attend daycare. You notice their wild, uncontrolled behavior, observe their mothers' futile attempts to discipline them, and believe these children to be more spoiled and demanding. Many children who attend daycare exhibit such behavior, but not of all of them do. Many children with two working parents are well-behaved, socially adept, and exhibit a strong family bond. Your observations may be based on misconceptions. First of all, you may see these children in situations that bring out the difficult behavior in all kids—unstructured scenarios such as birthday parties or play time at the park—that are conducive to exuberance. Secondly, your bias alters your interpretation of what you see. You may perceive normal, free-spirited, age-appropriate behavior as wild and undisciplined simply because of your bias. The third reason could be the result of another self-serving tool employed by those who don't want to leave the comfort zone of their own beliefs—the double standard.

A *double standard* is the use of two different sets of rules to judge evidence and information. For example, parents often apply a double standard to children's behavior—one set of rules or expectations for their own kids, and another set for other people's kids. Two children may exhibit the same behavior. The parent of one child may see the behavior as releasing pent up energy or exerting independence. That parent may see the other child's behavior as out of control. The labels we apply to others are powerful. Labeling a child as a "brat"—even privately, in one's mind—results in a different interpretation of behaviors than perceiving the child as energetic, independent, or precocious. Because assigning labels can be a form of stereotyping, it should be no surprise that double standards in judgment often result.

CONSIDER COUNTERARGUMENTS

Bias, stereotypes, and double standards are difficult to overcome because they can be subconscious. When you are aware that you have strongly held beliefs and that it takes a lot to convince you otherwise, at least you know your limitations and that you must make an effort to get past them. Assumptions and biases that are so deeply ingrained that you don't even know they are influencing you are more problematic. A history of influences and experiences makes it challenging to gain a clearer and more accurate understanding of the world. This is why it is important to make an effort to think critically until it becomes automatic.

An effective means of dealing with personal bias is to seek counterarguments. Look for evidence or expert opinions that provide a convincing contradiction to your initial response. This takes some humility and integrity when it involves beliefs that you hold near and dear, but only through acknowledging your personal perspective can you then look beyond it.

Let's return to the example of raising children. To be a true critical thinker you would need to recognize your bias, that you are basing your beliefs on your own personal experience. You then must seek supporting evidence of situations involving working mothers and approach it with an open mind—specifically, looking for valid information to disprove your original assumptions. Most issues don't have a definitive right or wrong side. Looking at both sides, though, gives you a complete, balanced view so you can make decisions for your family and judge the choices made by others.

 ## GETTING CREATIVE

Creative thinking results in the development of new ideas. It can involve critical thinking, but the purpose is to put together information and ideas in unique ways. Creativity reflects a person's particular talents and interests and is the manifestation of the workings of the imagination. Like critical thinking, creative thinking involves such mental processes as assessing, analyzing, synthesizing, and applying information. In the case of creativity, the outcome is something that didn't exist before. (Read the Future Focus to learn the power and payoffs of creative thinking.)

Many people believe that being creative is a gift—something you are born with. Some people claim that they are not creative, that they can't draw or paint and that even Play-Doh modeling compound offers a challenge. They are mistaken in a couple of ways. First of all, being creative is not necessarily the same thing as being artistic. Artistic ability is one manifestation of creativity. Ultimately, though, creativity is a way of thinking. It means taking what you know and visualizing how it can be molded into something different—something other than what is immediately obvious. Secondly, creativity can be developed and enhanced.

The human brain has capabilities beyond our understanding. Engaging in mental exercises that introduce you to new ways of looking at the world can boost creativity. By regularly practicing such exercises you get accustomed to a new, dynamic way of processing information. You have learned how creative thinking can enhance your success as a student and open doors in your career. Now consider some things that can help you become a more creative thinker.

FUTURE FOCUS: THE PATH OF CREATIVITY

My story begins with earning a Ph.D in Developmental Psychology, a field that interested me but one in which no research jobs were available. I therefore began teaching introductory psychology courses. The information for these courses is standard, and there are many textbooks and workbooks available. At first I worked from existing materials but wasn't satisfied.

I thought about the students' experience in class. I wondered how I could make it more interesting and dynamic. I wanted to entertain them as much as teach them. So I began creating my own teaching tools. My approach to lecturing was varied and colorful, because I acted out many of the psychological phenomena students needed to understand. My efforts didn't go unnoticed.

I was asked to create interesting exercises and activities to accompany other textbooks. Plenty of standard questions and projects were available already, but publishing companies wanted new, different, and creative student materials. My work in developing these materials resulted in the opportunity to travel and present my creative teaching ideas to other instructors at college campuses around the country. I now write, present workshops, and still teach—the ideas flowing from my effort to do things differently. I would never have predicted that I would be where I am today, doing what I do. The path of creativity has led to a wonderful and fulfilling career.

GET IN TOUCH WITH YOUR CREATIVITY

Developing your creativity should not be a chore. Stressing about developing new ideas stifles creativity. In most cases, thinking flows best when you are relaxed and don't feel intense pressure. Let your mind go by listening to music, stretching out in a hammock, going for a run, or taking a warm bath. These often are the times when you are likely to get in touch with your creative self, when your mind tends to process more effortlessly the ideas you've been concentrating on in the recent past. Use your downtime to allow your mind to wander, but pay attention to where it goes.

HOLD THAT THOUGHT!

You never know when inspiration will strike. You may think of an interesting topic for a course paper while dozing. While driving to school you may envision a new look for your living room. While taking a shower you might see a way to resolve a personal issue with a family member. You don't want to lose new ideas that come to you, so be prepared to jot them down. You may want to keep a small notepad in your backpack, handbag, car, or nightstand so you can record your thoughts. When you review your notes later, they may inspire additional ideas. Consider setting up a small file to keep these ideas for future reference, particularly for school papers and projects. Create specific categories like "Biology Research Ideas," "Homecoming Float Themes," or "Pro Arguments for Art History Debate" for easy identification. You will be glad to have a resource of ideas at your fingertips to use for instant inspiration.

FEED YOUR MIND

The more mentally stimulated you are, the more creative you can be. The greater your knowledge and experience base—that is, the more material you have to work with, to make connections between, and to draw inspiration from—the greater your ability to generate new ideas. Read a lot of books on a variety of topics. Reading exposes you to the thinking of others from different backgrounds, generations, cultures, and perspectives. It takes you around the world and lets you travel through time. It immerses you in circumstances that would otherwise be unfamiliar. Diversity in your personal library provides a tremendous tool for developing your creativity.

Experience the world yourself. Take in concerts, theater productions, and art exhibits. Travel to new places. Build relationships with people who are different from you. Get involved in activities you've never tried. The richer your life experiences, the richer your thinking.

PUT THOUGHTS INTO WORDS

Sometimes it can be challenging to translate what you are thinking and feeling into words. When you make a concerted effort to do so, however, you can reveal some enlightening things. Keep a journal as you experience life on a daily basis, and make it a goal to record those experiences as they affect you. Don't be satisfied to simply record the technicalities of your experiences:

> *Had a guest lecturer in history today. His father fought in World War II. Presentation will be covered on the upcoming exam.*

Instead, strive to dig deeper and describe as accurately as possible your emotional response to things:

> *The guest speaker whose father fought in World War II really moved me. I had always viewed war as such a completely evil and destructive force. I felt a new sense of patriotism as he spoke of his father's pride in the role he served in this nation's struggle for peace and democracy around the world. I was unaware of*

how this seemingly awful event brought people together and created a unity and common purpose that seems nonexistent now.

When you get in the habit of writing about your experiences in this way, you tend to think more fully and less rigidly. You are likely to look more comprehensively at the world around you. Being able to recognize and understand your experiences leads you to make new connections and seek considerations beyond the immediate and obvious. It's the starting point for creativity.

USE TECHNIQUES FOR THINKING CREATIVELY

You can apply several techniques to become more creative. Begin with your goals. Then get in the habit of brainstorming, creating mind maps, and letting your mind wander using random words to stimulate ideas.

ESTABLISH YOUR GOALS

Clearly map out what you hope to accomplish with your creative ideas. Otherwise, you will have no framework on which to develop new ideas. For example, if you are writing a speech on Freud's defense mechanisms, begin by identifying what you want your audience to learn. Perhaps they need to know the specific terminology when talking about defense mechanisms or, more important, how these defense mechanisms contribute to human behavior. Keeping these goals in mind, you can then consider how to help your audience understand the connection between defense mechanisms and behavior. To present an interesting and successful speech, you may decide that highlighting the audience's own use of defense mechanisms— even while listening to you—would be a fun and personal approach to teaching the material. Your next challenge is to determine how to get audience members to identify their own defense mechanisms so you can incorporate the topic to your presentation. When you use your end point to guide you, you have the inspiration to keep your creativity on target.

BRAINSTORMING

One of the best ways to get your creative juices flowing is *brainstorming*—a technique in which you quickly and without restriction generate ideas on a topic. The critical element in brainstorming is that you do not evaluate ideas while generating them. You write down everything that comes to mind, without assessing if it is good, feasible, silly, or impossible. Brainstorming is essentially a flurry of mental activity— hence the word part *storm*. In brainstorming, you allow yourself to follow the path of your thoughts as they travel. The greater the expanse they cover, the better.

Once you have generated your list, review the ideas one by one. This process is likely to spur more ideas. Some ideas may appear to be related whereas others may appear illogical. Some will be as ridiculous as they seem and you will eliminate them. Others can be modified to have potential. You may combine several ideas or rework one or two, or you may even discard the list and start fresh. The primary goal of brainstorming is to let your thoughts flow freely and unhindered. Consider everything and eliminate nothing at first. Then look at each idea as if it has potential.

MIND MAPPING

If you want to guide your brainstorming, you can create a *mind map*—a diagram that shows the connections between concepts and ideas. Begin by writing a topic or an issue. Then note any idea that comes to mind, as an offshoot of the main idea. The secondary ideas often will generate offshoots themselves, and so on. As with brainstorming, refrain from editing as you go along. Whatever connections you make between items, regardless of whether someone else would agree, write down the idea. See where your thoughts can take you.

Figure 6.3
Mind Map—A Diagram
That Shows the Connections
Between Concepts and
Ideas

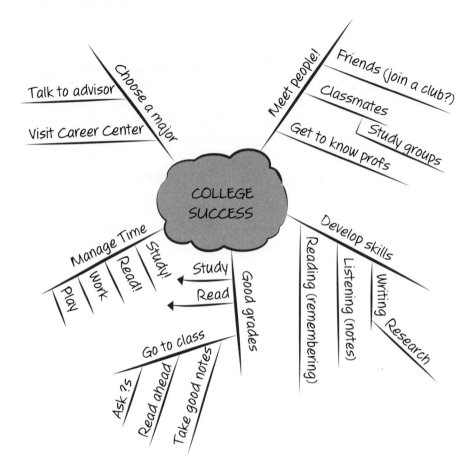

A mind map resembles an intricate connection of roads (see Figure 6.3) and provides numerous points of view from which to consider the central issue. The more connections you make between ideas, the more substance you have to work with for generating new ideas.

RANDOM WORD TECHNIQUE

Another strategy for thinking creatively is the *random word technique,* a tool used in problem solving. Begin with a randomly selected word (suggested by another person or chosen by flipping open a page in the dictionary or a magazine and pointing to any word) and consider the characteristics of that word. Then apply the characteristics to the problem at hand. Here's an example of the random word technique in use.

> *Your company wants to develop a new consumer product to release right before the holidays. Your random word is* leaf. *Your thoughts include ideas of Christmas trees, which have needles instead of leaves. The needles often drop off and get sticky sap on the floor, as well as making a mess. You begin considering ideas along two different lines: (1) how to prevent tree needles from dropping off the trees and (2) how to make it easier to clean up the sap once the needles have fallen. You think of developing a clear spray coating for Christmas trees that seals the needles so they won't fall off, at the same time preserving the natural look of the tree. You also consider a tree skirt made of several disposable layers, each with a holiday design imprinted on it. Consumers can easily tear off and discard the layers, along with the fallen needles that have gathered.*

You can also use the random word technique in combination with mind mapping and brainstorming to think about an issue in general rather than to solve a problem. You can then connect the results to generate some new thoughts.

By definition, creativity has unlimited possibilities and inspirations. Whatever technique helps you think in different ways, make use of it. Try a variety of techniques to find your favorite, or develop your own method for enhancing your thinking. Every one of us is unique and therefore takes a unique look at our environment. Your mind has the power to do amazing things in a multitude of ways.

CHAPTER 6 REVIEW QUESTIONS

1. Define critical thinking. What are some characteristics of critical thinkers?

2. Why are critical and creative thinking important to develop while you are in college?

3. What should you consider when assessing the information you gather from a media source?

4. How do inductive and deductive reasoning differ?

5. What are the ways in which personal thinking can be limiting?

6. What techniques can you use to enhance your creative thinking?

SKILL PRACTICE

1. Visit three different websites of your choice and evaluate them.

Identify the URL (website address). What does it tell you about the type of website it is?

Can you identify the individuals or organization responsible for the information on the website? If so, who are they and what are their credentials and professional affiliations? Do you believe they are qualified to present valid information on the site? Why or why not?

Does the site list the sources of its information? Are the sources respectable? How can you tell?

Does the site provide links to related sites? Follow one or two links. Do these appear to be trustworthy sources of information? Why or why not? Does the site confirm information presented by the linked sites?

Do you find anything questionable about the sight—anything that makes you doubt the integrity of the information presented? If so, what?

2. Consider each of the following claims:
   a. Regular exercise can reduce the potential for heart attacks.
   b. The space shuttle Columbia exploded due to a faulty heat shield.
   c. Adult human behavior is shaped by unresolved childhood issues.
   d. Rampant images of model-perfect looks in the media cause most women to feel inadequate.
   e. Violence in television and video games affects behavior.
   f. Turmoil in the Middle East is the result of the Israeli-Palestinian conflict.
   g. Giving in to children's every whim spoils them.
   h. Going to college expands your career options.

3. Answer the following for two of the previous claims.

   Is the claim a fact or an opinion?

   How could you concretely prove or disprove the claim?

   What part of the claim could you establish as being true, based on your own observations, experiences, or knowledge? What biases or stereotypes might cause you to be wrong?

   What information in the claim has not been disclosed?

4. Tune in to the media.

   Identify a claim that was made by a media source you consider respectable and reliable and that you believe is true. Discuss why you think it is true.

   Identify a questionable claim made by a media source you consider respectable and reliable. Explain why it is questionable.

   Identify a questionable claim made by a media source you consider to be of doubtful integrity. Explain.

   Identify a claim that was made by a media source of doubtful integrity and that you believe is true. Explain.

5. Analyze each of the following arguments:
   a. *Premise:* You must be 18 years of age or older to vote.
   Premise: Joe is 20 years old.
   Conclusion: Joe votes.
   b. *Premise:* Good professors provide several chances for students to earn grades.
   Premise: Dr. Jones gives four exams and assigns daily homework and a research paper.
   Conclusion: Dr. Jones is a good professor.
   c. *Premise:* When lightning strikes, there are clouds in the sky.
   Premise: There are clouds in the sky.
   Conclusion: Lightning is striking.
   d. *Premise:* Boulder is a city in Colorado.
   Premise: Ian is in Boulder.
   Conclusion: Ian is in Colorado.

6. Brainstorm one of the following topics for five minutes. Write down everything that comes to mind.

   Your own business you could set up and run before you graduate from college

   The perfect weekend

   Topics for a paper (assigned or not) for one of your classes

   Ways to help freshmen adapt to their new college life

7. Choose one of the previous topics and create a mind map for it. Can you see beyond the obvious?

8. Can you see beyond the obvious? Identify the total number of squares in this figure.

CURRENT COURSE APPLICATION

1. Begin approaching your time in class from a more critical perspective. As you listen to lectures or read the material, ask more questions. If you do not have the opportunity to ask questions or engage in group discussions during class time, jot down your thoughts. When you study for exams, refer to your notes for a more complete understanding of the material. Consider the following questions:

Does this information make sense? Why or why not?

How does this relate to other issues, subjects, arguments, and findings?

Do I agree with the points being made?

Is there supporting evidence? Are the sources of information sound?

What possible contradictions could I find?

Could I approach this issue from a different perspective, and what would be the implications?

2. Incorporate these questions and others into a group study session. Debate the issues and answers to gain the input and insight of others.

3. Think critically and evaluate your instructors' presentation of information. Consider the following questions:

Does the presentation make it clear when something is a fact compared to a personal opinion, concept, or theory?

Does the instructor cite the source for the information presented?

Does the instructor discuss the means of obtaining information, such as research methods or surveys?

Does the instructor insert acknowledged personal opinions into the presentation of material?

Are opinions supported with an explanation—are they expert opinions?

Does the instructor welcome being challenged on the information presented? Does he or she address questions that ask for counterarguments or opposing evidence, or acknowledge different viewpoints?

What does the instructor look for in subjective exams—a rigid account of facts and figures as presented, or your own summation, consideration, and interpretation of the critical ideas presented?

4. Identify any biases you may have with regard to issues presented in your current courses. For what topics did you feel comfort or discomfort with the ideas and theories presented? Did you enjoy learning some facts purely because they appear to confirm your original beliefs on the topic? Did any subjects irritate you because they challenged long-held beliefs about the way things work? Think critically about contradictory possibilities. How could you alter your emotional response to some topics?

5. Identify ways in which you can be more creative in your courses. What projects or assignments can you enhance by thinking about them differently? How can you make the most of the assignments through a unique approach? What can you do that is different but that still accomplishes your instructor's goal for the assignment? Consider your assignments in a new light. Break away from standard thinking, planning, organizing, and writing. Imagine how to inject dynamics into the material and your learning.

6. Analyze your own thinking patterns by asking yourself the following questions.[4]

What influences have shaped my identity? How have they done so? In what situations am I less an individual because of these influences?

How careful am I about separating hearsay and rumor from fact? About distinguishing knowing from assuming, guessing, or speculating?

How often do I take the trouble to make my opinions informed?

To what extent do I think that my way is better (both personally and ethnocentrically)? How has this kind of thinking affected my view of personal problems and public issues?

In what areas do I most resist change? Is the cause of my resistance insecurity or fear? If so, of what?

To what or to whom do I feel the strongest urge to conform? In what situations has this tendency interfered with my judgment?

How strong is my need to maintain my pride or dignity? What aspect of my image is precious to me? Which of my roles am I most sensitive about? In what situations have my image-protecting maneuvers affected my thinking?

Do I tend to make generalizations (stereotypes) about members of my own race or other races? Religions? Political or social organizations? What caused me to first form these views, and how have they interfered with my evaluation of people, places, or ideas?

To what extent do I oversimplify complex matters? Am I unwilling to deal with the complexity of truth, or do I feel threatened by answers that are not neat and tidy? What has made me this way?

To what extent do I jump to conclusions? Do I tend to do so in some areas but not in others? Why? Do I draw conclusions prematurely out of convenience or to sound authoritative and impress people? In what recent situations have I formed hasty conclusions?

In what areas am I most inclined to assume too much, to take too much for granted?

To what extent have any of the issues mentioned combined to undermine my thinking about important personal and public issues?

TAKE A LOOK ONLINE

A good website for further insight into critical thinking, particularly as it relates to academics and writing assignments, is

http://webster.commnet.edu/libroot/workbook/critical.htm

The following website offers techniques for developing creative thinking:

www.mindtools.com/pages/main/newMN_CT.htm

[4] Adapted from V. R. Ruggiero, *Beyond Feelings: A Guide to Critical Thinking,* 2nd ed. (Mountain View, California: Mayfield, 1984). Reprinted with permission from McGraw-Hill Companies.

SUGGESTED ANSWERS FOR SKILL PRACTICE

1. Visit three different websites of your choice and evaluate them.

Answers will vary depending on websites chosen.

2. Consider each of the following claims:

a. Regular exercise can reduce the potential for heart attacks.

Fact or opinion can be established.

Lab studies can prove (and have proved) the claim.

Compare people who exercise regularly to those who don't and monitor health and number of heart attacks.

Numerous reports of such findings continue to be published regularly.

If you like to exercise, you may hope the claim is true. If you don't exercise regularly, you may dismiss the findings or focus on those that are weaker in proving their case.

Exercise is known to be beneficial because it directly strengthens the heart. The claim does not indicate how much exercise is required.

b. The space shuttle Columbia exploded due to a faulty heat shield.

Fact or opinion can be established.

NASA has studied data along with pieces of the shuttle to determine the likely cause of the explosion.

Knowledgeable experts understand what happened and can identify the problems that led to the explosion.

Some information has been disclosed to the public in pictures and reports.

Biases might include any strong beliefs about NASA operating like many other large bureaucracies and appeasing the public with false information.

Columbia exploded upon reentry, the point at which the shuttle relies on the protection of the heat shield. NASA has explained that several heat-resistant tiles had fallen off during take-off. This explains the cause of the disaster, but the public may not be aware of other factors.

c. Adult human behavior is shaped by unresolved childhood issues.

It is difficult to establish as fact.

Human behavior is complex and the term *childhood issue* is vague. This claim is not likely to be proved or disproved.

Studies could only be done if the terms *human behavior, unresolved,* and *childhood issues* were specifically defined.

Most people can identify certain adult behaviors or motivations as stemming from experiences they had in childhood. Most people acknowledge that the things we encountered while growing up can influence our current behavior and that any difficult issues still lingering negatively in our minds have the potential to affect how we act at times.

If you don't feel you have any unresolved issues, you may reject this claim. If you believe you have many issues that heavily influence you, you may assume this claim to be fact.

What we learn in childhood—through the classroom, from parents or siblings or friends, and through personal experience—does in fact influence us in a variety of ways. Because this claim lacks definition and specificity, it could not be considered fact.

d. Rampant images of model-perfect looks in the media cause most women to feel inadequate.

It is difficult to establish as fact.

It might be possible to do a large-scale survey to find out how women (representing a cross section of the population) feel about themselves and what they attribute those feelings to. There is no guarantee that women would respond truthfully.

Most forms of entertainment media present attractive individuals of both genders. Advertising also employs images of attractive, fit people to promote products and services. It is rare for the media to present average individuals with less-than-perfect faces and bodies. Many women (and men) are concerned with their appearance, which is indicated by sales of clothing and cosmetics as well as self-improvement products for dieting, tanning, hair removal, cellulite reduction, and so on.

Women who feel confident about their appearance may reject the claim. Women concerned about how the media influence children may assume the claim is fact.

It is true that the media display images of women as primarily beautiful and thin. The effect that those images have can be disputed.

e. Violence in television and video games affects behavior.

Fact or opinion can be established.

Studies can and have been done to assess this connection.

Studies compare individuals who have viewed violent images with those who have not. They examine how behaviors differ in a variety of situations. Children are highly influenced by what they see others do—either in life or on a video screen. They often repeat what they have witnessed, either in reality or in their play.

You may be biased if you have strong feelings about watching violence— whether you enjoy action-packed scenes and believe that viewing violence is cathartic, or you abhor it and avoid it in any form.

Extreme violence is portrayed in movies and in some video games. People of all ages can get ideas for behavior from what they observe others doing— real or portrayed. *Violence* is not well defined in the claim. Furthermore, the claim doesn't indicate what degree of violence is powerful enough to influence behavior or in what ways the behavior is affected.

f. Turmoil in the Middle East is the result of the Israeli-Palestinian conflict.

It is difficult to establish as fact, as stated.

There are too many elements of Middle East turmoil to get a definitive answer. The closest we might come is to poll the primary figures involved in the issue, but then we would only have their opinions.

A critical study might ask qualified experts to assess the situation and speak with key figures involved. It would not be possible to get feedback from the general population, who may not be free or comfortable to speak their minds. It is a well-established fact that the Israeli-Palestinian conflict is at the root of a great many problems in the Middle East, and many powerful and influential people acknowledge that the conflict has far-reaching repercussions.

A strong tie to either side of the conflict will likely influence how someone views the claim.

A major Israeli-Palestinian conflict exists over the occupation of land. *Turmoil* has broad implications and does not specify issues of concern.

g. Giving in to children's every whim spoils them.

It is difficult to establish as fact or opinion.

Psychologists can study elements of this phenomenon. However, the claim involves too many factors to establish a fact that is true for everyone. A study could only be done on a small scale that identifies some specific elements related to the larger phenomenon of spoiling children.

The claim assumes the following information: Most people are aware that individuals who are used to getting their way expect to get their way all the time and behave negatively when they do not. A commonly used term to describe this—in adults or children—is *spoiled.*

If you have had a fortunate life so far and have received most of what you've wanted (and you don't believe you are spoiled) or have experienced deprivation, struggling for the things you want, you are likely to view this issue differently.

It is true that when people get used to something happening on a regular basis they tend to expect it, and it is difficult to accept when the event no longer occurs. The claim does not specifically describe what the result of "spoiling" is.

h. Going to college expands your career options.

This is easy to establish as fact.

A study can compare the jobs that don't require a degree (which individuals with and without degrees may apply for) and the jobs that do require a college degree (which only individuals who have college degrees can apply for). Obviously the extra qualification of the degree expands one's career options.

Employers for jobs that require college degrees will only hire individuals who have college degrees. Employers of jobs that don't require a college degree still may hire individuals who have college degrees.

Someone who is particularly creative, ambitious, or well-connected may believe that a college degree is not necessary to have a large expanse of career opportunities.

It is an indisputable fact that having a college degree qualifies you for more jobs than if you don't have one.

3. Answers will vary depending on claims selected.

4. Tune in to the media.

Answers will vary depending on claims cited.

5. Analyze each of the following arguments:

a. *Premise:* You must be 18 years of age or older to vote.

Premise: Joe is 20 years old.

Conclusion: Joe votes.

Each premise is true but the conclusion is not necessarily true. Just because Joe is old enough to vote doesn't mean that he exercises his right to do so.

b. *Premise:* Good professors provide several chances for students to earn grades.

Premise: Dr. Jones gives four exams and assigns daily homework and a research paper.

Conclusion: Dr. Jones is a good professor.

Each premise is true but the conclusion is not necessarily true. Although Dr. Jones exhibits one of the qualities of a good professor (giving several chances for students to earn grades), he may exhibit characteristics that are not consistent with being a good professor (such as refusing to answer questions, poorly explaining the material, and not being available during office hours).

c. *Premise:* When lightning strikes, there are clouds in the sky.

Premise: There are clouds in the sky.

Conclusion: Lightning is striking.

The first premise is true. Even if the second premise were true, the conclusion would still be false. Clouds are required for lightning, but they don't ensure it. It can be cloudy without lightning striking.

d. *Premise:* Boulder is a city in Colorado.

Premise: Ian is in Boulder.

Conclusion: Ian is in Colorado.

The first premise is true. If the second premise is true, then the conclusion is also true. All considerations are met with the premises and the conclusion.

6. Answers will vary.

7. Diagrams will vary.

8. Can you see beyond the obvious? Identify the total number of squares.

There are 30 squares, including 16 individual squares, the entire shape, 9 different groupings of four individual squares, and 4 different groupings of nine individual squares.

STUDENT SCENARIO DISCUSSION RESPONSES

- **What made Mark's roommate's comments so noteworthy that Amanda acted on his advice?** The roommate probably spoke about Dr. Goodwin with a lot of passion. Amanda needed to make a decision immediately about which biology class to take, and the roommate said some unpleasant things about Goodwin, suggesting that her tests were unfair. The emotion and the need to decide quickly led Amanda to focus only on the hearsay.

- **What factors would Amanda have considered if she had thought critically about the message she received?** Amanda would have first considered the source. She didn't really know Mark's roommate, but what she did know of him indicated that he was not a dedicated and responsible student. Therefore, his input should not have held any meaning to her—at least, not regarding the quality of a professor. Complaints from a student who hardly goes to class and is upset at not doing well are not valid pieces of information on which to base an important decision.

    Amanda would also have realized that the roommate's information was purely opinion, without hard facts to back it up. Words like *horrible* and *unfair* are questionable as fact. The point about test questions coming from out of the blue carries no weight coming from someone who misses lectures and doesn't read the book. Critically thinking would have led Amanda to take into account the reason that Mark's roommate would tell her these things.

- **Does this scenario represent a common occurrence? Explain.** Yes, it occurs regularly. It is much easier to see, read, or hear something and take it at face value to make a quick and easy decision than to take the time to question it and think it through. We want to believe that others are telling us the truth and that their intentions are good. It takes effort to be skeptical. It also is time-consuming.

LEARN ACTIVE LISTENING

In this chapter you will learn

○ Why you need to be an active listener in college

○ What it takes to concentrate

○ Specific strategies for active listening

○ Cues that instructors use to communicate important information

○ How to deal with difficult lecturers

● PAY ATTENTION

It might seem strange to think that there are skills involved in something as basic as listening. This chapter explains how students can learn and refine their listening skills to become more successful.

Hearing is what your ears do, but listening is what your brain does. Hearing is the passive process that occurs when sounds stimulate the auditory nerve. Hundreds of thousands of sounds make their way into your ears every day, but you notice only a small portion of them and you pay attention to even fewer. Those are the sounds that you actually listen to. Listening is the active process of focusing on and attending to auditory input.

DEGREES OF LISTENING

Listening is not an all-or-nothing experience. That is, you don't simply listen or not listen. There are varying degrees to which you pay attention to the sounds around you. Imagine, for example, that you have the television on as background noise while cooking dinner, ironing clothes, or studying. You are aware of the steady noise coming from the television. However, you simply hear it. You aren't really aware of anything that was said, who said it, or even what program is on.

Now imagine that the television is on and you are "listening with one ear." In other words, you are occasionally paying attention to what is being said, catching portions of the dialogue, and recognizing who is speaking and when. This is how you might "watch" television while chatting with a friend or talking on the phone.

When you actually sit down to enjoy a television program, you engage in a much higher level of listening. You focus on the content of the program—the words and who says them. You laugh at the jokes and follow the plot. Although you pay attention to the show, you may stop paying attention once the commercials come on.

The greatest degree of listening engagement occurs when you become more involved mentally. When you listen to the dialogue, you might recall what happened with the characters in previous episodes. You predict how the characters will respond to each other and anticipate changes in the story line based on the verbal exchanges. You are not just listening, but rather you are actively listening.

WHAT IS ACTIVE LISTENING?

Active listening is the highest level of listening possible. It involves not only hearing information but also working to process that information mentally and physically so it is more meaningful. Active listeners purposefully listen to what they hear so they understand it as completely as possible.

It is important to be an active listener in college because much of the information is conveyed through the spoken word. Concentration plays a key role in listening. You can learn to minimize the impact of disruptions to listen more effectively. You also can apply your knowledge of the structure of professors' lectures to become a better listener and a better student. You can then build on these skills to lay the groundwork for effective note taking, reading, and studying.

 LISTEN UP!

Before you learn specific strategies for how to listen better, let's take a look at why listening is so important. Doing well in school involves more than simply studying and staying awake in class.

LECTURES: THE FOUNDATION OF COLLEGE LEARNING

Most college courses involve lectures, which enable instructors to share important information about a topic. Lectures can introduce and expand on concepts, explain processes, present theories, provide evidence, and describe critical events. The instructor may use a lecture format to identify the most important material for students to learn in the course and may share personal opinions and experiences related to the subject matter through lecture.

Sometimes lectures parallel what your textbook says. Sometimes they expand on it, and sometimes they provide completely new and different information. Regardless of lecture content, there is no substitute for experiencing it firsthand. Sometimes students figure out that the instructor's lecture is a recap of the reading assignments and decide that there's no need to attend class as long as they do the assignments. They may plan to show up only on scheduled test days. Instead, they may not skip class entirely but may have a liberal policy of missing class. They may ask to borrow a classmate's notes so they can copy them. Such behavior is risky for students who want to earn a good grade in a course. Read the Student Scenario to see how some students learned the hard way that their plan was seriously flawed.

STUDENT SCENARIO: TAKE GOOD NOTES FOR US!

Shelley, Kim, Denise, and Becky were excited that they got into the same European history course. They sat together each day for the first several weeks of the semester before Kim had what she thought was a great idea.

"There's really no reason for all of us to go to class every day," she told her friends. "Why don't we give ourselves a break? Shelley and I can go every Tuesday, and Denise and Becky can go every Thursday."

"Great idea!" replied Becky. "As long as we copy each other's notes, we'll have all the information we need for the tests. And, of course, we'll all be there for those."

"Cool!" said Shelley. "I would really love not having to sit through that class twice a week. Once is bad enough."

"I agree," said Denise. "We can do just as well if we go half as often. I'm all for it!"

"So it's a deal?" Kim asked.

"Yeah, it's a deal," everyone chimed in.

"Just remember," added Becky. "Take good notes for us."

The girls really enjoyed their new arrangement and were reliable at copying their class notes for each other. However, they weren't very happy when they got their first exam scores. Three of them earned a C and one of them got a D.

Figuring they simply had to take better notes or study harder the next time, they continued their practice of paired attendance. The second exam yielded no better results than the first. When Kim met with her professor to discuss the problems she was having with the material, she was surprised as well as embarrassed when her professor said, "It appears that the clever arrangement you have with your friends isn't working. I suggest you start coming to class regularly from now on if you want to improve your grade."

Consider the following questions:

- Assuming the girls took good notes and made regular copies for each other, what went wrong?

- What insight did the girls' initial conversation provide as to why the plan didn't work?

- The girls have a right not to attend each and every class. Why should it matter that their professor seemed displeased with their arrangement?

- What should the girls have done after they received their first exam grades?

- Are there any circumstances in which such a plan might be successful? Explain.

A DIVERSITY OF TOPICS

Sharpening your active listening skills is especially important when you are learning a variety of topics. The method of teaching students how to solve math problems is likely to be completely different from that used to teach about the French

Revolution or Freud's theory of psychoanalysis. You must adapt your listening to each particular type of communication style so you can effectively follow the presentation for that subject. Active listening enables you to meet the different lecture demands so you can understand the diverse concepts presented in your courses.

A VARIETY OF INSTRUCTORS

Not only does the class content vary, but instructors also are diverse. Because you are responsible for learning the information they teach, you must be able to listen effectively to many different styles of speaker. Instructors differ in their tone of voice (imagine the stereotypic monotone instructor who reads notes without any hint of inflection), their body language (standing stiffly behind a lectern or pacing the room and gesturing wildly), their level of organization (following an outline as opposed to spontaneously talking without any obvious starting point or conclusion), and general ability to communicate effectively (that is, to explain concepts clearly, to provide examples, to present analogies, and so on). Some instructors make the material easy because they have a highly effective lecture style. Others make it challenging because they do not speak well in public. Some learned strategies can help you deal with challenging instructor styles.

VARYING LEVELS OF INTEREST

The greater your level of interest in a topic, the more you will be able to process and remember information on that topic. The effect of your level of interest on learning is so significant that it overrides the effect of both your prior knowledge on the subject and your intelligence.[1] You probably don't have the same degree of interest in all of your classes, though. No matter how uninspired you may be in a class, you must still learn the material, and the grade you earn will still go on your transcript. Therefore, you must figure out how to maintain your motivation and function effectively even in the classes you find downright dull. Active listening helps you succeed even in the courses that are least interesting to you.

OTHER SPEAKERS

Besides your instructors' lectures, you also hear other speakers. Some classes bring in guest speakers, each with a unique presentation style. Some instructors occasionally use videos to convey information. In those cases you must listen for the necessary facts without being able to ask questions.

The greatest additional input, however, is likely to come from your classmates. When your classmates ask questions, make comments, or engage in discussions with the instructor and other students, it is important for you to listen actively. Instructors often make significant points as a result of such exchanges, and these points may show up on the exams. (See the Professor's Perspective for an illustration of how this might work.) Don't make the mistake of tuning out when the lecture is interrupted by someone asking a question or seeking an example. When class members engage in a discussion that develops from a question posed by the instructor, you can gain a more complete understanding of the topic. Therefore, when your classmates talk, listen. You may discover something new through their contribution or see the big picture more clearly.

[1] Andreas Krapp, "The psychology of learning motivation," *Zeitschrift für Pädagogik* 39 (1993): 197–206.

PROFESSOR'S PERSPECTIVE: I'M GLAD YOU ASKED THAT!

Typically, professors lecture because it's an efficient way to deliver a lot of material. Although many professors are good speakers, some of them would prefer to teach by interacting with their students—something that a limited amount of class time doesn't often allow for. However, when you ask questions about the material, professors can get excited. Asking questions shows them that you are listening and want more information. They may take the opportunity to elaborate on the topic and present additional information. Professors use student questions to launch into a more detailed explanation and sometimes even inform the class about the extent to which an exam will cover the material. They may sense students' enthusiasm and interest and may believe that by sharing information about the exam, students will study more and will learn the material more thoroughly.

Next time someone asks your instructor a question, listen carefully. You may just hear, "I'm glad you asked that. It's important that you understand this issue because it's going to be on the next test." You should also plan to ask some questions. You might get more than a simple answer.

 ## CONCENTRATE

Concentration and active listening go hand in hand. In fact, you can't engage in active listening without fully concentrating. *Concentration* is the act of paying attention to an activity in progress. You concentrate when you are reading, exercising, painting, and listening. The more you concentrate during a lecture, the better listener you will be.

WHAT IT TAKES TO CONCENTRATE

Concentrating requires strong effort on the listener's part. It's important to understand the relationship between concentration and listening. As a listener, you can learn how to make yourself focus, maintain that focus, and reduce the scope of what you concentrate on at one time.

THE PARALLELS WITH LISTENING

Just like listening, concentrating is not an all-or-nothing activity. You can concentrate to varying degrees that parallel those of listening. Light concentration requires little effort but doesn't yield much information from the experience. Recall the examples presented earlier about listening to television. The example of watching a program while also holding a conversation illustrates light concentration. When you turn your attention to what is happening in the program—following the dialogue, laughing at the jokes, and so on—you are in a state of moderate concentration. Most people watching television are in that state. They want to focus enough to be entertained but don't want to work too hard at it.

The example in which you not only listen to the dialogue but also think about what is being said so you can follow the story lines and predict upcoming plot twists demonstrates active listening. It also exemplifies deep concentration. When all of your attention is focused on a particular topic, so much so that you are mentally involved, you are concentrating at the highest level.

College work requires intense concentration. There are three basic components of concentration: (1) the ability to focus at will, (2) the ability to sustain that focus, and (3) the need to limit that focus.[2]

FOCUS AT WILL

We don't just wait around for concentration to set in. Rather, we can actively pursue it. In fact, it is necessary to focus at will to establish a state of deep concentration. You must recognize when it's important to give all of your attention to a situation and then tune in with all you've got. For class lectures, this involves being an active listener, which takes initiative and determination. No one can lead the way to effective concentration. You must do it on your own. People differ as to how easily they can get into a zone of concentration. Take the Skill Check to help you determine your ability to concentrate on listening.

SKILL CHECK: ASSESS YOUR ACTIVE LISTENING

Read each statement and think about how it describes your behavior. Circle YES in the appropriate column. Be honest in your answers. How to score your responses is presented at the end of the chapter.

Statement	Always True of Me	Sometimes True of Me	Never True of Me
I sit close to the front in class.	YES	YES	YES
I show my instructor I am listening.	YES	YES	YES
I don't watch the clock in class.	YES	YES	YES
I constantly assess my understanding.	YES	YES	YES
I ask for clarification if needed.	YES	YES	YES
I seek things that interest me in a lecture.	YES	YES	YES
I ignore distractions in the classroom.	YES	YES	YES
I prepare before class by reading the text and reviewing previous notes.	YES	YES	YES
I establish a purpose for listening.	YES	YES	YES
I relate everything to the big picture.	YES	YES	YES
I determine my instructor's strengths and weaknesses and adapt my listening.	YES	YES	YES
I listen with an open mind.	YES	YES	YES
I believe my notes are a good representation of what was said in class.	YES	YES	YES
I consider how the information might affect me.	YES	YES	YES
I use my desire to succeed in class to motivate me to listen effectively.	YES	YES	YES

[2]Becky Patterson, *Concentration: Strategies for Attaining Focus* (Dubuque, Iowa: Kendall Hunt, 1993).

SUSTAIN YOUR FOCUS

Once you have reached a state of deep concentration, you must sustain it. Brief periods of concentration are inadequate. To gain from active listening, keep your attention properly focused for a significant period of time. Apply strategies for active listening to maintain an effective state of concentration.

LIMIT YOUR FOCUS

If your attention is on several things at a time, you aren't truly concentrating on any one thing. Everyone tries to mentally multi-task on occasion—jotting down a grocery list while listening to a lecture, watching approaching storm clouds and wondering how to avoid getting wet while walking to the next class. But the truth is, a person isn't focused on anything at all while multi-tasking. When you are in class and need to attend to the information being presented, your instructor's voice is all you should focus on. Concentration is achieved only through choosing a single topic and giving it your full attention.

As you may know, the three elements required for concentration are not simple tasks. Many things can distract you from establishing and maintaining a high level of focus. The next section discusses these distractors and how to overcome them.

DIFFERENTIATE EXTERNAL AND INTERNAL DISTRACTORS

Our sense organs are bombarded continuously with information that they pass on to the brain. Many things in the world around us, as well as physically and mentally within us, compete for our attention. Even in the classroom, there are many sights, sounds, and smells to focus on. Anything in the environment that you could pay attention to instead of what you should concentrate on is an *external distractor*. You are trying to listen to a lecture, for example, but the people behind you are having a conversation in hushed whispers, someone in the back of the room just popped the top on a can of soda, and the picture window to your right offers a view of the beautiful spring day. Before you know it, your attention is divided among the various sensations around you—only one of which is the professor's voice.

As if the external distractors aren't enough, imagine that you're also hungry. You didn't have lunch before class, and you're daydreaming about the pizza or hamburger that awaits you after class. In addition, suppose that the jeans you are wearing shrunk in the wash last night and feel like they could be cutting off the blood circulation in your legs. Usually you don't put them in the dryer, but you forgot because you were studying for an economics exam. The last exam was very difficult, and you are worried about remembering all of the theories and formulas. At this point, the lecture you are supposed to be concentrating on has no chance, with all of the *internal distractors* you are dealing with—personal and mental issues that overwhelm the ability to concentrate.

You can't completely escape distractors to your concentration. (See Figure 7.1 for a list of both external and internal distractors you might encounter in the classroom.) You can, however, limit them so you can concentrate and actively listen in class.

DEAL WITH DISTRACTIONS

The first step in concentrating and listening actively is to reduce the threat of distractions. Once you know how to keep your attention from wandering, you can free your mind to effectively take in the necessary information presented in class.

MINIMIZE EXTERNAL ELEMENTS

Successfully mastering the three components of concentration requires that you actively deal with any distractions. Start by sitting in the front row, in the center of

Figure 7.1
Distractors in the Classroom

External Distractors	Internal Distractors
Traffic noise	Hunger
Rustling papers and books	Fatigue
Cell phones and other electronic devices	Body aches and pains
Noisy food and gum wrappers	Tight clothing
Talking and loud whispering	School-related anxiety
Extreme hot and cold temperatures	Concern over personal problems
Windows with a view	Anxiety over a family crisis
Coughing and sneezing	Personal responsibilities
Instructor mannerisms, such as wild gesturing, tone of voice, pacing	Daydreaming

that row. Being close to your instructor and in front of the board gives you an edge in being able to listen actively. Not only do you have an unobstructed view of visual material, but you reduce your exposure to noise from the rest of the room. Many students report a difference in their ability to hear what's being said, even in a regular-size classroom that seats 30 to 40 students, just by moving to the front of the room. They say they didn't even realize how much harder they were having to work to catch everything when sitting further back in the room. Straining to discern all of the words (consciously or not) uses up a portion of your attention. More important, it lessens your capacity to focus on what's really important—the meaning of what the instructor says.

When you sit in the front row, you are also more likely to ask questions. You perceive yourself in a more intimate setting with your instructor, because you are less aware of the people sitting behind you. Not only do you benefit from asking your own questions, but you also are more likely to hear everyone else's comments and questions when you sit in the front.

Another consideration is to avoid sitting where you have a good view out the window. Even the most studious among us enjoy watching the world go by. If you are easily distracted by what others are doing and the classroom isn't full of people, try to find a seat in an area by yourself. You can at least minimize the subtle noises created by other people writing, eating, and generally moving around. If you struggle with maintaining your concentration throughout the class period, sit where you can't see the clock—and, of course, don't wear a watch. The easier it is to keep track of time, the more you are likely to focus on how much class time is left rather than listening with full attention.

PRECLUDE PHYSICAL PROBLEMS

To reduce internal distractors, take care of yourself as much as possible in preparation for your time in class. Get enough sleep. You can't listen carefully when you're tired. Eat and drink something before class, but don't come to class with a full bladder. Don't plan to eat during class. Some instructors allow students to eat in class, but the activity competes for attention. You cannot focus fully on the lecture if you are trying not to smudge orange powder from your cheese puffs onto your notes or chocolate on your textbook. Eating also tends to distract others who are trying to listen.

Always carry aspirin or other pain medication with you. Take it when necessary to avoid losing a whole class period worth of material due to a bad headache. If possible, wear comfortable and weather-appropriate clothing. It's difficult to focus on the task at hand if your mind is wandering to the fact that you are cold or your pantyhose are slipping. You may not always be able to control these distractions, but planning ahead can make a difference.

INHIBIT INTERNAL ISSUES

Other concerns—internal struggles—are more difficult to control. These take greater effort and more extensive planning to overcome. As you know, it is extremely important to take control of your schedule. When you map out all your obligations and designate specific times to accomplish tasks, you greatly reduce your level of stress. That's because you know that everything will be done at a specific time, including going to class. Also, knowing that you have designated time to carry out each of your responsibilities lets you focus on what you are doing right then. For example, you don't need to concern yourself with grocery shopping while you are in class. You know when shopping will get done, and you know when you will do your homework, do the laundry, exercise, and so on. Putting the effort into being organized and effectively managing your time frees your mind to concentrate in class.

If personal challenges disrupt your concentration, consider this: As long as you have paid your tuition and continue to attend class, you need to make it worthwhile. Whatever difficulties you must deal with in other areas of your life, you certainly don't want to add to them by creating problems with school. Make it your goal to keep schoolwork on track. Allowing other things to disrupt your concentration could result in getting poor grades, which only makes things worse. Commit to making school one area in which you achieve success, and remain determined to focus fully in all school-related activities. The reward is a positive and inspiring result that helps you counteract the current problem.

Barriers to effective concentration are not limited to environmental and personal distractors. Other factors play a major role in your ability to focus on academic tasks. These factors include attention, interest, and motivation.

AIM YOUR ATTENTION

Attention plays a major role in your ability to concentrate. Remember that one of the components of concentration is being able to focus at will—deliberately directing your attention to where it needs to be. With so many potential distractions, this is a challenging task. Sometimes the lack of attention opens the door to the distractors in the first place.

A CONVENIENT EXCUSE

Attention and distraction work a little like the age-old question of which came first, the chicken or the egg. You may claim that you simply can't concentrate in class because of everything going on around you, but maybe you perceive the environment as distracting only because you are not paying attention. A specific part of the brain, called the *reticular formation,* eliminates unwanted and unnecessary sensory input. It controls attention, enabling you, for example, to go to a crowded, noisy party and carry on a conversation with a few friends. Although you are bombarded with a tremendous number of distractions, you can focus on what's important to you—the words spoken by your friends. If you can focus your attention at a party, you can focus your attention in class. Don't use distractions as an excuse. Most instructors try to keep students quiet and incidental noises to a minimum as they take command of the room.

PLAN OUT A PURPOSE

To help you direct your attention to the lecture, develop a *listening goal*. In other words, determine what it is that you want to get out of class each day. The following is a list of reasons for paying close attention to a lecture.

- To clarify points made in previous lectures or reading assignments
- To identify the main points and supporting evidence
- To find examples and analogies illustrating the concepts
- To support or refute opinions on the topics
- To find information applicable for use in an upcoming paper or research project
- To improve note-taking skills
- To gather the information needed to perform well on the exam
- To succeed in the course and maintain a high grade point average

The first several goals involve listening for the sake of thinking about the material more thoroughly. Other items express more personal goals. Whatever reason you have for focusing your attention on the speaker is a worthwhile goal.

INCREASE YOUR INTEREST

Because concentrating and listening effectively are actively carried out by you, you must really want to do these things. It is easier to focus and listen in a course that you find interesting. You enjoy hearing about the material and you actively listen to and become involved in lectures without much effort. You probably don't need to be concerned about the classes you enjoy.

The classes that you are less than passionate about are more likely to challenge you. The less interested you are in the course, the harder you have to work to succeed in it. Life can seem unfair when you have to put twice as much effort into a class that bores you to tears. The fact is, the greater your interest, the more information you take in and understand.[3] Therefore, it is extremely important to increase your interest

---

PERSPECTIVE CHECK: WAKE ME WHEN IT'S OVER

Everyone ends up with a dull class now and then. What should you do when it happens to you? You have to get through class somehow, but how?

When you dread going to class, do you still attend regularly? Do you try to find someone to take notes for you on a regular basis instead? Do you just try to copy the words your instructor says so you can review them later for the test? Perhaps you see the class as a chance to tune out and work on assignments from other classes or even take a nap, especially if you believe that you can't stay awake anyway.

If the instructor is dull, it's not your fault, right? Isn't it the instructor's responsibility to attract your attention and get you to learn the material? If instructors fail to do this, isn't it their fault that you aren't able to do well on the exams?

A mediocre grade isn't less painful just because the class was boring. If you get a poor grade in a dull class, do you explain it away later as not counting just because the class wasn't what you thought it should have been?

---

[3] Andreas Krapp, "The psychology of learning motivation," *Zeitschrift fur Padagogik* 39 (1993): 197–206.

in classes that don't inspire you. Consider your approach to uninteresting classes as you read the Perspective Check.

EMPLOY ELABORATION

When you take a class that you immediately find dull, you can do one of several things. First, see if you can find some aspect of the course—any aspect—that might spark a desire to become actively involved. It could be the jumping-off point for you to generate additional interest. One proven method for increasing your interest in a topic is through a variety of *elaboration strategies*—techniques that make information more meaningful because you mentally process it in numerous ways. Here are some elaboration strategies worth trying.

- *Mental imagery.* Try to picture the information. What does it look like? If it is an event, envision it as it happened. (For example, envision Allied troops landing on the beaches of Normandy on D day.) If it is a personal or social behavior, imagine what people would look like engaged in it (for example, peer pressure in high school). If it is a work of art, try to picture what the city and people might have looked like at the time the work was created. (For example, what was the French countryside like in the time of Monet?)

- *Expansion.* Go further with what is presented. What experiences might have led someone to develop a particular theory? What might the world be like if this information were not yet known? (For example, recall the days prior to worldwide Internet access and cell phones.) How has this information changed individuals? Society? Culture?

- *Prediction.* Once you have the initial information, consider what will come next. What might it lead up to? Where might the field of study focus its attention next? What might you need to know about this information?

- *Compare and contrast.* How is the information similar to and different from what was already presented in the class, what you already know personally, or what you can imagine? (For example, how was the battle of Gettysburg similar to the battle at Fort Sumter, or how were combat strategies in Iraq similar to those used in the Civil War?) What things contrast greatly with it? How might you categorize information based on the similarities? How might you reconcile the differences?

- *Debate.* If you were required to debate on the topic, which side would you choose to support? What supporting evidence or examples would you use to make your points? If you had to argue for the opposing side, what information could you use to make a strong argument?

- *Real-life application.* How could you apply the material to real-life circumstances? (For example, why is it important to understand the dynamics of the Civil War, politically or logistically?) Who would make use of the information and how?

- *Personal application.* How could you relate the information to your life? What could you gain from knowing this information? Consider how other people in your life could benefit.

- *Discussion.* Talk about the material with your roommate, friends, and family. Do they know anything about it, or are they interested in learning about it? What can you tell them that might be interesting? Do they have any opinions related to the information itself or its application?

Not all of these strategies apply to all course topics. Find those that work for you and consider how to use the information in ways you ordinarily wouldn't. Engage in some internal dialogue about what the lecturer is saying. Usually, students listen and process information faster than lecturers deliver it. An internal dialogue helps you maintain your active thoughts on the subject matter.

FIND A FRIEND

Besides enhancing the course material to make it more interesting, you could also focus on other aspects of the class that might be of interest. Perhaps the information is dull but the instructor has some great qualities—either as a speaker or as a personable, caring individual. Get to know a couple of your classmates. Knowing people in the class may motivate you to attend regularly. You also might arrange to study together before the exams. Even if you don't like the course, you'll be in good company.

SEEK SUBTLETIES

It could be that the topic as a whole is uninspiring but one or two aspects of the material interest you. Psychology, for example, is a tremendously diverse field. Sometimes students are disappointed with the first unit, which typically deals with the scientific method and how to conduct research. However, when they look through the text, they eagerly anticipate when the focus turns to social psychology and its dramatic experiments on obedience and social control. If you happen to find an element of the course that seems more tolerable to you, talk with your instructor about the possibility of doing some extra credit work on the subject. If you are required to write a paper or conduct some research of your own, you may be able to explore the topic that interests you the most. This will motivate you to work hard at learning the material and ultimately succeed in the course.

ASSESS ALTERNATIVES

If you simply can't tolerate a particular course, look at your academic options. If it is an elective course, consider another choice. You may do much better in a music appreciation class than an art history class if you are required to take a humanities course. If the course is part of your degree plan, consider taking it with another instructor at another time. Sometimes the same course can be a completely different experience in the hands of a different professor. Researching classes and instructors before registering can help you avoid a class that is so uninteresting you simply can't tune in.

You cannot always love what you do, so it is important to learn how to adapt to situations with high demands and low interest. Read the Future Focus for some insight on how the ability to concentrate in the face of boredom comes in handy.

FUTURE FOCUS: I DIDN'T THINK I'D BE DOING *THIS*!

School is not the only place people have to learn information that is less than interesting. Unfortunately, jobs also demand uninteresting tasks. Of course, if you want to keep your job and succeed in your career, you must adapt to work requirements that you hadn't anticipated. As you read this story about Tad, consider if what he is going through is similar to what you have experienced in any of your courses. How will your ability to listen actively and participate in those challenging classes serve you well in the future?

Tad was really excited about his new job as an electrical engineer. He was working for a premier telecommunications company, earning a great salary, and enjoying his coworkers. One day Tad received a memo about a mandatory meeting that everyone on his design team had to attend. Apparently there would be some changes made in the department, and the meeting would describe the new protocol.

It was difficult for Tad to pull himself away to attend the meeting. He was on a roll with his latest design and hated to shift focus. The meeting began slowly and Tad thought it was going to drag on forever. His boss was not an eloquent speaker and the room was packed and stuffy. He needed to pay close attention because he'd be learning about his new responsibilities. Much to his dismay, Tad found out that he wouldn't be able to spend all of his time doing design work but would now have to write weekly status reports, research potential customers and their equipment, and attend frequent marketing meetings.

Tad was devastated. He was an engineer, not a marketing professional. Not only was he clueless about market research and customer relations, but he really wasn't interested in that part of the business. All he wanted to do was design the parts and let others handle the issue of how they would be used and by whom. After calming down, Tad realized that he needed to adapt his focus.

Tad briefly considered looking for a new job. Then he realized that the new scope of his job was the situation for engineers everywhere. Tad was not pleased with his new job responsibilities, but he knew he had to learn how to approach them positively. The new tasks were going to make up a significant part of his career, and he needed to learn how to do them successfully.

 ## STRATEGIES FOR ACTIVE LISTENING

Now that you know the skills for listening effectively and the reasons it is critical to master these skills, you are ready to learn the techniques for getting the most out of class.

DEMONSTRATE ACTIVE LISTENING

You can tell when people are listening actively just by looking at them. If you ask what they are doing mentally while they listen to a lecture, you'll get an even clearer picture of what active listening involves.

LOOK LIKE A LISTENER

When students are really listening, they usually appear to be paying attention. It is difficult to listen and pay attention and *not* be focused. Active listeners have definite body language. They sit up straight and make eye contact with the speaker, they routinely nod to show understanding or to acknowledge points made, they take notes, and they speak up in class.

Sitting close to the front of the room makes all of these things easier to do. Being close to your instructor enables you to see the board clearly and watch as they speak. Making eye contact with the instructor demonstrates that you are following what he or she is saying and helps you maintain your focus. Active listeners take notes but do not write down everything the speaker says.

When you listen actively, you can participate in class because you follow the information presented. Active listeners ask questions to clarify points and assess their understanding. They also ask for additional examples or suggest their own to see if their interpretations are correct. They elaborate on points and make general comments on the topic, which can inspire class discussions. All of these interactive contributions both demonstrate and enhance the mental activity taking place while listening actively.

MENTALLY MANIPULATE THE MATERIAL

The key elements to active listening take place in your head. Recall the earlier examples of watching television. The active listener doesn't just mindlessly watch a favorite program but rather thinks about the dialogue as it occurs. Active listeners consider the dialogue's relationship to previous events. They conjecture what it indicates about the relationships between characters and anticipate upcoming plot twists based on what they hear. This is the same kind of mental activity that happens when you actively listen in class.

The elaboration strategies presented earlier demonstrate some active listening techniques. Here are some additional ways to work with the information presented during a lecture.

- *Assess.* State the topic to yourself. Is it new or have you heard it before?

- *Make connections.* Is the information related to something you've learned before? Is it a subcategory of a larger topic? Did you read about it in your textbook? Does it lay the groundwork for additional information to come? What topics might follow now that this information has been presented?

- *Ask questions.* How does the material relate to what you've been discussing in class? What is the point of learning the information? How might someone apply it to real life? Who uses information like this? What does it lead up to?

- *Interpret.* What is the meaning of this information? Consider how it fits in with the subject matter of the course as a whole.

- *Draw conclusions.* How is your understanding more complete now that you have this information? What more do you know about other topics since having learned this information? Develop summaries for sets of information with this material.

- *Judge.* What is the value of this information? How could it help you personally?

Engaging in all of these mental manipulations not only keeps your attention focused on listening, but it also helps you understand and learn the material. Having a true understanding of something doesn't come just from listening, taking notes, and repeatedly reading those notes. Learning arises from thinking about information, working with it mentally, and processing it to make sense of it. The meaning of specific information comes from understanding its elements, its purpose, and its connection to other information. Active listening starts this learning, but you must follow up, review, and seriously study to remember all that is presented to you over time. As you concentrate on what your instructor says, listening not just to translate the words onto a piece of paper but to make sense of the material, you begin to learn it.

THE FIRST STEP: PREPARE TO LISTEN

When you attend a lecture, you can give yourself an advantage by preparing for what you are going to hear. Going into a lecture unprepared makes it much harder to focus your attention, and the information may seem foreign and difficult to process. On the other hand, when you do some background work prior to class, you may have an easier time listening effectively.

Reading your syllabus helps you prepare for class. Most instructors list the topics planned for each class day. Familiarizing yourself with the upcoming week's material gets your brain in gear for learning. Reading about the topic before your instructor discusses it in class actually brings about active listening. If you already have the concepts in mind before the instructor presents them, you can engage in elaboration and questioning more easily. Class time can provide the opportunity to follow up on any questions you have about the reading and to discuss evidence, examples, and applications with your instructor. Doing any related homework assignments and problem-solving exercises also helps prepare you.

A CLOSER LOOK AT LECTURES

Lectures usually are not haphazard ramblings of your instructor. In most cases they are well planned out and have specific goals for covering the topic. This is to your advantage when you are an active listener, because you can learn to identify cues that show a pattern of presentation. When you identify the pattern, you can immediately make more sense of the material, create effective notes, and prepare better for the exam.

PICK OUT PATTERNS

You can determine the organizational patterns of lectures through the language your instructor uses. When you can quickly recognize how your instructor is teaching, you have a framework for mentally processing the information. This helps you organize your thoughts and enables you to feel more in control of what you are listening to. Here are some standard elements of a lecture.

- *Reviewing.* Some instructors begin each lecture by reviewing what they have already presented. They do this to help students recall important information that paves the way for the new material to come. Signal phrases include *to review, to recap,* and *to summarize where we left off.*

- *Introducing.* When instructors start a new topic, they may begin by introducing the main points. Signal phrases include *we will now turn to the topic of, today we will begin discussing, I will now introduce you to,* and *we will now talk about the topic of.*

- *Lists.* Instructors often present lists of basic facts or concepts of a new topic. Listen for cues such as *first of all, secondly, next, in addition, then, another,* and *lastly.*

- *Topic expansion.* After explaining the basics, the instructor may expand and elaborate on them, focusing on one detail at a time and subsequently presenting evidence and examples. Listen for phrases such as *let's look more closely at, expanding on, an example of this would be, this is composed of,* and *going further with regard to.*

- *Sequences.* Instructors often present material according to its sequential parts—for example, steps for solving math problems, stages of development, or events in a history time line. Listen for phrases such as *beginning with, preceding, followed by, next, then,* and *ending with.*

- *Cycles.* When instructors discuss the trends and patterns of a topic, especially related to the point of origin, they might use phrases such as *we begin with, it starts with, followed by, next we see, which leads to, subsequently, resulting in, coming back to, ending up with,* and *once again we see.*

- *Visual-spatial.* Some material—such as anatomy, biological structures, and geography—requires a knowledge of visual-spatial orientation. Instructors may draw diagrams on the board or refer to pictures and maps. Listen for *next to, above, below, adjacent to, bordering, inner, outer, anterior, posterior, north, south, east,* and *west* as indicators of a visual-spatial mode.

- *Compare and contrast.* Higher-level thinking often involves looking for similarities and differences between paired concepts, theories, processes, or events. Instructors may present these comparisons in lecture. Listen for phrases such as *on the one hand, similarly, along the same lines, likewise, also, in contrast to, on the other hand, however, but,* and *in opposition to.*

- *Cause and effect.* With some subjects, the causal relationship between elements is important. Instructors may present information in terms of its role in bringing about a change or with regard to the factors or events leading up to it. Cues include *initially, then, brings about, leads to, as a result, followed by, because, due to, thus,* and *as a result.*

- *Problem solving.* Some lectures involve explaining how to identify and work through the steps to solve a problem. Listen for words that signify problem solving, including *identify, issue, decide, hypothesize, begin with, calculate, estimate, predict, determine, proceed, conclude by,* and, obviously, *solve.*

- *Examples.* To make their points clear, instructors often provide examples, analogies, or supporting evidence. Listen for phrases such as *for example, in support of, to demonstrate, to illustrate, like, think of it as,* and *such as.*

CONCENTRATE ON CRITICAL CUES

Lectures can provide you with cues that demonstrate what information the instructor finds particularly important. Whenever your instructor writes anything on the board, uses prepared slides, or presents transparencies on the overhead projector, write down the key points. The instructor's efforts to present the information graphically indicate that it is important and that you should pay attention to it. He or she is likely to discuss the material, so be prepared to listen carefully. Likewise, if your instructor distributes any additional readings, articles, charts, graphs, or tables, he or she probably expects you to understand them. The use of videos, film clips, or computer presentations also indicates the significance of the material they cover. Make sure you actively listen during these presentations and related discussions, because you are likely to see the material on an upcoming exam.

Instructors also use body language and speech patterns to emphasize important points. You may notice a pause after your instructor presents a specific piece of information. The pause may give everyone the chance to write down the fact and think about it. The instructor also may begin to speak more slowly during a portion of the lecture. Use this opportunity to focus more intensely on the information being presented. An instructor may repeat a critical piece of information to indicate its significance. The repetition may be accompanied by a change in the tone of voice— either in volume or intensity. Sometimes professors get excited about information they find particularly important, and you can tell when this happens. Their eyes may widen and they may begin gesturing more. They may leave the lectern to approach students and may pound the desk or break their chalk in the process of overzealously marking on the board. Sometimes instructors do these things to get students' attention, and it usually works. Don't be distracted. Instead, take these signs as a cue to listen up.

DEALING WITH DIFFICULT INSTRUCTOR STYLES

Most college professors are not trained speakers. Usually they are experts in their field of study who must teach what they know to others. Some enjoy this opportunity and feel comfortable with it, but others do not. Some instructors have a knack for public speaking and communicating effectively with students. Other instructors may be incredibly knowledgeable but have difficulty explaining the concepts to students. You are likely to experience a variety of lecture styles during your college career, so prepare to listen effectively in different situations.

BATTLING THE BORING

Regardless of how interesting the material is, the instructor's presentation can make it seem boring. Tedious lecturers are challenging because they don't inspire active listening. Their style may be so slow or so bland that listeners don't have the auditory input to motivate their thinking. During a dull lecture, you might have to create interest by engaging in elaboration, visual imagery, forming opinions, interpreting, and summarizing. Tedious lectures provide ample opportunity to make connections between concepts.

You can also try to liven up the lecture by asking questions that prompt examples or even an elaboration of particular points. Your question may prompt your instructor to tell a story or share additional information, or it may lead to questions from others and perhaps even a class discussion on the topic. Your attempts to interact with the instructor may be greatly appreciated and may enable him or her to break from the rigid presentation format. Vocal students sometimes can help instructors discover how to cover the material in a more casual, personable manner.

SURVIVING THE SPEEDY SPEAKER

At the other end of the spectrum from the boring lecturer is the fast talker—an instructor who naturally tends to speak quickly, either because of nervousness or to cover a lot of material in a short class period. Either way, it's challenging to keep up and gather the information adequately. The situation doesn't allow much time for additional mental processing when you can barely stay on top of what is being said.

With instructors who speak rapidly, you may be able to control the situation. Ask your instructor to slow down or to repeat portions of the lecture. Ask for additional examples or explanations if you couldn't follow the original one or if you just need a moment to catch up. You may even ask the instructor to write the key points on the board. Make it your goal to listen actively for the main points. If you simply can't get all of the details, make sure you can get them from the textbook. If you still have concerns, visit your instructor during office hours. Make an appointment to talk about any gaps you have in your notes. Don't hesitate to do this on a regular basis if necessary. You are entitled to get the information you need.

STAY WITH THE SOPHISTICATED SPEAKER

You may find that some instructors talk above your level of understanding. They may do this because they have a hard time adapting the material for undergraduate students, or they may be trying to challenge students to see if they can rise to the occasion. If your instructor uses unfamiliar vocabulary and complex explanations, come to class well prepared. Do your reading and homework assignments ahead of time so you have the background information to help you interpret what your instructor says. Meet regularly with others in the class to discuss previous lecture topics. Someone else may feel more comfortable with the instructor and may understand the material better.

Ask your instructor to clarify points or explain unfamiliar terms. He or she may not do this to your satisfaction, but it is worth asking. If enough students question the advanced vocabulary and conceptual presentation, the instructor may get the point. You could also bring a pocket dictionary to class to look up critical words as they are presented. Use your active listening skills to gather meaning from the information that you *can* follow, which provides context for better understanding the difficult concepts.

DEAL WITH THE DISORGANIZED LECTURER

Disorganized speakers are difficult to deal with and require a little extra work. First, prepare for class. As with other challenging lecture situations, when you read ahead of time and work through assignments, you have significant exposure to the material already. This enables you to get an idea of what the instructor will present during the lecture, which prepares you for it. If your instructor fails to organize the information, you can do so in your own mind. Active listening during a disorganized presentation helps you make connections and categorize information to see the whole picture. Try to recognize the main ideas, related points, and relevant examples. Find a way to structure your notes most effectively during a disorganized lecture.

If you find an instructor to be particularly disorganized, chances are that your classmates also do. Plan weekly study sessions to compare notes and discuss the material from class. When you collaborate, you may see the structure of the information emerge.

CHAPTER 7 REVIEW QUESTIONS

1. What is the difference between hearing and listening? What specifically is active listening?

2. Discuss several reasons why it is important to be an active listener in college.

3. How are concentration and active listening related?

4. Identify some internal and external distractors and ways to deal with them.

5. What roles do attention, interest, and motivation play in active listening?

6. What are some positive and productive things you can do if you find yourself in a boring class?

7. How can you look like an active listener? Why might you want to ensure that you look like an active listener?

8. Discuss the role of preparing to listen actively during a class lecture.

SKILL PRACTICE

1. Identify each of the following distractors as either external or internal. For each one, explain what you could do to minimize it or eliminate it completely.
   a. You regret not having brought a sweatshirt to class. It is 85 degrees outside, but the school has cranked up the air conditioning and you are freezing.
   b. Your instructor has a cold and is clearing his throat about every 30 seconds.
   c. You had a fight with your boyfriend last night and went home crying. When he arrives in class, he takes a seat across the room, next to an attractive young woman, instead of sitting next to you as he usually does.
   d. You drank a large soda with lunch right before class. Now you are wondering if you should tough it out or disrupt class by getting up to use the restroom.
   e. You just realized that you forgot to return your mom's phone call. You are never going to hear the end of it.
   f. One of the lights in the room is buzzing and flashing, creating an annoying pattern.

2. List several things that indicate the characteristics of an inactive listener.

3. For each of the following excerpts of lectures, identify the specific lecture pattern and underline the cue words and phrases.
   a. A self-fulfilling prophecy is a prediction that comes true not because it was right but simply because it was made. Let's look at how this works. First, you make some kind of prediction or judgment about something that will happen. For example, you believe that you are going to have a miserable time with the blind date your friend set you up with. You believe that if the woman has to be set up on blind dates she is likely to be dull. She probably has nothing interesting to say, has no sense of humor, and won't be any fun to be around. You promised your friend you would go as a favor. So, despite your lack of enthusiasm, you drive to her house to pick her up and then you drive to a restaurant for dinner. At this point, you feel relieved to have the radio to listen to on the ride to the restaurant. At least you don't have to try to make conversation. Once you get to the restaurant, though, it's another story. Now you have to interact with this woman, but you just can't imagine what you can talk about. You offer comments on the weather and the meal choices and she responds politely. Next, you mention the latest movie and she tells you her life keeps her so busy she doesn't have time to go to the movies very often. Clearly, she is very dull. The remainder of the evening involves no humor, depth, or passion. It appears you were right—she is a loser. Confirming your original prediction, you believe you are a very good judge of character. All of your original expectations were met. However, you didn't happen to consider your own contribution to the evening. Speaking about the weather doesn't inspire others to vivid and substantial responses. And when she mentioned her busy life, you failed to inquire what might keep her so busy. The woman may have thought that you were dull, humorless, and uninteresting to be around. Your own actions made your predictions a reality. This is what is meant by a self-fulfilling prophecy.
   b. Let's take a look at some of the structures of the brain. The brain is made up of two hemispheres—the right and the left, which are connected by a band of fibers known as the *corpus callosum*. These fibers are located toward the top middle part of your brain—about eye level. The outer portion of the brain, called the cerebrum, is divided into four regions, or lobes. The back portion of each hemisphere is where the optic nerve connects to the brain. Thus, these areas are called the occipital lobes. Above the occipital lobes, in an area that doesn't extend quite to the front, nor down as far as ear level, are the

parietal lobes. Just below the parietal lobes, extending back to border the occipital lobes, but stopping before reaching the front section of the brain, are the temporal lobes. These portions of the hemispheres are responsible for auditory processing, so it makes sense that they correspond closely to the location of the ears. The fourth lobe of the brain is the frontal lobe. Like the name implies, it is located in the front section of the hemispheres, beginning where the parietal lobes and temporal lobes end at the top and bottom, respectively.

c. Speech and language development occurs in a series of ordered steps. The first stage begins at birth. Newborns have a one-tube resonator—that is, their larynx is not yet fully developed. The one-tube resonator limits the sounds that babies can make to reflexive crying, coughs, sneezes, burps, and so on. By the time the baby is six to eight weeks old, the larynx has completely dropped and the infant is able to make cooing noises and elicit sustained laughter. Stage three is marked by vocal play—the infant's experimentation with different tongue and mouth positions and the sounds that result. In stage four, babies engage in reduplicated babbling, which consists of combining a consonant and a vowel sound and repeating them. Babies eventually progress to non-reduplicated babbling, in which the vowel and consonant sounds are different from each other ("me-da" and "bo-da"). This stage also involves expressive jargon, which is the intonation that the babbling takes on. The sixth stage of language development is identified by the child's use of protowords—sounds that have specific meaning but are not actually words ("ga" for *cookie*). The use of protowords is followed by vocables, a more advanced form of sound with meaning. The next stage, which is the final one of infancy, occurs on average between 9 and 12 months. This is the stage of the one-word utterance. At this stage, children can speak and properly use some words from their native language.

d. Let's look at two distinct theories of human behavior—that of Sigmund Freud and that of Carl Rogers. Freud believed that the origin or cause of all of our behavior is ultimately the result of the ego trying to satisfy the id in accordance with the superego's rules—all taking place out of our conscious awareness. The id seeks immediate gratification of sexual and aggressive impulses, whereas the superego tells us these are bad. The way in which the ego goes about pleasing both the id and the superego is manifested in our behaviors. Rogers's humanistic theory on the cause of behavior couldn't be more different. Rogers believed that all humans are fundamentally good and that behavior reflects an individual's constant striving to be the best person possible. Both theories acknowledge that problems can arise in human behavior, with Freud claiming that problems are due to the ego failing at its balancing act. The ego's efforts to satisfy the id according to the conscience—the superego—are ineffective, so problems such as fixations and neuroses arise. Again, Rogers's theory takes a very different view of the root of behavior problems. Rogers believed that although we are striving to attain the ideal self, it is sometimes difficult to get there. Problems develop when we become aware that the *actual* self is very far from the *ideal* self. In the most severe case, we become what Rogers termed *incongruent*. Despite these differences with regard to the origin of behavior and the cause and manifestation of problems, the two theories share a common theme with regard to therapy.

e. It has come to my attention that many students do not know how to calculate their grade point average, or GPA. I will now take you through the steps for how to do this. You are probably aware that an A is worth 4 points, a B is worth 3 points, a C is worth 2 points, a D is worth 1 point, and an F is worth no points. First, list your courses and the number of credit hours. Note the grade you earned for each class and the number of points for that grade. Next, multiply the number of grade points by the number of credit hours for that class. For example, you earned a B in biology, which is a three-credit-hour course. You multiply 3 (points for the B) by 3 (number of credit hours). You have a total of 9 points for biology. Do this for each course for the semester. Once you have obtained a number value for each course, add the numbers. Divide that total value for all courses by the number of credit hours of the courses. The resulting answer is your GPA. So, if all of your course values total 38 and you took 12 credit hours for the semester, your GPA is 3.17. That's pretty good.

CURRENT COURSE APPLICATION

1. Assess each of your instructors using these checklists. Given the profile you discover for each one, determine what specific things you can do to be a more effective listener and overcome challenges with each instructor.

Speech Patterns

- Does the instructor speak loudly or so softly that it's difficult to hear?
- Does he or she speak very slowly and repeat a lot, or does he or she speak very quickly, making it difficult to keep up?
- Does he or she have clear pronunciation, or are some words difficult to understand?
- Does he or she speak dynamically with varying intonation, volume, and expression, or in a monotone?

Body Language

- Does the instructor sit or stand in one place while lecturing or does he or she move freely around the room?
- Does he or she use gestures and motion toward items written on the board?
- Does the instructor primarily keep his or her back to the class while writing on the board, or does the instructor face the students and attend to their level of interest?

Organization

- Does he or she provide handouts or write outlines or lists on the board to guide the lecture?
- Does he or she review previous material or introduce new information without a review?
- Does he or she stray from the topic with incidental stories and examples?
- Does he or she stray from the topic while responding to students' questions and comments?

Concern for Students

- Does he or she immediately respond to questions when students raise their hands, or put them off until that portion of the lecture has ended?
- Does he or she accept requests to slow down, repeat information, or provide additional examples, or are students expected to research information on their own?
- Does he or she willingly engage students' attempts to discuss topics and accept personal comments, or are interactive behaviors discouraged?
- Does he or she come to class early or stay after so students can ask additional questions?

2. For any class in which you typically sit in the back row, try sitting in the center of the front row for the next class period. Answer the following questions:

Were you able to hear your instructor better?

How did being up close affect your experience in the class?

Did you feel a stronger connection with your instructor? In what ways?

Did you find it easier to ask questions or participate in class discussions?

How did it affect your ability to listen actively?

3. Identify your least interesting class. Make a list of at least three things that you can do to increase your interest and motivation in the course. Discuss your specific plans for carrying out your ideas.

4. Make an effort to prepare for one (or more) of your classes. Review the syllabus to find out what topic will be covered. Read any related material in your textbook, even if none has been assigned. Review your notes from the past several lectures. Meet with some classmates to talk about the material presented so far. After class, write about how being prepared affected your experience in class.

In what ways were you able to listen more actively?

Were you able to make more connections among the information?

Were you able to gain more meaning from the lecture?

Was it easier to follow the lecture and take notes?

Were you more relaxed in class?

Do you feel you learned more than you usually do?

TAKE A LOOK ONLINE

For some tips and interesting facts on listening in class, go to

www.quinnipiac.edu/x2917.xml

For an in-depth look at the difference between hearing and listening, along with details as to what sounds prompt our attention and why, check out the following website:

http://interact.uoregon.edu/MediaLit/mlr/readings/articles/earlids.html

---

STUDENT SCENARIO DISCUSSION RESPONSES

- **Assuming the girls took good notes and made regular copies for each other, what went wrong?** No matter how complete the girls' notes were, they couldn't convey all of the critical points made in the lectures. When you must rely on someone else's notes, you are limited to that person's
  - Decisions about what was important enough to write down
  - Understanding of the material
  - Ability to convey the meaning of the information in writing
  - Interpretation of the material (ability to capture the essence of what the instructor was trying to convey)
  - Method of organizing the information

When you don't go to class, you don't have the opportunity to ask questions, ask for clarification, or hear firsthand accounts of experiences and examples of the information. There is no substitute for listening to a lecture in person.

- **What insight did the girls' initial conversation provide as to why the plan didn't work?** The fact that they agreed to the plan in the first place demonstrates the girls' lack of understanding as to the true value of being in class. Believing that you can rely on another person's class experience to enhance your learning is a mistake. They also demonstrated a fundamental lack of motivation for the class. (Shelley said, "I would really love not having to sit through that class twice a week. Once is bad enough.") If this was the girls' attitude, then it is not likely they were good listeners when they were in class. Their notes probably reflected their lack of interest.

- **The girls have a right not to attend each and every class. Why should it matter that their professor seemed displeased with their arrangement?** Conscientious students are always concerned about what their instructors think about them as students. Courses often involve written assignments, oral presentations, essay exams, and other subjective elements. Instructors must make decisions about their students' knowledge and abilities. Therefore, students should provide teachers with the best set of information possible. This is also the case when semester grades are borderline. Do you want your instructor to perceive you as a student who does everything possible to learn the material and demonstrate an interest in succeeding, or as someone trying to succeed with the least amount of effort?

- **What should the girls have done after they received their first exam grades?** Individually, they should have figured out where they went wrong on the test and met with the instructor to discuss the difficulties. Each one of them should have resumed attending class regularly.

- **Are there any circumstances in which such a plan might be successful? Explain.** Under very difficult circumstances, a student with well-defined goals but a challenging schedules might reasonably try such a plan. Consider an individual who must support a family and also go to school. If the degree plan required a course that had limited offerings—particularly if it were an important prerequisite course—and the time of the class conflicted with work or childcare, having an arrangement such as the girls' plan might be the only way. It is not optimal and it would be best for the student to explain the situation to the instructor. The student could plan to meet with the instructor outside of class periodically to review the material and ensure that the notes were complete.

ANALYSIS OF RESPONSES FOR SKILL CHECK

Count how many times you circled YES in each column.

14–15 YES responses for Always True of Me

You're probably a fantastic listener, both in a classroom setting and among your friends. Keep up the good work.

12–13 YES responses for Always True of Me

You are a good listener but need to fine-tune a few of your listening skills. Choose behaviors to modify that you think will easily improve your listening and classroom performance.

10–11 YES responses for Always True of Me

You need to change some behaviors so you get more out of classroom lectures. To improve your listening skills, start with any item that you marked as Never True. Then move to the Sometimes True column.

9 or fewer YES responses for Always True of Me

or

7 or more YES responses for Never True of Me

You need to master listening skills for academic success. Most college classes include lecture, class discussion, or group work—all of which require listening skills.

SUGGESTED ANSWERS FOR SKILL PRACTICE

1. Identify each of the following distractors as either external or internal. For each one, explain what you could do to minimize it or eliminate it completely.

   a. You regret not having brought a sweatshirt to class. It is 85 degrees outside, but the school has cranked up the air conditioning and you are freezing. This is an external, physical distractor. The best way to avoid it is to be prepared with an extra layer of clothing for when the air conditioner is running at maximum capacities or the heat is not working.

   b. Your instructor has a cold and is clearing his throat about every 30 seconds. This is an external distractor and may involve some internal mental distractions as well (wondering if it will stop, thinking about how distracting it is). Try to focus on what the instructor is saying in between the coughs instead of focusing on the coughing.

   c. You had a fight with your boyfriend last night and went home crying. When he arrives in class, he takes a seat across the room, next to an attractive young woman, instead of sitting next to you as he usually does. The emotional situation is an internal distractor. The boyfriend and the attractive woman are external distractors. Your best strategy would be to move to a place in the room where you are not able to see your boyfriend. Secondly, you must convince yourself that you will not let him deal you another blow by interfering with your learning and success in the class. For you to give your attention over to concerns about your relationship would cost you at least one lecture's worth of important information.

   d. You drank a large soda with lunch right before class. Now you are wondering if you should tough it out or disrupt class by getting up to use the restroom. The most immediate distraction is physical—the need to use the restroom. The mental debate over whether to leave class is another internal distractor. The best strategy is to go to the bathroom and return to class as quickly as possible. You can get the few minutes of missed notes from a classmate after class, and once your physical distractor is gone you can give you full attention to the lecture. To avoid the distractor, don't drink a soda before class.

   e. You just realized that you forgot to return your mom's phone call. You are never going to hear the end of it. The mental turmoil is an internal distractor. Make a note to yourself to call her the first chance you get. Then focus on class.

   f. One of the lights in the room is buzzing and flashing, creating an annoying pattern. This external distractor is likely to bother everyone in the room. If you concentrate on the lecture, the distraction will fade into the background and you won't even notice it.

2. List several things that indicate the characteristics of an inactive listener. Answers may include characteristics such as the following:

   Arrives late for class

   Comes to class unprepared

   Brings food and drink to consume during the lecture

Sits where he or she has a good view out the window

Sits in the back of the room in case he or she wants to take a nap

Brings work from other classes to do during lecture

Focuses on any number of external and internal distractors

Tries to copy every word said by the instructor during lecture

Refrains from asking questions, even though not all of the information is clear

Tunes out when classmates ask questions or engage in a class discussion

Writes things down occasionally but spends more time doodling and making to-do lists

Concentrates on how boring the material is and what a waste of time it is to be sitting there

Carries on conversations with classmates while the instructor is speaking

Leaves the lecture and doesn't think about the material again until the exam

3. For each of the following excerpts of lectures, identify the specific lecture pattern and underline the cue words and phrases.

   a. This lecture uses a cycle pattern. Terms and phrases that provide important cues for listening include *let's look at how this works, first, at this point, next,* and *confirming your original prediction.*

   b. This lecture uses a visual-spatial presentation. Terms and phrases that provide important cues for listening include *the right and the left, connected by, located toward the top middle part, the outer portion,* and numerous other positional words and phrases.

   c. This excerpt presents a sequence of ordered events. Phrases that provide important cues for listening include *in a series of ordered steps, the first stage begins, by the time, stage three, in stage four, at this stage, eventually progress to, this stage also involves, the sixth stage of language development,* and so on.

   d. This lecture compares and contrasts two theories. Terms and phrases that provide important cues for listening include *let's look at two distinct theories, couldn't be more different, both theories, takes a very different view, despite these differences with regard to,* and *the two theories share a common theme.*

   e. This lecture presents steps for problem solving. Words and phrases that provide important cues for listening include *calculate, I will now take you through the steps, first, multiply, once you have obtained a number value, add the numbers,* and *divide that total value.*

8 TAKE EFFECTIVE NOTES IN CLASS

In this chapter you will learn

◌ The numerous benefits of taking effective class notes

◌ The fundamental elements of an effective set of notes

◌ The circumstances in which you should take notes

◌ The basic note-taking formats

◌ How to adapt to different class demands for taking good notes

THE MANY BENEFITS OF CLASS NOTES

Taking notes is both a precursor and a result of active listening. When you establish the goal of writing down in a clear and organized fashion the information you hear, you are prepared to listen attentively. You have greater incentive to listen and to process what you hear. In turn, active listening, which involves questioning, thinking critically, challenging ideas, and finding meaning in the material, makes your notes more thorough and useful. Beneficial notes contain the most critical information and the details that make them more meaningful on later viewing.

Most college classes require heavy note taking because of the oral presentation format, which is very common. However, developing your skills as an effective note taker benefits you long after graduation, because many job experiences involve similar demands. Read the Future Focus to see how note taking could be part of your career.

FUTURE FOCUS: GET THIS DOWN

Imagine a life with no more lectures or hours of note taking. Once you leave college and begin your career, you're not likely to have such demands on your penmanship. However, you will still encounter situations in which you must listen and write down critical information that you hear.

Whenever you begin a new job or transition into a new phase of your career, you have an orientation. No one ever just sits down at a new desk and starts to work. A new job usually begins with a period of learning your exact responsibilities and the numerous details of your work environment. An orientation is likely to take the form of a series of presentations, lectures, demonstrations, and meetings. You must be able to take good notes that you can understand and refer to during the introductory months of your job.

Throughout your career you will be required to attend meetings: board meetings, staff meetings, interdepartmental meetings, client meetings, sales meetings. At each meeting, you learn important information that you will be responsible for, requiring you to compile an effective record of what was said. You also may attend training sessions, workshops, or conferences whose purpose is to provide new material that you will be expected to incorporate into your job responsibilities.

Your future success depends upon your ability to take in information, understand it, and apply it effectively. When you are skilled at taking notes, you will be prepared to make the most of oral presentations, and you will have confidence that your efforts will pay off.

JOGGING YOUR MEMORY

The most common perception students have about why it's important to take notes in class is that it is the only way to remember important information that can't easily be found somewhere else. When the instructor lectures on material that is not in the text, it is critical that you create a set of notes from which to study for the exam. This is note taking at its most basic, but it is only a small part of your in-class experience.

Most college professors do not see it as their job to present to students the material from the text. They expect students to read what is assigned and to learn on their own the information contained in the book. In fact, instructors often present new material in lectures—material that can be obtained only from being in class and hearing what the instructor says. Considering how much time instructors spend preparing for class and sharing information, you can almost count on this material making an appearance on the exam. To have a record of the information so that you can refer to it at a later time (and so you can study it before the exam), you need a reliable set of notes. If your notes are sloppy, disorganized, or inaccurate, they will be useless. When you listen actively and take thorough notes, you have an effective tool for helping you understand and recall what your instructor said in class.

JUMP-START YOUR LEARNING

What if the information presented in the lecture mirrors your textbook? Do you still have to take notes during the lecture? Just because the same information is available in your text is no excuse to forgo either of the two fundamental class experiences—listening and taking notes. On the contrary, your time in class listening actively and taking notes of what the instructor says helps you learn the material thoroughly, setting you up for greater success on papers and exams.

Every class period is a learning opportunity. Unfortunately, many students see it simply as a means of jotting down information from lectures to file away for studying at a later date. In fact, note taking can help you make the most of your time with your instructor and classmates.

ACTIVE LISTENING AND CRITICAL THINKING

When you concentrate and process information as it is presented, you establish the foundation for learning that information. When you listen carefully and think through what is being said, as well as identify and record the critical points made, you broaden your learning opportunity. The goal of producing a set of clear, organized notes provides an excellent motivation to listen actively. It gives you the purpose for listening and being in class—not just because you must accurately record facts and figures, but because you must convey a connected picture through the elements of your notes.

College lectures typically contain a great deal more material than high school classes. In high school, your teachers probably presented all of the material so there would be no question as to the main points or the relevant details you would be responsible for knowing. With the greater level of complexity in college courses, it follows that the lectures are often more challenging. Instructors do not necessarily provide an overview or context. Instead, they may expect you to piece it together and draw your own conclusions. College material often is not clear-cut. Multifaceted issues involve unresolved conclusions. Your notes must capture all of the elements involved, and it is not always immediately obvious what those elements are. Only by applying the skills of active listening will you be able to capture the complete essence of a lecture in your notes. Learning the skills required for effective note taking drives and enhances your active listening.

Listening actively to a lecture involves critically thinking about the material. You consider not only the content of the lecture but the source of the information, the relationship and relevance to other points made, how the information can be applied, and the significance of learning it.

Another term for critical thinking is *active learning*. This term describes exactly what you are doing when you process fully what your instructor presents. It may seem like a lot to keep track of now, but once you develop your listening and note-taking skills, you will automatically approach information in this way. Remember that it is your goal to capture and convey the subject matter as completely as possible in written form. If you simply sit back and attempt to transcribe words that you hear into words that you write, you miss the opportunity to begin understanding and learning the material, and you may completely miss the critical lessons that you will be responsible for on the exam. The Student Scenario demonstrates how passive note taking catches up with you and hinders your ability to do well.

STUDENT SCENARIO: THREE DAYS AND COUNTING

Shreta had always been an excellent student in high school and was excited, if not a little overwhelmed, by her new college experience. She had a full schedule of demanding classes and made sure she attended every class. She came ready to take notes each day. Although the subjects were challenging, class time was quite relaxing for her. She felt confident in her note-taking skills. She was attentive and quick to write down just about everything her instructors said with incredible accuracy. She had notebooks full of words, lists, and even diagrams copied from those illustrated on the board. Because transcribing lectures came easily for her, she took the opportunity to sit back and put herself on autopilot during her hours in class. The studying would come later.

Shreta believed that her optimum time frame for studying for exams began about three days prior to the test. At this point, she knew she would pull out all of the notes she had gathered over the past several weeks and would read through them. This way, Shreta thought, she would be able to learn and remember everything for the test, as she had done successfully in high school. She had even talked with several of her college classmates and discovered that this was their basic study time frame as well.

With three days and counting for her history exam, Shreta opened her notes to the first page. She read through them and began identifying the pieces of information that she believed were important to know. She was a little frustrated, however, to discover that her notes didn't seem to make much sense now. She remembered a few points, but page after page of the notes seemed to run together and the content felt disjointed—with some phrases appearing as if they were stuck in as an afterthought. Afterthoughts to what? She didn't even know. It all appeared to be a tremendous amount of information to learn in a fairly short period of time. Realizing she had to do what she could, Shreta set out to memorize as much as possible—names, dates, places, and events—reviewing the major elements repeatedly in the time she had. By exam day, she felt confident she had committed everything of significance to memory and felt prepared to ace the test.

To her dismay, Shreta discovered the exam was not at all what she expected. Instead of presenting questions requiring simple recall of individual facts, the exam called for students to apply the material to a varied set of scenarios and theories. Her rote memorization of isolated names and dates was useless. Instead, she needed to understand and relate entire collections of events and their participants, highlight the significance of particular time periods, discuss specific actions as precursors to subsequent occurrences, and elaborate on the validity of different historical perspectives. Even the objective questions required knowing how facts were interrelated. Shreta made a meager attempt to complete the test, relying on her limited knowledge, but was not surprised to find her grade was barely passing.

Consider the following questions:

- What were Shreta's strengths as a student?

- Why didn't those qualities help her in this instance?

- What was Shreta's fundamental mistake, and why do you think she felt comfortable with this choice?

- How might Shreta have discovered her error prior to the exam?

- What could she have done if she had realized her mistake once she started studying for the test?

- What should she do, now that she understands what the exams involve?

CRITICAL CLUES

In addition to being a collection of facts and figures and a written record of your thoughts, questions, and understanding, good notes provide you with other important information.

INSTRUCTOR'S INSIGHT

When you effectively capture the information and the message of a lecture, you record your instructor's particular interest and insight into the topic. Most professors are experts in their field, and every field of study has several schools of thought on the subject matter. Not every piece of information you receive is up for debate, but each instructor has a personal perspective and an area of emphasis that he or she is likely to pass along. What your instructor says may echo the perspective of the textbook to some extent, or he or she may present an additional point of view or even a contrasting or conflicting perspective. This is part of the richness of your college education. You will hear numerous theories and interpretations of the topics you study. Enjoy it and use it to stimulate and discover your own perspective.

Your instructor's insight, personal interpretation, and emphasis on the subject matter can be critically important. In all likelihood, it is the perspective that the instructor wants you to learn, or at least to apply on papers and exams. When you discover a difference between what you read in your book and what your instructor presents in class, ask the instructor about it. Analyzing differences is part of critical thinking and stimulates class discussion. Ask about the instructor's perspective on concepts presented in the book, and learn the reasons for the differences. Of course, be certain to record their responses in your notes. Make clear references to ideas you recall from your reading and link the references to what your instructor says. Recognize the importance of your instructor's input. Read the Professor's Perspective for a relevant anecdote.

Instructors also have their favorite topics and ideas they find enthralling. It may be easy to tell through their body language, tone of voice, facial expressions, and the words they use what interests and excites them. When you see these indicators, include them in your notes. Draw stars or underline the phrases that made your professor come alive. When he or she begins speaking in an animated way, make note of it. The reason is that if the content excites your instructor, he or she will most likely test you on it. Ask questions about these points in class, and mark these cues in your notes as being critical for study.

Sometimes instructors just come right out and tell the class that something will be on the exam, or they present a sample question or two. When this happens, write the information as explicitly as possible. By providing potential test questions, instructors give students an idea of what to expect on the test, and help them better prepare for it. Instructors want students to do well. They don't want you to fail simply because you don't know the optimal way to study for the course. Use your notes as a means for recording all of the hints and pointers you can for upcoming assignments and exams.

PROFESSOR'S PERSPECTIVE: IT'S ALL FAIR GAME

Professors' time is valuable. They don't want to spend it on meaningless issues or information in classes. You are responsible for learning everything you hear in class. In other words, anything you hear in class is fair game as test material. Be sure to record all important details in your notes.

The tricky part is that you may not recognize some information as being necessary to include in your notes. Some lectures are highly structured and easy to notate. Other lectures, however, may involve a presentation style that leaves you wondering just what it is you should think about and take notes on. For example, some instructors use personal experiences and storytelling to illustrate key points. They may present these in a personable and enjoyable way—a way that encourages students to sit back, relax, and just listen. And they may want students to do that, so long as they get the significant lesson out of it at the end. Don't ignore the vignettes and apparent tangents to the topic. Be sure to mention the story, its elements, and critical conclusion in your notes.

The same holds true for questions from students and class discussions. If your instructor is answering someone else's question or several individuals pull the instructor into an elaboration of the topic, don't take the opportunity to tune out. Professors often use prompts to address critical points. Discussions enable them to cover the material in ways that appeal to the class and that capitalize on the group's understanding. Taking notes is not optional during those times. It is tremendously important for you to actively listen to group discussions, think about them, and include them in your notes for future reference.

MONITOR YOUR UNDERSTANDING

If you have any concerns about how well you are following the important ideas or about your ability to convey the ideas effectively in your notes, make an appointment with your instructor. Bring your notes and be ready to show what you have recorded so far. Use your notes to talk about the main ideas briefly so you can demonstrate your degree of comprehension for the lectures. Find out if you have omitted any major points and if you have successfully captured the essence of the lecture in your notes. Ask for pointers on note taking and studying for the upcoming exams.

You should always meet with your instructor after you receive a disappointing test grade. Bring your class notes with you so you can review them with your instructor to determine if there was a problem with how you recorded the information from class. Compare items that you missed on the exam with those areas in your notes. Your instructor can help you identify the reasons your notes may have been insufficient for you to prepare successfully. You can then work on improving your note-taking methodology. If possible, follow up with your instructor prior to the next exam.

OTHER PEOPLE'S NOTES

Notes are notes, right? If they contain all of the necessary information that enables you to prepare for an exam, you should be able to achieve success. It's not unusual for students to use each other's notes to help them through a course, but you should consider some important things before doing so. Read the Perspective Check and assess your position on the nature and source of class notes.

PERSPECTIVE CHECK: THE NATURE OF NOTES

How do you use your course notes? Of what benefit are they to you? Does it matter where they come from? Is it critical that you take your own notes, or would you be just as happy to borrow notes from someone else? Do you feel you could do better in your courses if you studied someone else's notes—someone you consider to be more skilled at taking notes? What if you could obtain notes from another source and simply sit back in class and listen, knowing you have the notes to study from? What if your instructor offered his or her own notes for you to study from? Would you accept them? Do you believe you could be part of a note-taking group and do it successfully? Why or why not? What are the pros and cons of taking your own notes in class?

CONSIDER THE SOURCE

Each set of notes reflects the note taker, and this is why you should always take your own notes. Only you can assess your level of understanding and the degree of thoroughness with which the information is recorded on paper. The experience of listening and taking your own notes sets the learning process in motion. Sometimes it may seem desirable or necessary to rely on someone else's notes. If you miss class for an emergency, you must catch up with what you missed. Many students regularly turn to other people as a source of critical class information. The reasons vary. Maybe they want to put in more hours at work, so they find a willing classmate who lets them copy their notes. Maybe they think the lecture duplicates the book and that it's not imperative they go to class. Getting someone's class notes wouldn't hurt, though. Maybe they have found class notes through their fraternity or sorority, an older student, or even the instructor, and want to take advantage of their good fortune. Under no circumstances, though, is it recommended to use someone else's notes as a replacement for your own.

When you rely on another student's notes, you are assuming that the person understood the topic clearly and that the notes are accurate. You are assuming that the person included all of the necessary information and didn't omit any critical points. You are assuming that the person copied charts, graphs, and illustrations effectively, correctly showing important visual information. You are assuming that the person picked up on the nuances of the instructor's message, including important cues, references, and connections within the material.

How likely is it that all of these assumptions are sound? Many students in your classes may be capable of taking excellent notes but, unless you have complete confidence that their notes are the best notes possible, you should be cautious about relying on them. You may think that your own notes aren't the best notes possible, but the difference is that you produced them. You were in class and experienced the information firsthand. Hearing the lecture, thinking about it at that time, and making an effort to convey the critical elements in your notes benefits you more than you know. When you use your notes to study for an exam, you are using them as memory triggers. What you have written prompts you to recall what went on in class. Another student's notes cannot do that for you.

Other people's notes also reflect their personal learning style, which may differ from your own. If you prefer ideas written out as completely as possible and the borrowed notes are in shorthand and include lots of pictures, symbols, and underlining, you will have a difficult time interpreting them. On the other hand, if you are visual and learn best when information is presented in small, compact units and the notes you borrow have lines and lines of text, you will tune out quickly. Learning styles manifest themselves in other ways besides a person's note-taking format. The content is also influenced by the way you take in information. Auditory learners are likely to have notes that reflect the fact that they gain a great deal from listening. Their notes may be substantial for them—filled with references to the lecture—but inadequate for others. Visual and kinesthetic learners often take notes vigorously and benefit from the activity. For an auditory learner, pages upon pages of detailed descriptions, explanations, and examples are overwhelming and have little appeal.

It's fine to exchange notes with someone else occasionally, but it's not a good idea to make it a habit. Here are some suggestions for how to use notes from other sources when it is necessary.

IF YOU MUST

Sometimes you must borrow notes from someone else. When this occurs, be particular about finding the notes to use, and put in the effort to understand them as completely as possible.

CHOOSE YOUR SOURCE WISELY

At times, you simply can't avoid missing a class and must get a copy of someone else's notes. To prepare for such an occurrence, get to know some of your classmates as soon as the semester starts. Chat with them before or after class, get together for coffee and talk about some issues from class (among other things), and, if possible, ask to compare your notes with theirs. (Claim that you'd like to be sure your notes are up to par.) This way, you can determine some things about your peers. From just a few conversations, you'll be able to tell if they are motivated, have a history of success, care about how they do in class, and are responsible regarding school—in short, what kind of students they are. When you find classmates with positive characteristics, you can feel confident that they are likely to go to class, listen well, and take good notes. Of course, if you can take a look at their notes, you can see if they are neatly written and complete, and you'll know whether you can understand the abbreviations, symbols, and diagrams. If you sense that a particular classmate is not concerned about grades, skips class often, or has notes that look like chicken scratch, cross the person off your list of potential note sources.

BE PREPARED

Once you have found a few reliable classmates, exchange phone numbers and e-mail addresses so you can contact each other if necessary. In addition to knowing you have someone to help you out when you unexpectedly miss class, you may even find a great study partner. If you know ahead of time that you won't make it to class, let your classmate know as soon as possible. When he or she understands that someone else will be reading the notes, the classmate may make a special effort to document the lecture more fully. It is also a good idea to tell your instructor that you won't be in attendance and that you have arranged to get a copy of your friend's notes. This shows your instructor that you have already made plans to catch up on what you must miss, and, if the instructor is aware of the strengths of the student you are relying on, your decision to use that person's notes will reflect positively on your efforts to succeed.

FOLLOW THROUGH

When you miss class, don't wait until the next class period to get the notes. Make arrangements about the logistics when you first call about missing class. Ideally, make arrangements to copy the notes (at your expense, of course) and have the classmate review them with you. Suggest that you'll treat for a cup of coffee and a doughnut. Not only will you have a chance to understand more fully what went on in class (and jot your own notes on the copies to help you assimilate them), but your classmate will also have a study opportunity. If the classmate isn't willing to do this, or if you want to be even more certain that you have everything you need to supplement the missing class, make an appointment with your professor. Bring your copy of the notes and ask to talk through them to make sure they capture the information sufficiently. If you've read through them at least once, prepare to briefly summarize what you believe to be the important points. Remember, professors expect you to do what it takes to learn and do well in their class. When you make such an effort as a result of missing class, you are communicating a strong desire to succeed. It's something they will remember.

DO UNTO OTHERS

Other students may ask you for a copy of your class notes. If so, make your decision wisely and be wary of students who may take advantage of you. Just as you assess others to determine if you would consider asking them for their notes, you should assess those who ask the same of you. If other students have noticed that you are always in class, listen attentively, ask good questions, are respected by the instructor, have confidence, and do well on exams, they may try to benefit from your hard work. If a student routinely asks to copy your notes and it becomes a nuisance, direct the person elsewhere—another classmate, the instructor, or the career center, which may offer seminars on note taking.

If you agree to share your notes with someone else, be sure to copy them yourself or go with the person to make copies. Under no circumstances should you let your notes out of your possession, because they are irreplaceable.

AN OFFER YOU CAN'T REFUSE?

Some professors place their own notes on reserve in the library for students to check out or copy, or they may offer them for sale through a local bookstore. If either option is available, should you go for it?

It depends on your approach. If the notes reflect what is covered in the lecture, then they may have some value as a complement to your own notes. However, if you are tempted to sit back and relax during class, believing that the instructor's notes are all you need, then it's not a good idea to acquire them. You still need to actively listen and take your own notes during class. But here's how your instructor's notes can help:

- They can give you a strong head start in understanding each day's lecture. Reviewing them before class prepares you for what's coming, primes your mind to think about the topic, and creates a more complete and effective set of your own notes.

- They can enable you to absorb more of what is said at the time it is presented. With your instructor's notes in front of you, you can follow the lecture and fill in the margins with notes of your own. Their version is likely to contain the substantial points, which relieves you of having to jot those down. You can then take more time to record details as well as your critical thoughts, questions, and ideas about the points that are already noted.

- They can enable you to prepare a set of questions to ask and topics to explore in class. When you read what your instructor plans to discuss during the lecture, jot down the questions that come to mind. You may find they are answered in the lecture. If not, you'll be ready to more fully explore the material. You can bring up any topics you find particularly interesting or would like more specific examples of. Be ready to record all responses and related comments.

- They can give you better insight into your instructor's approach to the material and what he or she considers important for you to learn. When in doubt about the test or the extent to which topics will be covered on the test, use your instructor's notes as a springboard to ask the best way to prepare for the exam.

 ## PREPARING TO TAKE EFFECTIVE NOTES

You can do many things to ensure that you leave class with a great set of notes. When you prepare for the task of effectively documenting the goings-on in class, you advance your chances for a successful learning experience for the day and in future study sessions.

GET SET MENTALLY

To make note taking easier and more productive, you can do several things before class even starts. Of greatest importance is preparing mentally for the information. When you know the topics that will be addressed, you lay the groundwork for greater understanding and clearer communication of ideas. Begin by looking at your syllabus. Most instructors indicate which chapters and topics will be covered each day in class. Another beneficial activity is to review your notes from the previous lecture. This helps solidify your learning and trigger your memory of the material for the exam, and it provides a good lead-in for the lecture to come.

Each unit is likely to refer to terms, people, processes, events, problem-solving methods, and theories. It's easy to forget important details, even after a couple of days, when the material from other courses interferes. When you refresh your memory shortly before class, the content from the previous class comes rushing back and you're ready to dive right in.

Another great way to get the most out of class is to read the related text chapter ahead of time. Some professors require this and expect students to come prepared to ask questions and discuss the material they read beforehand. When you read about the topic before the lecture, you prime your mind to smoothly incorporate the lecture material. Being familiar with the material enables you to take more effective notes. You can do more critical thinking because you already know the basics of the material. You can incorporate this additional insight into your notes to help convey the big picture. If the lecture material is new but related to the reading material, you will have the foundation for understanding and interpreting it more fully. Some students prefer to read the chapter after hearing a lecture, and this strategy is also valid. But if you have not yet established a preference, try reading prior to class to see how much more you can gain.

BE READY IN CLASS

The classroom is where it all happens. Set yourself up for the experience. Everything—from your choice of seat to the materials you use—can influence the quality of your notes. Go prepared to tackle the note-taking task.

TAKE A (GOOD) SEAT, PLEASE

Note taking and listening are inseparable class partners, so it should be no surprise that where you sit in class can make a difference in the effectiveness of your notes. As you know, sitting as close to the front and the center of the classroom as possible provides the best opportunity to listen and watch what is going on in class. The more clearly you can see and hear, the better your opportunity to take good notes. Don't strain your ears or sit there wondering if you heard something correctly. Sit closer if possible, and ask questions if necessary.

BRING THE RIGHT MATERIALS

Good organization plays a role in successful note taking. Notes are critical to future comprehension, so it is imperative that you use the right tools to create notes. A three-ring binder is the best way to organize notes because you can use loose-leaf, hole-punched notebook paper and place the sheets in any order necessary. If during the course of taking notes you need to add an additional sheet, you can do so easily, wherever the information fits. Also, if the lecture takes a particular turn and your instructor inserts something he forgot to mention earlier, you can place your note sheets in the appropriate order in your notebook (despite the mixed-up lecture order). Also, you may receive supplemental handouts that accompany the lecture. A three-ring binder allows you to insert these additional sources where applicable. If you don't wish to carry around a large number of notes from previous units, you can remove them from the binder, file them away, and bring only your current course notes to class. Consider a small binder for each course or a large one with dividers to separate class material. Also, hole-punch each syllabus and place it at the beginning of the class section for easy reference.

Pens are preferable to pencils for the fast-paced note taking of college courses. Pencils can break, the writing can be difficult to read, and you don't want to be tempted to erase while taking notes. Erasing takes too much time and can cause you to fall behind while following a stream of ideas. It also can tear your paper and create messy, hard-to-read pages. Writing in ink allows you to simply cross out mistakes quickly and move on. Just remember to bring a few with you so you don't run out of ink. The same goes for paper. Keep plenty of extra paper so you can feel free to space out your notes and use as many sheets as necessary.

THE PROS AND CONS OF LAPTOP COMPUTERS

Laptop (and notebook) computers are becoming more popular as note-taking tools on college campuses. Technology does not necessarily bring benefits in this case, as you can see from the following list of pros and cons of taking notes on a laptop:

Pros

- Laptops produce clear, legible notes that are easy to read.
- Some students can type faster than they can write, so a laptop reduces the chance of omitting important information.
- Students can print out multiple copies of notes for free.
- Laptops can store extensive notes and enable students to compile notes from different courses (prerequisites and corequisites) for easy comparison.
- Laptops provide a stable, portable source for storage and retrieval.

Cons

- Laptops limit note taking to words only. There are few options for personalized symbols or graphics such as mind maps. (Graphics programs are too cumbersome for note taking.)

- Word processing programs capture information in a linear fashion. The options for inserting side notes are either time-consuming (for example, using the Comments function) or confusing and disjointed (for example, indenting text or inserting notes between parentheses or dashes).

- Laptops hinder the use of rapidly drawn symbols, so the note taker must describe ideas, concepts, and relationships more fully, which makes note taking more time-consuming.

- Laptops don't allow for easy recording of charts, graphs, tables, or illustrations during class time. Additional note sheets are required for those.

- Students may spend more time looking at the computer screen than making eye contact and watching the instructor, thus losing many important elements of the classroom experience.

- Instructors may consider laptops distracting and even rude. Intense typing—even to document the lecture—makes students appear tuned out.

- The key clicking that occurs during typing can be distracting to other students and the instructor.

- There is greater potential for losing valuable data. If the batteries are not properly charged, the user loses power (and possibly data) and the computer becomes inoperable. The same consequences result from a hard drive crash.

- Laptops can be cumbersome to carry around and set up. Students must get to class early enough to find an outlet (assuming the user is plugging an AC adapter into an external power source, which requires being close to the outlet) to power up, open the file, and so on. It also takes more effort with a laptop to call up notes for a quick review.

- Laptops can be stolen from backpacks left unattended and may suffer damage from being jostled around regularly or getting wet in the rain.

GETTING STARTED

Several tasks can make note taking more effective for learning. Good notes are a study tool. They do not just replicate what you hear. Rather, they are a compilation of critical information.

CREATE A HEADING

With organization as key, begin by dating and labeling your notes. The date tells you where the information falls in relation to all of the other information presented in a unit. When you prepare for your exam, you will be relieved to see the date of the lecture clearly displayed in your notes. The date helps you locate information and keep things in order.

Next, title your notes for each class period. If the syllabus doesn't provide a title and your instructor doesn't give one at the beginning of class, make one up. The title reflects the basic subject matter contained in your notes. You may have a few titles throughout a single day's notes. If your notes have large, clearly marked titles, you can quickly and easily find notes from a specific lecture or topic.

PREPARE TO BE BRIEF

Although your notes should be complete (containing all of the critical information required for the exam) and thorough (including all of the information relevant to the topic that enables you to gain a full understanding of the topic and its application), your actual notation must be brief. You should not expect or attempt to write down every word spoken during a lecture. Most professors quickly present a lot of material. Even if you could keep up for a while, your ability to transcribe the lecture word-for-word would not last.

You must develop your own style of rapid, effective note taking, primarily through the use of paraphrasing, abbreviations, and symbols. Sometimes just writing faster than normal is necessary, but be careful. You must be able to read what you've written. If increasing the speed at which you write results in illegible chicken scratch, you'll have to do something else.

Even if you can write quickly and neatly, using shortcuts in your notes frees you to listen more closely and record the important information more efficiently. It is rarely necessary to write complete sentences that include every article, verb, and object. Using telegraphic speech (writing only the key words—just enough to get the meaning across—as in telegrams) and paraphrasing (putting ideas into your own brief wording) reduce the amount of writing you must do, as well as the time it takes to record the information. Here is a brief excerpt from a lecture, followed by notes using telegraphic speech and paraphrasing.

> *The economic growth of the 1920s rested on consumer spending. Advertisers developed new and effective ways to persuade Americans to acquire the products coming out of the nation's factories and workshops. The advertising business boomed. Radios brought advertising into the home, billboards attracted the attention of millions of motorists. Advertising, said one of its practitioners, "literally creates demand for the things of life that raise the standard of living, elevate the taste, changing luxuries into necessities."*[1]

Telegraphic notes

Economic growth—1920s—consumer spending. New advertising methods—prompt purchases—American products. Exposure—radios (home)—billboards (driving). Advertising—increase demand—raise living standards—elevate taste—luxuries become necessities.

Paraphrasing

U.S. economic growth turned to consumers in the 20s, and the advertising industry grew. More widespread ads via radio and billboards exposed people to American products and prompted purchasing on a greater scale. Advertising itself would change consumer behaviors—creating the perception of what would be a necessity instead of a luxury, and promoting a higher standard of living, thus increasing consumer spending.

When you take notes, you don't need to write individual words in full, either. Figure 8.1 presents a list of the most common abbreviations in note taking and Figure 8.2 shows some suggested symbols. You can use your own abbreviations and create your own personal symbols. Just be sure you make yourself a key to remind you later what each item means.

BE SURE OF YOUR VOCABULARY

Sometimes you *do* need to write sentences completely and word for word—namely, when defining new terms. When your instructor introduces vocabulary words, be as accurate as possible when writing them down in your notes. Instructors may

---

[1] Adapted from Edward L. Ayers, Lewis L. Gould, David M. Oshinsky, and Jean R. Sodurlund, *American Passages: A History of the United States,* brief edition, p. 565. (Belmont, CA: Wadsworth, 2003).

b/c—because	re—regarding	pt—point	ft—foot
ex—example	subj—subject	co—company	in—inch
imp.—important	ch—chapter	max—maximum	mi—mile
w/—with	ea—each	min—minimum	c—centimeter
w/o—without	def—definition	lg—large	m—meter
i.e.—that is, that is to say	cont'd—continued	sm—small	km—kilometer
e.g.—for example	pos—positive (+)	amt—amount	g—gram
p—page	neg—negative (−)	lb—pound	yr—year
pp—pages	imp't—important	oz—ounce	mo—month
sol—solution	pol—political	soc—societal	vs—against
thru—through	sum—summary	concl—conclusion	gen—general
sig—significant	prim—primary	2ary—secondary	orig—original
info—information	no.—number	beh—behavior	incl—includes

Figure 8.1
Common Abbreviations
for Use in Note Taking

+	positive, plus, more	∞	infinity, infinite
−	negative, minus, less	∟	right angle
=	equals	↑	increasing, rising, higher
≠	does not equal	↓	decreasing, declining, lower
>	greater than	→	leads to, results in, causes
<	less than	←	results from, refers to, is affected by
~	approximately	"	repeating the same information
#	number, pounds	¶	paragraph
&	and	♀	female
@	at	♂	male
%	percent	*	important

Figure 8.2
Common Symbols for Use
in Note Taking

highlight terms and even tell you that you need to know them. They may then offer their own definitions or direct you to the definitions in the text. As with any other information presented one way in your book and another way by your instructor, you would be wise to focus more closely on the one expressed by your instructor.

You may hear an unfamiliar term used in the lecture. Underline or highlight the term so you can go back and fill in the definition later. Some instructors use sophisticated vocabulary, and it is important that you don't let new words slow you down while taking notes. Make it a point to look up the words later so you can grasp the full meaning of the lecture. Consider leaving a blank space by these words to complete your notes after class.

TAKE NOTES ON EVERYTHING

Instructors present information in a variety of ways during class time. They may invite guest speakers to share their knowledge and personal perspectives with the class. They may show a video, a television program, a documentary, or a movie. Some classes may involve role-play or live demonstrations. Unless your instructor tells you otherwise, you should take notes just as thoroughly during these events as you would during a lecture. Just because an instructor introduces a different mode of covering the material doesn't mean you won't need to remember the information for the exam. In fact, the opposite is likely to be true. Unique classroom experiences often reflect the most important aspects of a topic, so it may be particularly critical to understand the content they explore. Don't think that simply because the presentation is not a long-winded lecture that you will remember it without taking notes. When you sit down to study several weeks later, the demonstration that seemed vivid and memorable in class may have faded with all of the input you received since then. You probably will have to adjust your note-taking format to the presentation, though.

DRAW IT

When your instructor presents graphical information—tables, charts, graphs, maps, or illustrations—try to duplicate it in your notes. Even if the instructor presents a reproduction of a visual from the course textbook, draw your own version anyway. If your instructor includes it in the lecture presentation, you can count on it conveying significant information that you need to remember. When you draw it yourself, you are more likely to learn and understand what is conveyed in the visual. The activity of drawing it causes you to notice the facts and figures in the labels, where they go, and how they relate to each other. You do not need any artistic ability. You just need a careful eye to capture the detailed information.

 DETERMINE YOUR PREFERRED FORMAT

There are many ways to take notes. Consider your approach thus far in school. Read the Skill Check and answer the questions to help you understand your current note-taking strategies.

SKILL CHECK: MY NOTE-TAKING SAVVY

Think about how you take notes, or look at the ones you have taken so far this semester. Are they neat, and can you read them? Do they make sense? Do they show a particular method or approach to recording the information? Can you distinguish the factual information from your own comments, thoughts, and questions? Are they organized? Can you follow an obvious thread of a topic, or do the notes seem to be a collection of randomly placed tidbits? Do your notes effectively help you remember the information presented in class? Are you able to make connections and understand a deeper level of meaning beyond the basic information noted? Do you think you could improve your note taking? Do you need to and want to?

BASIC NOTE FORMATS

You need to be comfortable with how you take notes. When you develop a rhythm for writing down critical information you hear, you are better able to listen and think about the material as it is presented. This, in turn, helps you produce more effective notes. A few standard note formats are recognized as the easiest and most effective means of recording information for future reference. The different methods tend to appeal to different types of people based on learning style and learning preferences. You can also create your own variation on the formats using the basic idea and adding your own elements that optimize how you write the information and how you use it later. You must practice these new techniques to learn them, and it may feel awkward at first. As you persist, though, the techniques will become second nature and you will notice an improvement in your ability to get what you need out of your time in class. Developing your skills requires a period of adjustment. In the end, you shouldn't feel like you are forcing yourself to take notes in a particular way.

OUTLINES

An outline is simply a hierarchical way of recording information. You begin with the main idea, then indent to write supporting ideas. For every additional subcategory of information, you indent a little more. Pieces of information and ideas that are on the same conceptual level, in other words, are part of the same subcategory, are indented to the same degree, and appear as a list. Figure 8.3 shows notes in an outline format. You may indicate the different levels or categories of information either with Roman numerals and letters or Arabic numerals and letters. If you are in a hurry or don't care to enumerate, you can simply use bullets and dashes to notate individual points.

Figure 8.3
Outline Format for Note Taking

October 20
American History
Prof. Joseph

Life in the United States: The Victorian Era

The Victorian era—late 19th century
- Public code of personal behavior
  Restraint
  Sexual modesty
  Temperate habits
  Hard work
- Characterized majority of white Americans

The rules of life
- Unmarried couples had to be chaperoned
  Kiss = engagement OR social disgrace
- No premarital sex
- Marriage for life
  Sex only for procreation

The moral code
- Focus on character: displaying virtues
- Expected to adhere to marriage vows
  Divorce rate <u>increased</u>
  Double standard: society looked the other way when men visited prostitutes or were unfaithful; women disgraced for same.
- Expectations for children
  Respect adults
  Discussion of sex—rare
  Entertainment found at home

Religion
- Permeated society
  145 Christian denominations
  Sunday = church, rest, quiet
- Morality challenged in several ways
  Science (e.g., Darwin) undermined beliefs
  Sigmund Freud's theories of repressed sex and aggression

This is a logical way to approach information, and some instructors clearly lecture according to an outline of the material. With spontaneous lecturers, though, what makes up the different levels (the categories and subcategories) of the outline may not be straightforward. You may find that some pieces follow a hierarchy but that other points seem to fit randomly. For the latter situations, you must indicate the relationships of information through explicit notes or arrows.

COGNITIVE MAPS

For visual learners, cognitive maps can be an appealing way to note information. Cognitive maps arrange individual ideas in shapes and link them through connected lines or pathways. They allow viewers to visualize conceptual relationships.

Cognitive maps are a good format for lectures that do not seem organized. However, the space constraints of notepaper may be a challenge. If your map grows too large and you must continue it on another page, it will be disjointed and you won't be able to see the full picture. Later, you can redraw the map on a larger sheet (or reduce the size of the shapes) and use it as a study tool. Label the shapes with the concepts they reflect, and make sure you clearly indicate evidence, examples, and side notes where appropriate. Figure 8.4 shows a cognitive map for the same topic as the outline in Figure 8.3.

Figure 8.4
Cognitive Map Format
for Note Taking

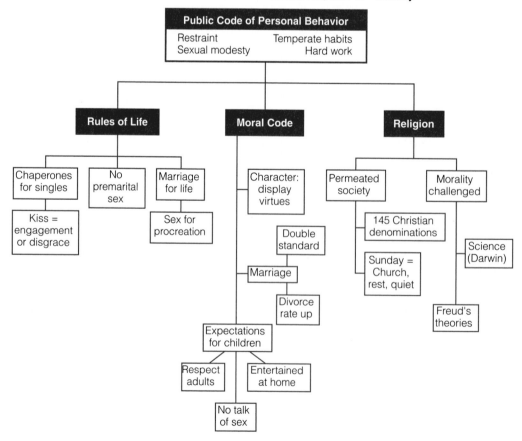

Life in the United States: The Victorian Era, Late 19th Century

THE CORNELL METHOD

The most popular and highly recommended note-taking method is the *Cornell method,* which provides both an effective format for recording information and a systematic means of learning from your notes. The Cornell method has five steps—*record, reduce, recite, reflect,* and *review.*

One key to this method is the layout of the note page itself. You leave a 2.5-inch margin of space on the left side of a letter-size page for a *cue column,* which allows six inches for notes. You also mark a two-inch margin at the bottom of the page for a summary, which you add after taking all pertinent notes. You mark only one side of the paper. After you have set up the pages, you are ready to begin. Here is a description of the five steps in the Cornell method.[2]

1. *Record.* The first step is to write the necessary information from the presentation—the key ideas and all critical supporting points including evidence, examples, tables, charts, and graphs. Use methods that help streamline note taking, such as paraphrasing and the use of abbreviations and symbols, as long as they make sense and convey complete ideas.

2. *Reduce.* After you have documented the important information, it is time to reduce it. This should occur soon after you take the initial notes so the ideas are fresh in your mind. Using the cue column—the 2.5-inch space on the left of the page—write basic recall cues to help you remember the content of the notes. These cues can take the form of single-word headings, brief summary statements, or even questions that the notes on the page answer. Write the cues in the cue column but next to the related information. Figure 8.5 illustrates a page of notes taken using the Cornell method.

3. *Recite.* Once you have reduced your notes to the set of cues in the left column, you can test yourself and recite the answers. With another sheet of paper, cover the notes on the right, leaving the cue column exposed. Progress down the column and for each keyword, phrase, or question, provide an explanation, description, or answer that demonstrates your understanding of the material contained in your notes. Talk through the material out loud and as completely as possible. The goal is to present the material in your own words, from memory, as if you are explaining the concepts to someone else. When you approach the topic with purpose and focus, you engage in a highly effective learning process. The more you recite using the cue column, the more prepared you will be for the exam.

4. *Reflect.* The fourth stage involves reflecting on the topic by using the information recorded in your notes. The purpose is to consider the context, the greater meaning, connections, and applications of the material. An effective means of reflecting is to write a summary of the information you recorded. Use the two-inch space across the bottom of each page to present your own synopsis. Instead of simply restating what you already wrote, think critically about the topic before summarizing it.

5. *Review.* The final stage of the process is to review everything you wrote. If you have not done so already, this is the point at which you should gather all of your notes from the unit or chapter, and collectively recite, reflect on, and consider them as a whole. When you place your note pages side by side with only the cue columns exposed, you gain a simplified but effective overview of the material. You can test yourself on the information in its entirety, in order

[2] Linda Wong, *Essential Study Skills,* 4th ed. (Boston: Houghton Mifflin, 2003).

Figure 8.5
The Cornell Method
Format of Note Taking

When was Victorian era?	October 20 American History Prof. Joseph
Personal behavior should demonstrate	**Life in the United States: The Victorian Era**
1.	Victorian era—late 19th century
2.	Public code of personal behavior included 1) restraint, 2) sexual modesty, 3) temperate habits, 4) hard work.
3.	
4.	* Lifestyle of most white Americans.
	The rules of life
Characteristics of relationships	Chaperones required for unmarried couples
—before marriage?	Kissing either led to engagement or resulted in disgrace!
—after marriage?	Premarital sex was taboo.
	Couples married for life, with marital sex being only for the purpose of procreation (possibly due to lack of birth control and the desire to reduce unwanted pregnancies).
	The moral code
What is character? Evidence for not holding true to societal expectations of marriage.	Focus on character—displaying virtuous behavior.
	People expected to adhere to marriage vows, but . . .
	The divorce rate was seen to increase.
	A double standard existed for men and women. Men who were unfaithful (with prostitutes or otherwise)—society looked the other way; women who were unfaithful were disgraced.
	Strict views on raising children:
Child rearing was strict.	Children were expected to respect adults; little or no talk of sex occurred; and entertainment took place at home.
	Religion
Religious climate, increasingly threatened by new ideas.	Permeated society as 145 Christian denominations existed, with more than 22 million members.
	Sundays were for 1) church, 2) rest, 3) quiet.
	Morality was challenged by scientific progress, along with views of Darwin and Freud.
	Summary: The late 19th century, also known as the Victorian era, was characterized by strict societal and religious expectations of personal conduct. Evidence shows that the moral code wasn't upheld as stringently as was purported, and a double standard applied to men's and women's behavior. Changes in society eventually threatened to undermine the morality of the time, with Darwin's theory of evolution and Freudian views on sex.

of presentation, by following the prompts you wrote in the cue column. You may then rewrite the cues in an outline format. Review often for early and long-lasting learning.

The Cornell method is the only formal note-taking technique that specifies an approach to reviewing your notes. However, no matter how you take notes, they should always be effective for future studying.

ADAPT YOUR FORMAT WHEN NECESSARY

Once you have found a note-taking style that is comfortable and successful for you, use it wherever and whenever possible. In some circumstances, however, you may need to alter your primary format for taking notes in order to record class information more effectively.

DIFFERENT COURSE TOPICS

Subject matter sometimes calls for a particular teaching method. When the presentation format makes it difficult for you to apply your usual approach to taking notes, find a successful method of recording the critical information.

MATH, SCIENCE, AND COMPUTER COURSES

The content of math and some science courses involves primarily numbers, symbols, formulas, and equations. The presentation may follow step-by-step processes using numerical elements, and your notes will reflect the processes. It is important to record the steps in precise detail, in the sequence they occur, and to write all numerals, letters, and symbols very clearly. It is also essential to keep pace with the presentation of the material to ensure that each piece of information is in the right place and fully designated.

When noting the ordered steps of an equation, you may need to make additional comments to describe the purpose and significance of each step along with explanations for applying theorems or formulas. The Cornell method is effective in these courses, because the cue column is ideal for explanations associated with each equation noted. Flow-style cognitive maps also are effective at documenting the progress of a process.

If you find yourself getting behind and missing a step or two, leave space to fill in later. To find the missing step, ask to see a classmate's notes, talk with your instructor, or look for an example in the text. This is also a good way to cross-check the accuracy of your notes. The instructor may walk you through a problem that you will solve again as part of a homework assignment. The textbook is likely to demonstrate the same processes and apply the same formulas that the instructor used, but this is not a certainty. Some instructors prefer that you use a different problem-solving method than the one shown in your text. Make sure you learn the instructor's way and use it on your exam.

LAB SECTIONS

Even in practical lab classes you need to be prepared to take notes. Although you may be busy conducting experiments, you still need to take notes—to define new terms, document procedures and observations, and explain experiment results. You may need to study your lab notes for an exam in the corequisite science course.

POETRY AND LITERATURE

When you study written works in depth, the notes you take are likely to refer to specific lines of the text. If the source of the work is your textbook, consider making a copy of the relevant pages to write on and add to your set of notes. Number the lines, the paragraphs, or the sections of the work for easy reference in your notes. Whatever system you use for referring to the piece of literature, make sure you take complete notes on the meanings and issues related to the work and minimize rewriting lines of the source work.

DISCUSSIONS AND SEMINAR COURSES

As you know, the content of class discussions should be included in your notes. Some upper division courses—*seminar courses*—are almost entirely discussion driven. When you take notes for a discussion, identify several things in your notes. Begin by stating the subject matter and any specific question presented for discussion. For example, if your instructor asks the class to consider the question, "Are journalists protected by the First Amendment to withhold evidence in a criminal trial, due to a confidentiality agreement with their sources?" you would begin by writing this as a major heading. Then write concisely the comments made by everyone in the class. (Don't forget to write your own thoughts and comments, too.) When your instructor makes a comment or poses additional questions based on an individual's input, highlight and specify the contribution.

The Cornell method is also useful with a discussion format because you can record the comments sequentially and add input (from your instructor, particularly) in the cue column later. Your instructor is also likely to wrap up the discussion with some summary comments, which will be critical to your understanding of the important points from the discussion.

DIFFERENT LECTURE DEMANDS

As you know, instructors can differ in numerous ways. Idiosyncrasies in the manner of presenting information can call for an adjustment in how you take notes in each class.

THE DULL LECTURE

When you are in a course that challenges you to stay awake, use note taking to help get you through it. Lectures can be dull if the information is presented in a slow, static way. The instructor may state the information in such a basic way that it takes little effort to record it on paper. Use the slow pace of the class to your advantage.

- Have your textbook open to the corresponding topic, if possible, and jot down some additional notes to enhance the information presented in the lecture.

- Refer back to your previous notes and begin noting the connections between concepts and ideas. Write specific links throughout the lecture material.

- Think of questions to ask in class or ways to start a class discussion. Your instructor may appreciate the opportunity for some spontaneity.

- Begin anticipating test questions. What is your instructor likely to ask on each topic? Make a list in the margin next to the lecture notes so you can quiz yourself later.

Don't be too lackadaisical during boring lectures. In fact, it sometimes requires extra effort to maintain your focus and not tune out. Consider dull classes a chance to improve your note-taking skills while essentially preparing for the exam each day in class.

THE RUSHED LECTURE

Some instructors always seem rushed, no matter how much material they cover each day. These are the classes that cramp your hands and leave your head spinning with the barrage of information. When faced with this kind of lecture regularly, prepare to tackle it.

- Read the text ahead of time. When you know what is coming, you will not feel as overwhelmed. You also will be ready to document the lecture because you will be familiar with the terms and concepts already.

- Leave lots of space in your notes. If you can't record the entire idea before your instructor moves on to the next idea, simply leave space and begin writing about the new concept. You can either ask the instructor later to fill you in on what you missed, look it up in the textbook, or compare notes with a classmate.

- Ask a classmate or two to routinely cross-check notes with you. If you feel rushed and overwhelmed, you probably aren't the only one. Make a habit of getting together with a few classmates after class to compare notes. This way you can help each other fill in the blank spaces in your notes.

Don't hesitate to ask your instructors to slow down or repeat themselves. Some don't realize how fast they are speaking and that it is difficult for listeners to follow. If they receive enough feedback from students, they may make an effort to slow the pace.

THE INTELLECTUAL LECTURE

Some instructors approach teaching from a high-level standpoint, neglecting (or choosing not) to adapt their manner to accommodate beginners. This can be quite challenging, particularly when the instructor uses sophisticated terminology, but you can do some things to be more comfortable in class.

- Read the text material before going to class. Although the instructor may present the material in a highly intellectual manner, the textbook is likely to take a more introductory tone. When you first encounter the material in a more simplified way, it prepares you to understand it in a different context.

- Be ready to ask appropriate questions. Your instructor certainly owes you explanations when you have difficulty with the concepts, but it is important that you demonstrate an initial effort to understand the basics. Try to resist raising your hand to say, "I'm totally lost" or "I just don't get it." It is difficult for an instructor to address such broad complaints in class, so they probably won't. Instead, be specific in what you ask about. For example, you might say, "I understand the origins and functions of the id, ego, and superego, but I am having trouble making sense as to how they interact. Could you provide another example, please?" This provides some solid ground upon which the instructor can formulate a useful explanation.

- You may have to forgo paraphrasing and do more word-for-word translation of ideas. It is more time-consuming and provides less of an opportunity to think about the material at the time, but it can help you get the right information down to begin with. If you write down the concepts as your instructor presents them, you can review them later and reflect on what was said. Then use your book and ask questions to help you make sense of the difficult concepts.

- Create a study group. Many heads are better than one when trying to decipher and interpret a highly intellectual instructor. When you work together with others who have heard the same things in class, you begin to understand the material from the student perspective.

THE SCATTERED LECTURE

For every organized instructor, there's a scatterbrain to match. Although they may be highly knowledgeable and accomplished in their fields, these instructors have a difficult time maintaining a step-by-step, easy-to-follow presentation of material— maybe because they are so well versed in their subject that they can't help but jump around when discussing certain topics. Such lecturers can be very interesting and even enjoyable to listen to, but they create chaos for note taking.

- Write what your instructor writes on the board (or presents with slides or an overhead). If it's important enough for the instructor to have written it down, then you should write it down. The information may serve as a sort of anchor for the direction of the lecture.

- Listen for certain phrases that can help you determine where your instructor is (or is going) contextually—for example, "That reminds me of . . . ," "Another way to look at this is . . . ," "In the case of . . . ," "Going back to . . . ," "Where are we?"

- Compare notes with someone else immediately after class. Don't wait to review the presentation if you want to make sense of it. Make it a habit to briefly compare notes to see that you were on the same track as soon as class ends. Spending just five or ten minutes will be worthwhile.

If you ever feel completely out of control with regard to note taking, meet with your instructor. Part of the instructor's job is to help students learn the material. Take advantage of office hours. Always bring your notes to show what you have been doing in class. Your instructor may offer some significant input to help you develop your skills specifically for his or her style of lecture.

A WORD ABOUT TAPE RECORDERS

Taping a lecture has benefits and drawbacks. First of all, not all instructors allow students to tape lectures, so if you are considering this you must get permission. Before you decide if this is right for you, think about the following issues.

THE BENEFITS OF TAPING A LECTURE

When you tape a lecture, you free yourself to listen more actively, because you won't be worried trying to write down everything you hear. Knowing you have a second chance to listen to the lecture, you are able to think through the information more completely as it is presented. You are more relaxed while you listen and you can participate more fully in the experience of being taught. Class may be more enjoyable to you and the instructor may enjoy noticing that students are really listening and thinking about what is being said.

When you listen to the tape-recorded lecture, you undoubtedly gain more from it. When you hear it for the second time, you have a significant background gained from the first time. You can then build on the connections and conclusions you have already made and develop a more complete picture of the material. You can fill in your notes and amend those that you took in class with additional observations and thoughts stimulated by hearing the lecture again.

There are many circumstances in which you might consider taping a lecture. For example, taping a lecture may help you deal with a particularly challenging speaker. If you are not yet confident in your note-taking skills, you may want to tape-record lectures so you have additional time to write, as well as a predetermined sense of organization before you finalize what you put on paper. Taping a lecture is also helpful if you know ahead of time that you have to miss class. Ask a classmate to tape the lecture for you, and provide a tape recorder and tape for the task. Also ask for a copy of the person's notes. If he or she is an active listener, the notes will reflect the intricacies of the presentation your tape recorder didn't pick up.

THINK TWICE ABOUT TAPING

In some cases, taping a lecture is a great idea, however, the practice has the potential to do more harm than good. Taping a lecture should not be considered a substitute for listening in class. Some students use this tactic to give themselves a break from the rigors of paying attention and taking notes. (They may even take the opportunity to do work for another class or daydream.) There is no replacement for listening to a lecture firsthand—not even hearing a recording of the lecture. Tape recorders can't capture gestures, facial expressions, or subtleties in your instructor's tone of voice. Obviously, they can't let you see what was written on the board, and they may not capture all sounds in the room, such as critical questions and discussion input from classmates. Lecture material is most valuable when you listen to it and think about it firsthand.

Taping a lecture for whatever reason requires that you actually listen to the tape. Many students set out with good intentions but never get around to playing the tape. If they tuned out during class, they lose a significant amount of valuable information. Their notes will suffer, their studying will suffer, their understanding will suffer, and their grade will suffer. Tape a lecture only if you schedule a specific time to go back and listen to it.

Lecture tapes also shouldn't replace effective note taking. The more you hear, write, work with, and think about information, the better you will remember it. Just listening in class and again in the car on your way home or while relaxing on your bed is inadequate. Translating the ideas presented in the lecture into words; organizing them as you write; adding comments and additional thoughts, ideas, and examples all bring about a more thorough learning of the information.

CHAPTER 8 REVIEW QUESTIONS

1. Why is it important to develop good note-taking skills? Discuss several reasons.

2. Why do you need to take notes on material that you can find in your textbook?

3. What are the dangers of relying on other people's notes—even your instructors'?

4. What are the pros and cons of using a laptop computer to take notes?

5. What are the three basic note-taking formats?

6. What are some strategies you can apply to adapt to a dull class? A fast-paced instructor? A highly intellectual lecturer? A disorganized instructor?

7. What things should you consider when deciding whether to tape a lecture?

SKILL PRACTICE

1. The following are excerpts from lectures. Create a set of notes for each using an outline format, a cognitive map format, and the Cornell method format.

2. Which format appeals to you the most? Why? Does your preference depend on the subject matter?

The Life Cycle of Plants[3]

Of the approximately 295,000 known species of plants, 35,000 of those are seed-bearing, vascular plants—such as pine trees—called gymnosperms, and the other 260,000 are the flower producing plants, called angiosperms. These include such species as roses, corn, cactuses, and elm trees. Clearly angiosperms dominate the plant kingdom, so we will focus on them for the remainder of the lecture.

The life cycle of an angiosperm progresses through germination, seed formation, then death. Not all plants go through their life cycle at the same rate. Annuals complete the life cycle in a single growing season. These tend to be plants such as marigolds and alfalfa, which are herbaceous rather than woody. If you want marigolds in your garden, for example, you'll have to reseed or buy new ones each year, because once they die their life cycle is over and they will not grow again. Biennials are plants that live through two consecutive growing seasons. A carrot is an example of a biennial. Plant them once and you'll have them for two years. During the first season, their roots, stems, and leaves form. During the second season they flower, seed, and die. Many gardeners prefer perennials—plants that continue to grow and develop seeds year after year. Once you plant perennials, you can enjoy them for a long time.

Basic Accounting Systems[4]

Today we are going to talk about developing an accounting system, which consists of the methods and procedures for collecting, classifying, summarizing, and reporting a business's financial and operating information. Accounting systems can be simple for smaller businesses but more complex for larger businesses. The larger the business, the greater the number and variety of transactions that must be collected, accumulated, and reported. A major airline is an example of a very large company that has a complex accounting system. The airline must collect and maintain information on ticket reservations, credit card collections, aircraft maintenance, employee hours, frequent-flier mileage balances, fuel consumption, and travel agent commissions, just to name a few. The company's accounting system must be able to handle all of this information accurately.

Developing an effective accounting system requires a three-step process that evolves as the business grows and changes. Analysis is the first step, and it involves identifying the needs of those who use the company's financial information, as well as determining how the system should provide that information. The second step requires designing the system so it meets the user's needs. The last step occurs when the system is implemented and used. Managers must determine whether the company will use manual or computerized processing methods to collect, summarize, and report the accounting information. There are many options to choose from. To create an effective accounting

---

[3] Starr, Cecie, *Biology: Concepts and Applications,* 5th ed. Copyright © 2003 Wadsworth Group, Belmont, CA.

[4] Warren, Carl S., Reeve, James M., & Fess, Philip E., *Accounting,* 20th ed. Copyright © 2002 South-Western, a division of Thomson Learning, Mason, Ohio.

system, the design team should obtain feedback, or input, from those who will use the system. This way, the effectiveness of the system can be analyzed and improved upon if necessary.

The company should have a set of policies and procedures to protect its assets from misuse, to ensure that the business information is accurate, and to make sure it follows applicable laws and regulations. These policies and proce-dures are called internal controls.

The Watergate Scandal[5]

It was just a little past 1:00 in the morning when a security guard at the Watergate office building in Washington, D.C., noticed something strange. A piece of masking tape had been placed on a door to prevent it from locking when shut. The guard removed the piece of tape and continued his rounds, only to come back a little while later to find another piece of tape had been placed in the same spot. He called the police to report what he thought was probably a burglary in progress. It took a while for people to realize just how serious the events were that had taken place.

Five men were arrested inside the headquarters of the Democratic National Committee, located in that Watergate office building. One of the men was James W. McCord, Jr., the director of security for the Committee for the Reelec-tion of the President (a committee referred to as CREEP). Another member of CREEP, G. Gordon Liddy, was also arrested. Liddy and E. Howard Hunt, Jr., were both former White House aides. In addition, some of the "burglars" worked for the Central Intelligence Agency (CIA).

The police soon discovered that the break-in had been ordered by high-ranking officials of the administration and of President Nixon's election cam-paign. It was funded by contributions to the campaign. Two young reporters from the Washington Post *pursued the story and discovered that the five men arrested had bugged the Democratic National Committee headquarters and intercepted telephone conversations of Democratic Party officials, listening in from a motel room across the street.*

As the elements of the story continued to break, Nixon's advisors tried to cover the links between the burglary and the president's campaign. Apparently, they did a good job, because Nixon was resoundingly reelected that November. However, the following January, five defendants in the case pleaded guilty, and two others who took the stand in court were convicted by a federal jury. In March, McCord suggested that White House and other government officials had advance knowledge of the Watergate bugging. Nixon denied prior knowledge of the bugging and the cover-up by his staff that followed. Two of his principal aides, H. R. Halderman and John Ehrlichman, resigned. Nixon's attorney gen-eral, Richard Kleindienst, also resigned.

Eventually a special prosecutor was appointed and the investigation revealed much damaging evidence. As early as 1970, Nixon had approved a plan for burglary and electronic surveillance of people suspected of endangering national security. Of course, he had been warned—very officially in writing— that burglary was "clearly illegal." Nixon himself, it was discovered, had ordered the secret wiretapping of 17 people, including some of his own assis-tants and several journalists. Nixon's personal attorney raised about $220,000 to secretly pay the burglars and their attorneys. The director of the Federal Bureau of Investigation (FBI) destroyed vital Watergate evidence, and the U.S.

---

[5] Cummings, Milton C., & Wise, David, *Democracy Under Pressure: An Introduction to the American Political System*, 9th ed. Copyright © 2003 Wadsworth, a division of Thomson Learning, Belmont, CA.

attorney general, John Mitchell, witnessed a discussion proposing to bug the Democratic Party's headquarters as well as a plan to kidnap American citizens and take them to Mexico.

CURRENT COURSE APPLICATION

1. Review some of the notes you have taken in one or more of your classes recently. Check each item that applies.

    The notes include the following information:

    _____ Date   _____ Course name

    _____ Title of lecture or subject heading   _____ Instructor's name

    _____ The notes are clearly legible.

    _____ They are written in ink.

    _____ They are in a notebook with other notes from the same course.

    _____ They are in chronological order.

    The notes use the following note-taking format:

    _____ Outline   _____ Cognitive map

    _____ Cornell method   _____ Other (explain)

    _____ They include abbreviations and symbols.

    _____ They highlight all new terminology and unfamiliar vocabulary words.

    _____ Sequential information is clearly numbered.

    _____ They include space for additional information to be added later if necessary.

    By completing this checklist, what have you discovered about your current approach to taking notes?

2. In what class do you have the easiest time taking notes? Why do you think this is?

3. In what class do you have the hardest time taking notes? Why do you think this is? What specific things can you do to help make it easier to produce good notes?

4. How do your notes differ from one class to another? How do these differences reflect the different subject matter, lecture formats, and level of interest for the classes?

5. Meet with several classmates from one course to compare notes. What strengths do your notes possess, and what ideas can you gain from others' notes?

6. Make an appointment with the instructor in one of your classes (perhaps your most challenging course or the one in which note taking is most difficult). Bring a set of recent notes to your meeting and ask the instructor to personally assess the effectiveness of your notes. Does the instructor think your notes provide a good study tool? What advice can the instructor give you for improvement?

7. Try tape-recording a lecture. Be sure to get permission from your instructor first. Schedule a specific date to listen to your tape. After class, write about how it changed your experience in class.

    • How did you approach the class differently, knowing you would have the lecture on tape to listen to later?

    • What did you notice about your level of listening and concentration?

    • How did taping the lecture change the way you took notes?

    • How do you think you benefited from this experience?

- Did it make your time in class more difficult in any way? Explain.

After listening to the tape of the lecture:

- Do you feel more knowledgeable?
- Did you find it easier to comprehend the lecture the second time you heard it?
- Did you notice an increase in active listening or a decrease in mental processing, due to having heard it already?

TAKE A LOOK ONLINE

The following websites offer additional tips and ideas for effective note taking:

www.usu.edu/arc/idea_sheets/index.htm (Under Study skills, choose Effective note-taking strategies or Note taking: Cornell method.)

http://muskingum.edu/~cal/database/notetaking.html

STUDENT SCENARIO DISCUSSION RESPONSES

- **What were Shreta's strengths as a student?** Shreta was a studious, conscientious student who understood the importance of attending class regularly, taking notes, and putting in the time and effort to study for exams.

- **Why didn't those qualities help her in this instance?** Shreta's strengths did not help in this case because she didn't realize the difference between high school and college lectures. She was confident that simply recording what the instructor said would be sufficient to learn and understand the material, but she discovered this was not the case. Because she believed that she could easily write down the spoken words without really tuning in to what the instructor was saying at the time, her notes did not make as much sense as she thought.

- **What was Shreta's fundamental mistake, and why do you think she felt comfortable with this choice?** Shreta's fundamental mistake was underestimating the significance of listening well and thinking critically about the content while the instructor was speaking. Assuming that her ability to take notes was sufficient, she mistakenly believed she could approach class passively and save the mental work for later. This approach had always worked for her in the past. She did not believe what she was doing was lazy or careless. She had confidence in her note taking based on its past effectiveness and simply continued to do what had always worked.

- **How might Shreta have discovered her error prior to the exam?** Spending time talking about the course with a classmate or two might have clued her in that her passive approach may not work to gain the understanding she needed to do well. She might have brought her notes to show the instructor to get some feedback. During a brief discussion, the instructor might have asked Shreta some questions to find out how well she understood the concepts. She probably would have learned that she needed to do more active listening and questioning during class.

- **What could she have done if she had realized her mistake once she started studying for the test?** Upon discovering that her notes were difficult to comprehend, Shreta could have called a classmate to study together. Working with someone who had taken a more active approach would likely have helped her piece her notes together to see the big picture. She also could have made an appointment to talk with her instructor—bringing her notes in and explaining that she's concerned that she's missing something. Her instructor might have taken time to help her pull the concepts together, or at least guide her as to how to make sense of her lecture notes in combination with the textbook.

- **What should she do, now that she understands what the exams involve?** Shreta needs to listen actively and mentally process what she hears during class. In addition to getting the critical information down, Shreta needs to incorporate in her notes some questions, connections, and thoughts regarding the material, and she needs to paraphrase the material rather than trying to write it down verbatim. She should follow up with a classmate or the instructor to see that she is on the right track. And, of course, having a regular study partner is beneficial.

READ PROFICIENTLY

9

In this chapter you will learn

○ The challenges presented by college reading

○ Common reading mistakes and how to avoid them

○ Specific techniques to help you read effectively

○ Strategies for reading professional journal articles, imaginative literature, and poetry

 ## THE NEW CHALLENGES OF COLLEGE READING

College reading assignments may take some getting used to, in terms of the presentation style and the amount. When you develop your reading skills and understand how to approach reading in college, then confidence will replace the feeling of being overwhelmed.

MORE SOPHISTICATED MATERIALS

You have probably noticed a qualitative difference between high school and college reading assignments. The assignments may take much more effort and you may even feel somewhat drained after completing them. This is natural, because most college reading material calls for a higher level of intellectual effort.

A HIGHER STANDARD OF WRITING

Authors of college texts write for their audience. They consider students at your level to be adults with a maturity and intellectual ability deserving of reading materials to match. Although their goal is to introduce basic concepts related to the topic, these authors—professors or professionals in the field—use a rich, advanced vocabulary and a writing style befitting an educated and inquisitive audience. College students are sometimes uncomfortable with the level of writing in their texts until they have gained more experience in college.

EXPANDED CONTENT

High school texts present a limited amount of content on each topic. By contrast, subjects are addressed more thoroughly in college, so college textbooks are more detailed. Instead of presenting the most elementary facts, figures, events, people, and processes, most college texts include a variety of concepts, theories, interpretations, and philosophies—sometimes for a single topic. You will study scientific experiments and the research findings associated with them. You will frequently read about scientific methodology, information on sample populations, experimental techniques, and numerous interpretations of outcomes. Because college textbooks present more detailed, complex material, you will need to adapt to the new level of difficulty in your reading assignments.

ORIGINAL WORKS

You are likely to read more original works in college. In your high school literature class, for example, you may have read excerpts from well-known works, and the text may have explained both the excerpt and its context thoroughly. In college, however, you are likely to be reading the actual works in their entirety, and it is your responsibility to understand and interpret their meaning. You also are expected to read articles from professional journals—for example, presenting a scientist's own record of experiments. Most college textbooks do not break down the source material and explain it piece by piece. Knowing how to approach different reading formats is important for your success in college.

SHADES OF GRAY

The new intellectual expectations include considering issues that are not straightforward. Many college subjects involve areas of thinking that remain unresolved. In other words, experts in the field do not all agree on the ideal theory or approach to explaining some phenomena. You will be presented with a variety of beliefs, theories, interpretations, and applications for which there is no definite right or wrong answer. Your professor may share his or her view on the issue, but it is not required that you adopt it as your own. True learning comes from thinking through all of the different approaches and developing your own perspective. Be prepared not to find absolute answers in your reading.

MUCH MORE READING

One of the most eye-opening introductions to college is the amount of reading assigned. College courses cover much more material in a shorter period of time than high school classes—about twice as much. Therefore, the quantity of reading to cover topics at this rate basically doubles.

College textbook chapters tend to be longer and are more densely packed with information. It is not unusual to find chapters of 40–60 pages in a textbook. When you haven't made a dent in your assigned reading and you see what's ahead, you can feel overwhelmed. Also, many college classes, particularly upper division courses, require not just one but several books—for example, a textbook and supplemental books, or a variety of novels for a literature course. It can be difficult to accomplish all of the assigned reading in a limited amount of time. Keep in mind that you are expected to do all of the reading in addition to attending class and turning in course assignments.

COMMON READING MISTAKES AND HOW TO SOLVE THEM

Making the transition to college takes time. Many students make mistakes during this time that can hinder their success in class. Here are some common mistakes that students make with regard to reading. You can avoid all of them if you are aware and know the best way to handle the challenges that your reading may pose.

MISTAKE #1: READING IN THE WRONG PLACE

We live in a world that bombards us constantly with sights and sounds. Television, music, computers, cell phones, traffic, and other people's conversations are so commonplace that we often feel immune to the distractions. New college students often believe they can read anywhere. So what if your roommate has a few friends over? Just close your door and the party noise is reduced to a low din. The stereo bass may actually be soothing. The living room of the fraternity house has a comfy couch and you've become adept at tuning out the television shows when reviewing for your Friday biology lab. Besides, the chaos keeps you awake. Maybe you consider your bed to be the best place for studying. It's warm and comfortable, and you can completely relax while reading novels for your English lit class.

Snap out of it! Your tolerance for background noise, chaos, and relaxation while spending time with your textbook is likely to keep you from focusing and learning. College reading assignments require concentration.

WHAT TO DO

A noisy environment provides an excuse for not concentrating. You need significant peace and quiet to read, learn, and remember important information. You cannot fully engage your reading with familiar songs and television shows in the background, or the cheers of your roommate as he completes another level of an action game on his PC. A minimum amount of stress is important for good concentration, though. Being relaxed to the point of feeling drowsy makes short work of any focus. A nice, soft bed is not a good place for college reading.

Choose an environment that is conducive to thinking about what you are reading and mentally processing it in a meaningful way. You should have no major, continuous distractions that compete with your attention. Sit upright in a comfortable chair, not in something soft or in a reclining position so you are likely to be lulled to sleep. Also, you want your bed to remain a relaxing, calming place to be. If you turn it into a workplace—reading textbooks instead of material for your personal enjoyment—you may begin to associate your bed with the stress of school. Don't alter one of your few personal refuges.

The library offers areas that are ideal for reading. Study carrels (individual desks with partitions) provide a roomy area in which you can spread out your text and notebook or other materials while providing privacy. They are typically located in low-use sections of the library, as opposed to major thoroughfares where students talk openly and meet with study groups. You also may find similar study areas located in the dorm, some classroom buildings, and the student union. When you find a place to study on campus, be sure that you are not positioning yourself in a place where other students socialize.

When you read at home, be sure to eliminate all potential distractions. Turn off the television and stereo, set the answering machine to pick up calls and turn off the ringer to your phone, and make sure you won't be interrupted by your roommate or your family. Sit at your desk or the kitchen table to establish a good working area, even if you only plan to read. You may eventually begin to take notes or create study materials as you sit there. View your reading as schoolwork and approach it as such.

MISTAKE #2: NOT ALLOWING ENOUGH TIME TO READ

As overwhelmed as students feel with all of the assigned reading, it's surprising how many of them don't make the time to do it. They find time to attend class and complete assignments to turn in, but they don't always plan to do the reading. Freshmen often view reading as something to fit in around everything else, when time permits. Time is always a precious commodity for college students. Many college freshmen might remark that they have a ton of reading to do for their classes, but if you then ask when they plan to do that reading the answer might be hazy. Reading often hangs like a dark cloud over students' heads. They know they have to read—and may even take occasional stabs at it—but don't have a specific plan for accomplishing the reading.

WHAT TO DO

Make a specific plan to read. Include it in your weekly and daily schedules, along with all of the other tasks you need to get done. Identify the best times of day for you to concentrate and commit to a period for reading. It may seem easier to forgo reading for something else, because you don't often have to turn in anything related to reading. But when it is integrated into your time management plan, you consider it a necessary use of your time.

MISTAKE #3: SAVING IT ALL FOR TEST TIME

When you don't have to prove that you've read your weekly assignments, you can easily save them to do right before the test, and many students do—sometimes intentionally. You may know you've got reading to do, and you may even plan to get it done at some point, but you also know that your deadline is any time before the next exam. You may even believe that doing the reading right before the exam—say, a day or two prior—ensures that you will remember what you read. Usually, though, you don't realize just how much reading you have, and just how long it will take to complete, until it's too late—too late to finish or just too late to read it carefully enough to learn something from it. When the pressure is on, you feel it, and it affects your concentration.

WHAT TO DO

Realize that you will regret waiting until the last minute. The stress that results from having a lot of reading to get through will interfere with your ability to make progress. Schedule specific times each day to read for your classes. With the volume and complexity of reading to tackle, you must work at it regularly.

Effective college reading is a time-consuming task that requires a great deal of thought and effort. When you keep up with your reading throughout the semester, you can link it to the information from lectures. This enables you to recall the information more effectively than when you cram it in on the eve of the exam.

MISTAKE #4: UNDERESTIMATING THE IMPORTANCE OF READING ASSIGNMENTS

Some students view their reading assignments as secondary to the so-called real class work. They feel that instructors assign reading just to increase the course requirements and make use of the textbook they are required to buy. Reading is critical to your learning and success in each course. The Student Scenario highlights how this common perspective results in problems.

STUDENT SCENARIO: HE COULDN'T POSSIBLY . . .

The semester was rapidly coming to a close when Juan's geology instructor realized they were behind in covering the material. With only three weeks left, there were several more topics—and reading assignments—left to cover. Dr. Ramos was a great instructor, and the students were used to his bringing up issues from the readings and incorporating them into class lectures. The pace of the course picked up in the few remaining class sessions, with Dr. Ramos clearly rushing to talk about all of the relevant material. As he wrapped up the last day of class prior to the final exam, he glanced at the syllabus, reminded them of a few remaining topics and readings, and wished them good luck in their studying.

Juan began studying in earnest and carefully worked through his class notes and the reading assignments he had completed already, but there were still some remaining topics left to read about. Dr. Ramos had reminded the students about these topics on the last day. One of the topics from the syllabus was from an entirely separate book, and Dr. Ramos hadn't mentioned it at all. Despite starting early and working hard to prepare, Juan was running out of time before the exam. He really wanted to spend more time thinking through the material he had already been studying, but there was still the one remaining reading to do—a 64-page article. Juan decided that, because Dr. Ramos had never even mentioned the reading, he couldn't possibly expect them to do this along with everything else. Juan opted to focus on what he believed to be important—the reading assignments from the main textbook.

Juan was shocked and disheartened to find two ten-point questions on the exam from the last—and neglected—reading assignment listed on the syllabus. His final grade reflected the fact that he was not fully prepared.

Consider the following questions:

- Can you make the argument that Juan's decision to abandon the final reading to better prepare with the rest of the material mentioned in class was a good one? Explain.

- Was Juan entirely to blame for his final grade? Why or why not?

- Can you make the argument that Dr. Ramos was unfair to include questions based on a reading he never mentioned in class? Explain.

- What can you do to avoid this situation yourself, even if your instructor gets behind schedule?

- What does this scenario teach about syllabi?

WHAT TO DO

If the Student Scenario isn't enough to convince you of the importance of all reading assignments, read the Professor's Perspective. Find out your instructor's expectations of the reading schedule early in the term. Some instructors try to make sure that students keep up with the assigned readings by giving unannounced quizzes. Some instructors generate discussion questions based on the assigned reading and expect students to participate in the discussions, or they expect students to come to class and ask questions based on the reading. Make sure you read regularly throughout the term, just in case. Even if you are not directly assessed on the assigned chapters, reading the material close to class time is beneficial.

Reading the relevant material in the textbook immediately before coming to class prepares you for the lecture and makes it easier for you to take effective notes. You can generate a list of questions from your reading to ask in the next class to help clarify points and enhance your critical thinking.

You may prefer instead to do your assigned reading after you've heard the related lecture. If your instructor is a good speaker and the lectures are clear and easy to follow, the lecture may pave the way for a better reading experience. When you begin reading with a prior understanding of the information based on the lecture, you read more productively. Regardless of the order in which you choose to read and listen to the lecture, make sure you include the reading in your daily class study plan.

PROFESSOR'S PERSPECTIVE: THE ROLE OF YOUR TEXT

They're expensive, they're heavy to carry, and they take a long time to read. Meet your college textbooks. Although students bemoan them frequently, instructors consider them a fundamental tool for learning critical course information. Either the academic department or the professors themselves screen numerous texts before choosing the one they believe best suits the course. They read through the content, consider the writing style and tone of the author, examine the graphics and the various features of the book, and assess the supplemental materials such as an accompanying CD and chapter exercises. A great deal of time and effort goes into selecting the right books. Once the decision is made, it's the students' responsibility to take advantage of the textbook.

Instructors vary as to how much they rely on the text to provide the important information, but assigned readings are not given lightly. Unless your professor specifically tells you otherwise, any readings listed in the syllabus are expected to be completed, in full. Any reading assignments can and should be considered potential test material. Information mentioned in the assigned reading, whether or not it was discussed in class, may be considered part of the course content. Readings are selected and assigned for a reason, so take them seriously. Instructors do.

MISTAKE #5: THINKING OF READING AS A PASSIVE ACTIVITY

One of the worst mistakes you can make when approaching your reading assignments is to think of academic reading as a passive activity—something that simply requires sitting there and making sure your eyes register the words and images on the page. Skimming each page does not constitute reading, not if the goal is to learn something. Relaxing with a best-selling novel may be a passive activity, but reading for your classes should not be. Read the Perspective Check and think about your approach to academic reading.

PERSPECTIVE CHECK: IF I CAN JUST STAY AWAKE . . .

What comes to mind when you sit down to read for class? Do you flip through the chapter to see how many pages you've got to plow through? Do you challenge yourself to see how fast you can cover it all? Do you get frustrated just thinking about the time you'll have to spend gazing at endless lines of text? Or do you look forward to the knowledge it holds and to what you can extract from the text? Get a clear picture in your mind as to how you perceive the reading you must do for class. Does your approach work for you in terms of academic success, or are you just happy to stay awake for the duration?

WHAT TO DO

The best way to read textbooks productively (and make sure you stay awake) is to read with an active mind. Here are some suggestions for how to learn from your reading.

- *Take notes.* Create a set of condensed notes from the information presented in your text—just as you do for a lecture. The goal is to process what you read so you understand it, then reproduce it in your own way for later reference and recall. Your notes can take any form, and you can record them in the margins of the book, on notebook paper (which you can then insert with your lecture notes), or on index cards (which you can use as flash cards when you study).

- *Highlight.* It takes some practice to highlight effectively—to mark neither too much text nor too little. Highlighting causes a reader to focus, looking for main points and supporting details, identifying individuals and their significance, noting events or processes that are critical to understanding the topic. To be even more active with your reading, use several different colored markers to indicate different elements of the subject matter. For example, mark all theories in blue, people in green, locations in pink, and new terminology in yellow. Having goals to guide your highlighting brings greater interaction with what you read.

- *Create flash cards, lists, charts, and tables.* After reading through the material once, reread it quickly and extract vital information to create study tools. Choose terms, people, places, concepts, processes, events, and dates for flash cards. Define and describe the facts on one side of the cards. Then provide a quick prompt on the other side. Create tables that compare and contrast pairs or groups of events, people, or theories, noting similarities and differences. Make pie charts, lists, or cognitive maps wherever appropriate. Don't hesitate to be colorful and detailed if it helps bring the book to life.

- *Talk and test.* As you read, stop periodically and sum up in your own words what you've read, and quiz yourself to see what you've learned up to that point. It may seem time-consuming, but by providing yourself with a specific activity to incorporate into your reading time you remain mentally engaged with the information and learn more. When reading alone, talk out loud to yourself. Summarize sections of the text as if you are teaching them to someone. Or verbally list all of the significant points you can remember from a section. If you think your list is incomplete, reread the section to obtain more information.

MISTAKE #6: BEING UNREALISTIC ABOUT WHAT YOU CAN DO

One of the most common reading problems that students have is spending too long trying to read. When you can no longer focus on your reading, there is no reason to continue staring at the book. Students often persist, thinking that "it's the college way" to read for hours at a time. Once you've exceeded your attention span, though, a minute longer is simply a waste of time.

WHAT TO DO

We all have a limited capacity for reading at a high level of concentration. Recognize your attention span and schedule your reading time accordingly. You may have hours of reading assigned, but that doesn't mean you need to accomplish the assignment all at once. If you can focus for only 30 to 40 minutes before you begin daydreaming or dozing off, do not plan to read longer than that. Your goal should be to read productively and make the most of your time. When you can no longer do that, stop. Take a break, change topics, work on another assignment. Don't reread the same paragraph repeatedly. When you gain something from your reading—even if you spent only a short period of time—you walk away feeling motivated to do more later.

MISTAKE #7: IGNORING HELPFUL FEATURES OF THE TEXT

Textbooks contain more than just the main body of information. They contain numerous features—outlines, cognitive maps, boxes, tables, figures, and summaries. Their purpose is to help students learn. Frequently, though, students ignore them. These tools can make it easier to read and understand the material, so they should be the first thing you look at when you open your book.

WHAT TO DO

Before you go any further, read the following excerpt:

> A seashore is a better place than the street. At the start, it is better to run than to walk. You may have to try several times. It takes some skill, but it is easy to learn. Even young children can enjoy it. Once successful, complications are minimal. Birds seldom get too close. Too many people doing the same thing can cause problems, because one needs a lot of room. If there are no strong conditions or mishaps, it can be very peaceful. A rock can serve as an anchor, but if things break loose from it, you will not get a second chance.

What was this passage about? Did it make sense to you? You probably understood the words, but what about the paragraph as a whole? Reread it and consider its title, "Flying a Kite." Were you able to derive meaning through an overall connectedness between the elements described? If you were tested on what you read, how well would you do? How well would you have done prior to seeing the title?

As you can see, it's beneficial to have an awareness of what you are reading before you receive the information. By simply reading the title of the paragraph, you bring to mind everything you already know about flying a kite. With this knowledge, you can then gain more meaning from what you read.

Consider what this means for reading your course textbooks. When you immediately start to read a chapter—beginning with the first paragraph and moving on to the next—you are skipping an essential step in being able to truly understand and make sense of what you read. When you take a few minutes to look through the significant features of the chapter, you do the equivalent of reading the title to the kite passage. That is, you prepare your brain for the information to come.

PREVIEW THE CHAPTER

Start by looking through the assigned chapter. Most likely you will find at least one of the following features on the first page:

- *An outline.* This presents the headings and subheadings contained within the chapter. You can get an overall view of what is covered, the main topics that are addressed, and their relationship to each other through the headings and subheadings. When you understand where you are starting and where you will end up, it enables you to see each section's place in context.

- *A cognitive map.* A visual representation of the headings and subheadings of the chapter shows any natural hierarchies of the subject matter and lets you visualize the relationship between main points and supporting points. As you read, you can have a mental picture of where the information fits in the big picture.

- *Chapter objectives.* This is a list of the specific concepts and information that you should gain by reading the chapter. When you know what the author's main points are, you can look for them and focus on understanding their importance.

- *Questions to consider.* Some texts present a list of questions on the first page that will be answered within the chapter. Keeping these questions in mind as you read helps focus your reading. Even when questions are not specified for you, you can create your own based on the headings and subheadings throughout the chapter. For example, if a section in your American history book is titled "Brown v Board of Education," you can pose questions such as, "What was this case about?" "What was the ruling?" and "What impact did it have, and on whom?" You can then read the section with the goal of finding the answers to your questions. Not only will you be more motivated to read, but what you read will seem more meaningful. The message will be clearer, easier to recognize, and, consequently, easier to remember. You may even figure out some of what your next exam will cover.

In addition to the material at the beginning of the chapter, your textbook is likely to contain helpful features at the end of the chapter, including:

- *Chapter summary.* The chapter may end with a brief synopsis of the most important points made in the chapter. When you read the summary before you read the text, you get a good idea of the scope and focus of the chapter.

- *Chapter review questions.* By reading through the review questions, you see what issues are highlighted in the chapter. Use them to guide your reading as you search for the answers along the way. Doing so directs your attention and motivates you to tune in.

Previewing the chapter takes very little time—ten minutes at the most. It is time well spent, because it makes the rest of your reading time much more productive.

PREVIEW THE TEXT

Another great way to gain more from your text is to preview the entire book when you first get it. This helps you develop a good understanding about what the course in general is like. When you get your new books, check out the following features:

- *Preface and introduction.* Most textbooks have a preface and/or an introduction. The preface, sometimes titled "To the Student," may seem like a letter in which the authors share their vision of the text. You can learn a lot from what authors have to say, especially if they explain how they designed and wrote the book to help you learn. Sometimes they also provide tips and hints for approaching the text in the most effective and enjoyable way.

- *Table of contents.* Looking over the contents of the entire book shows you the scope of the text—the expanse of material that you will cover during the semester—and the sequence of the material. You can also see what each individual chapter covers. The authors decide which topics should precede others and what information should come later in the course. Sometimes professors alter the order in which they cover the material. Cross-check your syllabus with the text's table of contents.

- *Common chapter features.* As you scan the table of contents or flip through individual chapters, look for recurring chapter features. For example, in this book, Student Scenario, Professor's Perspective, and Future Focus are three features found in every chapter. They are considered important learning tools for this material. When you become familiar with the features, you know to look for them and determine how best to incorporate them in your reading as you progress through a book. If you have favorite features, use them to spark your interest in each new chapter.

- *Exercises and activities.* Most textbooks include problems, exercises, or activities for students to practice the concepts they learn. They may be placed at the end of each chapter, section, or other grouping of pages. Identify what kinds of exercises are available to assist you in learning the material and whether an answer key is provided.

- *Appendixes, references, glossary, and index.* The back of the textbook is likely to have many helpful resources, including one or more appendixes (supplementary material), a reference section (a list of sources cited within the text and provided to give proper recognition), a glossary (a list of key terms found in the text, usually in boldface type, and their definitions within the context of the subject), and an index (a list of topics, issues, people, concepts, and terms discussed in the book and the page or pages where they are mentioned). Take a look at what features are available for you to use as you read.

TECHNIQUES TO MAKE YOUR READING MEANINGFUL

Like most academic skills, effective reading is developed through practice. You may feel comfortable with your current method of reading right now. However, if you are performing less than ideally on quizzes or exams in spite of keeping up with reading assignments, it is time to try something more methodical—something designed specifically to yield the maximum gain from reading assignments. As you read the Skill Check, think about your current approach to reading.

SKILL CHECK: MY READING PLAN

You look up the assigned pages, open your textbook, and then what? What's your plan? Is there something you always do first, then second, then third? Is there a pattern to your approach to assigned reading? How do you know if the information is sinking in? Do you monitor your understanding? What do you do if the reading is particularly challenging, with new terms and concepts that are unfamiliar? What if the amount of required reading is particularly great? Do you have a plan to cover it all and remember what's important? How do you go about making your time spent reading more meaningful?

SQ3R

The most popular method for effectively approaching reading of an academic nature is known as *SQ3R*. The letters stand for the five steps in a series that create a complete process for learning from text. The number 3 refers to the fact that there are three important activities that begin with the letter *R*. SQ3R involves several of the ideas presented in the previous section as solutions for common reading mistakes. Together, they fulfill the most important element of effective reading—that of getting learners to be active with what they are reading. It is not possible to simply sit back and stare blankly at the page when you employ this approach.

S IS FOR SURVEY

In SQ3R, the survey step is essentially previewing the chapter. You begin by examining all of the elements of the chapter you are about to read. Read through any features contained at the beginning of the chapter, such as an outline, chapter objectives, and cognitive map, as well as each heading and subheading within the chapter, noting the hierarchy of information. Note any terms in boldface type or italics. Turn to the back of the chapter to read the summary and review questions. By surveying all of these features, you have a picture in your mind of what is to come, the manner in which it is presented, and what you can expect to get out of it.

Q IS FOR QUESTION

Imagine that you are trying to decide on an elective course to fill in your schedule next semester. You can't decide between philosophy or social psychology, primarily because you don't know the difference in the classes. However, there is a description of each one in the college catalog. You have read these descriptions previously but can't recall much from them. Now that you need some specific information, those course descriptions seem different. Why? Because you have a set of questions in mind that you want answered. You want to know, "What is the course about?" "What topics does it cover?" "How might it be related to my major?" "What kinds of activities are involved?" As you read the synopsis for each course, you look for answers to these questions. The otherwise dull passages now become interesting and informative as you read them with purpose.

This same phenomenon occurs when you ask questions of your textbook readings. Developing and asking questions are two of the most important aspects of SQ3R. You don't even have to create your own questions. Simply change the headings and subheadings in your chapters to questions. Here are some examples.

Chapter Heading	Questions
Types of Plant Tissues	"What are the types of plant tissues?"
	"How many are there?"
	"What makes them different from each other?"
Financing Corporations	"How is a corporation financed?"
	"What kinds of corporations are financed?"
	"Who can finance a corporation?"
Bureaucracy and Public Opinion	"How are bureaucracy and public opinion related?"
	"How do they influence each other?"
	"What are some examples of their relationship?"

Chapter Heading	Questions
Prohibition	"What was prohibition?"
	"When did it occur?"
	"What caused it?"
	"What was the result?"

As you read each chapter looking for answers to your questions, you discover how significant and meaningful the material is. You also have a basis for remembering the information—even details. Questioning works because it motivates you to learn something from your reading and provides the focus for obtaining that information. Having a particular goal in mind while you read also keeps you focused on what you are doing. Also, the questions that you pursue answers to in your reading may be the same questions that show up on the test. You can't prepare much better than that.

THE FIRST R IS FOR *READ*

After making an overview of the chapter and developing a set of questions for the first several sections, it is time to read. Reading, of course, is the whole point. It is through this activity that you learn the information, so you must read carefully and critically. You can use your questions to guide you. As you search for answers, also incorporate a recognition and understanding of new terminology—words that have a particular meaning in relation to the topic. If you don't know what a specific word means, look it up in the glossary of the textbook or a dictionary. Unless you can derive the meaning from the context, don't continue reading when you encounter unfamiliar words.

In your search for answers to the questions you've developed, be aware of the connection between pieces of information. The answer to one question may be related to the answer to another. If so, how? Consider how the material relates to lectures and class discussions. Where does it fit in with the big picture? As you read, integrate all of the information you know about the subject matter. The more you can mentally manipulate what you are reading, the more you will get out of the assignment. Is this time-consuming? Yes. Careful, critical, effective reading takes time. You cannot read quickly or without effort. Allow sufficient time to read for class.

THE SECOND R IS FOR *RECITE*

This is your chance to discover what you accomplished when you did your reading. Recite (yes, out loud) your questions and answers, as well as any other important points you gained from a particular section. This step is meant to be carried out, at least initially, after you have read a particular portion of your chapter.

Breaking your reading down into smaller chunks is easier for several reasons. You are more motivated to do it in the first place, knowing that you are not facing an entire chapter. A portion is more likely to fit into your reading attention span—which, for most of us, is within the time frame of an hour. And it allows you to concentrate on one area, get to know and understand it clearly, and prepare for the next section.

When you recite what you've learned, you need to step away from your notes and explain the material in your own words. Imagine that you are an instructor introducing the material to students in class for the first time. Attempt to communicate the critical points clearly, anticipating any questions a naïve person might ask. When you can recite successfully, you have read well and are ready to move on.

THE THIRD R STANDS FOR *REVIEW*

The purpose of reviewing is to monitor and cement your knowledge. You can review after reading to check how focused you are, but you can also review after reciting, to check your understanding and recollection of the information.

Reviewing can involve many activities that help you refresh your memory about what you read. Answering the chapter review questions helps you assess how well you understand and remember the most important concepts. Answering the questions you developed from the headings and subheadings serves the same purpose. Once you have covered the entire chapter, you can recite, or "lecture," your imaginary class on all of the chapter concepts or simply write a summary—in your own words—of the key points and supporting information.

Reviewing also involves creating and working with any study tools you find helpful—flash cards, time lines, charts, lists, graphs, tables, or diagrams. When you make these tools and review the information contained in them, you further embed the critical material in your mind. These are highly effective ways to learn and remember information you are responsible for.

SQ4R

In light of its tremendous success as a reading technique, the SQ3R method has been broadened to include another step. That fourth step—the new *R*—stands for either *record* or *reflect*.

THE FOURTH R FOR *RECORD*

Educator Linda Wong specifies the additional step of *record* immediately following *read*.[1] According to Wong, the SQ4R method includes taking notes on the reading assignments, using any format—outlines, cognitive maps, or the Cornell method. The reader can take notes in the margin of the text, on notebook paper, or on flash cards. Recording is a purposeful effort to translate important concepts and information from your reading into written format of your own.

THE FOURTH R FOR *REFLECT*

Educator Walter Pauk describes the importance of reflecting on what you have read.[2] This is really the critical thinking activity in reading, and it takes place after the reader has surveyed, questioned, read carefully, recited, and reviewed. (Pauk also advocates recording.) As a final step, the reader further engages learning by considering the facts and ideas that he or she has just read about. In reflecting, you ask yourself questions such as the following: What makes the facts and ideas important? How might they be applied? Why are you learning about them? Of what use are they to you? How do they relate to other things that you know? What else might you learn about them?

The goal of reflecting is to discover and enhance your interest in the topics you read about. It can motivate you to explore issues further by talking with your instructor or reading supplemental materials. Through these activities and the application of your knowledge, you grow not only as a learner but as a thinker.

RECOGNIZING PATTERNS IN TEXT

Textbook authors take special care to present material in an organized way that is clear and makes sense to students. They use specific patterns of presentation, depending on the information they are introducing. When you are aware of the

---

[1] Linda Wong, *Essential Study Skills,* 4th ed. (Boston: Houghton Mifflin, 2003).
[2] Walter Pauk, *How to Study in College,* 7th ed. (Boston: Houghton Mifflin, 2001).

patterns while reading, you can use your knowledge of the pattern to help you read most effectively and better remember the information. You will have even greater success with each step of the SQ3R (or SQ4R) process when you also recognize the particular way in which the information is organized.

- *Definition pattern.* This pattern is not likely to make up an entire chapter. However, some sections of texts may use a pattern of introducing a new word and then taking a couple of paragraphs to develop the concept thoroughly. For example, your political science text might introduce the term *veto,* explaining what it is, how it works, when it can be used, and how it has been used in the past.

- *Example pattern.* This is another simple pattern, also likely to make up only a portion of the chapter. In this pattern, the text presents an idea, explains it, and provides examples that demonstrate the concept. The section you currently are reading is an example pattern. Each item in the bulleted list is an example of a pattern found in textbook organization.

- *Chronological pattern.* This pattern presents information in a specific order—typically, from first to last or from earliest to latest. Time lines in history, life stages in developmental psychology, and how a bill becomes a law are examples of content that might follow this pattern.

- *Spatial pattern.* This pattern describes how things are physically located relative to one another—usually through a systematic approach. For example, a description of the layout of a city might go from west to east or from the city center outward. A chapter might discuss the bones of the body beginning with the skull and working down to the toes, for example.

- *Process pattern.* This pattern describes the steps in a process—the order in which things should be carried out for a desired result. In chemistry, you might read about the process for making salicylic acid in the lab. In English, you might read about how to write an opening paragraph of an essay, what to include in the body of the paper, and how to develop a conclusion.

- *Compare or contrast pattern.* When a text discusses any set of people, items, issues, or events in terms of their similarities, the items within the set are being compared. When the text discusses differences between such things, it is contrasting them. In some cases, you read about similarities and differences between things at the same time. Your history text might compare and contrast presidents of the twentieth century or leaders from countries around the world. Your psychology text might compare and contrast theories of personality.

- *Cause and effect pattern.* This method is often used to explore problems. The text states the problem and its cause, explains the effect it has, and describes a solution (if there is one). An example is a psychology text's discussion of insecure attachments between mothers and infants. The cause is maternal neglect and unresponsiveness, and the effect is a baby that doesn't seek proximity and comfort from the mother. The solution is to present new mothers with models for nurturing and tending to their infants, particularly throughout the first year of life.

When you recognize the presentation pattern your text is using at each point in the reading, you can set your mind to expect specific kinds of information. This makes it easier to interpret, understand, and remember what you read.

USING CHARTS, GRAPHS, TABLES, AND FIGURES

Not all information is best presented in written form. In some cases, a table or a figure makes the information easier to understand. What may seem like a long-winded description or explanation in paragraph form may be immediately understood when presented as a pie chart or a bar graph. Pay attention to these features in your texts. The content may or may not be fully explained in writing, but the graphical features contain valuable information nonetheless. Visual learners particularly benefit from these features.

Tables and figures sometimes simplify material discussed in the text. They make it easier to grasp and remember the information. If you are having difficulty making sense of a text passage and there happens to be a related figure, examine it carefully and then reread the passage.

All supplemental features are important to include in any notes you take from your reading and the quizzes you give yourself. When you use SQ3R, examine the features during your survey step and develop questions about them in step 2. As you read the chapter, refer to them in combination with the related section. Recitation of what you learned during a portion of the chapter should include any charts, graphs, tables, or figures. When you explain what they represent in your own words, you gain a more thorough understanding of that material. Of course, reviewing at any stage should include the graphical representations of the important information.

 ## DIFFERENT KINDS OF READING

Most of your reading in college will be from textbooks, but you also will encounter some other types of reading materials. Science courses may require that you read articles written by researchers who conducted experiments. Literature courses in college almost always involve a variety of literary works.

PROFESSIONAL JOURNAL ARTICLES

Facts and ideas in textbooks are often followed by a name and date in parentheses. This is known as a *citation*—a reference to the original source of the idea or information. Citations give credit to those who revealed the fact or proposed the idea. They refer primarily to books and professional journal articles. When you encounter a citation in your textbook, you can look it up in the references section in the back of the book and find out about the original source that first presented the fact, concept, or theory. Then, if you want to, you can locate the source article or book and read it.

Sometimes instructors assign readings from professional journal articles so their students can have direct experience with the format. The articles can be overwhelming at first, particularly if you are not aware of how they are organized and what information they contain. Most, however, contain basic variations of the following information:

- *Abstract.* The abstract is the first element of a professional journal article. It is a brief summary (usually no more than 250 words) of what the article itself contains. You can read the abstract and get an overview of what the study did, how it was conducted, what it found, and the author's interpretation of those findings. When you are required to write a research paper using professional journal articles, you can use the abstracts to determine if the article will be useful to you.

- *Introduction.* The author begins by providing background information—typically, past research and significant findings related to the topic. The introduction is presented in a narrative format. The author describes what researchers already know regarding the topic, what others in the field believe about the issues, and what questions are still unanswered. This section usually contains numerous citations because it mentions important discoveries in the field. Professionals may read the cited articles before continuing to read the current article or may read them as a follow-up. The introduction often ends with the author stating the purpose and hypotheses, or predictions for what will be found in the study described in the article.

- *Methods.* This is a detailed description of what the research investigation actually did. It presents the research procedures so that anyone else could carry out the same steps. The article explains the subjects of study, the equipment used, the amount of materials and time, the location and lab conditions, and the step-by-step procedure carried out.

- *Results.* The article then describes what happened in the study. The author addresses everything that occurred when carrying out the steps described in the methods section. This is the raw data.

- *Analysis.* This section applies the relevant statistical manipulations to the data to determine the significance of the findings. (For example, did the findings occur by chance?) The analysis may be technical and mathematical in nature. Instructors don't usually expect freshmen or sophomores to read or truly understand the analysis.

- *Discussion.* The author then discusses the interpretation of the results, addressing each specific finding and the reasons it did or did not turn out as expected. The discussion section may conclude with the author's statement on the importance of the findings, what the research contributed to the discipline's body of knowledge, and ideas for new studies.

- *References.* The last section of a journal article lists sources that were cited or discussed in the article. This section includes all of the necessary bibliographic information for readers to locate the sources on their own.

Professional journal articles vary in their writing style and ease of understanding. Some researchers are able to communicate their ideas and methods simply and clearly. Researchers do not always write well, which makes it more challenging for readers. The vast number of topics addressed in professional journal articles also contributes to the variety of reading experiences you will have. Some topics are simply easier to understand and follow than others. Being familiar with the design and presentation of the articles should help you, though. The Future Focus illustrates the importance of becoming comfortable with reading at a professional level.

 FUTURE FOCUS: GROWING AS A PROFESSIONAL

When you begin your career, you will be expected to keep up with the latest developments in your field, whether in medicine, another science, business, or education. Numerous publications present new findings and applications regarding work in your field. Journal articles are written by professionals in the field and often involve in-depth descriptions, explanations, and interpretations of research conducted on a variety of topics. To maintain your status as a valuable employee or to be considered for advancement in your line of work, it is important to keep up your professional journal reading. You may not have a lot of extra time for this activity. Therefore, the more effectively you can read and learn the necessary information from these articles, the better. Having an understanding of their format and keeping in mind your goal for reading enables you to gain the maximum benefit in a reasonable amount of time.

LITERATURE

The word *literature* officially refers to any written work, either factual or fictional. However, most people think of literature as creative writing—novels, short stories, plays, and poetry. Indeed, this is how it is used in the college curriculum. Literature classes focus on fictional works. Figure 9.1 highlights the distinctions between the two basic types of reading material—expository and imaginative.

The key to reading imaginative literature and learning from it is understanding and appreciating the reasons for reading it in the first place. Imaginative literature enriches our lives. It conveys the human condition so we can connect with the familiar and be swept away to places we've never been. It shows us who we are as individuals, as a society, a nation, a species, a planet. It enables us to experience the range of human emotions—touching the greatest joy, falling into the lowest depths of being—without having to live through the experiences ourselves. Imaginative literature can change us through our perceptions of the world and the people we meet, through our goals and the things that motivate us, and through awakening our compassion and understanding. It teaches us things we never knew and opens our minds to fresh ideas and the ways of the world. Imaginative literature is one of the most powerful personal, social, and educational tools.

Expository Literature	Imaginative Literature
Examples	
Fact	Fiction
Essays	Novels
News stories	Plays
Magazine articles	Short stories
Most college textbooks	Poems
Characteristics	
Journalistic: Goal is to convey or teach.	Goal is to produce pleasure.
Relates to real experiences people have had or can have.	Presents experiences we can only have through reading.
Written for our intellect.	Written for our emotions.
Uses precise language with direct meaning.	Uses words with layers of meaning.
Reader should be focused and alert.	Reader should be relaxed or passive.
Concerned with truth.	Truth comes from what may be possible in unique situations.

Figure 9.1
A Literary Comparison

SOURCE: Based on Mortimer Adler and Charles Van Doren, *How to Read a Book.* Copyright © 1972. Simon and Schuster, Inc.

When you set out to read a novel for your American Literature course, one of Shakespeare's plays for British Literature, or a collection of short stories by twentieth-century authors for a Contemporary Literature course, prepare to take a journey. Immerse yourself in the story, visualize it, imagine what it would be like if you were part of it, and try to see things through the eyes of the characters. As you read, consider the following questions to help you gain more from the story:

- Scene by scene or chapter by chapter, what do you think the author was trying to convey?

- What qualities does each of the characters have or lack? Might they represent an archetypal virtue or vice? Why do you think the author developed each character that way?

- What is your emotional reaction to the characters, places, and events? Do you think the author intended for the reader to feel those things? Why?

- Does the story have a message? Does the author state the message directly? Is the message subtle and open to individual interpretation? What makes you think so?

- Does the author provide clues to any upcoming events, messages, or morals within the story?

- What events and actions by the characters surprised you? On the other hand, which major elements of the story could you predict?

Consider taking notes for fiction assignments, using any formal note-taking format or a more casual method. Jot down interesting aspects of the characters and settings. Note your reactions to situations and events. Record random thoughts as prompts to help you transition back into the story after setting it aside for a while. Use your notes to help you during class discussions and for essay exams.

Good time management is just as important for reading literature assignments as it is for reading textbooks. Read only for as long as you are able to focus on the story and concentrate. Stopping in the middle of a chapter is okay if it means you aren't daydreaming or falling asleep. Because fiction books are not subdivided as much as textbooks, it is helpful to be on the lookout for good stopping places—a change in location, a shift in the story line, or a new time frame. Remember, when you read and think about a limited portion of the story at each sitting, you become more fully absorbed in the story, you pay attention to the details, and the entire text has more meaning. If you try to read too much at once, you may focus on reaching the end rather than savoring the experience of reading the piece of literature.

POETRY

Poetry is a unique form of imaginative literature, and one that is intimidating to many people. Poets tend not to use conventional writing techniques to convey their message. For this reason, it can be more challenging to discover the meaning and to feel confident in your understanding of what the poem says. As you approach poetry, keep in mind that poets write to share something personal. They may tell a story (*narrative poems*) or convey a collection of thoughts (*lyric poems*). In either case, they aim to draw us in emotionally and touch us in some way. They may contain elements of humor, sadness, longing, joy, pain, sorrow, or love. Some poems may even contain all of those emotions. Recognizing that a poem is a creative attempt to express the poet's feelings and to stimulate a response from the reader, you have the right frame of mind to proceed.

SCRUTINIZE

When analyzing poetry, you can operate on the microscopic level (looking for and noting the details), and the contextual level (examining how all of the elements come together to produce an overall message). The best strategy for challenging poems is to read them through once or twice and then begin studying the smallest elements, such as:

- *The title.* What meaning can you derive just from the title? What predictions can you make about the poem?

- *The speaker.* Whose thoughts or words does the poem contain? Is the speaker clearly identified?

- *Sentence or phrase structure.* Subject, verb, object. Try to determine who is doing what.

- *Word use.* Locate and define any unfamiliar words. Use contextual clues for additional understanding. Do any words or phrases have two or more meanings?

- *Imagery.* Does the poem contain detailed descriptions of places, people, things, behaviors, or emotions?

- *Figurative language.* Locate metaphors, similes, instances of personification, and other uses of figurative language. Identify the significance for each use.

- *Rhyming.* Does the poem use rhyming? Do rhyming words appear at the end of lines (sequential lines or every other line) or within each line? What is the rhyme scheme?

- *Meter.* What is the poem's rhythm (for example, iambic pentameter)?

- *Sounds.* What writing techniques does the poet use to create poetic "sound effects"? Does the poet use words that sound like their meaning? Do many of the words begin or end with the same sound?

STEP BACK

Once you have noted the detailed elements of a poem, take a step back and examine the work as a whole. Think about the following questions:

- Is it a narrative poem or a lyric poem? Does the poem tell a complete story?

- What is the tone or the mood of the poem? Does it seem happy, sad, remorseful, excited, fearful?

- Does the poem convey its mood through the use of sensory descriptions—phrases that appeal to any of the five senses?

- Does the poem use irony, understatement, or hyperbole (exaggeration) for dramatic effect? How do these elements contribute to the message of the poem?

- How do the detailed elements (such as word use, imagery, sentence structure, and meter) fit with the broader features (such as the type of poem, mood, and dramatic effects) to create a literary experience?

Reading poetry is a critical thinking activity. Few poets intend for their readers to passively approach their words. Working through a poem is like putting together a puzzle that first requires identifying the individual pieces. Don't forget to consider your personal reaction to the poem. Did you like it? How did it make you feel? Were you transported by the poet's use of sound, meter, and description, or did it fall flat emotionally? How would you have written about this topic? What poetic elements appeal to you and how would you use them? The experience of reading poetry offers limitless opportunity for critical and creative thought.

CHAPTER 9 REVIEW QUESTIONS

1. In what ways does college reading pose new challenges?

2. What are some common mistakes that college students make with regard to reading, and how can you avoid making these mistakes?

3. Describe the steps in the SQ3R method for reading.

4. What additional steps might you want to include in SQ3R?

5. How are most professional journal articles organized, and what information are you likely to find in each section?

6. What are the main differences between expository and imaginative literature?

7. What are the two main ways to analyze reading poetry? Provide some examples of each.

SKILL PRACTICE

1. Read the following passage and try to determine the meaning.

> *First you arrange things into different groups, depending on their color and texture. If there is not much to do, one pile may be sufficient. If you lack the necessary equipment, you must go somewhere else. It is important not to overload. It is better to do too few things than too many. Complications can arise if you don't follow directions, and a mistake can be expensive. At first, the whole procedure may seem difficult, but soon it will become just another fact of life. You can get caught up but never ahead on this task.*

Reread the passage with the knowledge that the title is "Doing Laundry." Describe the difference in the ease of reading, understanding, and remembering what you read.

2. Turn each of the following chapter subheadings into a question.
   a. Bank Accounts: Their Nature and Use as a Control Over Cash
   b. Nonfinancial Performance Measures
   c. Sputnik and Its Aftermath

d. The Northern Election of 1864

e. Sunlight as an Energy Source

f. A Closer Look at Bones and Joints

g. The Image of the Legislator

h. Cities and Suburbs: The Metropolitan Dilemma

3. Use what you have learned about reading poetry to analyze these two poems by the nineteenth-century American poet Emily Dickinson[3] and answer the questions that follow.

a. *'Twas such a little, little boat*
That toddled down the bay!
'Twas such a gallant, gallant sea
That beckoned it away

'Twas such a greedy, greedy wave
That licked it from the coast;
Nor ever guessed the stately sails
My little craft was lost!

b. *To fight aloud is very brave,*
But gallanter, I know,
Who charge within the bosom,
The cavalry of woe.

Who win, and nations do not see,
Who fall, and none observe,
Whose dying eyes no country
Regards with patriot love.

We trust, in plumed procession,
For such the angels go,
Rank after rank, with even feet
And uniforms of snow.

- What would you title each of these poems?
- What does each poem describe?
- What writing techniques does Dickinson use to create a sensory experience?
- How do those techniques create a greater understanding of the poems?
- What are your favorite aspects of each poem? Why?
- What do you find most challenging about each poem?

CURRENT COURSE APPLICATION

1. Check each item that applies to you.

_____ I do not complete all reading assignments because I attend class regularly.

_____ I am aware of how long I can read without losing my focus.

_____ I plan only to read for as long as I can fully concentrate on what I'm reading.

_____ I have specifically scheduled times to read in my weekly and daily planner.

_____ I make reading as much of a priority as accomplishing my other assignments for school.

_____ I do my reading assignments before class.

_____ I do my reading assignments shortly after attending the lecture on the material.

_____ I wait to do most or all of my reading assignments until a few days prior to the exam.

_____ I have a systematic approach to my reading assignments.

[3] Emily Dickinson, *Collected Poems: Courage Classics* (Philadelphia: Courage Books, 1991).

_____ I focus primarily on the main body of the text and don't pay too much attention to material in boxes.

_____ I struggle when I have long reading assignments such as entire books for literature classes.

_____ I dread having to read poems.

What have you learned about your approach to college reading? What issues do you need to work on? Identify each area for improvement and develop a plan using information from the chapter.

2. Designate reading time for your classes and mark your weekly planner accordingly, if you haven't already done so.

3. Preview (or survey) an upcoming chapter in one of your textbooks. Use the following list as a guide.

Chapter title

Number of pages in the chapter

Number of major sections in the chapter

Features at the beginning of the chapter (outline, objectives, cognitive map)

Charts, graphs, tables, figures, illustrations throughout the chapter

Special chapter features, usually boxed (story vignettes, cartoons, quotes)

Exercises, activities, or websites embedded in the chapter

Chapter summary

Chapter review questions

End of chapter exercises

Are you ready to read the chapter? Do you have a good idea of what you are going to learn about?

After reading the chapter, describe how your experience was affected by your having surveyed the chapter ahead of time. What features, either at the beginning or the end of the chapter, helped prepare you the most?

4. For an upcoming section in a textbook chapter, create a set of questions from the subheadings. Proceed with your reading. Then test yourself on the answers. Recite them out loud in your own words.

5. If you don't usually take notes on your reading, try it the next time you work on a reading assignment. First, decide whether to make notes in the margin or on a separate piece of notebook paper. Then review them and consider how helpful they will be when you study for your next exam.

6. Create flash cards, lists, tables, graphs, cognitive maps, and other dynamic study tools from one of your course textbooks. Use your study tools when you prepare for the exam. Which ones were most helpful? Why?

7. Write a brief summary of some imaginative literature you are reading for one of your classes, if applicable. Include answers to some of these questions as you write your summary.

What is the story line?

What is your reaction to the story and the characters?

What are you gaining from reading this literature?

Why do you think your instructor assigned this work?

Are you enjoying the work? Why or why not?

TAKE A LOOK ONLINE

For tips on taking notes from text, highlighting, becoming a critical reader, and reading literature, go to

www.readingmatrix.com/reading/reading_texts.html

For information on reading your math textbooks, check out

www.usu.edu/arc/idea_sheets/problem-guided_reading.htm

Check out this site for a new poem each day:

www.poems.com

STUDENT SCENARIO DISCUSSION RESPONSES

- **Can you make the argument that Juan's decision to abandon the final reading to better prepare with the rest of the material mentioned in class was a good one? Explain.** It clearly wasn't a good one but it may have been necessary. Juan was a conscientious student, but he did not allow enough time to prepare sufficiently for the exam. His desire to fully focus on the topics covered in class was well-intentioned and may have served him well for the majority of the exam. However, completely neglecting a reading assignment listed on the syllabus proved to be a bad decision.

- **Was Juan entirely to blame for his final grade? Why or why not?** Yes, Juan was entirely to blame for his final grade because he consciously neglected a required reading assignment.

- **Can you make the argument that Dr. Ramos was unfair to include questions based on a reading he never mentioned in class? Explain.** Students have the right to be frustrated when the instructor loses track of time and rushes through the course work at the end of the semester. Despite getting behind and having to rush, he still reminded students that he hadn't covered all of the material from the syllabus.

- **What can you do to avoid this situation yourself, even if your instructor gets behind schedule?** Read the syllabus thoroughly at the beginning of class and refer to it on a regular basis. Ask the instructor if everything listed on the syllabus is still valid, particularly if the class falls behind schedule. Keep up with the reading. Even if lectures get behind, read ahead to fit all assignments in before the end of class. Even if the instructor doesn't get a chance to cover all of the assignments or mention them in class, it's important to study all of the required materials for exams.

- **What does this scenario teach about syllabi?** Constantly referring to the course syllabi is crucial for success in class. You can't rely on the instructor to tell you what to do. Keep the syllabus for each course in the front of the class notebook and review it frequently. If something is stated on the syllabus, consider it a requirement unless the instructor specifically says otherwise.

10 WRITE AND SPEAK ELOQUENTLY

In this chapter you will learn

- ⦿ The power of words and the importance of increasing your vocabulary

- ⦿ The process for putting together a paper or speech

- ⦿ How to gather research materials

- ⦿ How to manage your time to prepare a good presentation

- ⦿ What constitutes plagiarism and how to avoid it

⦿ THE VALUE OF VOCABULARY

The building blocks for written and spoken language are words. By stringing them together in just the right way, we can generate any message we want and share it with others. It sounds so simple, but the options are vast. Individual words can be powerful, so the more of them you know the greater your ability to communicate.

RECOGNIZE THE POWER OF WORDS

Imagine some different possibilities for the title of this chapter:

Write and Speak Good

Write and Speak Better

Be a Better Writer and Speaker

Be an Effective Communicator

Communicate Well

How do they compare with "Write and Speak Eloquently"? The first option is simply incorrect because *good* is an adjective, not an adverb. The two words *write* and *speak* are verbs, so they require the adverb *well* as a modifier. The second option is grammatically correct but uninspiring. "Be a Better Writer and Speaker" is lengthy and clumsy. The last two choices are acceptable but eventually were dismissed in favor of the existing title. For a chapter on enhancing communication skills, it's appropriate to use the word *eloquent* because it conveys the essence of the chapter content. The title itself shows the power of words.

You don't need to be a sesquipedalian (a person who uses long words) to choose words that have more impact. Consider the following options for expressing the same idea:

Why Say It This Way?	*When You Can Say It Like This?*
Butterflies show the beauty of nature.	Butterflies exemplify nature's elegance.
I have always wondered about things.	Being inquisitive is one of my characteristics.
It is not something that will work.	It isn't a viable option.
She always did everything right.	Her efforts were infallible.
Everyone always argues when she's around.	Her presence is divisive.

You are probably aware of the strong effect that some words and phrases have. Consider major advertising campaigns. The slogan for athletic equipment producer Nike, "Just do it," now enters many conversations without any reference to sports. The elegant simplicity of using three words to express a whole range of meaning—a directive for getting something done, an inspiration for overcoming obstacles, a motivation for putting aside self-doubt and connecting with personal abilities—is clearly powerful.

EXPRESS YOURSELF

One of the most famous speeches in history was the "I have a dream" speech by Dr. Martin Luther King, Jr. Imagine if he had stated "I have an idea" instead. John F. Kennedy inspired millions with the line from his inaugural address, "Ask not what your country can do for you; ask what you can do for your country." What do you think would have been the effect if he had said, "Find out what you can do to help the United States instead of how it can help you"?

King and Kennedy's eloquent presentations have solidified in our minds and hearts who these men were. Their character and what they stood for become clear through the words they spoke. The same is true for you. The way in which you express yourself reflects you as a person. Your communication style conveys your thoughts, ideas, and efforts in life's endeavors. It demonstrates to others how you think, what you may be feeling, and your reactions to those emotions.

Contrast King and Kennedy's timely words of wisdom with what you typically see in an interview following a sporting event. Suppose the reporter asks a player a predictable question about what happened in the game. The player is likely to respond with something like:

Well, I knew this was a big game and the other guys would be tough, so I knew I had to go out there and, like, do my best and give it everything I got. They came out, played us hard, and, like I said, I just went out there, worked hard, did my best, and hoped for the best, and am really happy that we won against such a tough team.

Besides containing a couple of run-on sentences, this communication is repetitious, unimaginative, and provides no new or interesting information. It is hard to imagine that people learn anything from post-game interviews, because they are too similar and say too little. You probably don't want to express yourself like this.

Having command of spoken and written language can provide you with self-confidence. When you can put pen to paper and get your individual message across, your thoughts or ideas can be preserved and read by one or many, and referred to time and time again. When you can speak your mind clearly and competently, you can command others' attention and make yourself heard. Eloquent communication in either form shows people who you are and promotes understanding and respect for your thoughts and ideas.

 FUTURE FOCUS: YOU HAD BETTER BE GOOD AT THIS!

According to a survey of the National Association of College Employers, oral communication, interpersonal relations, and teamwork are the three most important skills that a potential job candidate can possess. Being able to express yourself effectively plays a critical role in all three skills. Oral communication refers to both formal and casual speech. You must be able to give professional oral presentations for colleagues and clientele in the workplace and speak knowledgeably, maturely, and eloquently in spontaneous and casual conversations.

Interpersonal relations in the work world involve a variety of elements including effective communication, both oral and written. Almost all career-track jobs require written communication skills. The documents you write describe critical aspects of your job. Written communication also includes personal letters and memos to important individuals with whom you work (or with whom you hope to work) and even e-mail. Connecting with others on any level as part of your job can be enhanced or hindered by your speaking and writing skills.

Consider the third skill, teamwork. It simply can't exist without clear, constructive communication between diverse people.

One last thing to keep in mind. Before you get your career started, you need to write and speak well about something of critical importance—yourself. Your résumé and job interview skills are founded in your ability to express yourself on paper and in person. Make an impact: Tap into the power of words.

LEARN THE LINGO

Whether you like it or not, you will be introduced to lots of new vocabulary in college. Each subject area has its own set of terms and meanings of words. You must recognize the terms when you hear them during a lecture and when you read them in the textbook. Terms are likely to appear on quizzes and exams, and classmates may use them during discussions. Take command of the language of your classes.

Most texts have a glossary of terms located in the back so readers can look up words specific to their use in the book. This is probably the best place to start when you encounter new terminology. If you can't find a term there, go to a dictionary. If you are not sure that the dictionary offers the appropriate meaning (based on how it is used in the field of study), then ask your instructor. Ask what he or she believes is the best way to define the term with regard to the context in which the term is used in class.

Sometimes you can determine the meaning through context, spoken or written. However, there are limitations to what you can learn about a word based on its use in a sentence. Here are some words of warning.

- You may need to understand the word itself to really know what the surrounding sentence or paragraph is talking about.

- Even if you can get enough of an idea about the word's meaning as it is used in the sentence, you still don't know the true definition of the word.

- You may misinterpret the sentence or paragraph because you are not familiar with the word.

Assuming the word's meaning incorrectly could hinder your understanding of important concepts. The best strategy is to persist in reading (or listening) as long as you think you have the basic idea of what is being discussed but to write any unknown words down to look up later.

When you communicate about the course topic in your assignments, exams, questions asked in class, and interactions with the instructor, use the correct terminology (and use it correctly). You are expected to learn how to write and talk about the course content as a professional would. Your success in class comes primarily through having a strong grasp of the course material, and the related vocabulary plays a major role.

BUILD IT UP

Learning in class helps you understand new course terminology. How can you build up your vocabulary in general, though? You can develop your command over the English language (or any language, for that matter) in many ways, the first and foremost way being to read. Reading is the key to increasing the number of words you know, as well as your ability to use them. In general, well-read people have rich vocabularies that not only include many words not commonly used but also make use of words in a different but appropriate manner. Take the word *exact,* for example. The word is an adjective in the sentence, *You need to give me the exact date of the battle to get the answer right.* But *exact* is also a verb, as in *I must exact a promise from you that you will not share the secret.* The verb form is less common than the adjective form but is correct nonetheless.

Knowing more words and more uses of words results primarily from exposure to them in books. Never underestimate the power of reading. To increase your vocabulary, read for school, for interest, and for pleasure. Read comedies, adventure, romance, biographies, history, travel diaries. Read novels about families, individuals, animals, places, and events. Don't limit yourself to a single *genre,* or type of book. The greater your experience of life through books, the greater your vocabulary will become, and the more interesting and eloquent a person you will become.

Making regular use of a dictionary and a thesaurus also paves the way to a larger *lexicon* (a selection of words in your vocabulary). Keep a standard dictionary at your desk and carry a pocket dictionary for quick reference throughout the day. When you come across a word you don't know, look it up in your pocket dictionary or write it down to investigate later. It takes time and practice using new words to feel comfortable with them and to have them readily come to mind when necessary. It is rare to learn a new word and be able to use it immediately so it enters your vocabulary. Consider writing each new word on a separate index card. Write the complete definition on the back, including the multiple uses of the word, and file it alphabetically into a small card file. When you have a few extra minutes, peruse your word file to refresh your memory of the new words you've accumulated. You may also want to do this while writing a paper or speech for one of your classes. Just take a quick look to see if any new discoveries stand out as more interesting options than an ordinary word you would have used otherwise.

A thesaurus also is helpful in this circumstance. A *thesaurus* is a book that lists words and synonyms. Writers use a thesaurus to increase the variety in word usage when they write. Think back to our sports interview. Imagine if the athlete had spoken as follows:

> *Well, I knew this would be an extremely competitive game, highlighting the serious rivalry between our two teams. The opposing team's players are well-conditioned athletes, so I was convinced we had to enter the game in top form and expend a great deal of energy. The opposition executed its game strategies proficiently and the players had the physical prowess to match. The competition spurred me on to focus mentally, exert effort skillfully, and perform at my peak ability. I considered the importance of all elements falling into place and was pleased that we were victorious, particularly in light of the difficult task at hand.*

This out-of-the-ordinary response is definitely more colorful than the earlier example. Using a broader variety of words does not necessarily mean using bigger words or words that are unfamiliar to most people. It simply involves choosing a variety of words—sometimes words that are not commonly used. Using a thesaurus, particularly when writing a paper or preparing an oral presentation, can help you break out of the word rut. It can spark ideas for new ways to express the same ideas, which is refreshing for the writer and the reader.

THE PROCESS BEHIND PRESENTATIONS

One of the most intimidating experiences early in college can be the assignment of a major paper or oral presentation. A distant due date for a presentation—either written or oral—listed on the course schedule can incite both panic and gloom. Take a deep breath, relax, and follow a step-by-step process that puts you in control and takes you from panic to presentation. Before you learn what to do, consider your beliefs about how to go about it. Read the Perspective Check.

PERSPECTIVE CHECK: MOUNTAIN OR MOLEHILL?

What goes through your mind when you've been assigned a long-term project? Do you take comfort in the fact that you have several weeks to put it together? Do you believe that you have more than enough time to write and practice your speech, so you don't even have to start for another couple of weeks? Or do you cringe at the weight of a presentation that you're allowed weeks to plan? Do you feel that the amount of time between the assignment and the due date is in direct proportion to the scope of the project? Do you become immobilized for days just imagining that you must prepare to scale a mountain with no map or compass? Or do you equip yourself to take on the task one molehill at a time, making your way toward the final presentation with confidence and relaxed grace?

TARGET A TOPIC

Regardless of the type of presentation you have been assigned, you must first begin by choosing a topic. College instructors do not typically assign specific topics to write or speak about, although they may require a general area of exploration or limit the possibilities to some topics covered in class. Enjoy the opportunity to select your own topic.

IDENTIFY YOUR INTERESTS

When searching for a topic, start with what interests you. It sounds simple and it is. The more interested you are in what you write or speak about, the better your presentation will be. If you must focus on something that you covered in class, review your notes and readings, and highlight all topics you find even remotely interesting. At this point, don't look for specific paper or speech topics. Instead, just look for areas within the course that capture your attention or imagination—a person, an event, a theory, a place, a time period, a process, and so on. Note elements of the material that can sustain your focus.

Once you have collected several possible areas of interest, list them according to preference. The reason you should identify several areas at this stage is that you may discover that what you thought would make a good topic doesn't, and what at first doesn't appear as interesting may become more so as you begin to explore it. Always have a back-up plan. As an example, consider that your psychology professor requires that you do a presentation on some aspect of child development—any period from infancy to adolescence. You recall what you've learned in class so far and realize you were most fascinated by events in infancy. Therefore, you select infancy as the main period of focus. With regard to development during this stage of life, you decide that the areas of greatest interest are language acquisition, theories of social attachment, and emotional maturity.

SPECIFY YOUR SCOPE

Probably one of the biggest challenges is to identify a specific topic that is just the right scope for the assigned project. Make sure your topic is neither too broad nor too narrow.

The first problem is more common. Freshmen are used to writing papers on topics such as "The Alamo" or "The Human Nervous System," which provide general summaries but are inappropriate for college courses. Presentations at the college level should be focused and in-depth. Instructors want to see that students have investigated the topic and discovered substantial relevant details. If your topic is too broad, you will be overwhelmed by the amount of information you need to cover and you won't be able to accomplish the project in the allotted time and page requirement. Your paper or speech will seem incomplete, with many issues untapped and numerous questions unanswered. The focus may appear random or biased.

On the other hand, if your topic is too specific you won't be able to put together a significant presentation. Your information will be too limited and the entire project may seem flimsy and, of course, too short. How can you tell if your topic is just right? By engaging in some preliminary exploration, you should get a feel for it after awhile.

Let's return to the example of the child development presentation. Suppose you review your class notes and textbook again to check the scope of information related to each of your potential topics. Referring to the section on language development in infancy, you find the following subheadings:

The eight stages of language development from birth to year two

Language development in infants born prematurely

Language development in deaf infants

A cross-cultural look at language development in infancy

Language development of infants placed in full-time daycare

You would decide which of these areas strikes you as most interesting, then look up the same information for the other areas of development that originally caught your attention. Then you would identify which of these more specific topics holds the most interest for you and list them in order of preference.

The last step in choosing a topic with the right scope is to do a brief search of recent, relevant information. Your notes and textbook are the best places to start. Check if your professor said very much during the lectures about the topic you selected as your first choice. Check how much space your textbook devotes to the topic. Does it cite many research studies for you to follow up with? If substantial information is available but you are still able to focus on a well-defined area, the topic is a good one to consider.

Suppose you investigate the topic "language development of infants placed in full-time daycare" and discover that the primary issues center around the age at which the infant began daycare, whether the infant has an intact family, and the quality of the daycare provided. There are several specific areas related to your main topic but not so many that you can't address them sufficiently. The topic seems appropriate for a presentation.

Get feedback from your instructor as to what constitutes a good scope for the project. It could save you a lot of grief trying to tackle something too large or producing something inadequate. By assuring yourself that you have a relevant topic of just the right scope, you can help ensure that the rest of the process goes smoothly.

COLLECT YOUR CONTENT

Your topic drives the next step in the process—that is, gathering your material. So far the focus has clearly been on writing or presenting a research paper. It is important to note, however, that college courses may call for other kinds of papers or presentations, including reports (in which you relate what you read or saw), descriptive papers (in which you describe a place, an event, or a process), reflective papers (in which you write about personal experiences and your thoughts regarding them), and creative papers (original works in which you develop characters, a story line, and other elements). In any of these presentations, choosing a topic you find interesting with just the right scope is no less important than for a research paper. You draw inspiration from working on a project that you care about and enjoy thinking about. Establishing a workable goal for what you produce and present enables you to do so successfully.

THE GATHERING PROCESS FOR NONRESEARCH PAPERS

Once you determine the parameters of your story, or you know the experience you would like to reflect on, you follow it up by brainstorming what to include in your presentation. This step begins with no rules or boundaries. It's just you and your topic. List thoughts and ideas and relevant information without limiting or censoring yourself. Produce as much material as you can, filling numerous sheets of notebook paper if you must. This gives you more to work with for completing the project.

Once you've finished brainstorming, take some time off. When you return to your earlier thoughts, begin by highlighting the ideas that you believe will work well in your presentation. After this first round of selection, begin eliminating some ideas. Continue the process until it becomes obvious which are the most substantial and appropriate elements to include in your paper. Don't get rid of your initial idea sheets, though, because you may want to review them again later.

THE RESEARCH PROCESS

The most common writing project in college is the research paper. You will certainly have to write at least one while in college. Many students cringe at the thought of these assignments—but only because they don't realize how easy they can be. Assess your knowledge of how to do a research paper in the Skill Check.

SKILL CHECK: THE ROAD TO RESEARCH

What is the first step down the road to research? Do you know what kind of information you need and where to get it? If you're unsure, who would you ask? What do you do with the information once you have it? How do you know if it's reliable and appropriate to use in your paper or oral presentation? How much of it do you need? If you find there is lots of material on your topic, how do you know which information to use and which to turn down? Are you confident in the steps you take, or are you immobilized at the mere idea of having to do research?

You will probably conduct any research required for your paper or speech in your school library. In college, professors usually expect you to use books, government documents, statistics, and professional journal articles to obtain information for a research paper. Popular magazines and newspaper articles usually are not acceptable because they do not provide firsthand accounts of the material of interest. A magazine such as *Psychology Today,* for example, presents journalists' summaries of research findings. The articles, which simplify the findings, are written to appeal to general public interest. Most likely your psychology professor will want students to read the original findings written by the researchers themselves. Professional sources make a big difference in what you learn.

To find these sources, your first stop is the card catalog or online catalog in the library. The catalog directs users to the books and documents that will help them obtain the information they seek. Use the *Reader's Guide to Periodical Literature* to read abstracts from professional journal articles relating to your topic. You can assess the scope of the information that exists on your topic and, through the abstracts, determine whether a particular article is potentially useful or not.

The Internet can be an unreliable means for research. Some instructors may not allow information obtained from websites, so be clear about their rules before pursuing this line of investigation. As you may recall, there are several things you can look for to evaluate the validity of a website. Do not use any information without going through this process, and, even then, exercise caution with the information you gather.

As much as possible, use recent sources of information in your research. A good rule of thumb is to search only for books and articles written within the past ten years. This way, you can be certain the findings are up-to-date and reflect the current state of knowledge and thinking on the topic. Using outdated materials could result in your paper reporting incorrect information, and your professor will spot this immediately.

Take notes as you peruse the catalog and the *Reader's Guide.* Copy the titles along with all of the bibliographic information so you can easily find the sources themselves. It's a good idea to list the details of each potential source on a separate index card for later reference. Once you have a substantial collection of sources to investigate, proceed to the stacks.

Using the bibliographic information in your notes, track down the books and periodicals you have listed. Once you locate each book, look through the table of contents to see if any chapters specifically pertain to your topic. Don't plan on reading entire books for a basic research paper. Points and quotes obtained from reading through a few target chapters should suffice. Glance through the journal articles for length and clarity of writing. The abstract may have sounded promising, but the article may be too complex for your purpose or may contain extensive information on a huge study. The best approach is to skim the introduction and the conclusion to check how easily you can read and understand them, as well as to determine whether the article provides the information you need. Be prepared to eliminate some of the journal articles as inappropriate for your purpose.

If you fall short of your required number of sources after investigating the materials, conduct another brief search. Once you have your sources, you can begin to read them carefully. With your topic and scope to guide you, read to learn about your subject matter and take notes on the specific information that you would like to include in your paper or speech—background information, known facts, current data, theories, conclusions, remaining questions, and so on. If you copy text straight from the source, use quotation marks to remind yourself that you used the writer's exact words, but be prepared to integrate all of the information together in your own words when you create your presentation. Again, one index card for each individual piece of information prepares you for the next step in the process.

ORGANIZE AND OUTLINE

The previous step should produce a stack of index cards or several notebook pages filled with individual ideas, information, or quotes, along with the sources from which they came. Spend a little time away from your material after you have worked on it for a while. This enables you to be fresh and open-minded when you return to it and ready for the next step.

After your break, reread each index card or all of the notes you gathered. An order and organization should now arise out of the mass of materials as you recall the ideas and information. Every time you read your notes, your mind tries to create a big picture out of the individual pieces. Eventually, the picture starts to come together. Through your research, you fill in the blanks, or round out what you read in your class notes and textbook about the topic. You see the issue in the real world—what researchers are investigating, what they are finding, and what conclusions they are drawing about it.

YOUR THESIS STATEMENT

With this knowledge, you can develop a thesis statement that provides a framework for your entire paper or speech. A *thesis statement* is a single sentence that communicates directly what the presentation is about. It simply and eloquently informs the audience of what they will read or hear.

It is challenging to write a solid, accurate thesis statement without a substantial understanding of the topic, which doesn't fully occur until the research phase of this process. Familiarity with the subject matter, gained from your research, helps you produce the best thesis statement. (Unless your instructor requires that you produce a thesis statement earlier in the process, wait until after you have conducted your research to do so.)

Returning to our earlier example, imagine you have collected a set of book chapters and recent journal articles that address some or all of the following issues:

Language development in infancy

Language development and daycare

Observations of infants placed in full-time daycare

Quality levels of daycare and the developmental milestones in infant participants

You read through everything—skimming the first time, reading sections more closely on subsequent readings—and eventually write this thesis statement:

Language development in infants who are placed in full-time daycare during the first year of life varies with the quality of that care.

This statement reflects the topic chosen (language development in infants in daycare) but specifies a particular focus that the assigned presentation can reasonably address. The thesis statement evolved from the research conducted and provides the foundation for what the paper or speech contains.

A TELLING TITLE

Just as it takes time and a little research to develop an effective thesis statement, you shouldn't rush into creating a title, which is the most basic and eloquent summary of your entire presentation. It should inform and interest your audience about what you will say, in very few words, which is a challenging task. Therefore, the more of your presentation you complete, the easier it will be to write an effective, telling title. The more you work with your topic and organize the information, the clearer the picture of just what it is you are talking about.

Titles can have a tremendous impact on our comprehension of the information that follows. Without a title to ready the mind for what will follow, the text may appear to be just a collection of words with no coherent message. When you read a title, your brain calls up what you already know about the subject and then integrates and makes sense out of what you read. Keep this in mind when you take on the task of creating your title.

Here are some possible titles for our example presentation:

The Daycare Dilemma: Risking Developmental Language Delays in Infancy

Daycare and Language Delay in Infancy: A Question of Quality

Babbling Babies: Boosted or Belated by Daycare?

Which title do you prefer? What others can you think of, based on what you know about the topic?

THE FORMAT OF YOUR PAPER

With your thesis statement established, you can organize your information to create a clear, straightforward presentation. The main points in our example are:

Characteristics of language development in daycare infants in high-quality care

Characteristics of language development in daycare infants in low-quality care

Factors related to daycare that contribute to language development differences

Imagine that this list represents the order in which you have determined the information will best be presented. It flows from providing the audience with the general findings of language development in each group and progresses to show the similarities and differences in language development by way of a comparison. The final point is to inform the audience about how factors related to quality of care contribute to the differences in language development. If you become familiar and comfortable enough with your research materials, your organization should readily present itself.

Once you identify your main points, you can then list your supporting information, evidence, and quotes along with them. Arranging the information in outline form essentially produces the skeleton of your paper or speech. Be specific in your outline so you know exactly what piece of information goes where (see Figure 10.1). This facilitates your task of writing.

Most papers follow the basic format illustrated in Figure 10.2. The first paragraph, represented by the first triangle in the figure, introduces your topic, providing general background information and explaining why it is an important topic to explore. Begin with a broad statement and gradually narrow your focus, ending the paragraph with your thesis statement. Each of the following paragraphs (represented in Figure 10.2 by three rectangles) begins with a *topic sentence* that introduces one of

Figure 10.1
Outline

1. General background information
   a. Children are the future.
   b. Attendance has increased in full-time daycare.
   c. Not all daycare programs are equal; they vary in quality.
   d. Developmental psychologists now study numerous issues related to daycare.
   e. Thesis statement: Language development in infants placed in full-time daycare during their first year of life varies depending on the quality of that care.

2. Language development in infants that attend high-quality daycare: on target and positive
   a. Characteristics of high-quality daycare
      1. Low teacher-infant ratio
      2. High percentage of caregivers' time spent interacting with children
      3. Visually and aurally stimulating environment
   b. Expected or target language development milestones in infancy
      1. Cooing and vocal play: 4–6 months
      2. Babbling: 6 months (reduplicated); 9 months (nonreduplicated)
      3. Expressive jargon: 9–18 months
      4. Vocables: 12–18 months
      5. One-word utterance: 12–18 months
      6. Sentences of two or more words: 18–24 months
   c. Characteristics of language development in infants attending high-quality daycare
      1. On target: expected level of comprehension and vocabulary
      2. Advanced: more words understood and uttered sooner

3. Language development in infants that attend low-quality daycare: delayed and problematic
   a. Characteristics of low-quality daycare
      1. High teacher-infant ratio
      2. Small percentage of caregivers' time spent interacting with infants
      3. Bland, nonstimulating environment
   b. Characteristics of language development in infants attending low-quality daycare
      1. Delayed: limited comprehension and few vocal utterances
   c. Concerns for language delays in infancy
      1. Delay in language development hinders social development due to difficulties with interpersonal interactions.
      2. By preschool age, children lag behind in vocabulary and comprehension.
      3. Preschoolers have difficulty with letter recognition and related sounds.

4. Factors contributing to developmental language differences in infants attending high-quality vs. low-quality daycare
   a. Amount of time that adults speak to infants
      1. In face-to-face conversation
      2. Reading stories
   b. Family factors
      1. Parents of infants in low-quality care are more stressed, spend less time interacting with infant (talking or reading to child).
      2. Parents of infants in high-quality care are less stressed and spend more time with infants at home (talking, reading, singing to child).

5. Language development in infants placed in full-time daycare during their first year of life varies depending on the quality of that care.
  a. Quality of care is reflected in affordability.
  b. Financial status of families determines quality of care and is related to parental time and interactions with infant.
  c. Due to "ripple effect" of delayed language development, quality daycare and parental support should be an important societal focus.
  d. Children are the future, so society should provide the best early-childhood experiences, regardless of family income and status.

Figure 10.1
(*Continued*)

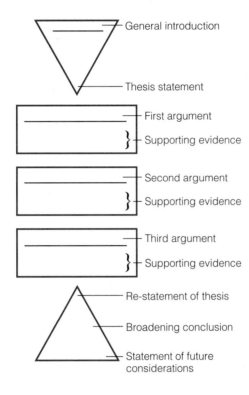

Figure 10.2
Basic Paper Format

the main points (identified earlier and indicated on the outline). The remainder of the paragraph presents your supporting arguments and discusses any evidence or data illustrating the main point. You should have at least one separate paragraph for each main point, presenting them in the order in which you organized your material.

Your last paragraph, or conclusion (represented by the triangle at the bottom of Figure 10.2), starts by restating your thesis statement. It includes a summary of your findings and broadens the scope to end with a general statement as to the importance or societal impact of the topic.

WRITE!

When you have successfully completed all of the steps to this point, you are ready to write. What may have seemed like the most challenging part of the task may now seem little more than a formality.

YOU'RE CLOSER THAN YOU THINK

When you write your outline, also arrange your index cards in the same order. Once you have each item in its place relative to all other items, your presentation is nearly done. All you need to do is communicate it in your own words, writing to connect the ideas and create a coherent whole and expanding your discussion of the individual facts to make them fit appropriately into the flow of the work. Otherwise, you have everything you need, in the correct order, along with the sources you must cite. You are not creating something from nothing as you face a blank screen or sheet of paper. The stack of organized and sequenced index cards *is* the prototype of your paper. All you have to do is bring it to life.

KEEP IT SIMPLE

Your writing should be clear, concise, and mature, reflecting that you are a college student. It does not have to be overly complex. Use the appropriate terminology related to your topic and a varied general vocabulary throughout your presentation. However, you should write for a naïve audience. In other words, imagine that whoever reads your paper or listens to your speech knows very little about the topic. Don't try to write for knowledgeable experts in the field. Instead, write as if you are teaching someone who is new to the ideas.

It is critical to show your instructor that you know and understand the topic. Instructors are your most important audience and the ones who determine your grade. The best way to be sure that they recognize your grasp of the issues is to specify all of the fundamental information in a direct and clear manner. If you try to write at a higher level, attempting to sound intellectual, you run the risk of leaving out important facts or background material that your instructor may be looking for. Don't omit elements due to thinking that the instructor already knows it so there's no sense including it. Your instructors may know it, but they need to see that *you* know it.

Another reason to keep your project basic is to practice for the future. The Boyer Commission Report on the state of undergraduate education mentions that students lack the ability to write for the purpose of teaching others. In the workplace, where these students end up, individuals need to communicate (through both written and oral presentations) to an uninformed audience. The commission report notes that when the emphasis is on technical writing, students do not develop the skills to explain new concepts to those who need to understand them at a basic level. Therefore, consider your presentation a means of communicating at a basic level. Your writing and speaking should be eloquent, easy to follow, and to the point.

REGROUP AND REVISE

Once you have written the first draft of your paper or speech, progressing through your index cards or notes and including all the necessary information, take a break. Leave your project for a day or two and don't think about it. Let others read it and provide feedback (you might distribute it to friends and family for their comments and suggestions), but don't look through the feedback immediately. After you have let your mind relax and regroup from the constant focus, return to your task.

Begin by reading your draft through in its entirety, out loud if possible. (Reading out loud helps you get a feel for the impact of the words, the sentence structure, length, and flow.) Jot down any ideas for changes on your draft. Then review the comments from others. Choose those suggestions you think will improve your work. Then revise it.

Once you have made all of the initial changes, read through your work again. If you feel like your mind is swimming in the material, distance yourself from it for a while and then revisit your paper to see how it is shaping up. There is no ideal number of times that you should review and revise your paper. The key is to gather feedback from others and to allow enough time to make the best effort possible. If your instructor ever offers to give feedback early on, take the opportunity.

THE PEAK OF THE PROCESS

The last step is to finalize your project to present to the instructor or class. All the hard work you have invested up to this point is demonstrated through your presentation. Make it impressive, because, as the Professor's Perspective shows, the culmination of your efforts carries a lot of weight.

PROFESSOR'S PERSPECTIVE: THE WHOLE PACKAGE

What is the point of written and oral presentations? What do professors want you to get out of them, besides a great deal of stress and strain over putting them together? The answer is that they want you to gain many things—probably the least of which is to learn the content you work so hard to obtain, understand, and organize. Instructors assign projects—whether papers or speeches— mainly to give students experience doing all of the tasks necessary to create them in the first place. Of course, through the time and effort involved, students also learn something about the course material. Just as important (if not more important) is that students must:

- Critically think through different subjects to identify a workable focus
- Follow the research process, making use of the library, locating sources, and obtaining information in various forms
- Create an order and an organization of a collection of information
- Communicate effectively about a particular topic

You cover a lot of ground in one assignment. When your instructors determine your grade on a project, they look at the whole package. They don't just consider your intellectual presentation of data. They also examine how you wrote about the topic—the vocabulary you used, the organization of the information, the transitions between ideas, the flow of the paper, the recognition of your audience, and following the guidelines of the assignments. Instructors read or listen to your work and ask themselves, "Does this reflect an understanding of what I asked the students to do?" "Does this demonstrate that a significant amount of time, effort, and thought went into it?" "Does this look like the work of a college student who cares about a grade in this course?" Remember the professor's perspective when you begin your next project.

PERFECTING YOUR PAPER

After working hard on your project for some time, you are ready to produce the final product. Don't burn out now. The paper that you turn in to your instructor should be as perfect as possible, in content as well as in appearance. The final product is the physical representation of all the work you have done. Make it look like the accomplishment it is. Every detail should shine.

Be sure that your spelling, grammar, and punctuation are flawless. There are no excuses for an oversight. Use the spell check and grammar check functions of your word processing application, but use them thoughtfully. If you have any doubts, go to your campus writing center for help, or ask a graduate student in the English department to proofread your paper. Imagine all of your efforts being marred by an error in word use or spelling!

If your instructor specifies margin widths or page layouts, follow them precisely. If the assignment calls for a title page, table of contents, reference page, page numbers, or footnotes, follow the requirements. Little things can add up to detract from a great deal of hard work. Use any recommended handbook to guide elements of style for citing references, such as the *MLA Handbook* or style manuals specific to some disciplines (such as the *Publication Manual of the American Psychological Association*). Follow page length recommendations if the instructor provides them. Instructors provide such recommendations to help students choose a topic with a suitable scope.

Last but not least, make your paper appear professional. Use high-quality, white printer paper for the final copy. Select a basic font style, such as Times New Roman, and do not correct last-minute typing errors with correctional tape or fluid. Fix the problem and reprint the page. Place the paper in a folder to prevent it from getting bent or creased or having coffee spilled on it. What your instructor sees represents you, your work, and your desire to succeed on the assignment. These impressions are powerful.

A SUPERB SPEECH

Oral presentations may accompany a written paper, which should follow all of the guidelines for achieving optimal presentation quality. However, when the peak of the process is to speak to an audience, you must do several things to succeed.

Don't underestimate the power of practice. If you must get up in front of a group and speak, the best thing you can do to prepare is to practice your presentation as many times as possible. This helps you become more familiar with what you are going to say and helps you relax when you do it for real. Practice in front of a mirror to check your posture and facial expressions as well as your ability to make eye contact with the audience. Although you may be allowed to use note cards, you shouldn't rely heavily on them or look down at them constantly. If possible, audiotape or videotape yourself practicing your speech. This gives the greatest insight as to what you need to polish before you present. Check yourself for unnecessary and distracting speech patterns, such as the repetitive use of *you know, like, uh,* and *um* or nervous behaviors such as pacing, tossing your hair, or cracking your knuckles. It's only when you become aware of how often you insert these into your presentation that you can make a concerted effort not to do it.

If you are using any visual aids, practice with them as much as possible beforehand. Whether this involves a set of note cards to use as personal prompts during your speech or visuals for the audience to view, make sure you can handle them gracefully as you incorporate them into your speech. Don't let them detract from what you are saying. Rather, let them enhance but not overpower your presentation. Work deftly to draw as little attention to the handling of your props as possible.

Before you go to class to make your presentation, consider what's best for you physically. Use the restroom and eat something light. You don't want to be uncomfortable or to have your tummy growl during your speech. Be careful about your caffeine intake. You don't want to appear jittery and overly boisterous or to feel revved up at the time of your presentation. Energized but relaxed is the ideal physical state to aim for.

Your appearance is important when you make an oral presentation—if not to your classmates then certainly to your instructor. Dress cleanly and in a manner that shows you have made an effort. To be "easy on the eyes," you may want to avoid overly bright colors, wild patterns, and bold fashion statements. Although you want to look pleasant, you don't want to detract from the presentation.

All speakers face the challenge of getting the audience immediately interested in what they have to say. Be careful about opening with a joke. Think about the topic of your presentation, the nature of the project, and the tone of the class. For some assignments, humor is a wonderful addition if used appropriately and incorporated seamlessly. For other presentations, it will not be acceptable at all and could cost you points toward your grade. An alternative to obvious humor or specific jokes is a personal story or vignette related to the subject matter. If you have just the right experience, sharing it at the beginning to introduce your topic can be an effective way to draw your audience in.

The last thing to consider when you make your presentation is allowing time for questions at the end. Ask your instructor if this is preferable, and then be prepared to interact with your audience and address comments and questions.

CREATE A WORKABLE SCHEDULE

Having a lot of time to plan and complete a project can produce anxiety or relief, depending on what you do with that time. You can waste it and become a stressed-out wreck or use it wisely, create a successful project, and remain relaxed. It's your choice.

YOU'RE NOT SUPERMAN

Some students equate writing a paper with leaping a tall building in a single bound or climbing Mount Everest from sea level. Taking the Superman approach to large projects is one reason students have a hard time getting started. As you know, any project that requires a great deal of thought and effort is really a series of smaller tasks, many of which don't take much time or a great deal of mental energy. Each step is important and provides invaluable experience, but that does not necessarily mean it takes hours of intense critical thought.

You already know the steps involved in creating an effective paper or oral presentation. Now you can learn how to approach those steps with regard to time and scheduling. Time management is critical for successfully completing a long-term project. Procrastination has an especially harmful effect on such projects. Once you run out of time, you simply cannot get it back. It sounds obvious, but you also must recognize the implications of facing a truly impossible situation, of literally not having enough time to do everything that needs to be done. If you can't give sufficient time to choosing an appropriate topic, the rest of your efforts will flounder. If you can't locate the source materials you researched, you will have nothing to write about. If you don't have time to organize the information you collected, your paper will appear to be sloppily thrown together.

THE SNOWBALL EFFECT: MAKE IT ROLL THE RIGHT WAY

Your efforts (or lack thereof) begin a cycle that gains momentum with time. Be sure that your momentum is building in the right direction. When you begin your project—with even the smallest task—you start off on the right foot, no matter what. If you briefly brainstorm possible topics, look through your notes and textbook to gather potential ideas, or sketch a story line, you have begun. You know it, and it feels good. For most people, being productive is all it takes to motivate them to do more. Every effort toward completing a project builds confidence and demonstrates progress. Checking things off your to-do list and watching your tasks diminish drives you to do more and to complete tasks sooner. Working this way tends to make people feel relaxed and ready to focus on each new step. When you produce a great finished product, you feel proud of what you have accomplished.

However, the outcome can take an opposite turn. When you have a long-term assignment but don't work on it, you still think about it and it doesn't feel good. It hangs over you like a dark cloud and stresses you out. The longer you put it off, the more anxious you become because you are aware that you have increasingly less time to tackle the project. As the project time frame diminishes, the harder it is to get started because the task looms larger. The initial frustration at having to do a long-term project turns to dread over having to do it in so little time. The momentum of your procrastination builds, along with your stress level, while your confidence and outlook for success fall. You soon realize that no matter how hard you try, you're not likely to do a very good job in the time remaining. And when you do begin to take on the tasks, you may be so stressed that instead of concentrating on the subject at hand you may only be able to think about how fast the clock is ticking. Some students say they work best under pressure, but don't believe them.

ANY TIME, ANY PLACE

The point is to get started right away and be productive. Make it happen whenever, wherever, and however you can. For example, your first task is to find a topic. Leaving class after just having received your assignment, you can read through your notes and textbook for ideas in the few minutes before your professor comes in for your next class or while getting a bite to eat or just before you turn off the light and go to sleep. Exploring general topics and identifying what interests you should take 10 to 15 minutes.

Once you have a basic idea of your focus, brainstorm specifics while taking a shower, driving to school, walking across campus, eating breakfast, or working out. Calmly think through the subjects related to the options you have chosen and consider which ones interest you. Jot down your reactions in a small notebook you carry with you for this purpose.

For research-based steps (such as looking up resources available to determine your scope), be as efficient as possible. If you have access to your school's library databases from your home computer, you won't even have to make a trip to campus. You might also do a quick Internet search to get an idea of how much information is available on your topic. General searches don't take long, so try to squeeze it in between other responsibilities. If you have a break between classes, head to the library to take some notes on potential resources. If you're at home waiting for a friend to show up to play basketball, surf the Internet for topic links while you wait. Use brief intervals of time to make progress on your project. Every little bit counts.

Eventually you need to spend longer amounts of time on project tasks. When you begin your research in earnest—reading abstracts to select useful sources, locating and viewing the sources to determine if you can use them, and then reading through them to gather relevant information—you need to plan ahead and commit to prolonged concentration. However, be realistic about what you can do. Remember, if you reach a point when you are no longer productive, it is a waste of time to go through the motions without making progress. Instead, designate 30 minutes to an hour for library time, reading articles, and even writing your draft. When you need to take a break, do so. When you limit your work periods to time frames that you are comfortable with, you are more likely to keep to your schedule and approach tasks with the determination to make the time count. The thought of sitting in the library for two or three hours may be so discouraging that you procrastinate instead.

THE SPECIFICS OF SCHEDULING

When you have a long-term project to plan for, begin with the due date. Working backward from this point ensures that you allow enough time to put the final touches on the presentation and prepare to present it to your instructor. Use the following process to help you develop the ideal plan for completing a large project efficiently. It is based on a six-week schedule, but you can easily alter it to fit a longer or shorter time frame.

1. Identify the due date on the calendar and note all other commitments that demand your time. Work around your other responsibilities.

2. Plan to have your entire presentation complete at least two full days prior to the due date. This will allow for computer or printing problems as well as any last-minute emergencies.

3. With this early deadline in mind, plan to work on your final revision three or four days prior to the actual due date.

4. You probably will benefit from taking a break for a day or two before you do your final revision, so allow for this in your schedule. It is a good time to work on other school tasks.

5. Schedule to finish the first complete draft of your paper no later than one week prior to the due date. Therefore, allow yourself several days to write this draft.

6. Once you have identified the date by which you want to start writing the full draft, go back to the beginning to schedule preliminary tasks.

7. Allow yourself two or three days to identify your topic. If necessary, include a basic search to assess information available for possible topics, enabling you to choose one of appropriate scope.

8. Consider another two or three days to research potential sources, which involves library time with the online catalog, databases, and the *Reader's Guide to Periodical Literature,* taking notes on books and articles that look relevant to the topic.

9. Depending on the number of possible sources noted, you may only need a day or two to find the actual sources themselves, skim them, and determine if they are useful.

10. Once you have a sufficient number of sources, allow yourself a week to read them and take notes. During this week, you can take breaks of a day or two. By the end of seven days, plan to have gathered the data, information, and quotes that you will use in your presentation.

11. Plan for two or three days to organize your information. This step may proceed quickly or may require some additional reading and thinking through the sources you have collected.

When you arrive at the last step, you should be closing in on what you have already mapped out for writing time. Make your adjustments according to how the previous steps meet up with the writing and revising steps. If you come to your allotted writing time too late in the schedule, you should shorten the amount of time you give to the earlier processes. Do not take away from your established writing time frame. It is much easier to develop your topic in a day or two or weed out resources in a single library visit than to write a whole presentation in a shorter period of time. Even if you are able to write quickly, don't take the chance of not having sufficient time to write.

If you have more time than six weeks to work on your project, consider making your own personal due date earlier. Giving yourself a cushion of time for last-minute

Figure 10.3
Schedule for Project
Completion

9/8	Assignment received
10/20	Assignment due (6 weeks)
September	
8–10	Topic exploration
11–14	Research potential sources
15–16	Find sources and narrow possibilities
17	Break
18–25	Read sources and gather useful information
26–29	Break (study for accounting exam)
30–31	Organize information
October	
3–4	Break
5–12	Write draft
13–14	Break
15–18	Revise
18	Paper in final form—print out, prepare to turn in
20	Turn in paper

issues is preferable to working up to the last minute. With a longer time frame for completing a project, you are also likely to find that you have periods when other assignments and exams require your attention. Use these as built-in breaks from your long-term project. You may have to take several days to study on a couple of different occasions, so take that into consideration when you schedule your presentation assignment.

However you choose to manage your time for a long-term project, plan to work on the early steps as soon as possible. Remember, putting them off—even when you know you have a great deal of time to complete the project—is likely to result in further procrastination and stress. Jump-start your momentum to guide your time management. See Figure 10.3 for a sample project schedule.

AVOID PLAGIARISM

Plagiarism is the act of taking another person's written work or ideas and passing them off as your own. This is a form of academic dishonesty—namely, cheating—and schools do not tolerate it. Consult your student handbook to find out how your own institution deals with instances of plagiarism. It's important to fully understand what this serious offense involves.

INTENTIONAL PLAGIARISM

Students who intentionally plagiarize are likely to do so for any or all of the following reasons:

Lack of time to do their own work

Laziness

Lack of confidence in their ability to succeed on an assignment

The belief they won't get caught

Plagiarism makes writing papers and speeches easier, because it relieves the need for original thought and extensive research. Perhaps most important, it saves a lot of time. However, the consequences for plagiarism are grave.

Plagiarism can take several forms. Any time that you take a passage from someone else's work and put it in your work, without using quotation marks around it and identifying who originally wrote them, you are plagiarizing. Furthermore, any time you take someone else's idea from a work and present it in yours without giving the person credit for it, you are plagiarizing. It is critical that you include citations for others' contributions.

A popular myth that goes around in high school and that remains with many college freshmen is that changing every third or fourth word in a sentence taken from an original source is acceptable. This is not true. Rather, it is a feeble attempt to disguise the plagiarism. The only acceptable way to include the ideas, findings, theories, and thoughts of another in your work is to give credit where credit is due.

Intentional plagiarism isn't limited to using excerpts from other people's writings. It also includes putting your name on another person's paper. Many websites today sell college level term papers. Students can submit a credit card number and just buy success—until they're caught. Just because these businesses exist does not mean that what they do is acceptable.

Most instructors are aware of these websites and recognize how to spot such plagiarism. There are many things that alert them to bought or borrowed papers, such as the quality. Many of the papers you can buy on the Internet are simply too good. If a freshman or sophomore turned in a paper that were this good, the instructor would immediately suspect plagiarism.

Papers are available online for just about every topic imaginable, but that doesn't mean that they all reflect the ideas, terminology, and scope of what an instructor or the textbook has presented in your particular class. A paper that approaches a topic from a very different angle or in an unusual manner, given what you have been exposed to in your course, would give you away. Also, instructors are likely to have a sense of the kind of student you are by the time you turn in a major paper in class. They will be aware of whether you regularly attend class, how you have performed on tests and quizzes, and your writing style on assignments. Any paper that isn't coherent with your work level in class will raise a red flag for plagiarism.

Given that most identified cases of plagiarism result in a failing course grade (at the least), or expulsion from the institution (at most), it is never a risk worth taking. Besides, you can't possibly feel worthy of your success when it isn't genuine. The best way to avoid being tempted to plagiarize is to manage your time wisely, find motivation to do well, and make the effort to get the work done.

UNINTENTIONAL PLAGIARISM

Not all plagiarism is intentional. You might engage in this behavior and not even realize it. However, the results are not necessarily less severe than if you plagiarized intentionally.

The primary form of unintentional plagiarism is sharing work. Suppose that the assignment for one of your classes is to write a computer program. You find that you are stuck on a step and ask a classmate for help. She offers you hers to take a look at, which you do, and you figure out what you were missing. It may seem innocent enough. You didn't set out to copy her work, and you made the effort to do it on your own. You just needed a little bit of help. However, your instructor may not see it this way. When you are assigned an independent project, your instructor may expect that you consult only the textbook or the instructor for assistance. Working together with a classmate (unless the instructor specifically assigned collaborative work) may constitute plagiarism. If you work math problems in the exact same way as a classmate, cite the same sources for a paper, or answer essay questions with the same arguments, you could be questioned about it. Instructors never like to see close parallels in students' work. They know that the same idea can be approached and expressed numerous ways, and they will be suspicious if two or more students have similar wording or methods in their work.

Typically, guilt is assigned to both the user and the provider of plagiarized materials. Whether you are the one who inadvertently copied the classmate's information or the one who shared your notes, calculations, or writing with a classmate to simply help out, you could be charged with plagiarism. The Student Scenario illustrates how dangerous our choices can be.

STUDENT SCENARIO: I JUST NEEDED A LITTLE HELP!

Kim was surviving the semester fairly well. She enjoyed school, for the most part, and her grades usually were good. After midterms, things began getting hectic, especially with the assignment of a research paper in her sociology course. It was due at finals time, so she had about eight weeks to get it done. Kim knew it would be tough with the demands from her other courses, her service learning project, and her job as a waitress. Eight weeks was a long time, though, and she felt confident that there would be ample opportunity.

With her busy schedule, time flew by and Kim became concerned when she realized that finals were fast approaching. With only four more weeks, she still hadn't given much thought to her paper. Even so, a month was enough time to produce a quality presentation. She was a good student and understood the course material well.

Despite her intentions to schedule time for her paper, Kim focused on other priorities and panic set in with only two weeks left until the due date. Seeing how stressed Kim was, her roommate, Rima, mentioned that a good friend of hers had taken the same sociology course a couple of years ago. He was an outstanding student and she was certain he had probably done well on this assignment. Because he saved all of his work, he was likely to still have it. Rima asked Kim if she would like to take a look at the paper for inspiration.

Kim thought that this might be a good idea. Seeing an example of what the instructor wanted was likely to serve as a good model for her to work from, and it would help guide her in choosing a topic and doing research. She obtained the paper, read through it, and worked with it by her side. Her time was running out and her anxiety was rising. Kim thought that by writing her paper on the same topic, she could complete it in time because the references were already supplied. The research phase could be greatly reduced and she could easily just change the wording around to make the work her own.

Kim ended the semester with confidence, believing she had performed well on all of her exams. She had completed her written project on time, handing in a beautifully typed paper. Her world came crashing down, however, when her sociology professor called to inform her that he was scheduling a meeting with the dean to discuss disciplinary measures for her plagiarism.

Consider the following questions:

- What went wrong for Kim?

- What specific things could she have done to avoid the panic that led her to desperate measures?

- Was Kim wrong to look at the other student's paper? Why or why not?

- Did Kim plagiarize intentionally or unintentionally? Explain.

- How might she have used the paper as a guide without plagiarizing?

- Should the student who wrote the original paper be held responsible for Kim's plagiarizing? Why or why not?

- What other options did Kim have for dealing with her situation, given that she did not have enough time remaining to write an acceptable paper?

GIVING PROPER CREDIT

How do you ensure that you are not plagiarizing? The most obvious step is to avoid using anyone else's previously completed work as your own (whether purchased on the Internet or obtained through a student network). Also, always be sure to do your own work. This does not mean that you can't have study groups prior to exams or even discuss aspects of class for assignments and projects. Simply be cautious when it comes to producing your work. Do your math and other science problems on your own. Develop computer programs or accounting worksheets without input from others (except your instructor or teaching assistant). When it comes to written or oral projects, choose a unique topic and gather your own sources. Support your classmates in their efforts, listen and provide input for their ideas, and encourage them to go with their interests, but don't work together or choose similar topics for presentations for the purpose of sharing resources.

When you do use information, ideas, and quotes from other sources, cite them properly. There are various ways to acknowledge your source, so check with your instructor for the preferred format.

An easy method for giving proper credit is to incorporate the name of the author and the work into the sentence that provides the information. This keeps the flow of the text and gives a clear reference for the reader. For example:

In his book, Your Guide to College Success, *John Santrock states that students should use direct quotations sparingly, relying only on the author's exact words if they are unable to convey the message as eloquently themselves.*

In some cases, this method may not be easy, as in the case of numerous authors. Also, if you have multiple references in a brief written passage, the writing stagnates if each sentence must include a citation. Other, more common options for acknowledging the original source of the idea or information are to place the reference in parentheses and to use footnotes. Each discipline has its own particular style for presenting bibliographic information and citations, but a reference made within the body of the paper looks basically like this:

When you write, only include direct quotes when they are so eloquently written that you feel you can't capture the same message yourself. Therefore, plan to use them sparingly (Santrock & Halonen, 2004).

You can also embed the citations within your sentence rather than after it. This is helpful when you need to present related ideas from different sources at the same time. For example:

Students who are more likely to plagiarize have been observed to have lower standardized test scores (Jones, 2001), *work more than 30 hours a week in addition to attending college* (Smith, 2003), *and reportedly are uncertain as to what they want to do after graduation* (Johnson, 1998).

The names and dates in the citation refer to the full bibliographic information presented in the References or Bibliography section of your paper. These pages are located at the end of your manuscript and list all works in alphabetical order by author. That way, readers can look up a particular reference and get all of the necessary information to read that original work themselves.

Unlike embedded citations, footnotes contain bibliographic information. A footnote is indicated by a superscripted numeral following the statement of a particular idea or piece of information. That numeral appears again at the bottom of the page, along with the full bibliographic reference. (You can see examples of footnotes throughout this text.)

When you develop your presentation, remember that it must be your work. This is in contrast with some assignments, such as research papers, in which students are expected to write about the theories, findings, and conclusions of others. A presentation can be more challenging because students are required to use their own words to present the ideas of other people. Just because the words are yours does not mean that you can take credit for the message. Acknowledge your sources fully and correctly to avoid plagiarizing.

CHAPTER 10 REVIEW QUESTIONS

1. Why is it important to build your vocabulary in college?

2. What are the two most common mistakes students make when choosing a topic for a paper or a speech? What can you do to avoid making either of these mistakes?

3. List the steps to researching a paper in the order in which you would carry them out.

4. What are the steps in the process of producing a written or oral presentation?

5. What are some of the key elements and strategies for managing your time when you have a long-term assignment?

6. What is plagiarism? Provide three examples.

7. How is it possible to unintentionally plagiarize?

SKILLS PRACTICE

1. Rewrite each of the following sentences to use more interesting and sophisticated vocabulary and communicative style.

The study shows that children watch more television the older they get.

There are a lot of different reasons for what the study found.

It is important that the company keep track of all of the money it spends and makes.

Many women were not happy that they could not vote, so they worked together to change the situation.

Some people agree with the professor's opinion on why the battle was so important, but other people don't.

2. Use a thesaurus to find synonyms for the following words. For each word, write at least two synonyms that you might choose if you wanted to convey their meaning in a presentation.

disagreement	invent
shy	natural
help	edge
cold	use
prove	right

3. Visit your library and become familiar with its resources. Flip through the card catalog or scroll through the online catalog. Check out several of the online databases to see what kinds of information are available to you. Read some abstracts in the *Reader's Guide to Periodical Literature,* wander through the stacks, find where the periodicals are located. Write about your discoveries.

4. Go to www.historychannel.com/speeches and listen to some of the famous speeches of the past. What makes them so dynamic? What words or phrases stand out? What do you notice about the delivery in terms of tone of voice, intonation, and phrasing?

5. Even if you don't have an oral presentation assigned, begin practicing how you communicate to others. Videotape yourself or stand in front of a mirror as you speak on a topic you know very well (such as a hobby, family, or hometown). Be as poised as possible, speak clearly, and make eye contact. When you see how you present yourself to others, you can begin working on those areas that need improvement. This can help not only in major class presentations, but with interpersonal communication with classmates, instructors, and job interviews in future.

What are your presentation strong points?

What elements need improvement?

What steps will you take to change your presentation style?

CURRENT COURSE APPLICATION

1. Are you keeping up with the new terminology from all of your courses? Do you feel comfortable with what your instructor says during lectures? Can you easily understand what you read in your textbooks? Do you highlight new words in your notes and the book? Consider creating your own minidictionary for each class. List all new terms and definitions (preferably in your own words) and practice using the terms appropriately before the exam or a class paper.

2. Which of your textbooks or other course reading materials do you like the most? What appeals to you about the book? What elements of the writing style stand out to make the book interesting to read? What do you find lacking or difficult with the writing in the books that are less appealing? Consider the books you read for pleasure. Do you have a favorite author? What makes his or her writing style effective? What kinds of books do you find unappealing? Why?

3. Do you have any upcoming papers to write or oral presentations to give? If so, have you designed a schedule for completing them? Are you sticking to it? Why or why not? If you don't have a plan or yours isn't working, try to manage your time using the suggestions in this chapter. How might this method help you?

4. Even if you don't have a paper or speech assigned in any of your classes, consider what topics you might pursue if you were required to develop a presentation for at least two of your classes. What topics look interesting to you? What aspects of those topics would you like to learn more about? Which ones lend themselves to a more in-depth investigation?

5. Consider situations in which you might be at risk for plagiarizing. Are you in the habit of working closely with classmates on individual assignments? Do you frequently share answers, ideas, or information? Do you try to be helpful to others by letting them view your work? Have you ever been tempted to copy someone else's work? Which work habits might you have to change to ensure that you aren't accused of plagiarizing?

TAKE A LOOK ONLINE

To listen to some great speeches of the past, go to

www.historychannel.com/speeches/

For an interactive website with vocabulary games and lists of terms for tests such as the Graduate Record Examination (GRE) and the Test of English as a Foreign Language (TOEFL), check out

http://supervoca.com/

The following website offers detailed information on writing:

http://nutsandbolts.washcoll.edu/

STUDENT SCENARIO DISCUSSION RESPONSES

- **What went wrong for Kim?** Kim failed to plan ahead and manage her time effectively. Had she mapped out a schedule for working on her paper as soon as she received the assignment, she would have incorporated it into her daily routine.

- **What specific things could she have done to avoid the panic that led her to desperate measures?** Besides getting off to a good start by scheduling, she should have created a plan from the moment she realized she hadn't started it yet. It would have been a tighter schedule, but a good student like Kim probably would have been able to stick to it. She could have broken down each step in the process into smaller steps to carry out whenever she could—brainstorming on the way to work, reading resources during breaks, going to the library during her lunch hour. Any small task to get her momentum going would have helped.

- **Was Kim wrong to look at the other student's paper? Why or why not?** She wasn't wrong to review a paper that modeled what the instructor was looking for. She was wrong to use it as the basis for her own and to rely on it to reduce her original work.

- **Did Kim plagiarize intentionally or unintentionally? Explain.** Kim plagiarized unintentionally because she did not set out to use the other student's work and thought that rewriting it was acceptable. However, she was still passing the other student's work off as her own. Because she used the same topic (when there are numerous choices for a sociology paper), incorporated the same references (instead of doing any research on her own), and just changed some of the wording, her paper is not an original piece of work.

- **How might she have used the paper as a guide without plagiarizing?** Seeing what constitutes a good paper in a particular course or with a given instructor can be helpful. Kim could have gained a clearer picture of the scope of the project and how a topic can reflect that scope. She could have assessed the type and number of references used to determine the extent of her own research and the detail expected by the instructor. She could have noted the writing style to understand an acceptable approach and the presentation of information to understand how to organize her own paper.

- **Should the student who wrote the original paper be held responsible for Kim's plagiarizing? Why or why not?** Just as Kim did not intentionally set out to plagiarize, the student who wrote the original paper did not intentionally provide his paper so it could be copied for a grade. In fact, he was probably unaware that Kim would do such a thing. Rima had likely just asked to borrow it so Kim could get an idea of what was expected. However, this would not necessarily relieve him of responsibility according to some instructors.

- **What other options did Kim have for dealing with her situation, given that she did not have enough time remaining to write an acceptable paper?** When situations become desperate in school, there usually are options, particularly for good students. With two weeks left, Kim might have tried to relieve some non-school-related obligations. She might have been able to take some time off work to write her paper. If money was a problem, she might have turned to her family for a small loan to get her through this difficult situation. Barring the possibilities of finding more time in her schedule, Kim could have talked with her instructor. Because she had demonstrated that she was a competent student who did good work and cared about her grade, she might have been able to receive an incomplete for the course and then finish any remaining work later, according to an agreed-upon schedule with the instructor. At that point, the incomplete would be replaced with the earned course grade.

11 PREPARE THOROUGHLY FOR EXAMS

In this chapter you will learn

⚙ The many benefits of exams

⚙ The various levels of understanding and the role of information processing

⚙ Study methods for making the most of memory

⚙ The nature and causes of test anxiety and how to reduce its negative effects

⚙ Important pretest information

⚙ THE PURPOSE OF EXAMS

Exams are fundamental to the college experience. They often cause dread and anxiety, especially when they are considered singular events of critical importance. In fact, they can be the greatest contributor to a course grade.

You may feel as if your instructors are out to make your life miserable when they place a heavy emphasis on exams. The truth is, they understand the many benefits provided by the test experience. Think about your perspective on tests. What does the experience mean to you?

MAJOR MOTIVATORS

Imagine if when you registered for college you received your books, a schedule of class times so you could attend lectures on the vital material, and then were left on your own to gather and learn the necessary information. If your institution simply trusted you to independently achieve the level of understanding and breadth of knowledge expected of a college graduate, would you do it? Despite your best intentions, you probably wouldn't. You might achieve success in a few courses directly

PERSPECTIVE CHECK: NOT ANOTHER TEST!

When you receive a course syllabus at the beginning of the semester, do your eyes go directly to the requirements? Do you hurry to find out how many exams you'll have and what kind they'll be—short answer, multiple choice, essay? Do you immediately feel apprehensive about a course in which the entire grade is determined by test scores? When you listen to the lecture or read the textbook, are you distracted by thoughts of how much information will be on the exam or how difficult it will be to learn?

Instead, maybe you actually like exams. Do you get a burst of adrenaline right before the test is distributed, knowing that you can release all of the information stored in your brain once the exam is finished? Do you look forward to the chance to meet the challenge before you? Your perception of college exams can make a tremendous difference in how well you perform on them.

related to your major. However, as for the rest of the experiences associated with your core courses and various electives, your approach most likely would range from "Forget this!" to "I just didn't seem to get around to it." Learning independently requires considerable self-motivation and willpower.

Exams provide periodic assessments of how much learning has occurred. At the most basic level, exams serve as a "kick in the pants" to help students achieve their goals. Suppose you're considering skipping class one day. Realizing that the lecture material is likely to be on the next test may override your thoughts of leisure. Daydreaming in class might be tempting, but knowing that detailed notes are critical for reviewing before the test helps keep you focused. The same motivating force helps you complete reading assignments, work problems in math and science, and prompts you to understand the material. Exams can provide you with the purpose for doing what it takes to learn the material.

THE LESSON IS IN THE LEARNING

You take your seat with sharpened pencil in hand. The blank pages of the exam stare up at you. It's the moment of truth—or is it? Taking exams can be an intense experience, and the results certainly are important. The test itself, though, is simply a final destination in the journey of learning. Everything you do to prepare for the exam is what really counts. The test just lets you demonstrate how far you've come.

Instructors give exams to evaluate what students have gained from the course up to that point. They want to see if you have understood the material and know how to communicate about it. They check that you have accumulated all of the important facts and details that make your knowledge complete. They need to know if you are able to apply the concepts in appropriate ways. Exams are ultimately opportunities for students to share their intellectual accomplishments with their professors.

Performing well on tests involves active listening, effective note taking, reading different kinds of materials written in a variety of styles, critical thinking, writing, time management, and other skills. When you identify important information, paraphrase it for reference, interpret the meaning, relate it to other information, and remember it all to share at one sitting, you are engaging in the true test. Through those activities, you enhance the skills that are valuable for future success, not for what takes place during the brief test time. If you do well on your exams, your instructors recognize that you learned the fundamental lesson of working to master the material. The Professor's Perspective shows how professors are tuned in to what students do to prepare for a test.

What if you *don't* do well on an exam? This is an important lesson as well. You probably recognize when you are not prepared. If it's obvious, you might admit that you just didn't do the necessary work. You may think you studied substantially and put enough time into preparing but are surprised by the difficulty of the test. Consider this a wake-up call. If you perform poorly on an exam, it means that something went wrong during the preparation phase. Did you go to class regularly? Maybe the information from the lectures is more critical than you originally thought. Were your notes sufficient? Maybe you didn't have a good record of the information you needed to learn. Did you understand your readings? Maybe you didn't pay enough attention or follow through with the concepts that you found confusing. Did you give enough time to studying? Maybe you believed you could put it all together and commit it to memory more quickly than was possible.

It is critical to assess your preparation strategies when you receive a low test score, rather than turning all of your attention to the test itself. If you tackle the learning process successfully, you have a good chance of performing well.

PROFESSOR'S PERSPECTIVE: ATTENDANCE OPTIONAL (BUT I'M WATCHING)

Sometimes professors or their teaching assistants arrange review sessions prior to an exam. You may have the option to attend and, if you opt out, there is no detriment to your grade—at least, not directly. Instructors organize such sessions on their own time, and you should view it as a generous gift. Review sessions offer a great opportunity to get last-minute questions answered. Because instructors take time out of their busy schedules for these events, they certainly aren't going to waste their time talking about things that are unimportant. Review sessions also are a great chance to learn what the instructor thinks is critical and the material that is most likely to be on the test. Instructors often reward students who attend such sessions by suggesting specific areas to study and the level of detail to expect. You may gain insight on anything from the exact format of the exam (how many of each kind of question) to some actual test questions. You have the chance to discuss the topics with classmates who also have taken the initiative to attend (and who are likely to be focused, conscientious students) and to get some additional time with your instructor. Instructors who offer review sessions notice which students are there.

Subjective test questions can be challenging to grade. Despite an instructor's certainty as to the desired answer, he or she may not have considered how students might interpret the question. Also, students may struggle to communicate effectively. When a response is ambiguous, the instructor must make a judgment call. Instructors are more likely to give the benefit of the doubt to a student who has taken advantage of a review session.

WHAT IT MEANS TO STUDY

Preparing for tests involves studying. Studying means doing something to enable you to remember all of the information to answer questions on the exams. Whether a person actually recalls the information depends on many factors.

LEVELS OF UNDERSTANDING

As you know, learning is not an all-or-nothing proposition. You do not either know something or not know it. Rather, there are degrees of understanding regarding topics. You know a little about some things, understanding in the most basic way. You may have a deep knowledge of other things and may grasp the most complex concepts for the entire scope of the issue. For example, you may know all of the rules of football, understand the play calling and team formations, and be able to call penalties faster than the referees. On the other hand, you may know very little about making music. You may know that it involves notes and rhythm, you might have heard something about scales and keys, but you might not be able to describe them. Whereas you may be an expert in football, you may have only a basic grasp of the elements of music.

In 1956, psychologist Benjamin Bloom recognized this phenomenon of different levels of comprehension and developed a *taxonomy,* or classification system, for intellectual behaviors associated with learning. Bloom's taxonomy describes six levels of thought that can occur when people think or read. Each level corresponds to a type of exam question and the thinking you are expected to do to successfully address it. When depicted graphically, Bloom's taxonomy takes the form of a pyramid. The base represents the most fundamental level of understanding. The levels higher on the pyramid represent increasing deeper understanding. Each level becomes more thorough and more intellectually demanding.

Imagine that you are learning about political polls in your political science class. Here are some descriptions of your thinking at each level of Bloom's taxonomy, beginning at the bottom of the pyramid and proceeding to the peak. The words in italics indicate the intellectual activity.

- If you are asked to *state* what polls are, to *identify* the different kinds of polls, to *repeat* some findings from polls, or to *recognize* what kind of population sample was obtained for a poll, your understanding is being assessed at the most basic level—that of recall or general knowledge of the subject matter.

- If you are asked to *explain* in your own words what political polls are and why they are used, to *describe* how they work, or to *discuss* their role in politics, you are showing your comprehension or understanding of the subject matter. To do so, you cannot rely solely on memorized facts but, rather, will have processed the information conceptually.

- Thinking further, you may be asked to *interpret* data collected by polls, to *use* polls to gather your own information, and to *demonstrate* how they yield significant information. Doing these things illustrates your ability to *apply* knowledge and understanding of political polls in appropriate ways.

- When you *compare and contrast* findings from different polls, *analyze* the distinction between various polls, *examine* the effects of using different populations in a poll, and *question* poll results based on how the poll was conducted, you understand the material to the extent of analysis. In other words, you can objectively assess the elements and draw conclusions by critically thinking about the topic.

- The next higher level of understanding is *synthesis*. It involves the ability to *design* your own polls, *formulate* a plan to use them to gain information, *propose* which populations you will use and collect the necessary demographics to help you prepare your idea for conducting the poll.

- The peak of understanding a subject is demonstrated through effective *evaluation*. When you are able to *argue for or against* the use of polls to obtain information, *assess the value* of a particular poll, and *estimate the outcome* of a poll based on the population polled, you are thinking at the most thorough and sophisticated level.

College exam questions may represent any of these levels of thinking, but you should see more of the higher level variety as you progress through school. College emphasizes thinking and learning, which means you must grasp the information more fully at a conceptual level. This occurs through deep processing—critically thinking and working with the material in significant ways. The good news is that you can control your level of learning. Through your own efforts, you can determine how well you understand the subject matter and what level of thinking you achieve.

THE INFORMATION PROCESSING MODEL

The phrase *mentally process the information* appears throughout this book. Mental processing involves actively working with information in your brain to make it meaningful. What happens exactly when you mentally process information?

Your brain is constantly bombarded with information from your five senses—sight, hearing, smell, taste, and touch. The information can be as bold and enthralling as the tune you crank on your CD player or as subtle as the squeak of your professor's shoes. What makes it easy to learn the lyrics to a song you like but nearly impossible to recall what Dr. Rickman's shoes look like? It's all a matter of what you choose to think about. When you pay attention to something, it stays with you. When you ignore it, it fades away (see Figure 11.1).

According to the information processing model, the first stage of the memory process involves weeding out information because the brain can't possibly attend to everything the body senses. This typically happens without your knowing it, or *unconsciously*. Sometimes you deliberately, or *consciously,* ignore some sights and sounds around you (for example, when you tune out your roommate's phone

Figure 11.1
Information Processing

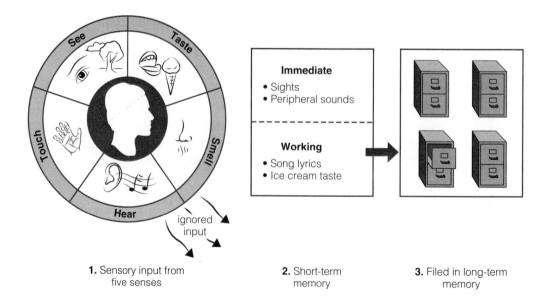

1. Sensory input from five senses

2. Short-term memory

3. Filed in long-term memory

conversation). More likely, you simply decide to focus on some things while letting other input fall by the wayside.

When you give something your attention, it enters what is known as *short-term memory (STM)*—the second stop along the memory path. It holds the information that you are currently thinking about. There are two elements to short-term memory. The conscious awareness of what you are doing at each moment may be viewed as a part of STM called *immediate memory*.[1] The words you are reading now are entering your immediate memory. *Working memory* is the portion of STM in which you actively think about information. For example, if you want to make sure you remember the distinctions between these two parts of STM, you may stop reading so you can think about them more thoroughly. You might consider how you have experienced each type of memory and think of ways to make them more vivid in your mind. (For working memory, you might envision little laboring brain cells lifting heavy pieces of information.) Whatever you choose to do—think, take notes, create images or examples—you are making an effort to keep the concepts in your mind to learn and understand them.

STM is aptly named because of its limitations. Information can stay active only for a limited period of time. Eventually, you move on and think about something else, and your previous thoughts are either forgotten or strengthened so they enter your long-term memory. The other limitation of STM is that it cannot hold a large amount of information at once. Generally, people can remember seven things at one time (plus or minus two things). For example, it's fairly easy to remember a phone number, but a string of numbers longer than a phone number can be challenging to recall.

You can use a strategy to help you remember a longer list of things. By *chunking*, or grouping together individual items in units of 7 ± 2 that make sense, you can increase the power of your STM. Consider having to remember everything on the following list:

robin	panther	Dalmatian	gecko	pig
snake	pug	gila monster	penguin	mutt
cow	Siamese	goat	leopard	ewe
kiwi	flamingo	salamander	coyote	calico

It probably seems like a daunting task to remember all twenty items. Organizing the list into meaningful units might help you. Consider the following organization:

Birds	*Cats*	*Canines*	*Reptiles*	*Farm Animals*
robin	panther	Dalmatian	gecko	pig
penguin	Siamese	pug	snake	cow
kiwi	leopard	mutt	gila monster	goat
flamingo	calico	coyote	salamander	ewe

You still have twenty items to remember, but now they are chunked into just five meaningful groups of four items. Sorting the information enables you to call up the categories. Then you can list the specific examples within each category.

Long-term memory (LTM) is the desired destination for any information you want to remember. It is believed to have unlimited storage capacity, so you can't overload it. Once something makes its way into LTM, you need to be able to retrieve it at a later time—hence, *remembering* it—and show that you have learned it.

---

[1] Diana L. von Blerkom. *College Study Skills: Becoming a Strategic Learner,* 4th ed. Copyright © 2003 Wadsworth, a division of Thomson Learning, Belmont, CA.

INFLUENCES ON INFORMATION PROCESSING

The information processing model describes three critical steps to successful learning: encoding information, storing information, and retrieving information. Look closely at each one and notice the things that affect your ability to carry them out.

ENCODING

Encoding refers to getting information into your long-term memory. How effectively you do this relates directly to how you think about the information while it is in working memory. That is when you must make the material meaningful in some way. The following factors affect your ability to encode:

- Your interest and desire to learn the information
- Your goals and reason for learning it
- Your ability to limit distractions (including stress) and concentrate on the information
- The associations you make between the new information you are trying to learn and your existing knowledge
- Stress

Your focused effort can help you encode new material into LTM. When you can't find any motivation or interest in learning something, then you probably won't learn it. It is difficult to put in the necessary time and thought it takes to solidify the information in your brain. Therefore, your greatest learning challenges come with classes that you find boring and irrelevant to your future career. However, if your ultimate goal is to achieve success in college and earn good grades in all your courses, you must find a way to make learning all required information a priority, even if it is less than inspiring. If you can find even one aspect of a subject that sparks your curiosity, or if you can maintain a strong focus on your desire to do well, you can find the motivation. It makes a difference.

STORAGE

Once the information is encoded, it moves into storage. A common analogy for LTM is a huge room of filing cabinets. When information is encoded, it must be placed somewhere in this storage facility. Where does it go, and how is it filed? That depends on how it is encoded. How you perceive the information and the degree to which you understand it determine how your LTM stores it. For example, when a zoologist hears the word *jaguar* he or she is likely to think of a large member of the cat family that lives in the jungle. A car dealer, on the other hand, probably thinks of the high-performance car. Both are aware of the other meaning, but their long-term memories have stored the concept of "jaguar" in different "files" based on the meaning that is important to them.

RETRIEVAL

Properly storing information in an organized rather than a haphazard manner is critical if you want to find it later. Retrieval is the process of going into the LTM files, locating the information you need, and pulling it out to use. If you know where to look among the vast filing cabinets, the task is quick and easy. However, if you have filed away ideas in no established order, you may never be able to find what you're looking for—or at least you could be in for a long search.

MAKE THE MOST OF YOUR MEMORY

Now that you have a basic understanding of how your memory works and what constitutes the key elements of learning, here are some specific ways to achieve your academic goals. First, consider your current approach to studying as you read the Skill Check.

SKILL CHECK: MAKING IT INTO MEMORY

When you need to learn something, how do you do it? Where do you start? What does it take for you to commit important information to memory? Do you engage in a specific process before an exam? Does it begin in the classroom and encompass the period of time it takes to cover a unit of material, or is learning something that only occurs in the few days prior to the test? Do you try to learn information for the long haul, or just for the time it takes to complete the test? What is your reaction to cumulative exams? What kind of plan do you have for tackling your finals if they are comprehensive? If you have trouble learning large amounts of information, do you think the problem lies in encoding, storage, or retrieval? Do you feel as if you know the material but that your mind "goes blank" during exams? How can you be certain you really have information in your long-term memory to begin with?

ENCODE WITH ENTHUSIASM

Encoding is the crucial first step toward learning. If you don't encode the information, it will not reach long-term memory and it won't be available to you later. Therefore, you must approach this task with the intent of seriously focusing on what you need to learn. Discover your motivation. Do you want to learn for the sake of learning so that you can become knowledgeable on the subject? Do you simply want to earn a good grade in the course to keep up your grade point average? Consider your short-term goals as well as your goals for the future. Each exam is a building block to later success, no matter how small and inconsequential. When you perform well on a test, you are one step closer to your goal.

You are in control of the outcome on your exams. Regardless of your instructor, the subject matter, the layout of the textbook, or the in-class assignments, you hold the power of learning. Use this power to find an approach to studying that works for you, making the most of your learning styles and preferences. Also, take charge of managing your time prior to the test. Don't get behind in class. Instead, make it a daily habit to briefly review class notes and complete assigned readings. When you keep up with the information throughout the semester, you will have done half of your test preparation. The more you read, think about, use, and discuss the information, the more strongly you encode it. You can do most of this with little effort, simply by staying on top of the material—going to class, taking good notes, asking questions, talking with classmates, and quickly reviewing before class. By the time you sit down to seriously study, you will realize that you already know a great deal of the material. This method works especially well with courses that you are not as interested in or find challenging. You may have to push yourself to use this method, but you will be glad you did. Here are a couple of ideas to try.

YOU'RE THE PROFESSOR

Understanding the big picture of course material is the key to succeeding on tests. When you see how all of the concepts are interrelated and how the details fit, you can answer questions about the information in many ways. A dynamic means of encoding the information is to teach it to others. You learn through teaching because when you explain the material to someone else you must demonstrate your knowledge of the terminology, concepts, and their relationship to one another. It also puts you in the position of having to answer questions about the material—for clarification, to provide examples, and to explain the same concepts in a variety of ways.

Of course, you may not easily find a willing student. Your roommate may claim to have better things to do than become enlightened about the principles of economics. However, you don't need a real student. You simply need to imagine that you have one. Find a place to be alone (always recommended for serious studying of any kind) and prepare to lecture. Auditory and kinesthetic learners may find this method of preparing beneficial because it involves the verbal recitation of information. Put your notes in front of you, open to the first page, and begin. You'll really get your energy flowing if you stand up to present the material. Glance at your notes to guide you at first, but gradually step away from them as much as possible. The value of this exercise is that you work with the information in a meaningful and significant way. This solidifies the information into your LTM and provides you with a sensible organization that enables you to retrieve it quickly and easily.

CREATE YOUR OWN EXAM

An effective way to encode information from your notes and readings is to anticipate the exam. If you have already had an exam in a class, you are familiar with the format your professor uses. Therefore, you know what kinds of questions to expect—multiple choice, matching, true-false, short answer, fill-in-the-blank, or essay. If you haven't had a test in that class, try to find out the test format by asking the instructor. He or she may tell you if you explain your study technique.

Prepare to write your own test for the class. As you read through the material, formulate relevant questions. If you expect multiple choice questions on your upcoming exam, consider what distracters (or additional answer choices) might be used to throw you off when asking about a certain concept. Think about what ideas or pieces of information lend themselves well to true-false questions. Larger issues are likely to be addressed in an essay format. When you review the material from this perspective, it provides useful insight as to how your instructor may consider both the content and the exam. Thinking about the ways in which you may be asked to work with the information makes it more meaningful to you. It also helps you organize it and connect the concepts. You may even discover that you can anticipate the actual exam through this activity. Don't forget to answer the questions you pose!

TEST YOURSELF

If you create your own set of exam questions, you should be able to answer them. Therefore, you can prepare for the real exam by answering your own test questions. Even if you don't predict the exact questions on the professor's test, you may be close. Being able to answer your own questions, then, is good preparation for retrieving the necessary information when you take the test.

Self-testing gives you the opportunity to step away from the material and assess how well you have encoded it, stored it, and are able to retrieve it. One way to help you make the most of your time and see how much you know is to test yourself orally. Make an audiotape, reading questions from your cue column (if you take notes using the Cornell method), the review questions from your textbook, questions from the study guide (if your instructor has assigned one), or those that you made up for your mock exam. After reading each question, let the tape roll to provide silence for the response time. Listen and respond to your audiotaped questions while driving, working out in the gym, or walking between classes. Next time you work with the material, review any questions that gave you trouble. The more you hear the questions and practice retrieving the information and communicating your answers, the more solidly the material will be stored in your memory.

TIME MANAGEMENT FOR STUDYING

Successful encoding requires time. Remember, the more you work with the material, the more strongly encoded it will be. You cannot quickly pass information on to long-term memory, because it won't have acquired any strong meaning. Therefore, you must plan a study schedule that allows for significant time to focus on what you need to learn. Daily reviewing gives you a big boost because it continuously develops your familiarity with the information. When you need to prepare for an exam, begin at least five days beforehand. This does not mean that you should only work with the test material for that entire time. Rather, it means you should schedule periods of time across those five days to study, giving you plenty of opportunity to encode all the information.

LIMIT DISTRACTIONS

Time is valuable, so you don't want to waste it when you study. Remember that your brain automatically drops information that you cannot pay attention to, and you can focus on a limited amount. If you decide to study in a noisy area of the student union or in your dorm room where your roommate is trying to get to the next level of a noisy video game, you probably will not be able to effectively encode much of the material you need for your test. No matter how good your intentions, other stimuli (such as noisy conversations and loud music) may overpower the details you are trying to commit to long-term memory. With the limitations on STM and the critical importance of deep processing (which requires concentration), noisy or visually distracting environments hinder the ability to study productively. When every minute counts in your busy schedule, choose a quiet environment for serious review, problem solving, critical thinking, recitation, and rehearsal. Find a place that doesn't tempt your attention to stray.

NARROW YOUR FOCUS

When you have an upcoming exam that covers a large scope of information, break your study time into small workable tasks. Divide the material into limited segments so you can give your full attention to unified portions of it at a time. One key to making progress is to work only as long as you are able to focus and be productive. When your patience and ability to concentrate run out, there is no reason to keep reading, writing, or studying any longer. Scheduling short study sessions throughout the week before your exam enables you to focus your learning so you aren't overwhelmed and so you can effectively encode all of the important information.

STUDY AT INTERVALS

Another benefit of distributing study time over the course of a week is that you can have a rest between the times when you work with the information. This is important because your STM becomes overloaded when you attempt to work with too many concepts at once. Piling up your study sessions can actually prevent some of the material from making it to LTM. Leaving longer periods of time between intense study sessions gives your LTM the time it needs to establish a place for the information in its filing system. Each time you resume studying, you can encode the next set of details with a clear mind.

Spaced studying is particularly critical for midterms and finals, when you have several exams in a short period of time. Because you must study for all of them simultaneously, it is necessary to take sufficient breaks between study sessions. If you happen to have courses that are somewhat similar in nature, such as psychology and sociology, or economics and accounting, you should designate exactly which course to study at what time. Then plan the intervals between the study times for those similar classes as far apart as possible. You may think that it would be helpful to study for classes in tandem when they are similar, but this is not the case. Courses that share concepts, terms, and information do not share all the same information. In fact, sometimes they approach the same concepts in different ways. It is easy to confuse the specifics of similar courses when you study them close together. Instead, plan to study your most divergent courses close together when you have to prepare for multiple exams at once.

CAUTIONS ABOUT CRAMMING

When you don't manage your time well before an exam, you have to learn most of the material immediately before the test takes place. Studying all at once at the last minute is called *cramming,* and it is something to avoid at all costs because it doesn't enable you to learn. Leaving your studying until the last minute results in numerous problems. First of all, you are likely to be highly stressed, which is a serious distraction when you try to concentrate. With your thoughts racing about the fast-approaching exam and the fact that you're not ready, you cannot give your full attention to the information in your working memory. Your memory drops the important course material to make room for your panic-stricken musings. The second problem arises when you try to force too much information in your head at once. Your STM just doesn't have enough room. A few details might get through to LTM but most won't. The information that does manage to get encoded and that moves on to storage is not likely to be filed effectively. Finding the right place to keep information so you can quickly and easily retrieve it is important for doing well on exams. However, when you encode quickly and under pressure, you may not establish a recognizable place for the information in an organized scheme. Basically, your LTM won't know where to put it. It may be in the system somewhere, but its location will be a mystery and you will have trouble finding it when you need it. If you can't retrieve the information when necessary, what good is it? For a further look at an all-too-common situation, read the Student Scenario.

STUDENT SCENARIO: I'VE GOT THE WHOLE WEEKEND!

Derek's geology exam was on Monday. After class on Friday, his best friend Li asked how the studying was going. "Oh, I haven't had time to study yet," Derek said. "But I've got the whole weekend!"

"Don't you have your history paper to work on?" Li wondered.

"Yeah, I'm going to hit the library for a few hours tomorrow. That still leaves most of the weekend to study." replied Derek.

"Wow, I'd be completely stressed if I hadn't even started yet," commented Li.

Derek didn't deny his anxiety. "I'm always tense before a test, but there's nothing I can do about it now."

"Good luck, buddy!" were Li's parting words.

In fact, Derek was anxious about the amount of material he had to learn before the test. He had already had an exam in geology, and knew that this exam also would be packed with details. He made a strong effort to sit down with his class notes, open the textbook, and find some flash cards he had made. When he realized just how much work was ahead of him, it made it even harder to concentrate. While he was trying to read and understand the material, Derek couldn't get rid of the mental monologue, "How will I ever remember all of this? If I don't do well, my grade will suffer." Sometimes it was all he was thinking about.

Derek put all of his free time into studying that weekend, but thought his grasp of the material was tentative at best. He knew a few concepts well, but a lot of the material was fading from his memory. Each time he began studying after a break, he felt like he was starting over.

When he sat down to take the test on Monday, Derek hoped that the questions would trigger his memory for the material. It didn't help that most of the test comprised subjective questions, which required recalling the information without any prompts or clues. Derek's answers were scant and disjointed. When he was asked to explain or describe concepts and their relationship to one another, Derek could only jot down some isolated, individual points. As he finished the test, he crossed his fingers in hopes that the instructor would award partial credit and vowed never to cram again.

Consider the following questions:

- Derek originally seemed confident that two days were enough to prepare for his exam. What changed his mind?

- What specific problems made it impossible for Derek to learn all of the material for the exam?

- How would starting to study earlier have eliminated these problems?

- Could a weekend ever be enough time to effectively study for an exam? Explain.

- Derek's limited study time hindered his exam performance. What problems might he have had during the exam to cause him to do poorly?

- How are those problems related to what took place during Derek's study time?

THE POWER OF ASSOCIATIONS

Imagine that you have to learn some new terminology for your biology class. You write the definition for each term, provided either by your instructor or the textbook, and repeat the definitions, word for word, over and over again until you have memorized them. You are confident you know the terms because each time you test yourself you can rattle off the exact definition. On the exam, however, instead of being asked to simply define the terms, you are required to discuss a particular biological phenomenon and include the roles and functions of the new terms.

Rote memorization, the process of simply repeating information so you can regurgitate it in the same way, constitutes *surface-level processing*. This means that, although you may be able to recall that information from memory, it holds no real meaning. You haven't thought about that information conceptually, so you are limited to reproducing it in the way you encoded it. Rote memorization restricts your ability to apply the information, and that hinders you on college exams.

Deep-level processing, which involves actively thinking and working with the material you want to learn, is necessary for true learning to take place. Deep-level processing occurs primarily through associations. The more you can link ideas, concepts, and phenomena to information you already know, as well as other material you are learning about, the more meaningful it becomes. Information that has meaning can be easily organized, stored, and recalled from long-term memory. Not only will you be able to recall it, but you will be able to explain it, discuss it, use it, think about it, and communicate it in numerous ways. Deep-level processing is the key to taking command of your test experience.

LINKING TO SCHEMAS

Associations are powerful because the brain organizes information in meaningful clusters, called *schemas*—categories of related experiences and the elements that make up those experiences. For example, if you are invited to a restaurant, you automatically think about all you know about restaurant experiences. This is your restaurant schema. You might envision being shown to your seat, being handed a menu, placing your order with the waiter, chatting with friends while waiting for your food, eating, and finally paying the bill. You might think of different restaurant experiences—fast food places (where you order at the counter, pay, receive your food quickly, then seat yourself), cafeterias (where you stand in line, select individual items off the buffet, pay, and seat yourself), and ethnic restaurants (where the waiter might bring chips and salsa or you might eat with chopsticks). Your restaurant schema enables you to predict what you will experience when you go out to eat and guides your behaviors when you are there.

When you are introduced to new information, your brain tries to place it in one of your existing schemas. This helps you make sense of it and categorize it in a way that is meaningful and helps you remember it. The more deeply you process new material, the more links you forge with various schemas. (For example, when you think about food, you are likely to call up schemas for food groups, eating, cooking, and restaurants, to name a few.) The more schemas are associated with a concept, the faster and easier it is to recall the information.

TECHNIQUES FOR MAKING ASSOCIATIONS

Deep-level processing is an active endeavor. It cannot happen when you just skim your notes or text. Remember that information enters the LTM through working memory. Therefore, you must work with the material intellectually. Consider how each of the following activities helps you learn:

- Highlighting critical information in texts and notes
- Using the Cornell method of note taking to provide a system for reviewing course material
- Elaborating on information through critical thinking
- Answering review questions at the end of each text chapter
- Writing your own questions on the material to answer at a later time
- Developing study tools such as flash cards, charts, graphs, maps, and illustrations

- Summarizing text passages and lecture notes in your own words
- Predicting possible test questions to gain insight into your professor's perspective and prepare for the exam
- Joining study groups to share ideas and discuss concepts with others
- Reviewing and reciting material to test your level of understanding

Each one of these activities requires you to think about the information and relate it to other concepts in some way. They help build associations as your mental links and schema for the course material increase.

Learning involves the integration of individual pieces of information. If you try to learn them as isolated units, they will not have as much meaning. For example, suppose your upcoming psychology test covers the fundamental attribution error, gender bias, and self-fulfilling prophecy. These terms may be difficult to remember, but they make more sense if you study them as the collection of ways in which we misjudge the behaviors of others and if you identify examples of the times that you have made such errors when trying to interpret others' behavior. The terms fit logically into the big picture of "judgment errors."

Actively thinking about a concept prompts you to form an image of it in your mind. When learning about vertebrates and invertebrates in zoology, you might envision a human and a slug to represent the two categories. When learning about a battle in the Civil War, you might call up movie images such as young soldiers dressed in blue and gray. Invoking mental images and expanding on them can help you make associations and learn new material. Incorporating as many sensory elements into your image as possible—chaotic scenes from the battlefield with soldiers charging each other, smoke from blasting cannons, sounds of men yelling commands and screaming in pain, the acrid smell of smoke in the air, even the fear of death—helps broaden your schemas and connect the new information into your already existing knowledge of the Civil War.

Kinesthetic and visual learners will also benefit from creating physical images through making lists, drawing maps, graphing relationships, and labeling diagrams. The act of translating mental concepts into concrete physical images requires understanding the relationship they have with other information.

As you work with your information frequently—highlighting, taking notes, jotting questions in the margins—you begin to associate it with different aspects of your experience. For example, you may think of specific concepts in terms of where they are located in the chapter (such as near the end) or on the page (such as below the graph). When you think about the information, it brings to mind the image of where you read it and triggers thoughts of additional information. You can also associate information with your own location. Memory experts suggest sitting in the same seat every day in class and for the exam as well. If you are in the same place as when you began learning the material, you can use cues from around the classroom to help trigger your memory for information. You can also create your own memory aid, or *mnemonic,* based on location. Envision a familiar place in your mind. Mentally distribute throughout that location the important information you want to remember. For example, think about your dorm room and begin by picturing the first step of a complex algebraic formula hanging on your door like a sign. Imagine the next step in the formula displayed on your computer screen, the next element lying on your bed, and the final part in the shower. Associating each part of the formula with a part of your room, in a natural sequence, can help you recall it on the test.

Acronyms are words formed using the first letter (or letters) of each word in a series. One familiar acronym is NATO, formed from North Atlantic Treaty Organization. You can devise your own acronyms as a memory aid. For example, to remember the names of the Great Lakes, think of HOMES (Huron, Ontario, Michigan, Erie, and Superior). You can even associate the acronym itself with an image, such as several homes sitting on the shore of a lake. You can also remember long lists of items, even in a specific order, by using *acrostics*—phrases or sentences in which specific letters stand for the letters in a set of target words. An acrostic is usually silly so it triggers the memory. For example, to remember the biological classification system in descending order from broadest to narrowest, you might consider this: King Phillip's Cat Ordered Five Greasy Sardines. The first letter of each word corresponds to Kingdom, Phylum, Class, Order, Family, Genus, Species. In this case, you would not try to remember KPCOFGS, because it has no meaning. Instead, the acrostic is likely to make an impression so you can recall the information easily.

In the 1970s, McDonald's ran an advertising campaign in which all the names of ingredients in a Big Mac hamburger were set to a simple tune:

twoallbeefpattiesspecialsaucelettucecheesepicklesonionsonasesameseedbun!

Even though the commercial no longer runs, many people can still recall the list of ingredients, which proves the effectiveness of setting words to music as a memory aid. Another example is the set of *Schoolhouse Rock* videos shown between cartoons on Saturday mornings. Children of all ages could recite the preamble to the Constitution of the United States as well as the process by which a bill becomes a law. Songs often contain rhyming words, which makes remembering the words easier.

Try creating jingles (catchy, repetitive verses or poems) or rap songs based on the course material. You can also use puns, jokes, or a play on words to help you remember concepts. For example, here's a joke to help learners remember that deciduous trees lose their leaves in the winter.

Question: *What did Doug the deciduous tree say to Jack Frost?*

Answer: *Leaf me alone!*

It's silly (and not very funny) but the pun serves as a memory aid. Naming the tree *Doug* emphasizes the *d* for *deciduous,* and the punch line prompts the image of leaves having fallen for the winter (the season of Jack Frost). If a strange or silly thought comes to mind as you are studying your material, take advantage of it. It is likely to help you out!

DON'T FORGET!

The reason you study is to learn the material and remember it for the exam. Do you worry that you might forget some or most of what you studied? When you know what causes forgetting, you are better equipped to prevent it. People forget important information for several reasons.

- *Decay.* This is the process by which information is simply dropped from your short-term memory, consciously or unconsciously. If information enters your STM and is ignored, it goes away. Information is constantly decaying from your short-term memory, because you receive more sensory input than you can possibly focus on. You may think that you are giving sufficient attention to all incoming information but you simply can't.

- *Displacement.* STM has a limited capacity, so if you try to cram too much information into memory too quickly, some of the information displaces the rest. Whichever input receives more attention wins out and overrides the other input. This is why it is important to allow plenty of time to prepare for exams and to spread out your study sessions. Limit what you focus on each time, and you'll minimize the potential for displacement of critical information.

- *Incomplete encoding.* Rote memorization may help you retain some information so you can achieve recall at a basic level, but you are not likely to remember any detailed information or have a solid conceptual understanding of the topic. This is an example of incomplete encoding. Deep-level processing is the best path to effective encoding.

- *Retrieval failure.* Getting information back out of your LTM is as critical as putting it in. After all, what good is having it in there if you can't retrieve it? If you have ever "blanked out" when trying to recall someone's name or while trying to answer a test question, you have suffered retrieval failure. This is the result of incomplete encoding (for example, not having established associations), a filing error (ineffective associations), limited practice with the material (not working with it enough), or similar causes.

- *Interference.* With all of the information coming and going from your LTM, concepts can easily interfere with each other, particularly if they are similar. There are two ways this can happen. In one case, deeply processing new information can hinder your ability to retrieve older, established information. Suppose you are learning the names for the bones in the hand and you need to recall the bones in the foot. With your current focus on the hand, you have difficulty retrieving something you already know but that may be stored similarly in LTM. The other type of interference works in the opposite way. As you are trying to encode new material, the stored information interferes with remembering the new. The stored information is firmly established and has been filed for a longer period than the new information. Your retrieval efforts are successful for what's established but don't work well for the newer information.

Forgetting is common in everyday life, but you want to minimize it during exams. When you understand how and why people forget, it can help you in your study efforts. Give sufficient attention to the concepts and details that are necessary for you to remember. Learn through deep-level processing. Don't try to learn too much at one sitting. To avoid interference in learning, tackle one concept at a time and intersperse the topics with diverse course content.

CONTROL TEST ANXIETY

Most students experience at least a little anxiety prior to taking tests. For some, it can be beneficial. The boost of adrenaline prepares them for action, keeps their thoughts flowing, and gets them through the exam. However, intense test anxiety can be counterproductive, damaging performance and resulting in poor test grades. Testing is an integral part of the college experience, so the sooner you reduce disruptive factors, the better. Understanding the nature and causes of test anxiety can help you take the necessary steps to control it.

UNDERSTAND THE NATURE OF TEST ANXIETY

When we think about the unknown and potential outcomes, we get nervous in the present. An upcoming exam may weigh heavily on your mind and you may react to that concern. You may think, "What if I don't have enough time to finish?" "What if the test has mostly essay questions?" "What if I draw a blank?" "What if I fail?" When test anxiety gets out of control, it can be debilitating.

EMOTIONALITY

Test anxiety has two fundamental components: emotionality and worry.[2] *Emotionality* refers to the body's physiological reaction to the upcoming test. You recognize its signs when your heart beats faster, your breathing becomes more shallow, your palms get sweaty, and you feel nauseated. In cases of mild test anxiety, you won't feel the nervousness and discomfort until just prior to the test, and the anxiety may dissipate once you begin to take the exam. This level of anxiety can help you if you feel confident and prepared for the test. However, test anxiety may set in so early that it disrupts studying and may not dissipate after the exam has begun.

WORRY

Does the following monologue sound familiar? "This test is going to be so hard. There was too much material to learn, and I don't think I really know any of it. If I do poorly on this test, I'll get a bad grade in the course and my grade point average will suffer. People will think I'm a lousy student and my parents will be really upset. This is a total disaster!"

The problem with worry is that the negative thoughts running through your mind use up valuable mental processing capacity. Instead of concentrating on the exam, you are dividing your attention between test questions and the monologue. The harder you perceive the test to be, the more your negative thoughts are confirmed and grow stronger. If you discover, however, that the test is not as difficult as you had imagined, your negative thoughts diminish and you free yourself up to focus.

RECOGNIZE THE CAUSES OF TEST ANXIETY

Several factors contribute to test anxiety, including lack of preparation and misplaced motivation. Not knowing the material and being aware that you are not prepared is bound to cause anxiety, and your worries are justified. Not being ready for an exam lowers your *self-efficacy,* your self-confidence and the belief that you are capable of succeeding.

Another factor contributing to test anxiety is motivation. Your reason for wanting to do well on the test has an effect on how well you learn the material and, ultimately, how anxious you feel when taking the exam. If you are learning the material for the sake of knowing it and demonstrating that you know it, you are likely to succeed. Your study methods are more likely to be effective and to result in a calm, confident approach to the exam. On the other hand, if you want to learn so you can do well on the exam to demonstrate your ability relative to others, you are not as likely to achieve your goal. Your test anxiety may be driven in part by the concern that you won't do as well as your classmates and that you'll appear to be a failure. When your goal is to learn rather than to earn a good grade, you are more likely to be cognitively and psychologically prepared to do well on your exams.

REDUCE YOUR TEST ANXIETY

Being sufficiently prepared for exams is the most effective way to rid yourself of the negative effects of text anxiety. Suppose you had to take a test on the subject of where you live. You probably wouldn't be nervous even if the test were worth a lot of points and you didn't even know the test format—multiple choice questions about your street name and number, drawing a map from campus to your home, writing an essay that describes your home, listing routes from your home to various locations. The reason you wouldn't be nervous is that you know the information

---

[2] R. M. Liebert and L. W. Morris. "Cognitive and emotional components of test anxiety: A distinction and some initial data," *Psychological Reports* 20 (1967), pp. 974–978.

and are comfortable dealing with it in numerous ways. The closer you can come to mastering material, the more relaxed you are when tested on it. It is not possible to overlearn material. The fact is, the more you read, study, manipulate, and talk about information, the more solidly it becomes embedded in your memory and the easier it is to retrieve. Recognizing the need to prepare for exams, regardless of your feelings about the class, is the first step toward reducing text anxiety.

Your next step is to persevere through the courses that least inspire you. You must master the material, if only for a semester. When you aim to succeed with the material rather than with your grade in the class, you lay the foundation for good test performance.

You can apply the following three techniques to reduce anxiety while preparing for exams and while taking them: (1) slow and deepen your breathing, (2) relax your body, and (3) eliminate negative thoughts.

FOCUS ON BREATHING

When the body senses a threatening situation, it reacts in a predictable way. One reaction is shallow breathing. In response to anxiety, we tend to breathe faster, which prevents us from filling our lungs to capacity. When we don't take in all the oxygen we need, we get lightheaded, dizzy, and confused. You may not be aware of this entire process or the extent to which it affects you when you get nervous. You notice the difference, however, when you take specific steps to ensure that your breathing pattern is optimal. Practice the following procedure at home when you have plenty of quiet time.

Steps to Abdominal Breathing[3]

1. Lie down on a rug or blanket on the floor in a "dead body" pose—your legs straight and slightly apart, your toes pointed comfortably outward, your arms at your sides and not touching your body, your palms up, and your eyes closed.

2. Bring your attention to your breathing and place your hand on the spot that seems to rise and fall the most as you inhale and exhale.

3. Gently place both of your hands or a book on your abdomen and follow your breathing. Notice how your abdomen rises with each inhalation and falls with each exhalation.

4. Breathe through your nose. (If possible, always clear your nasal passages before doing breathing exercises.)

5. If you experience difficulty breathing into your abdomen, press your hand down on your abdomen as you exhale and let your abdomen push your hand back up as you inhale deeply.

6. Is your chest moving in harmony with your abdomen or is it rigid? Spend a minute or two letting your chest follow the movement of your abdomen.

7. If you continue to experience difficulty breathing into your abdomen, an alternative is to lie on your stomach, with your head rested on your folded hands. Take deep abdominal breaths so you can feel your abdomen pushing against the floor.

When you become at ease with breathing into your abdomen, practice it any time during the day when you feel like it and are sitting down or standing still. Concentrate on your abdomen moving up and down, the air moving in and out of your lungs, and the feeling of relaxation that deep breathing gives you. Use this whenever you feel yourself getting tense.

[3] Davis, M., Eshelman, E. R., and McKay, M. *The Relaxation & Stress Reduction Workbook,* 5th Edition. Copyright © 1995 by New Harbinger Publications, Inc. Reprinted with permission.

BREATHING TO RELEASE TENSION[4]

Fear and relaxation are physiological opposites. Therefore, when you can get your body into a completely relaxed state, you will not suffer from test anxiety. Here are some methods for releasing the tension in your body.

Breath Counting

1. Sit or lie in a comfortable position with your arms and legs uncrossed and your spine straight.

2. Breathe in deeply into your abdomen. Let yourself pause before each exhale.

3. As you exhale, count "One" to yourself. As you continue to inhale and exhale, count each exhalation by saying "Two...three...four."

4. Continue counting your exhalations in sets of four for five to ten minutes.

5. Notice your breathing gradually slowing, your body relaxing, and your mind calming as you practice this breathing meditation.

The Relaxing Sigh

1. Sit or stand up straight.

2. Sigh deeply, letting out a sound of deep relief as the air rushes out of your lungs.

3. Don't think about inhaling—just let the air come in naturally.

4. Take eight to twelve of these relaxing sighs and let yourself experience the feeling of relaxation. Repeat whenever you feel the need for it.

Letting Go of Tension

1. Sit comfortably in a chair with your feet on the floor.

2. Breathe in deeply into your abdomen and say to yourself, "Breathe in relaxation." Let yourself pause before you exhale.

3. Breathe out from your abdomen and say to yourself, "Breathe out tension." Pause before you inhale.

4. Use each inhalation as a moment to become aware of any tension in your body.

5. Use each exhalation as an opportunity to let go of tension.

6. You may find it helpful to use your imagination to picture or feel the relaxation entering and the tension leaving your body.

Shorthand Procedure for Deep Muscle Relaxation

1. Curl both fists, tightening biceps and forearms (Charles Atlas pose). Relax.

2. Wrinkle up forehead. At the same time, press your head as far back as possible, roll it clockwise in a complete circle, reverse. Now wrinkle up the muscles of your face like a walnut: frowning, eyes squinted, lips pursed, tongue pressing the roof of the mouth, and shoulders hunched. Relax.

3. Arch back as you take a deep breath into the chest. Hold. Relax. Take a deep breath, pressing out the stomach. Hold. Relax.

---

[4] Davis, M., Eshelman, E. R., and McKay, M. *The Relaxation & Stress Reduction Workbook,* 5th Edition. Copyright © 1995 by New Harbinger Publications, Inc. Reprinted with permission.

POSITIVE SELF-TALK

A quick but powerful tool for overcoming the disruptive impact of worry is positive self-talk.[5] Replacing negative thoughts with statements that emphasize self-efficacy helps you focus on the demands of an upcoming test. Think to yourself, "I can do this. I have participated in class, done my assignments and reviewed my notes. I have the information I need to perform well on this test." Positive self-talk instills confidence and frees your mind so you can do your best on exams.

The sooner you address problems with test anxiety, the better. If you need help working on these methods or would like more suggestions, visit your campus counseling center. College tests are not the only trigger of debilitating anxiety. Read the Future Focus to find out how taming general anxiety is critical for career success as well.

FUTURE FOCUS: SWEATY PALMS

If you suffer from high levels of test anxiety, you probably are anxious in other high-pressure, performance-based situations and are likely to encounter such situations throughout your career. If you have a career that involves obtaining a license or certification, you may face tests periodically. Many careers have occasional training seminars in which participants are expected to demonstrate their mastery of information presented over a short period of time. Your performance may affect your standing in the company or your potential for a promotion or a raise.

The job interview itself is a pressure-filled experience. High levels of anxiety can disrupt your ability to make a good impression and may hinder your opportunity to be considered for the job. Oral presentations to business partners, clients, or customers that require recall of vital facts and information must be carried out with finesse to be effective and to make a positive impact.

Learning to control your anxiety is a skill that rewards you all your life. Incorporating effective relaxation techniques into your routine and practicing positive self-statements may help you overcome the limiting effects of anxiety now and in the future.

PREPARE FOR THE TEST EXPERIENCE

TAKE CARE OF YOURSELF

You can't take a test when you're sick. And it's not likely that you will perform optimally when you are hungry, tired, or have a headache or sore muscles. It seems almost silly to mention the importance of taking care of your health, but college students often neglect themselves physically, particularly when they've got a test coming up. There couldn't be a worse time to forgo sleep, deny your body (and brain)

---

[5] Carol Malec, Liz Young, Bryan Hiebert, Jane Rose, Samara Felesky-Hunt, and Kelly Blackshaw, *Stress Medicine: You Matter Too (An Intervention Guide for Building a Healthy Lifestyle)* (Calgary: LifeLong Wellness Research Institute, 1997).

nutrition, and wear down your immune system. To ensure that you can function at your maximum capacity during an exam, you must begin caring for yourself beforehand.

SLEEP

Even though you may feel pressured to squeeze in more study time, plan to get a full night's sleep for several consecutive nights prior to your exam. If that is not possible, at least make sure you sleep seven to eight hours the night before the test so you can think clearly. New research has found that sleeping well after studying helps more solidly encode information into memory.[6]

EAT WELL

Regardless of your usual meal schedule, try to eat something before your test. If you tend to get queasy, eat something bland like crackers or a bagel. Don't load up on sugar or caffeine, because you may come down from your sugar high or may need to use the bathroom during the exam.

MAINTAIN YOUR ROUTINE

Getting regular exercise is always a good idea, but don't start a new workout regimen or increase your bench press repitions the day before an exam. You could be distracted by aching or cramping muscles. Remember, your brain functions best when your body is in good shape. Eating right, getting enough sleep, and staying moderately active helps you feel good, both physically and mentally. When your immune system is strong and you maintain a good energy level throughout the day, you can concentrate more effectively.

PREVIEW TEST POLICIES

Most instructors provide test-related policies on the course syllabus. Review these policies when you study for the exam. If your instructor has not specified any particular policies or ground rules, inquire about the following:

- *Test location.* Will the test be given in your regular classroom or at a testing center on campus? If you must go to a testing center, find out the center's hours of operation and the time by which you are expected to complete the test.

- *Time of test.* Is the test scheduled during regular class hours or at another time? Final exams and some midterm exams usually operate on different schedules.

- *Time allotted for the test.* How much time will you have to take the exam? The entire class period or less than the class period? Will you be able to work as long as it takes to complete it? Find out your time limitations so you can gauge your pace.

- *Instructor's presence.* Will your instructor administer the test or will there be a proctor? If you have a proctor, will it be a teaching assistant from the class, someone else in the department, or a person outside of the department?

- *Questions.* Will students be able to ask questions once the test has begun? If so, what is the protocol? Do you simply raise your hand or do you approach the teacher or proctor?

- *Required materials.* What materials are you required to bring to the exam? Do you need an essay book (often called a blue book) or an electronic Scantron

[6] K. M. Fenn, H. C. Nusbaum, and D. Margoliash. "Consolidation during sleep of perceptual learning of spoken language," *Nature* 425 (2003): 614–616.

sheet? Might you need more than one of each? Do you need a pen or number 2 pencil? Whatever you need, you should always bring a few, just in case.

- *Optional materials.* What additional testing aids are you allowed to bring with you? Can you use a calculator? Are you restricted to the kinds of functions it can perform? Can you have a cheat sheet with formulas or terms? If so, are you limited in size?

- *Exam protocol.* Will you be expected to write on the exam itself, or should you be prepared to bring notebook paper? If you do write on the exam, can you use your own notebook paper to work problems or ask for additional pages for long essay questions? (Be aware that some instructors do not allow students to bring any papers to the exam because it raises concerns about cheating.)

- *Guessing and partial credit.* Will you be penalized for guessing? Will instructors award partial credit on subjective questions such as essays and some math problems?

- *Food and drink.* Are you allowed to bring food and drink to the exam? (If so, be considerate of others and don't bring items with crinkly wrappers or foods that are noisy to eat.)

- *Restroom breaks.* Are you allowed to get up when necessary to use the restroom? (If the testing period is long, breaks may be scheduled.)

- *Makeup exams.* Some instructors simply do not give makeup exams unless the student makes arrangements before the exam has started. If that is the case, be sure to call the instructor immediately upon discovering that you can't make it to the exam. Recognize that makeup exams can have a different format and different time restrictions than the original exam. Also, a makeup exam may require you to accommodate the instructor's schedule.

BE ON TIME

Take all necessary steps to ensure that you arrive on time, or even a little early, for your exam. Allow extra time for unexpected traffic conditions, construction, or accidents if you are driving. Consider parking conditions when you arrive on campus. Does it typically take you a long time to find a place to park? Do you have to walk far to your class or rely on campus transportation? Plan for delays.

If you have a class prior to your scheduled exam, choose a seat near the door, if possible, so you can leave quickly once class is over. If your earlier class is far away from your test location, you might ask your instructor if you could leave a few minutes early that day. However, don't plan to skip classes entirely simply because they fall on the day of your exam. What you think you might gain in terms of test points by giving up class for extra studying, sleeping, or relaxing, you may lose later on. The instructor of the class you skip may give critical information and insight into an upcoming exam, and you may find yourself behind.

Arriving late for an exam is disruptive to both you and your classmates. Despite your best attempts at discretion, your entrance is likely to be noisy and to distract those who are trying to concentrate. You may have a more difficult time relaxing and may feel flustered from starting late. You are also at risk for missing important announcements prior to the exam, which the instructor may not repeat for latecomers. In most cases, instructors won't give extra time for latecomers to complete the test.

CHAPTER 11 REVIEW QUESTIONS

1. What are the various purposes of college course exams?

2. Briefly describe how information is processed in the brain, and discuss how knowing this can help you study more effectively.

3. What are some common reasons that we forget important information?

4. Why should you avoid cramming for a test?

5. What are some of the basic causes of test anxiety?

6. Why does test anxiety tend to diminish performance?

7. What are some critical things you should find out about your instructor's exam policies before you take a test?

SKILL PRACTICE

1. Go to http://faculty.washington.edu/chudler/chmemory.html and test your memory. Choose the assessments for the highest grade levels. Complete them and then scroll to the techniques section. Use the suggested tips to try and remember the word lists provided. How did you do? Which strategies seem to work best for you? Why do you think that is?

2. Create some acronyms and acrostics for information you are currently working on in any course. Remember that they should stand out in your mind so you can easily recall the information.

3. Pretend that a friend is concerned about his or her ability to do well on college exams. Teach your friend what you know by lecturing on this chapter so that he or she could understand and benefit from the information. Describe in your own words the purpose of exams, how information is processed mentally, and how to study effectively, relax, and prepare for exams.

4. Try to answer the chapter review questions from any of your textbooks without studying. How much do you remember of the information you have already covered? What does this tell you about how well you have encoded the information so far? What should you do to prepare for the next exam?

5. Find a time to be alone in your room to work on relaxation techniques. Spend some time relaxing and controlling your breathing. True relaxation that you can achieve quickly takes practice. Make it a point to schedule times to do this regularly.

CURRENT COURSE APPLICATION

1. Create a variety of study tools for a course in which you have an upcoming exam. Consider making flash cards, developing comparison charts, graphs, illustrations, or diagrams. How much do you think you learned just by making the study tools? Be sure to refer to them when you study, explaining the visuals in your own words.

2. Try the encoding technique in which you assume the role of lecturer, presenting material from your favorite class. See if you can present the material in a different but organized way that makes it easier to learn and remember. Note how meaningful the information becomes and how easy it is to see the big picture when you are responsible for describing it.

3. Write a test in preparation for your next exam in any course. Based on what you know of the exam format, develop questions of various types for highest level information. Try to anticipate what your instructor will focus on and which topics will take which test format (multiple choice, true-false, essay). Take your own exam to see how well you know the material. Do you feel better prepared for the actual exam in that class?

4. Consider your most difficult and intimidating class as the stimulus for practicing relaxation techniques. Work toward slowing your breathing and relaxing your muscles as you prepare for the lecture. Employ your visualization and relaxation before or during homework or while studying for this course. Try to achieve a state of relaxation when you take your seat for the next exam.

5. Review all of your current course syllabi to see if the instructors' test-taking policies are clearly stated. Do they address all of the important items presented in this chapter? If not, which policies should be clarified? If you have had an exam in the class already, was there anything regarding the testing situation that you learned the hard way because your instructor did not clarify the policies? Keep the list from this chapter and be sure to inquire about test-taking policies in your future courses.

TAKE A LOOK ONLINE

For some fun tests of memory as well as methods and techniques to help you remember things, check out

http://faculty.washington.edu/chudler/chmemory.html

Many interesting memory facts and assessments can be found at

www.exploratorium.edu/memory

To assess the extent of your test anxiety, go to

www.wright-counseling.com/checklists/TestAnxietyAssessment.html

STUDENT SCENARIO DISCUSSION RESPONSES

- **Derek originally seemed confident that two days were enough to prepare for his exam. What changed his mind?** When he began studying, he discovered the problems he created by waiting.

- **What specific problems made it impossible for Derek to learn all of the material for the exam?** Derek had to learn too much information in the time frame. To work with the information sufficiently enough to get it solidly into LTM, he would have needed a great deal more time. Too much information at once overloaded Derek's STM and only a portion of it entered his LTM. Also, once Derek realized how much information he had to learn over the weekend, he began to panic. His stressed state was a distraction. His anxious thoughts competed with the material he was trying to study. He also was not able to fully concentrate on the course material because he was worried.

- **How would starting to study earlier have eliminated these problems?** Had he had more time, Derek would have been relaxed and able to focus on learning, thus encoding the material more effectively. Also, he could have spread out his study sessions, giving him the chance to limit the amount of information he had to focus on at a time. This would have enabled him to work with a set amount of materials and concentrate to get the details from working memory into LTM. By spacing his study sessions, he could give his LTM time to absorb the information and file it appropriately so he could recall it. More time means more practice. Derek could have reviewed what he had studied previously and then set a foundation for additional learning, creating significant associations between concepts.

- **Could a weekend ever be enough time to effectively study for an exam? Explain.** A weekend might be sufficient if you have kept on top of all course material and have spent significant time working with it prior to that point. If you read through your notes daily, read and highlight assignments regularly, prepare flash cards, make lists, draw graphs, and then review these tools fairly often, you probably have encoded a great deal of the information without designating specific study sessions. Group discussions and sessions (for example, with shared problem solving of additional math or science exercises) give you the chance to work with the information often. With all of these regular study events occurring beforehand, you could probably solidify your knowledge and memory for the significant material in a weekend.

- **Derek's limited study time hindered his exam performance. What problems might he have had during the exam to cause him to do poorly?** Derek probably had difficulty retrieving some of the information stored in his long-term memory.

- **How are those problems related to what took place during Derek's study time?** If he did not make enough meaning out of the material or establish enough associations between concepts and his existing knowledge, then it is likely he was not able to remember information that he had spent time working with. Those processes were compromised when he was rushed. In the end, he was not able to demonstrate that he had learned some of the important material.

PERFORM OPTIMALLY ON EXAMS

In this chapter you will learn

- General strategies that can help you perform better on any kind of test

- Strategies to help you succeed on multiple choice, true-false, and matching test items

- How to perform optimally on essay questions, including what to do if you don't know the answer

Once you have prepared for your exams, it's time to demonstrate what you know. This is your chance to shine and make it clear that you have worked hard to learn the material. Even when you are more than ready to share your knowledge, though, exams can still pose a challenge. When you become skilled at the process of taking tests, you are in an even better position to do well.

APPLY GENERAL TEST-TAKING STRATEGIES

Regardless of the course or test format, there are several tactics you can use to help achieve success on your exams. Begin by assessing your current test-taking savvy by answering the questions in the Skill Check.

At the end of this chapter, you will have the opportunity to take a sample test that includes all of the elements discussed in this chapter. Not only can you apply what you learn, but you can see firsthand how an actual exam presents these elements.

SKILL CHECK: HOW TEST-WISE ARE YOU?

What do you typically do when you receive an exam? Do you approach all tests the same way, regardless of the course or format of the test? Do you immediately dive in and try to answer the questions in order, starting with the first one? What do you do if you can't answer a question? Do you stick with it until you come up with the answer? Do you quickly guess and move on? Do you use any personal strategies to help you with questions, such as cross-checking for clues in multiple choice questions or identifying limiting terms in true-false items? Do you deal with all essay questions in the same way, or do you approach them differently depending on the question? After thinking about your test-taking skills, consider how effective they are—or aren't!

AIR OUT YOUR THOUGHTS

Right before an exam, you may feel that you are about to burst, trying to hold in all of the information you've been accumulating during the long hours of studying. One way to relax, get settled, and gain confidence before you begin a test is to "dump" some of the critical facts you've been trying to keep in your head. Find a blank space on the back of an exam page and quickly jot down some critical facts and concepts that you can refer to during the exam. You may or may not use them, but you may feel better once you know that you've remembered them long enough to write them down. You also will have freed yourself to approach the test.

Continue this process as you work through the exam. When you encounter questions that jog your memory, don't wait for a specific question to apply what you remember. Make some brief notes in the margins to refer to later if necessary. Taking a few seconds to release your bundles of knowledge, memorized lists, or outlines of concepts is well worth it when you can use them to help you through the test.

ASSESS THE TEST

Begin all tests by looking them over thoroughly. Take a minute or two to size up what lies ahead of you. Find out the following information:

- How many pages there are
- If the questions are on one side or both sides of the page
- How many questions there are
- How many questions of each type there are
- How many points each section of questions is worth
- If any questions have multiple parts

These may seem like trivial issues, but you want to be sure you know what you are responsible for. Imagine if you let the time expire and then realized you didn't do the last page. You also don't want to overlook questions on the back side of each page. In your haste, you could easily have flipped the pages without realizing that entire sets of test material are missing. Once you know the parameters of the exam, you can then plan how to tackle it.

STRATEGIZE YOUR APPROACH

Systematically working your way through an exam ensures that you remain as relaxed as possible and that you complete the exam on time, achieving your desired results. Two important things to consider are how to allot your time and in what sequence to answer the questions.

After reviewing the test elements, make a rough estimate of how much time to allow for each section, question, or problem. If your test includes different types of questions, grouped together in sections (multiple choice, true-false, essay), determine the amount of time you think you will need to effectively complete each section. True-false typically require the least amount of time, because your answer options are limited to two. Multiple choice questions require more reading and thinking to process, and essay questions demand the most time and concentrated effort. As you make your time estimates, also consider the point values for each section. Suppose the exam you're taking has only three essay questions, each worth eight points (for a total of 24 points), and a multiple choice section that contains 20 questions at three points each (for a total of 60 points). You'll want to be sure you have sufficient time to work through the multiple choice section carefully.

If your exam consists entirely of essay questions or math problems to solve, base your estimates on the scope of the questions or problems and your knowledge about the particular question or problem. Consider how time-consuming the problems are and whether they have multiple parts. Ask yourself if the topic of the question is something you can write about easily. Those that are the shortest and that you immediately feel confident about are not likely to require as much time. As you progress through the exam, keep your eye on the clock. Make adjustments to your timing as you go.

The best place to begin an exam is with a question you can answer easily. Many students think they have to start with the first question and then become flustered when they can't answer it immediately. Tackling items that are easy for you builds your confidence and lessens anxiety.

After answering the questions you know, focus on the more difficult, high-value questions. These are likely to be essay questions or math problems that require more thought and preparation, thus requiring a greater portion of the allotted exam time. Although they may be the most demanding items on the test, you can't spend all of your remaining time on them if you still have unanswered questions. Give yourself a time limit for working through these items. After that, shift gears and complete the other remaining sections. The change in focus can refresh your mind and expose you to other questions that may prompt your thinking regarding the difficult questions. Once you have finished the remainder of the test items, return to the challenging items and complete them in the time you have left.

LOOK FOR CLUES

Sometimes test questions provide clues to the answers of other test questions. It's usually inadvertent, and instructors usually try to prevent this when they write exams. It's difficult, though, to make certain that no test item makes reference to information contained in other test items, especially if the exam contains a variety of formats. Thus, simply reading certain questions can provide you with the information you need to answer other questions.

Multiple choice questions may reveal clues through the questions themselves or the answer choices that follow. In the following example, notice how the second question provides the answer for the first question.

1. The supercontinent _____ is believed to have combined with other land masses to form a single world continent called _____.
   a. Eurasia, Pangaea   **b.** Pangaea, Gondwana
   c. Tectonica, Pangaea   **d.** Gondwana, Pangaea

2. Geologists believe that the early supercontinent Gondwana drifted in which direction before combining with other land masses to form the single continent Pangaea?
   a. north through the Arctic Circle, then east toward the Pacific region
   b. south from the Tropics, across the southern polar region, then north
   c. south from the northern polar region to the southern polar region
   d. north through the Tropics, drifting west, then south to the pole

The answer to question 1 is *d* and is clearly stated in question 2. These two items would not likely be next to each other on an exam or even in this order. However, if you did not know the answer to the first question, you would find it once you continued reading through the remaining questions.

True-false questions may bring out aspects of relationships between concepts, the presence or absence of an event, phenomenon, or process, or an individual's involvement. Consider what you can learn from the following questions.

1. President Warren G. Harding was implicated in the numerous scandals that took place during his presidency. ____ True ____ False

2. Warren Harding's presidency was rife with scandal. ____ True ____ False

Whether the first question is true or false, the statement informs you that Harding's presidency was associated with numerous scandals, which answers question 2.

Essay questions also can give clues and make use of clues. Sometimes essay questions provide explicit background information to prompt students to write more completely. These detailed questions can include information pertaining to some of the objective items on the test. On the other hand, some of the objective questions on an exam provide you with information you can incorporate into your essay responses. For example, the following essay question would help you with the multiple choice questions in the earlier example.

Discuss the theories that contributed to our understanding of macroevolution, such as the idea of continental drift, the supercontinent Gondwana's migration south through the south polar region, then north to combine with other land masses to form the single world continent known as Pangaea.

The details presented in this question actually answer both of the multiple choice questions. Thus, by reading through your entire exam before beginning, you may discover information that helps you answer questions and jog your memory for the material.

The following essay question offers very little information, but the true-false questions in the earlier example could prompt your answer for this essay question.

What were some of the problems that plagued Harding's administration?

The earlier questions remind you that numerous scandals occurred during Harding's presidency. Therefore, you could identify at least one topic to address for this essay.

LET THE CLOCK RUN OUT

Some students finish exams as quickly as possible and leave early to have free time to relax, hang out with friends, or get a head start for another class. Instructors rarely plan to give students significantly more time for an exam than they expect is needed. Unless you are absolutely certain that you have answered every item correctly, you should make use of every minute of the testing period available to you. The Professor's Perspective illustrates how leaving before the exam time is finished can actually be detrimental to your grade—in more than one way.

PROFESSOR'S PERSPECTIVE: I'M OUTTA HERE!

Students who leave before exam time is up usually make an impression on the instructor, but it's probably not the one they want to make. Most instructors want to obtain a substantial look at what their students have learned, so they try to create exams that assess students' understanding of the material as completely as possible in the time provided to take the exam. If you hurry through your test and dash out of class before time is up, your instructor is going to know that you didn't demonstrate your understanding of the concepts to the extent of his or her expectations.

When grading exams, particularly those with subjective elements, instructors often recall how quickly a student turned in a test. In some classes, the time of completion is even noted on the exam. Instructors may use this information to judge how much effort a student put into the test performance. They may not grade kindly any answer that is less than ideal if the student completed the exam quickly and left early.

If you should happen to complete all of the questions before time runs out, check your answers, particularly those that you did early on in the test. Symptoms of test anxiety are likely to diminish over time, and you become calmer as you progress through your exam. As this happens, you are able to think more clearly and concentrate more fully on what you are doing. You may find that in your early moments with the test, you rushed through items or didn't read them properly, and you will be glad to have had another chance to answer them when you aren't so anxious. If you continue to feel stuck on questions after answering everything else, use all of the time you have left to reread the other questions to see if they offer any clues. If not, you can continue to reflect on the course material and something may come to you. You'll also want to check for technicalities in your responses. Did you mark the answer you intended to mark? Did you fill in the bubble carefully so the computer can read it properly? Is there a clear distinction between your T's and F's? Do all of your matched items match the right response? Take this extra time to eliminate as many inadvertent errors as possible.

If your exam involves any writing, take the time to look over your work. First, make sure you read the questions correctly. Occasionally, students complete a lengthy essay response and find out later that they had misread or misunderstood the question. Even if you don't have time to rewrite an entire answer, should you spot your mistake before time runs out, you can begin to make changes, which could help your grade tremendously.

If you are certain that you have read all questions correctly and your answers are organized and well supported, look at the details. Make sure each word is legible. Check your grammar, spelling, and punctuation. If you have continued your writing on the back of the page or a different sheet of paper, make sure the order is clearly marked. Being thorough in your exam review can only benefit your grade.

 ## TAKE ADVANTAGE OF OBJECTIVE TEST TIPS

You can use some test strategies that are entirely unrelated to your knowledge of the test material.[1] The ability to use these strategies is called *test-wiseness*.[2] This chapter examines some tips you can use to successfully work through your exams.

MASTER MULTIPLE CHOICE

Most students consider multiple choice questions to be fairly easy because they only have to recognize the correct answer among several options. However, multiple choice questions actually can be tricky—and often are intentionally so. Any topic that involves subtle distinctions between concepts or theories lends itself to multiple choice questioning. Answer choices may be confusing if you don't know the material in detail. They also may closely resemble the correct answer. In addition, answer choices may cause you to second guess your knowledge of the topic. At the college level, it is less likely that you can rely on the method of eliminating obviously wrong choices to identify the correct answer.

BEGIN WITH WHAT YOU KNOW

As you know, you don't have to answer test questions in order. In fact, you shouldn't if you find that the first few items are difficult. Find a question you feel confident with and start from there. Pay close attention to all answer choices to see if they provide clues.

READ CAREFULLY AND THOROUGHLY

A multiple choice question may be worded so as to confuse students who don't read carefully. For example, the question may take an unexpected form. Consider the question, "Which of the following items is not a component of the theory?" Students who read the question quickly may overlook the word *not* and may envision an entirely wrong potential answer.

The answer choices themselves may be tricky. Instructors often can anticipate how students might read questions in haste and what information students are likely to confuse with the correct answer. They may purposefully include such answer choices to make the test challenging.

Of course, there's no excuse for selecting the wrong answer if you don't read every option thoroughly. Even if you are certain that choice B is correct, read C and D, too. These subsequent choices may elaborate on the answer in B to make it more applicable for the question asked, or you may simply have been wrong when you thought it was correct in the first place.

ELIMINATE SYSTEMATICALLY

Sometimes the best way to find the right answer is to identify the wrong answer. When you read through your answer choices, mark those that you are certain are not correct. If you are lucky, you will have only one option remaining. Usually, however, there are two possible choices. In this case, reread the question to see if it

[1] J. Millman, C. H. Bishop, and R. Ebel, "An analysis of test-wiseness," *Educational and Psychological Measurement* 25 (1965), pp. 707–726.

[2] G. Samson, "Effects of training in test-taking skills on achievement test-performance: A quantitative synthesis," *Journal of Educational Research* 78 (1985), pp. 261–266.

provides any reason to choose or eliminate either of your remaining options. If not, move on to other questions and see if they shed any light. When you come back to the troublesome questions, look for these elements:

- *Grammatical incongruence.* Consider eliminating answers that make the complete sentence ungrammatical. Also, answers that don't agree in tense or number with the question are suspect. Here's an example.

  Notes receivable
  a. *are amounts that customers owe.*
  b. *are notes indicating what customers have already paid.*
  c. *is a lump sum remaining to be paid on an item.*
  d. *are records of transactions involving the exchange of money.*

  Each answer choice except *C* completes the sentence that the test item begins. Choice *C* results in an ungrammatical sentence.

- *Unfamiliar terms.* Answer choices that include terms that you have never seen before but that supposedly relate to the topic are suspicious.

- *Attractive distractors.* Sometimes instructors write answer choices using terms that are similar to those used in the question. A choice might stand out because of its use of terminology, but it may have been placed there as a distractor.

- *Opposite options.* If two answer choices are exact opposites of each other, one of them is likely to be correct. Here's an example.

  Quaking aspen (Populus tremuloides) *are propagated by*
  a. *sexual reproduction*   ***b.*** *asexual reproduction*
  c. *germination*   ***d.*** *meiosis*

  Choices *a* and *b* obviously are opposites. Analyzing the other choices could help you select *b* with confidence.

- *Synonymous statements.* If you find that two or more answer choices essentially say the same thing, chances are good that none of those are correct. They may even be true relative to what is asked in the question, but because they all say the same thing in a slightly different way, it is likely that the remaining answer is actually the correct one. Of course, this is not the case when *all of the above* is an option. The previous example illustrates clues provided by synonymous statements. Given that germination and meiosis are aspects of sexual reproduction, it is unlikely that any of these choices is correct.

- *"All" or "none" statements.* When *all of the above* or *none of the above* is offered as a choice, you can fairly easily determine if it is correct or should be eliminated. If you find even one of the answer choices to be wrong, you can eliminate *all of the above* as a possibility. Likewise, if you find just one of the statements to be correct, you can eliminate *none of the above* as the answer. If you find more than one option to be correct but aren't sure of the others, the answer is likely to be *all of the above.* Unless you have a choice of *A and B only,* the only way to account for multiple correct statements is to assume they are all correct.

LOOK FOR SPECIFICS

Answer choices that include specific terms and information related to the topic are better candidates than vague, abstract answers. Instructors most likely provided details to help you thoroughly understand the answer choice and relate it to the question. Often, distractor options do not contain much detail so they look appealing without giving themselves away as incorrect.

Answer choices that are significantly longer than the others often are correct. They tend to be lengthy because they include more detailed information, which often makes them a safe bet.

TACKLE TRUE-FALSE QUESTIONS

True-false questions are all or nothing. If any portion of a true-false statement is false, then the entire statement is false. It's as simple as that. Some test items contain multiple sentences, all or portions of which may be true whereas others are false. Those that are false are the determining factor.

Absolute terms, such as *always, never, entirely, completely, all, none, only,* and *every* do not usually make for a true statement. True extremes are rare. At least one instance is likely to contradict a statement that contains an absolute term, and all it takes is one example to render the statement false.

Moderating terms, such as *sometimes, often, rarely, some, many, few, often, may, can,* and *generally,* indicate that a statement is true. The opposite of the statement that something "may happen" is that it won't happen—an absolute that is likely to be false.

True-false items can be tricky when they involve double negatives—statements constructed to contain two negative terms. They often are awkward to read and unclear in their meaning. Sometimes—but not always—the two negative statements cancel each other out, resulting in a positive statement that may or may not be true. Identify what the following statement means:

> *Americans didn't believe that it wasn't in their best interest to remain neutral in the early years of World War I. True or False*

The two terms *didn't* and *wasn't* initially make it hard to understand exactly what the Americans believed. At first, it gives the feeling of a negative belief. Then, when you consider that Americans felt negatively about something *not* happening, you realize that the statement says that Americans were *in favor* of neutrality.

MANAGE MATCHING

Matching is a lot like multiple choice. For each item, you have a list of choices. As in multiple choice, the more potential choices you eliminate, the better your chances of choosing the correct answer. Thus, the best place to start a matching section is by completing certain matches. Here are some logistical tips for matching.

- *Begin with the lengthy descriptions.* If one column contains single word names or terms and the other column provides detailed information, start with the more descriptive items. Read the first detailed description and then survey the list of short items to find the one that matches the description. You save time and prevent confusion if you do this as opposed to reading one simple word and continually reading through the lengthy presentations in the other column to find your match.

- *Mark off choices carefully.* Once you've made a match, mark off the items to eliminate them from your subsequent searches. However, crossing through them so you obscure the text may cause problems if you later discover you need to reassess your answers. Mark a substantial X through the number or letter of the item or draw a faint line through it in pencil.

- *Be certain of all answers.* When you are down to your last match, be sure to read through your items to confirm that they are in fact a match. If you find a problem with the two remaining choices, you must go back and find the error.

The danger with matching items is the potential chain reaction of wrong matches. Don't assume the two remaining items are a match without checking to make sure.

LOOK FOR COHERENT TERMINOLOGY

When you are trying to determine matches but are unsure of them, consider the wording of the choices. When an item was discussed in class, what terms were used to describe it? If a description uses unfamiliar or seemingly unrelated vocabulary, it's a good candidate for elimination. Likewise, if the terminology in the description sounds familiar with regard to one of the choices, it may be a likely option.

FIND THE TERM AS PART OF THE DESCRIPTION

If you are trying to find a description of a particular term and you find one that includes that term, it probably is not a match. For example:

    1. Appropriation _____   ***A.*** *Legal appropriations used to restrict retained earnings*

If you were trying to eliminate possible matches for the definition of the term *appropriation,* you would eliminate option *A* because it includes the term in its definition.

    Some matching tests involve using choices more than once. Some provide more choices than you need (that is, some choices won't match anything). Both of these alternatives make the task more difficult, but you can still apply the tips presented here. In the case of multiple matching options, consider each item in the second column every time you look for a match. Do not cross off any choices to eliminate them from consideration. When the test provides more choices than you will use, check all items for a potential match and then eliminate items as you use them. When you think you are finished, check the remaining unmatched items to make sure they are the ones to eliminate.

SUCCEED ON SCIENCE AND MATH EXAMS

Science and math tests primarily involve solving problems, which can intimidate some students. Solving problems may seem involved, complicated, and challenging, particularly under the time constraints of an exam. The reality is that science and math tests are really just extensions of homework assignments. As mentioned previously, repeatedly working through problems is your best study strategy, because that's what you'll find on the test. Here are some things to keep in mind when taking science and math exams.

WORK TO SOLVE PROBLEMS

Problems on science and math exams, as with other subject areas, can provide clues for other problems on the exam. Begin by working the problems you know. Doing so is likely to spark your memory for how to solve other problems on the exam. Instructors often develop exams hierarchically, with the most basic problems presented first, followed by more complex problems that incorporate the methods and formulas you have already used to solve earlier problems.

    The first step in solving a problem is to determine precisely what you are supposed to do. To help you understand your task, briefly write the problem in your own words. Identify the elements involved in the problem, including the known variables and the unknown variables—most likely what you are expected to find. Also jot down what you know about relationships between any of the elements involved in the problem. This helps you identify more clearly where to start and the steps you need to take.

Most math and physics homework consists of solving problems—the same kinds of problems, most likely, that appear on the exams. They may have different stories and involve different numerical values, but the types of problems are likely to be the same. As you approach each problem, try to relate it to your homework. This may help you to relax and tackle the problem with greater ease. Keep in mind that some test questions may require you to combine formulas or procedures that you practiced individually as homework. Although they may be more involved as a result of the combined procedures, their formats are familiar and they are not different kinds of problems.

PROVIDE A COMPLETE RESPONSE

It takes knowledge and skill to answer problem solving test questions optimally. Even under pressure, though, it is important to be neat and complete and to attempt at least some of every problem on the exam.

SHOW ALL OF YOUR WORK

Showing your work is often the most critical element of math and science tests. Instructors may be more interested to see that you use all of the right formulas and approach the problem in the correct way than if you make a slight calculation error and get the wrong answer. This is why it is critical that you include—and document—every step of your process on your exam. Don't skip a step because you can do it mentally. Write it all down.

WRITE LEGIBLY

It may be hard to write neatly when you are under pressure and time is running out, but, given the tremendous value of showing your work, your instructor must be able to read it. You want to make sure that your instructor can understand every effort you made in solving the problem. Do not simply rely on a correct final value to earn you the grade.

WORK AS MUCH OF THE TEST AS YOU CAN

Most instructors who give exams that involve extensive problem solving offer the opportunity for partial credit. Thus, even though you may not get an answer completely right or you don't finish a problem, you can still earn points for what you've done. Remember, the goal of most science and math exams is to demonstrate that you've learned to approach and solve specific kinds of problems. Knowing which formulas to use and when to use them is as critical as reaching the correct answer. If you find you just can't figure out some problems, don't abandon them entirely or erase what you've written so far. Preserve your attempts (even if you've tried more than one) so that your instructor can see what you did. You may earn substantial points for the effort.

PAY ATTENTION TO THE UNITS OF MEASUREMENT

As you work through a problem, keep track of the units—feet, meters, pounds, liters, and so on. For some problems you may have to convert units of measurement (Fahrenheit to Celsius or kilograms to grams), and a fully correct answer may call for the correct unit of measurement.

 ## EMPLOY ESSAY TEST SKILLS

Many of the strategies already discussed pertain especially to succeeding on essay exams. Understanding your task, keeping track of time, and proofreading are particularly important skills. As you consider the following tips, keep in mind that subjective questions vary in length (from short answer to essay) and in number (from one essay question tagged on to the end of an objective test to an entire essay exam).

BE CLEAR ABOUT YOUR TASK

The kind of writing produced depends on the purpose of the communication. In descriptive essays, you describe something, helping to draw a mental picture for the reader. In procedural essays, you take the reader through a step-by-step process. In comparative essays, you highlight the similarities and differences between ideas or things. In perspective essays, you are expected to present your particular opinion on a topic and support it through evidence and examples. Finally, summary essays present a general look at the elements that make up a particular topic or issue. To provide the appropriate response to an essay question, you must fully understand what's expected of you.

READ CAREFULLY—TWICE

Begin by reading and rereading each question carefully. Make sure you understand the point of the question before you begin writing. Some exams give you a choice of questions to answer. If you overlook the instructions and answer all of the options, you spend valuable time responding to questions that won't count for anything. Instructors typically grade the first answers on the exam, so it won't count if you do a better job on the later questions.

When students read the questions too quickly, they often miss critical portions of text. Essay questions often have multiple parts and require the learner to write about several issues or various aspects of one issue. If you do not read the question thoroughly, and formulate a response before you begin writing, you may end up answering only part of the question. As you read through the questions, put a number next to each element of the question. As you plan your response, make sure you have incorporated each numbered item in your answer.

IDENTIFY THE DIRECTIVES

As you scrutinize the question, underline keywords that tell you what you need to do in your essay. Your response should carry out the task requested by the directive in order for you to receive full credit. See Figure 12.1 for a list of directives and their meanings.

Identifying the kind of essay to write should help you determine the scope of your answer. Notice that some directives require more information than others. Familiarize yourself with this list and practice writing in each format to help you perform optimally on your essay exams.

TUNE IN TO TIMING

Previewing the exam and allotting time to complete each portion of the test is especially critical for essay tests. Begin by assessing (1) how many items you must answer, (2) the point values for each question, and (3) how prepared you feel to answer each question. Use the combination of this information to estimate how long to spend on each item. Leave yourself some time at the end for proofreading and last-minute corrections.

If you have 80 minutes to complete an exam that contains six questions, prepare to stop writing after about an hour. This allows you 20 minutes to review your answers, proofread and correct errors, clarify or add information that you have recalled since you originally wrote your answer, and rewrite illegible portions. Count on about 10 minutes per question for your initial effort—less time for questions you know you can answer fully and quickly. This enables you to tag on a few minutes for those questions that take a little more thought and development time.

Figure 12.1
Directive Terms Used in
Essay Exams

Analyze—Break into separate parts and discuss, examine, or interpret each part.

Compare—Examine two or more things. Identify similarities and differences. Comparisons generally assume similarities more than differences.

Contrast—Show differences. Set points in opposition.

Criticize—Make judgments. Evaluate comparative worth. Criticism often involves analysis.

Define—Give the meaning, usually specific to the course or subject. Explain the exact meaning. Definitions are usually short.

Describe—Give a detailed account. Make a picture with words. List characteristics, qualities, and parts.

Discuss—Consider and debate or argue the pros and cons of an issue. Write about any conflict. Compare and contrast.

Enumerate—List several ideas, aspects, events, things, qualities, reasons, and so on.

Evaluate—Give your opinion or cite the opinion of an expert. Include evidence to support the evaluation.

Illustrate—Give concrete examples. Explain clearly by using comparisons or examples.

Interpret—Comment on, give examples, or describe relationships. Explain the meaning.

Outline—Describe main ideas, characteristics, or events. Outlining does not necessarily mean using a Roman numeral and letter scheme.

Prove—Support with facts (especially facts presented in class or on a test).

State—Explain precisely.

Summarize—Give a brief, condensed account, including a conclusion. Avoid unnecessary details.

Trace—Show the order of events or progress of a subject or event.

Essay questions require more focus and concentration, so it is easy to get wrapped up in writing and lose track of time. Keep your watch on the desk for frequent reference, or sit where you can easily glance up and see the clock.

If you find you are running out of time and determine that it is not possible for you to finish writing your answer, condense your presentation. Much like math and science tests, essay tests often allow for partial credit. Writing a complete and correctly structured essay is not as important as communicating that you know the information. Therefore, if you find yourself pressed for time, briefly jot down any remaining facts, data, definitions, or ideas you had intended to discuss. Convey them in outline form, if possible, or simply itemize them.

PLAN, WRITE, PROOF

When you are certain about which questions you are responsible for and have scrutinized your first item for the number of questions and directives, you are ready to plan your answer. You may be tempted to just start writing, but preparing your approach is critical to a successful answer. In fact, you can usually write a well-planned test essay more quickly and eloquently. The time you spend organizing your answer is saved when the writing flows confidently and effectively. See the Future Focus on page 288 to learn how developing these skills is imperative not only for doing well on exams, but for career success as well.

DEVELOP AN OUTLINE

Create a basic outline of your ideas, identify the main points, and plan to devote a paragraph to each one, with supporting points, evidence, and examples. If you jot your outline in the margin of your paper or briefly at the beginning of your essay, you can use it to guide you as you write. The outline is also helpful if you run out of time, because your instructor can see your train of thought and your scope.

As you create your outline, note any specific facts relevant to the material—facts that you've been trying to remember to use on the exam. Write each one in the appropriate place in the outline to establish where to present it. Once you have completed your outline, check it to make sure the points are in the order you want to discuss them. If the question itself doesn't call for a particular order, begin with your strongest points. Write about what you know best and can present with the greatest specificity. This establishes the strength of the essay and builds your confidence so you can communicate with ease.

CREATE YOUR RESPONSE

Ideally, your test essays will take the form and contain the primary elements of a standard essay. Your best strategy for creating an effective first sentence or thesis statement is to simply restate the test question. This serves as the springboard for an introductory paragraph in which you give an overview of the main points and the order in which you will discuss them. Be brief, however, so that you get on with the body of your essay.

Begin each paragraph with a topic sentence that introduces the point you will discuss. Provide as much detail as possible. General statements are ineffective and won't earn you many points. However, avoid providing excess, unrelated information that takes your essay off topic.

Use transition terms as you progress from one paragraph to another and from one point to another. Words such as *next, therefore, consequently, in addition,* and *nevertheless* help you maintain the flow of your essay and suggest your organization. If you have time, complete your essay with a concluding paragraph. Restate your main points and make any final statements that connect your ideas, arguments, or evidence.

RESPOND COMPLETELY

To perform optimally on essay questions, you must define important terms, discuss pertinent relationships, cite relevant research—in short, provide adequate details. Instructors look for details in a complete answer. Students may omit details, thinking that the instructor already knows them thoroughly. They may claim that defining basic terms and pointing out correlations between issues is not necessary and even seems silly, because the instructor is well versed in the subject matter.

The details could be the very pieces of information that determine whether you receive full credit on the question. They are at the core of the answer, and instructors establish these elements as concrete points to look for when they grade an essay. To ensure that a response is written to the fullest extent possible, assume that your reader is naïve about the subject. Write as if you are trying to teach someone everything you know about that subject. When you approach your response in the role of teacher writing for an uninformed learner, your essay will be more complete and will contain the level of depth and detail expected.

PROOFREAD YOUR WORK

If you don't have enough time to write a conclusion and proofread your work, then opt for proofreading. Review what you've written to make sure it is legible and doesn't contain grammar, spelling, or punctuation errors. Basic errors demonstrate carelessness and immaturity in writing skills. If the instructor has to decipher sloppily written words and misspellings, it is unlikely that the essay responses will make a favorable impression.

DON'T BLUFF WHEN YOU BLANK

At times, you may need to include details that you cannot recall specifically. In these instances, provide as much information as possible to make your point, but generalize if necessary. For example, suppose you were writing an essay describing Freud's psychoanalytic theory of personality. You know it's critical that you mention Freud's three fundamental constructs, but you cannot recall the names. As concisely as you can, provide all of the information you know about each construct, demonstrating that you know what distinguishes them from one another, their functions, psychic domain, and so on. You may write something like this:

> *Freud identified three specific elements or constructs of the human psyche. The most basic of these resides completely in the unconscious mind and is driven by aggressive and sexual instincts. This construct seeks immediate gratification and causes serious problems should it be allowed to control behavior. Because this construct needs to be held in check, another, more rational construct emerged and functions both at the unconscious and conscious levels of awareness, controlling daily behavior and making choices in accordance with societal rules. To help this construct make appropriate choices, a third construct develops during childhood as the notions of right and wrong are integrated. The internalization of rules gives this third construct the role of conscience, or guide to acceptable behavior. All three constructs interrelate and influence each other, the result of which is overt, observable human behavior.*

If you find yourself facing a question you simply can't answer or can't answer sufficiently, refrain from bluffing. Instructors are adept at identifying students' attempts to fake a specific response. Bluffing usually takes the form of rambling, disorganized statements that only tangentially relate to the question and have no valid examples or evidence to support them. Not only are instructors likely to see through any attempts at bluffing, but they also won't appreciate it. Most instructors would much rather see a set of partial outlines or itemized points that demonstrate an effort to realistically answer the question.

You may consider writing a brief note stating that you cannot recall some aspects of the concepts, issues, or topics but that you have presented those aspects that you do remember, and their relevance to the question. In this case, write anything that you believe might demonstrate at least some understanding on your part.

FUTURE FOCUS: BE BRIEF AND TO THE POINT

Being able to perform well on essay exams prepares you to communicate quickly and effectively in the workplace. Particularly with e-mail and other advances in communication tools, most jobs demand that workers be able to translate their thoughts into words for others to read. Proficient essay exam writing requires you to recall, organize, and disseminate detailed information to others. These skills will be a routine part of your future career. You will be called upon to write memos that communicate vital information to coworkers (especially at remote sites), to summarize meeting minutes, to maintain e-mail correspondence with customers and clients, and so on. In each situation, you must be able to communicate important information effectively on relatively short notice. Much of your job will involve thinking quickly on your feet—and communicating those thoughts nearly as fast.

LEARN FROM YOUR TEST

Once you finish your test, you will have completed two parts of the three-part learning process that takes place in college courses. The first part of the process is studying—understanding, processing, and encoding the information. The exam, which represents the second part of the process, involves working with, retrieving, and communicating the information in a variety of ways. To round out the experience, you receive feedback on your performance when your test is returned to you. Do not overlook the importance of this step. What you gain from reviewing your test performance—what you did right and particularly what you did wrong—can be invaluable to your success in college.

FOCUS ON FEEDBACK

When you receive your graded exam, review it carefully. If you are allowed to keep it, set aside time to review it in detail. Pay attention to several specific points as you read through your test.

ASSESS YOUR PREDICTION

Most students have a sense of how they performed once the test is over. When you first see your grade, consider whether you are surprised by it. (Read the Perspective Check for some insights into evaluating test performance.) Ask yourself the following questions: Did you get the grade you expected? Did you lose points on the questions you thought were most challenging? If so, you can feel comfortable knowing that you are able to monitor your performance effectively. If you are surprised by your weak performance in some areas, spend some time assessing your test-taking habits.

PERSPECTIVE CHECK: GETTING YOUR TEST BACK

What do you do once you get your test back, after checking the grade? Do you review tests differently depending on whether you did well? Does getting a bad test grade cause you to feel like you can't do what it takes to succeed in the class? Does it dampen your interest in the class and lessen your enthusiasm? When you receive a test with a low score, do you throw it away because you don't ever want to look at it again? Would keeping the test feel like a blatant reminder of failure?

If you succeed as you had hoped and earn a high score, do you think it's unnecessary to keep your test? Do you keep it to boost your confidence for future assignments and exams? After reflecting on how you deal with returned tests, consider how you might use the feedback in future.

DETERMINE THE SOURCE OF ERRORS

Students miss objective test questions for several reasons. When they understand the problems, they can take steps to ensure that they don't repeat those mistakes. When you review your test, consider if you:

- *Suffered from test anxiety.* If your problems were the result of nervousness and the negative impact of anxiety, begin practicing relaxation and deep breathing techniques. Consider visiting the counseling center to get assistance before the next exam.

- *Failed to recognize the material.* If some of the questions looked completely foreign to you, maybe you did not receive the information to begin with. Did you complete the reading assignments and attend all classes? Is your note taking inefficient? Determine the possible sources of the missed information. If you are not certain as to when or where information was presented, ask a classmate who responded correctly to the questions.

- *Failed to learn the material.* If you just didn't know the answers, ask yourself why. What information did you not study enough? Did you not effectively read or complete reading assignments? Were your lecture notes incomplete or vague? Did you know the material in general but were lacking in specifics? Did you not allow enough time to learn everything as completely as you needed to?

- *Rushed through the questions.* Were you rushed and careless as you read through the test? Did you fail to read through all of your answer choices? Did you miss a grammatical incongruence or overlook a double negative? Keep in mind the value of working a little more slowly next time so that you use clues and become more test-wise.

- *Misunderstood the question.* If you missed several questions due to misinterpreting them—thinking that they were asking for one thing when they were, in fact, asking for something else—follow up with your instructor. He or she may write questions in an unconventional way or may use wording that is more challenging than you're used to. If this is the case, learn how better to approach what your instructor is asking.

- *Were confused by the concepts.* Perhaps you missed items because they were conceptually difficult for you. If this is the case, commit to asking more questions in class or visiting your instructor during office hours. Ask for clarification on the course material as you encounter questions. You can't possibly succeed in a course when you don't have a fundamental understanding of the material. It is not a good idea to take an exam when you still have questions about the meaning of basic information related to the course.

- *Ran out of time.* If time was an issue, causing you to rush through parts of your exam or to not finish, then try to work more quickly and efficiently in the future. Learning the material more thoroughly enables you to recall information faster, making time less of an issue. If you had trouble completing essay questions, practice outlining and writing on a class topic in a short period of time. Practice usually improves the ability to write under time constraints.

Figure 12.2 provides a checklist for reviewing returned exams. Apply what you discover about your performance to improve your grade on subsequent tests.

STUDENT SCENARIO: BUT I JUST READ IT WRONG!

Maya approached her professor at the end of class to discuss an item she missed on her psychology exam. She was a good student in the nursing program and believed that if she could simply explain what had led to her error she could regain most of her missed points.

The test question asked students to sequence the stages of development for speech and language in infancy. The stages were listed in random order in a column with a space next to them in which students were instructed to write the number of the stage. The first stage begins with a one-tube resonator and the eighth and last stage is marked by the onset of a one-word utterance. Maya mistakenly reversed the first and last stages but placed all of the remaining stages in the correct order relative to one another.

Maya brought her exam for her instructor to see and explained how she had just misread *one-word utterance* as *one-tube resonator.* She believed that, because she simply confused the two similar terms but otherwise knew the order of development, she should receive credit for her answer.

Her instructor knew that Maya was a good student who had performed well on assignments and previous exams. She listened to Maya's argument with an open mind but did not agree that Maya should receive credit for the question.

Consider the following questions:

- What did Maya do right in this situation?

- Was Maya's request unreasonable? Explain.

- What factors contributed to the instructor's decision not to give Maya credit for the question?

- Why is it important to consider that Maya was a good student?

MEET WITH YOUR INSTRUCTOR

If your exam grade is less than you had expected, discuss it with your instructor immediately. Prepare for your meeting by going through the checklist in Figure 12.2 to help you understand what went wrong. This provides a good starting point for your meeting.

Understanding your errors on subjective questions often requires personal input from your instructor. He or she can give you specific ideas to apply in the future. It is also important to show your instructor that you are not satisfied with a mediocre exam grade. When you schedule a meeting right away to discuss your test results, you communicate your desire to understand your mistakes and take steps to

Figure 12.2
Post Exam Checklist

As you review your returned exam, check off each item that applies. Write the related test question numbers next to the factors that contributed to your unsatisfactory responses. Determine what you need to do prior to the next exam to avoid a similar outcome.	
Reason for Deducted Points	*Question Number*
____ Test anxiety was high.	_____
____ Didn't have all the information to study from.	_____
____ Didn't learn the information thoroughly.	_____
____ Rushed and didn't think carefully before answering.	_____
____ Misunderstood what was being asked.	_____
____ Never fully understood the concept.	_____
____ Ran out of time.	_____

improve your performance. This makes a good impression on your instructor and could help you when the instructor has to make subjective judgments about your next exam.

Even if you performed well on the exam, you should follow up with your instructor if you have any questions about it—answers to particular questions, reasons for points having been deducted, or what to expect next time. In this case, it's better to wait awhile before approaching your instructor, who is likely to be bombarded by many other students with questions and concerns and requests for grade changes. Call or e-mail the instructor to make an appointment.

SAVE YOUR TESTS

After you have reviewed your exam (and discussed it with your instructor if necessary), file it away. Saving tests can be beneficial for several reasons. First of all, you can refer to it while you study for future exams—to jog your memory about the length, format, and style of exams in that course. If your class has a cumulative final exam, items from previous tests may provide you with a good idea of the kinds of questions and topics that may be emphasized on the final. Reviewing past exams is an excellent strategy for preparing for the final.

Another reason for keeping your tests is to ensure that you receive the correct semester grade for the course. Errors can occur. Your instructor might enter your grade wrong in the grade book, make a calculation error when tallying your final grade, or mix your grade with another student's. Should you find an unexpected and incorrect grade on your report card, you can bring your collection of exams to the instructor to verify. Your instructor will greatly appreciate this.

Of course, determining whether the grade on your report card is correct assumes that you are aware of the grade you earned in the course. If your instructor returns all homework assignments, quizzes, and exams, or at least posts grades for all of the work you do in class, you should keep a running record of what you've earned. You should know your current grade at any point in the semester by calculating based on your file of returned work. Remaining aware of your performance in each class helps you recognize when you need to spend more time and effort and seek help should you need it. Also, it prevents surprises when the report card arrives.

CHALLENGE GRADES WITH MATURITY

If you believe points have been deducted in error, make an appointment to meet with your instructor. Review your exam adequately and acknowledge possible causes for your mistakes. If you still feel certain that a mistake was made, meet with your instructor and arrive prepared. Have your exam paper with you, along with your class notes and textbook. If the issue relates to a question of whether you presented factual information correctly, highlight or bookmark the material so you can easily show your instructor.

Approach your instructor with maturity and respect. Regardless of what you think you deserve, he or she is the authority on the topic and is qualified to judge your work. When you calmly and positively present your case along with your evidence, your instructor is more likely to listen with an open mind. Rude or demanding behavior probably will be met with resistance and most likely will not achieve the outcome you desire. A bad attitude gains neither respect nor the benefit of the doubt.

CHAPTER 12 REVIEW QUESTIONS

1. What does it mean to strategize your approach to an exam?

2. Why is it important to spend the entire allotted time for an exam?

3. What strategies can you use to eliminate answer choices on multiple choice items?

4. What are the key elements to succeeding on an essay exam?

5. What are some of the directives found in essay exams, and what do they require you to do?

6. What are the benefits of reviewing and keeping a test after it has been graded and returned to you?

SKILL PRACTICE

1. Take the sample psychology exam presented at the end of the chapter. Even though you have not prepared for the exam, use what you have learned about test-wise strategies to help you answer as many questions correctly as possible. As you work through the exam, find examples of the following:
- Clues for the answers to other questions
- Multiple choice questions worded in a tricky manner
- Misleading multiple choice options
- Grammatical incongruence in multiple choice options
- Seemingly unfamiliar or unrelated terms as answer options
- Attractive distractors as answer choices
- Opposite statements as answer choices
- Long, specific answer choices among brief, vague choices
- Complex true-false items that contain just one false statement
- True-false items with absolute terms
- True-false items with moderating terms
- True-false items with double negatives
- Matching items with coherent terminology
- Matching items with terms contained in the description
- Clues to specifics to be used with essay questions

Check both your answers and your guesses against the answer key and explanation.

2. Rewrite each of the following questions as an opening statement of an essay response.
   a. Describe the nature of *depreciation*.
   b. Evaluate the two-party system of government.
   c. Illustrate the detrimental effects that some species have on an environment by discussing the Australian rabbit infestation of the mid-nineteenth century.
   d. Prove that animals communicate with each other.

CURRENT COURSE APPLICATION

1. Apply the strategies you've learned in this chapter on your next quiz or test. Keep a list or journal of the strategies you try and how they worked. Afterward, write up a brief report on what you did and how it changed your testing experience. Which strategies worked especially well? Which ones were easy to carry out? Were any of them too difficult to apply? Did any strategies not help you?

2. For each of the directives presented in Figure 12.1, develop an essay topic using relevant material from some of your courses. For example, if you are taking a government course, you might make use of the *contrast* directive to write: *Contrast the three branches of government*.

3. Out of the 16 test items you created using the directives, choose one and develop a brief but complete outline for it as if you were starting to take a test. Be vigilant about the time. If any of your courses include essay questions on the exams, you might want to pursue writing one of the essays as preparation for your next test.

4. Review past exams from your college classes, if possible. Address each item on the suggested list in this chapter. Did you notice anything about your performance that you hadn't considered before? What did you discover that may help improve your performance on the next exam? When you are finished reviewing your tests, file them and label the folders neatly with course names. Add any other work that the instructor has returned to you.

5. Calculate your current grade in each of your classes. Do you have all of the information you need to do this? If not, what grades are you missing? If possible, meet with your instructor to get a complete picture of your grade to date. Now consider what assignments, quizzes, and tests remain. Determine the level of performance necessary for you to earn the grade you desire in the course.

TAKE A LOOK ONLINE

For some additional sources of test-taking strategies, check out the following websites:

   http//mit.edu/arc/learning/modules/test/challenge.html

   www.byu.edu/ccc/Learning_Strategies/test/strategy.htm

   If you are concerned about math-based tests and need some information on math anxiety, go to

   www.rvc.cc.il.us/classes/plc/mathanxiety.htm

STUDENT SCENARIO DISCUSSION RESPONSES

• **What did Maya do right in this situation?** Maya reviewed her exam and discovered the items on which she lost points. Because she felt strongly that she could explain the error and restore the lost points, she maturely discussed it with her instructor.

• **Was Maya's request unreasonable? Explain.** Her request was not unreasonable, because she simply asked the instructor to listen to her explanation and reconsider her grade. Maya made no demands. Nor did she approach the instructor as if she were entitled to the points. It is not unreasonable to discuss issues or concerns over grades on an assignment or a test. It may not change your grade, but it will at least provide greater understanding that can help you in the future.

• **What factors contributed to the instructor's decision not to give Maya credit for the question?** Although the instructor was able to see that Maya had a portion of the question fundamentally correct (the sequential order of several of the items), Maya had made a basic mistake. Knowing the first and last stages of development were critical to the exam, and Maya's answer did not demonstrate such knowledge. Succeeding on exams also involves reading the questions carefully. Not only was Maya careless in her initial reading of the question, but she probably didn't review her test or she probably would have found the error.

• **Why is it important to consider that Maya was a good student?** Whenever students demonstrate dedication and commitment to succeeding in a class, it can work to their benefit. Maya's instructor listened to her with an open mind, knowing that she had worked hard and proved herself in the past and wasn't likely to be looking for an easy break. If Maya had a track record of poor attendance or low test scores, or if she failed to turn in homework assignments, the instructor may have regarded her appeal for additional points with more skepticism.

SAMPLE TEST IN PSYCHOLOGY

Choose the one best answer for each item.

1. The primary goal of personality theories is to
   a. test behavior hypotheses
   b. describe behavior
   c. understand and explain behavior in order to develop methods of increasing individuals' quality of life
   d. treat problematic behavior

2. A personality theory that describes a person in terms of loyalty, sensitivity, extroversion, and so on is a
   a. trait theory   **b.** learning theory
   c. humanistic theory   **d.** psychoanalytic theory

3. The behavior-genetic approach to personality focuses on
   a. nature versus nurture   **b.** congenital factors
   c. genetic variations   **d.** genetic constants

4. When using an assessment tool for personality traits, making sure that you are measuring exactly what you intend to measure is referred to as checking for
   a. reliability   **b.** validity
   c. the personality coefficient **d.** vicarious acceptability

5. According to Freud, feeling desire for the opposite-sex parent indicates that the child is experiencing a _____ fixation.
a. oral   **b.** anal   **c.** phallic   **d.** genital

6. According to the humanistic approach, an individual who has a very large gap between the actual self-image and the ideal self is
a. efficacious   **b.** evasive   **c.** elusive   **d.** incongruent

7. Trait theorists generally make a basic assumption about human behavior. This assumption is that
a. human behavior tends to be largely inconsistent from one situation to the next
b. human behavior tends to be largely consistent from one situation to the next
c. each person tends to fit into one category or another
d. personality is dominated by unconscious processes that are largely beyond the person's control

8. Resolution of the Oedipus complex comes when a boy
a. abandons his desire to possess his mother and begins to identify with his father
b. recognizes the absurdity of fearing castration and identifies with his mother
c. recognizes his love for his mother and competes with his father for her attention
d. realizes that his father knows about his love for his mother

9. Which of the following topics would most likely not be considered by the behavior-genetic approach to personality?
a. alcoholism   **b.** attachment   **c.** sociability   **d.** IQ

10. The trait theory approach to the study of personality emphasizes the study of
a. the conflict between conscious and unconscious motivation
b. measurable, relatively unchanging characteristics
c. behavior driven by the desire to reach a self-ideal
d. genetic influence

11. The theorist who studied individuals who experienced life to the fullest through their positive outlooks and achievement of their goals and dreams was
a. Sigmund Freud   **b.** Carl Rogers
c. Albert Bandura   **d.** Abraham Maslow

12. A Freudian defense mechanism is *best* described as an attempt by the
a. ego to lessen anxiety by keeping conflicts out of awareness
b. id to avoid conflict by simply doing whatever comes naturally
c. superego to create guilt by reminding the person about morality
d. total personality to coordinate the actions of the id, ego, and superego

Respond to each statement by writing true (T) or false (F).

_____ **13.** Freud believed that childhood experiences were always the cause of problems in adulthood.

_____ **14.** Freud attributed a great deal of the workings of personality to the unconscious mind. Thus, he emphasized the role of the fundamental animal instincts of sex and aggression in his humanistic theory of personality.

_____ **15.** Abraham Maslow didn't believe that it wasn't possible for some people to become self-actualized.

_____ **16.** Erikson discovered that some infants develop a sense of mistrust during their first year of life.

Match each concept with the appropriate definition.

_____ **17.** intimacy versus isolation

a. Freudian defense mechanism that involves an unconscious barring from awareness of unwanted thoughts, feelings, and desires

_____ **18.** ego

b. Stage of psychosexual development when the libido lies dormant

_____ **19.** trait

c. Erikson's stage of psychosocial development in which the individual is either able to enter in a relationship with another person or face a lifetime alone

_____ **20.** repression

d. One of Freud's three psychological constructs, and the one that functions in reality

_____ **21.** behavior-genetic

e. A relatively permanent and enduring personal characteristic

_____ **22.** projection

f. A theory of personality that focuses on genetic variation

_____ **23.** id

g. One of Freud's three psychological constructs, and the one that acts as our conscience

_____ **24.** superego

h. Repression, plus the attribution of unwanted desires to another person

_____ **25.** latent

i. One of Freud's three psychological constructs, and the one that uses the pleasure principle

Write a brief essay on the following topic:

26. Compare and contrast Freud's theory of personality with that of the trait theorists. How do they fundamentally view behavior? What are the critical elements of each theory? What do they claim contributes to problematic behavior?

SAMPLE TEST ANSWER KEY AND EXPLANATION

1. Answer: c. This is the longest and the most descriptive answer. If you consider the notion of a _theory,_ you could readily eliminate option _d,_ because the purpose of a theory is never treatment itself. When left with the remaining three choices, all of which seem plausible, c provides the most specific response.

2. Answer: a. If this question completely eludes you despite the specific examples of "loyalty, sensitivity, and extroversion," note that other test items are related to a couple of the options. Question 6 presents some information on the humanistic approach, and four other items on the test (4, 7, 10, and 19) are related to trait theory. By reading through the test items and the answer choices, you can gather more information that might help you determine the answer. For example, item 10 addresses the specific focus of trait theory, with one choice being "measurable, relatively unchanging characteristics." This is stated in nearly the same form as option *e* in the matching section, "a relatively permanent and enduring personal characteristic," with "trait" as one of the matching options. Of the other options on item 10, one mentions the unconscious, one mentions a self-ideal, and one mentions genetics. All of these could be related to yet other items on the test. As you read through the questions to identify those that you can answer right away and then reread them for further information, the connections become apparent.

3. Answer: c. You may not have known this answer, but you could have narrowed it down quickly to either c or d because they are opposites of each another. You could confirm your answer after completing the matching section of the exam, which includes "behavior-genetic" as an item.

4. Answer: b. This question is challenging if you don't fundamentally know the answer, but you can still apply some strategies. First, the terms *reliability* and *validity* are often used in conjunction with each other, so you might have been able to infer a relationship, whether synonymous or opposite. The topic of the test item, personality theories, makes "the personality coefficient" a plausible choice. Even if you've never studied psychology, "vicarious acceptability" is likely to stand out as an unfamiliar and unrelated term. If you reduce *reliability* and *validity* to their root words, *reliable* and *valid,* it may clarify the meanings for you. The portion of the test item, "making sure that you are measuring exactly what you intend to measure" might prompt you to think about the word *valid.*

5. Answer: c. Two options—*a* and *b*—can be eliminated immediately because the words begin with vowels and therefore are incongruous with the article that precedes the blank. This leaves two possible answers, *phallic* and *genital.* An additional clue is the word *child* in the question. Anyone who has studied the stages would be aware that the phallic stage occurs during childhood and the genital stage begins at puberty and continues through adulthood.

6. Answer: d. The first three choices are similar to each other. On occasion, test writers create attractive answer options that confuse students. It is usually likely that the odd word out is the correct response.

7. Answer: b. This question contains a couple of clues. Like question 3, it has two options that are exact opposites of each other ("human behavior tends to be largely inconsistent from one situation to the next" and "human behavior tends to be largely consistent from one situation to the next"). You can eliminate the option that refers to "unconscious processes" because one of the true-false items discusses Freud and his emphasis on the unconscious. One of the matching items also mentions this fact.

8. Answer: a. This option is a paraphrased restatement of the stem in question 5. The phrase "feeling desire for the opposite-sex parent" is similar to the concept of a boy's "desire to possess his mother."

9. Answer: b. The behavior-genetic approach, mentioned in question 3, deals with genetic variations, which refers to differences. The behaviors of alcoholism, sociability, and IQ are indicative of variation among people. However, the question is looking for something *not* evidenced by variation. This leaves your remaining option. Confirm your answer by thinking about attachment behavior. Indeed, children tend to be attached to their parents.

10. Answer: b. This exam covers the trait theory extensively—in items 2, 4, 7, and in the true-false and matching sections. You should be able to gather enough information from those items, particularly from the matching definition, to answer this question.

11. Answer: d. Had you only remembered that the first names of important humanistic psychologists begin with an *A*, you might have marked choice *c* and immediately moved on. This demonstrates the value of reading through all of the choices before identifying the answer.

12. Answer: a. You may need to know the material to answer this question correctly, particularly because it highlights the word *best*. However, the highlighting suggests that more than one (if not all) of the statements may be true to some extent. Therefore, just identify the item that addresses the specific question the best. Whether or not you choose the correct response, this item can be useful on the essay section.

13. Answer: F. This question contains an absolute term (*always*), so it's safe to assume that the answer is false.

14. Answer: F. This multifaceted statement provides considerable information about Freud's theory. Every single point is true except one—Freud's theory is not humanistic (a point clearly evident through numerous other items on the test). With even one false point, the entire statement is false.

15. Answer: T. This statement is awkward to read because of the double negative. It really says that Maslow believed that it was possible for anyone to become self-actualized. In this case, despite the seemingly absolute term *anyone,* it is a true statement.

16. Answer: T. The use of the moderating term *some* suggests a true statement.

17 through 25. The best place to start with the matching section is with the column on the right. Read through the first description and then glance through the short list of terms on the left. The following text reveals the correct answer for each item and walks you through the process of discovery for those items.

Choice *a* is a description of a Freudian defense mechanism. You can eliminate several of the options on the left as follows:

- "Intimacy versus isolation" refers to a conflict or stage, not a single concept.
- "Trait" has been established throughout the test as a separate theoretical approach, not a mechanism.
- "Behavior-genetic" also has been established as a theory.

The remaining terms are all related to Freudian theory. If you still cannot determine the answer, move on to further eliminate your choices.

The second item in the right column, *b*, refers to a stage of development. Which items can you eliminate from the left column? Another clue lies in the term *dormant,* which has a similar meaning to the word *latent*—number 25.

The description of Erikson's stage of development, option *c*, explicitly states an either-or situation. Among the choices in the left column, item 17, "intimacy versus isolation" is the only one that sets up an either-or situation.

Option *d* refers to one of Freud's three constructs. With multiple references to Freudian theory, you may choose to move on for now.

The definition in option *e* was presented earlier in multiple choice item 10. You should easily be able to match it with item 19, "trait," and cross it off your list.

Option *f* also has been well established on the test and shares the term *genetic* with one of the answer choices. This makes it an easy choice to be paired with item 21, "behavior-genetic."

Option *g* offers another Freudian construct. If you're still not sure, despite the notion of "our conscious," continue trying to match and eliminate items.

With option *h*, it is unlikely that item 20, "repression," matches because the term would be contained in the definition. Option *h* has similar terminology to option *a*—"unwanted thoughts, feelings, and desires," so you might consider these related. If *h* doesn't match item 20, then there's a good chance that *a* does. The only other defense mechanism mentioned in the left column is item 22, "projection," so you now have the match for *h*.

You are now left with identifying which of Freud's three constructs are which, from the three remaining choices, "id," "ego," and "superego." You must use the clues and draw from your knowledge to pair these up correctly. The term *ego* has made its way into our everyday vocabulary, so even those who aren't studying psychology should know the term. Therefore, this term seems most related to reality. Match 18 with *d*. You are now left to determine which of the constructs—"id" or "superego"—relates to our conscious and which one uses the pleasure principle. Any recall of the id and its relation to the animal instincts of sex and aggression (mentioned in item 14) might help you determine that the id uses the pleasure principle. Match item 23 with option *i*. Then confirm any knowledge that the superego acts as our conscience—the only remaining pair (item 24 and *g*). They are indeed a match.

Your process for completing the matching section may have been different. The important factor is that you start with what you know, then systematically eliminate options to reduce your remaining choices, then look for clues among them to make your matches. Always check that the last two items work with each other, in case you made an error along the way.

26. This essay question requires multiple tasks. First, underline *compare and contrast*. These are the two directives that dictate what your response should do. Not only does the question ask you to compare and contrast the two theories, but it also gives you specific aspects of each theory to address. Therefore, your second step should be to enumerate the elements of the question, like this: Compare and contrast:

- How each theory fundamentally views behavior
- What the critical elements are in each theory
- What each theory claims contributes to problematic behavior

Once you have identified each task for the essay, you can develop an outline based on the elements. Include your supporting facts and information, some of which you can glean from items on the test. To begin your essay, write an opening sentence or two that restates the question. Here is an example.

> *Freud's theory of personality shares similarities with the trait theory but also contrasts with that theory. These similarities and differences will be examined with regard to (1) their fundamental views of behavior, (2) the critical elements of each theory, and (3) the factors that contribute to problematic behavior.*

SUGGESTED ANSWERS FOR SKILL PRACTICE

2. Rewrite each of the following questions as an opening statement of an essay response.

a. Describe the nature of *depreciation*.

> *The following essay will provide a detailed look at the nature of depreciation.*

b. Evaluate the two-party system of government.

> *The two party system of government has both advantages and disadvantages.*

c. Illustrate the detrimental effects that some species have on an environment by discussing the Australian rabbit infestation of the mid-nineteenth century.

The Australian rabbit infestation, which occurred in the mid-nineteenth century, illustrates the detrimental effects that a species can have on its environment.

d. Prove that animals communicate with each other.

There is no doubt that some animals communicate with each other.

INDEX